Social Change and Education in Greece

A Study in Class Struggle Dynamics

Spyros Themelis

SOCIAL CHANGE AND EDUCATION IN GREECE
Copyright © Spyros Themelis, 2013.

Softcover reprint of the hardcover 1st edition 2013 978-0-230-33822-7

All rights reserved.

First published in 2013 by
PALGRAVE MACMILLAN®
in the United States—a division of St. Martin's Press LLC,
175 Fifth Avenue, New York, NY 10010.

Where this book is distributed in the UK, Europe and the rest of the world, this is by Palgrave Macmillan, a division of Macmillan Publishers Limited, registered in England, company number 785998, of Houndmills, Basingstoke, Hampshire RG21 6XS.

Palgrave Macmillan is the global academic imprint of the above companies and has companies and representatives throughout the world.

Palgrave® and Macmillan® are registered trademarks in the United States, the United Kingdom, Europe and other countries.

ISBN 978-1-349-34122-1   ISBN 978-1-137-10861-6 (eBook)
DOI 10.1057/9781137108616

Library of Congress Cataloging-in-Publication Data

Themelis, Spyros.
   Social change and education in greece : a study in class struggle dynamics / Spyros Themelis.
      p. cm.—(Marxism and education)
   Includes bibliographical references and index.

   1. Education—Social aspects—Greece. 2. Social mobility—Greece. 3. Social change—Greece. 4. Social classes—Greece. I. Title.
LC191.8.G8T47 2012
306.43'209495—dc23   2012028021

A catalogue record of the book is available from the British Library.

Design by Newgen Imaging Systems (P) Ltd., Chennai, India.

First edition: January 2013

10 9 8 7 6 5 4 3 2 1

Transferred to Digital Printing in 2013

MARXISM AND EDUCATION

This series assumes the ongoing relevance of Marx's contributions to critical social analysis and aims to encourage continuation of the development of the legacy of Marxist traditions in and for education. The remit for the substantive focus of scholarship and analysis appearing in the series extends from the global to the local in relation to dynamics of capitalism and encompasses historical and contemporary developments in political economy of education as well as forms of critique and resistances to capitalist social relations. The series announces a new beginning and proceeds in a spirit of openness and dialogue within and between Marxism and education, and between Marxism and its various critics. The essential feature of the work of the series is that Marxism and Marxist frameworks are to be taken seriously, not as formulaic knowledge and unassailable methodology but critically as inspirational resources for renewal of research and understanding, and as support for action in and upon structures and processes of education and their relations to society. The series is dedicated to the realization of positive human potentialities as education and thus, with Marx, to our education as educators.

Series Editor: *Anthony Green*

Renewing Dialogues in Marxism and Education: Openings
Edited by Anthony Green, Glenn Rikowski, and Helen Raduntz

Critical Race Theory and Education: A Marxist Response
Mike Cole

Revolutionizing Pedagogy: Education for Social Justice Within and Beyond Global Neo-Liberalism
Edited by Sheila Macrine, Peter McLaren, and Dave Hill

Marxism and Education beyond Identity: Sexuality and Schooling
Faith Agostinone-Wilson

Blair's Educational Legacy: Thirteen Years of New Labour
Edited by Anthony Green

Racism and Education in the U.K. and the U.S.: Towards a Socialist Alternative
Mike Cole

Marxism and Education: Renewing the Dialogue, Pedagogy, and Culture
Edited by Peter E. Jones

Educating from Marx: Race, Gender, and Learning
Edited by Sara Carpenter and Shahrzad Mojab

Education and the Reproduction of Capital: Neoliberal Knowledge and Counterstrategies
Edited by Ravi Kumar

Social Change and Education in Greece: A Study in Class Struggle Dynamics
Spyros Themelis

This book is dedicated to all those individuals and families who hosted, trusted, and helped me with researching this book in the wonderful community, which I call Protopi.

It is also dedicated to my family—Pavlos, Aleka, Yiannis, and Agelos Themelis—for all their constant support, love, and understanding all these years.

Contents

List of Illustrations   ix

Acknowledgments   xi

Introduction   1

Part I   11

1   Social Stratification and Class Analysis   13
2   Social Mobility: Issues, Trends, and Critique   31
3   The Political Economy, Social Stratification, and Class Formation in Postwar Greece   53
4   Education, Social Mobility, and the Question of Meritocracy   75

Part II   97

5   Contextualizing the Case Study   99
6   Quantitative Aspects of Social Mobility   111
7   Occupational Trajectories and Experiences of Mobility   133
8   Educational Experiences and Pathways to Social Mobility   153
9   Alternative Pathways to Social Mobility: The Role of Migration, Marriage, and Political Patronage   177

Conclusion   199

Appendix 1: The Major Political, Economic, and Social Events in Greece, 1936–2011   217

Appendix 2: The Register 221
Appendix 3: Quantitative Data Analysis 225
Notes 227
Bibliography 239
Index 261

Illustrations

Figure
7.1 The proto-capitalist division of labor in Protopi   136

Tables
3.1 Primary-sector output in the Greek GDP,
   1950–2008 (in %)   65
3.2 Primary-sector employment, 1961–2010 (in %)   66
3.3 Secondary-sector output in the Greek GDP,
   1950–2008 (in %)   67
3.4 Secondary-sector employment, 1961–2010 (in %)   67
3.5 Service-sector output in the Greek GDP,
   1950–2008 (in %)   68
3.6 Service-sector employment, 1961–2010 (in %)   69
4.1 Number of students in Greek secondary education,
   1971–2001   81
4.2 Number of students in Greek tertiary education,
   1956–2001   82
4.3 Greek students studying abroad, 1956–2007   84
5.1 Survey sample (by gender, generation, and ethnicity)
   ($N = 1,248$)   107
5.2 Interviews participants (by gender, generation, and ethnicity)
   ($N = 40$)   110
6.1 The class scheme   118
6.2 The core mobility table (class origins and destinations)
   ($N = 1,248$)   123
6.3 Absolute mobility rates   124
6.4 Long- and short-range mobility   124
6.5 Inflow analysis table, in % (columns)   126
6.6 Outflow analysis, in % (rows)   127
6.7 Dissimilarity index (in %)   128

6.8	Structural and exchange mobility	128
6.9	Class 1 (service class) vs Class 4 (farmers)	129
6.10	Class 2 (intermediate class) vs Class 4 (farmers)	130
6.11	Class 3 (manual workers) vs Class 4 (farmers)	130
A1	Survey sample (by gender, generation, and ethnicity) ($N = 1{,}248$)	225

Acknowledgments

This book would not have been completed without the advice, support, encouragement, help, and care of a number of people to whom I am indebted.

First and foremost, my gratitude and unreserved thanks go to all the people and families in the community of Protopi, where the research took place. I owe them more than a few lines of appreciation, for they taught me most of what appears in the remainder of the book and much more that will stay with me for life.

This book draws on a PhD degree I attained at the Institute of Education (IoE), University of London. I am grateful to the receptive and stimulating community of the IoE, where I took part in one of the most exciting intellectual journeys I could ever imagine. Funding for this PhD degree was provided by the Economic and Social Research Council (ESRC), which I would like to thank for having ensured the material conditions that made the degree and the pursuant journey possible.

I would like to cordially thank Eva Gamarnikow, who supervised this degree and has provided me with endless moments of cherished human contact, critical sociological insight, unstinting support, and unique sense of humor. Many special thanks go to the best series editor one could ever have, Tony Green, for his inspirational pedagogical practice, intellectual acumen, advice and care for my ideas, and generally for his love for (critical) thinking and people who still strive to do that: dare to think!

Joyce Canaan has not only offered me comments and outstanding feedback, more than that she has also given me the precious gift of her intellectual company. I would like to thank her for being the inspiring role model, her humility, enthusiasm, encouragement, and our many a sparkling conversations. Many people offered pertinent suggestions and found the time to read various parts of the book. Especially, Dave Hill and Panayiotis Sotiris took time away during conferences and discussed some ideas I explore in this book. I want to thank them for their invaluable comments and precious time. My thanks extend to Kostas Skordoulis for our inquisitive discussions over topics related to this book, his unique listening skills, and astute comments. I would like to thank the organizers and the participants of the International Conference on Critical Education during the consecutive (and very hot) summers of 2011 and 2012 in Athens, where I enjoyed the camaraderie and conversations with many of them. Many thanks go to Natasha Beranek and Giovanni Picker for their prompt and thorough comments on chapters of this book. I am grateful to Farah Mendleshon, from Middlesex University, who understands like few the importance of academic research and offered me a grant to do that, that is, research at the University of Utrecth during Spring 2011.

I would like to thank the editors at Palgrave Macmillan, the production team, and all other parties involved in the publication of this book for their understanding, cooperation, and professionalism.

Completing a book has been known for inducing to its authors many a cranky or even tempestuous days and nights. It is thanks to some dear friends that I found refuge and courage to move on. Hence, I would like to thank Tristan McCowan, Ayman Salem, and Alpesh Maisuria for our humor-infused moments and the hope and relief they have offered me.

More than anyone, though, it is Esther Jillett who has offered me her understanding, advice, and support. I have her to thank for lifting up my spirits at critical times and encouraging me to the end, as well as for her excellent comments. A special "thank you" is a mere token of recognition for someone who has been very special to me indeed.

For many years now, while researching, thinking about and writing this book, I have deprived my family, Pavlos, Aleka, Yiannis, and Agelos Themelis, from treasured moments we could have had together. Now that the book is completed, I hope this ameliorates some of the hardships of the last 11 years or so and the compromises endured by all. It is impossible to thank my family for all they have been to me and offered me throughout these years, yet my appreciation has to be registered somehow. A cordial "thank you all" is well in order here, as is the dedication of this book overleaf. My brother, Yiannis, has been an outstanding supporter throughout and has never let me down no matter how short-noticed my requests to read parts of this book have been. A special "thank you" is extended to him.

This book comes out at a time that the country it is concerned with, namely Greece, is in great difficulty. I hope the book can offer some hope to the Greek people and all those who are tried by the socioeconomic ordeal that has been unfolding in Europe and elsewhere since 2008. It would galvanize me to keep writing in the future, if I knew that with this book I managed to spark up some debate and action for a better future that we urgently need to start working on.

Introduction

Themes

On the last day of primary school, Phokion and Theophilos bid farewell to the 40-pupil strong class, received their graduation certificates, and went home. That evening, they both went to the crops to give a hand to their families. This is early 1960s during harvest time, a labor-intensive period for almost everyone in our little provincial town, which I henceforth refer to as Protopi. That day was the last time Phokion and Theophilos saw each other at school. In September, Phokion moved out of Protopi to study in the nearby city, which was in geographical proximity though it felt like worlds apart in almost every other aspect. Phokion's family had the financial ability to hire landworkers and hence release their son from agricultural duties so that he could advance his academic career. Phokion made the most of it. He completed both lower and upper tiers of secondary school and was one of the first in his generation to enter university and become a teacher. In the late 2000s, he told me that he was looking forward to him retiring in the next few years. Both his children were university graduates, which was enough to make Phokion proud, though not sufficient to give him peace of mind. Unemployment is very high and rising among graduates, albeit Phokion was optimistic that "they will find their way." For Phokion, education became the catalyst for a life that was considerably better than his parents'. He achieved all that people of previous generations could not. That is to say, a white-collar, highly respected, permanent, secure job, which was performed under conditions insurmountably better than those in agriculture. His upward social mobility was impressive not only in socioeconomic, but also in cultural terms. Phokion entered a new social class, the middle class, and was ambitious, highly aspiring, and motivated. The values of this new class evolved largely around the significance of education in enabling individuals to fulfill their potential. The middle class achieved some economic prosperity, high social status, and good living conditions. In due time, they wanted their kids to lead a similar life and they knew that the best way to achieve this was also through education. In other words, the middle classes started reproducing themselves, just like their counterparts in Western countries.

Phokion's location, therefore, in the social world of Protopi is relatively easy to fathom, though much more intriguing and complex than this vignette has allowed to surface.

Theophilos, on the other hand, did not attend secondary school. He was one of five siblings and his parents could not afford to let him stay on at school. Instead, they deployed him in the family farm. When he turned 14 years, his uncle offered him an apprenticeship as a builder, which is the job Theophilos has held ever since. In the late 2000s, he was unemployed and seriously concerned about his occupational future. He was proud of his two sons, though neither of them was in secure employment: The elder one was a musician and the younger a semiskilled builder working alongside his father. But what can explain Theophilos's difficult socioeconomic situation? Is it due to choices he exercised or lack thereof? Why did he not transcend the manual versus non-manual divide and thus secure a better career and easier life like Phokion? Which struggles, forces, choices, strategies, impediments, preferences, and barriers led him to semiskilled manual labor and attendant employment precariousness? As we shall see in the next chapters, family resources paved the way for Phokion's educational attainments, which became the passport to a better life, the signifier of success. They allowed him to get a self-fulfilling job, improve his living conditions, marry someone who was a teacher herself, and in this way entrench their position in the emergent middle class and pass down to their offspring their good standing in society.

Theophilos came from a Roma family whose size was much larger than Phokion's. Although his parents had their own land, it was not enough to make ends meet. Some family members had to become landworkers and Theophilos was one of them. Had they afforded it, Theophilos perhaps would have joined Phokion at secondary school and, who knows, even university. Educational and occupational careers, though, take more than wishful thinking and retrospective speculation to be realized. They need family support, financial resources, and an environment that fosters aspirations to flourish. In the neighborhood where Theophilos and his family lived, there were no families with such characteristics. Most of the residents were landworkers and/or smallholders. It was a neighborhood occupied predominately by Roma families. Many people in Protopi held a belief that being of Roma origin was already a bad start in life. Others maintained that Roma families' values and cultural attitudes did not pay enough attention to their children's education; hence they missed out on occupational opportunities and attendant social advancement. In spite of this, Euriklea, Theophilos's wife, also of Roma background, strongly disagreed. Her eyes were full of passion when she spoke to me about education. When I last met her, she offered a rapturous offensive against the hurdles poor people face in their quest for a better future, which she vehemently believed could be achieved through education. For her, it was racism and discriminatory attitudes of the dominant group, the non-Roma, which did not allow people from humble origins to flourish. Although Phokion was from an affluent family, he was very sensitive to various forms of discrimination too. According to him, it was class differences that separated, ranked, and allocated people into different social groups and determined their success in life. Venus, a young woman from non-Roma background believed that women had a harder time finding a job, especially those who married to Roma men, like herself. Marrying out, for example, a non-Roma person marrying a Roma, was usually the equivalent of marrying down, that is to say entering a lower social class and even becoming an outcast in the community. Females like Milena believed that marriage was a family strategy that could determine one's social status and class position. However, marriage was neither preferable nor available as an option for everyone. Vryon's parents, for example, were both of non-Roma background without any private land nor advanced skills, which they could exchange in the labor market. For them, occupational opportunities had to be sought outside Protopi. As a result, they emigrated to Belgium and then to Germany. Upon repatriation, Vryon applied for a job in what was perceived by many locals to be the "golden sector" within the postwar labor market, namely the civil sector. It was the time when vocational qualifications, in fact any qualifications higher than primary school, conferred high socioeconomic returns and rewards to their incumbents. Pericles, by contrast, attempted twice to emigrate abroad, but did not succeed in settling down. When he returned to Greece, he managed to find a job in a factory, though more insecure than Vryon's, under worse working conditions and not as well-paying. This, though, begs the question: If Vryon and Pericles were contemporaries with similar material assets and family history of emigration, why did only one of them, namely Vryon, manage to avoid employment insecurity and achieve a career that offered him better material and symbolic rewards? Was it because Pericles lacked formal qualifications or was it due to his Roma origin? Phaedon would say that formal qualifications do not carry any value these days. For him, it is all about who knows whom, not who knows what. He might come from a family with an established tradition in university attainment (his father, sister, and, of course, himself were all university graduates), but success in the microcosm of Protopi passes through the meanders of political power. Political mediation or "meson" as it is widely known is perceived by many as the most salient force in the allocation of opportunities. I last met Phaedon in a public place outside Protopi where he was having a drink with Heliad, another recent university graduate who was devastated by the lack of opportunities for new graduates. They both come from Protopi, but they avoid meeting there unless in secret. Heliad is of Roma origin, whereas Phaedon is not. As Phaedon told me on a different occasion, "it's ok to be progressive, unlike our parents, but you've got to be careful not to be seen hanging out with a Roma woman." When I last recorded their career movements, they were more or less in their mid-thirties. One of them, Heliad, had migrated to Athens to find a job, while Phaedon had just launched a start-up company. They were both nervous, cautious, and impatient to see their dreams take off the ground. This was the beginning of the economic crisis that has since hit Greece very badly and has plunged young people, Roma and non-Roma alike, into precariousness, unemployment, underemployment, and labor market insecurity. Social mobility has not totally vanished as a social practice and personal experience; it has however diminished or taken different forms.

These are some of the issues I discuss in the following chapters. Several other topics of distinct importance and direct relevance to the overarching themes are also examined and integrated into the analysis. These include social-class formation and its significance in the transmission of socioeconomic (dis-)advantages and occupational opportunities; the impact of modernization on people's careers and social mobility pathways; the differential allocation of rewards to members of different gender and ethnic groups; the way social, cultural, and family values impinge on career aspirations; and social mobility outcomes. These topics are embedded in a systematic analysis of class struggles as a means of understanding the development of the relations of production and their articulation to the Greek version of capitalism.

TheS tudy

The main aim of this book is to examine some key aspects of social change and class struggle dynamics in postwar Greece. In particular, this is a case study of a community, which has undergone significant changes in its political organization, occupational structure, labor market, economy, and educational provision since the 1940s. The focus of my exploration is on the differential distribution of occupational opportunities and rewards and the significance of education in this process. In other words, my interest evolves around the impact of postwar educational expansion on occupational and social-class outcomes for respondents from three adjacent generations who belong to diverse class, ethnic, and gender groups. The material of the book draws on three levels, which are intertwined in my analysis. The first, namely the macro-level of analysis, deals with the structural and institutional transformations in liberal democracies and mainly in Greece, and some key aspects in their political economy, occupational structure, labor market, economy, politics, and education from the late 1940s until 2008. The second or meso-level is concerned with occupational and social mobility patterns and trends, and their association with the changing role of education in respect of Protopi as a community. Finally, this book explores the microcosm of lived experiences of residents in Protopi in order to gain an understanding of the social, political, and cultural factors that impinge on their occupational and social mobility outcomes and their relationship with education (micro-level).

Given that social mobility research in Greece remains largely undertheorized and underexplored, I draw on studies from countries with a long tradition in the pertinent field (e.g., Britain) in order to develop a conceptual framework and an appropriate methodological design. Social mobility is explored both within the lifetime of the families and individuals (*intra*generationally) as well as over three adjacent generations (*inter*generationally). In this way, I explore the diverse mobility strategies of families and individuals and the relationship between educational attainments and occupational outcomes both in comparison to their peers as well as to their parents and grandparents. Differential practices of allocation of rewards and penalties, benefits and detriments, advantages and disadvantages, are not approached as instances or accidents in the history of Protopi, but as embedded practices in its social and cultural fabric. I show how they permeate every domain of social relations and cut across all institutional arrangements: from politics to education and from employment to marriage. In other words, economic, political, cultural, social, and educational institutions constitute a constellation of totality of the respondents' milieu.

This book argues that education has been a key mechanism in social mobility outcomes of individuals and families in Protopi for the best part of the postwar era. The positive impact educational attainments have had on the improvement of people's life chances has been unequivocal. However, the benefits of the main mechanism associated with achievement, namely education, have not affected equally all relevant social groups, such as the majority of Roma people and women born before the 1980s. What is more, alternative mobility pathways, such as emigration and marriage in the past, as well as political patronage and clientelist relations diachronically seem to mediate the impact of educational credentials and compromise the importance of education in individuals' occupational and social mobility success. In other words, mechanisms related to ascription, such as class-based mating practices and political patronage, have limited the potential of institutions that were expected to act as mechanisms of equalization of opportunities, such as education. This book exposes the new political economy that emerged in Greece after the Second World War and its unequal, inequitable, and socially unjust structural foundations upon which the Greek version of postwar liberal democracy was founded.

The Research Design

Up until the 1990s, the interactions of the Roma people with the dominant groups in society were principally interpreted and studied in terms of their relevance to the economy, while the social aspects of Roma life were often approached with the intention of "exposing" the problems they allegedly created to the dominant society. Roma people have only recently been studied in their contemporary urban contexts, albeit not unproblematically so. For example, Sibley (1981) and Williams (1989) argue that the urban environment transforms the former nomads and pariahs into an urban ethnic group that competes with other groups for strategic resources and a legitimate social identity. Such a conception that perceives two different groups of the same society like two cars in separate lanes of the road fails to recognize the dynamic nature of social relations, especially in rapidly changing contexts. In this book, the Roma are not contained into such a "separatist" framework but they are perceived as active agents, who also shape their personal, collective, and social identity through various processes of interaction with other groups. The dynamics of such processes need to be explored not in isolation with other social collectivities nor in an ahistorical manner, which presupposes the always and already existing ethnicity of Roma or any other group. In breaking away from this hegemonic theorization, the research design of my study includes both dominant and marginalized groups, the non-Roma and the Roma, respectively. In this way, this book demarcates from the study of minority groups as part of ethnic or minority, or even "racial" studies and from prevailing, "othering" theorizations of the differential social mobility of minority groups, such as the Roma.

In addition, my focus is equally on both genders since the social mobility of women can reveal the gender inequalities that exist within the family as well as in the labor market (Dex, 1987). This is another original element that characterizes this study and distinguishes it from conventional mobility inquiries and their typically male-centred approach.

At present, there is a conspicuous dearth of studies that have explored social mobility and its interrelated dimensions through the use of qualitative data, while there are probably no studies that have utilized a mixed-methods design. This book breaks new ground in the relevant field by treating qualitative and quantitative methodologies not as competing but complementary. Specifically, this study uses elements from both the quantitative (Goldthorpe, 1980, 2000) and the qualitative traditions (Bertaux and Thomson, 1997) in the study of social mobility. It is argued that this mixing of methods adds both to the originality of the book and the production of new knowledge. The quantitative component is based on a representative survey and illustrates the distributional aspects and diachronic patterns, trends, and fluctuations of intergenerational, occupational, and educational mobility. The qualitative component draws on critical ethnography, which consists of extensive observations, semi-structured interviews with 40 participants, and informal discussions with a large number of interlocutors (and, in some cases, their friends and families), and it reveals the complexity of the lived experiences and subjective understanding of individuals of their intra- and intergenerational, individual and family mobility. The research design draws on the transformative–emancipatory approach and is concerned with issues of social justice (Olesen, 1994; Kincheloe and

McLarean, 2000; Truman et al., 2000; Mertens, 2008a). This approach is particularly important in this book as it underlines the class struggle dynamics through the unequal distribution of opportunities and rewards and tries to reach an understanding of discriminatory processes and power differentials. A key overarching commitment to this approach is its search for a more egalitarian and fair society, which is embraced in this book.

The findings I present and the ideas I develop in the following chapters are not idiosyncratic to Protopi, but resonate with other areas in Greece and further afield. Educational practices and mobility pathways tend to vary from place to place, depending on local resources, values, strategies, networks, and so on. As a result, the micro-processes and experiences of individuals of their own occupational and educational lives in Protopi comprise an original case study. However, through the examination of occupational and educational trajectories of individuals and families, I was able to dig deeper into the socioeconomic, cultural, and political history of Protopi too. Despite the importance of the historical and geographical conjuncture that occupational and educational trajectories relate to, they are ineluctably interwoven in the mode of socioeconomic production and organization. After the war, the way production, society, and economy have been organized is similar in many Western countries, including Greece, albeit with local variations. In this vein, Protopi has to be seen also as an analogy to Greece, as a "microcosm" of a broader context, which incubates an unambiguously complex reality. While, then, the story of Protopi that is explicated in the remainder of the book is to be viewed as a spatially and temporally bounded account of some key aspects of a multifarious reality, I make no mistake to believe that there might not be other dimensions that have remained partially heeded to, suppressed, or relegated to oblivion. Nevertheless, the criteria for judging the success (or not) of this book should be consistent with its stated aims. In terms of "what can this book tell us?" then, I would be content if my reader approached it as a magnifying lens, a "splinter in the eye" (Adorno, 1974) that can allow for the wider and much more elaborate "story" of class struggle dynamics through education in postwar Greece to come to the foreground rather than the definitive account of the story I am about to tell. Given the historical character of some of the processes I discuss, such as modernization, as well as the widespread application of the model that Greece followed after the war, which prioritized educational expansion in a state-supported but marketized economy, insights can be drawn for other countries too. If anything, since 2009, the economic crisis that has plunged Greece into economic recession has brought its society on the brink of disarray and its political system in international ignominy; this is an array of developments that makes this study more apropos and timely than ever. I hope this book is esteemed for both its academic value and intellectual contribution as well for its social usefulness for the lessons it can offer from history and hope for the future.

The Organization of the Material of the Book

PartI

This part comprises four chapters. Each one of them touches upon a different aspect, namely social stratification and class analysis, issues of social mobility, the Greek political economy and society, and the connection between education and social mobility. This part of the book aims to contextualize the case study that will be presented in Part II by furnishing the reader with the broader socioeconomic, political, social, and historical underpinnings of the study (macro-level of analysis).

More specifically, chapter 1 offers an overview of the way social stratification, modernization, and social change have been researched and theorized. It argues that social inequalities have been systematically explored after the Second World War because of the need to safeguard peace and secure the conditions for social and economic progress that seemed to prevail in the first few postwar decades. In other words, the interest in social stratification stemmed partly from an interest in gauging capitalism's potential to ensure the conditions of its own reproduction. In doing so, the chapter examines how social class was theorized in the works of three classical theorists whose work is important to the study of social mobility, namely Marx, Weber, and Parsons.

Chapter 2 develops further these issues by discussing the diverse theoretical traditions in the study of social mobility. I delineate two key dimensions in mobility analysis, the epistemological and the ideological/political one. I argue that both are inextricably linked to the way mobility is studied and the outcomes that are generated. I demonstrate how findings from major mobility studies in Britain have given rise to debates and policy initiatives on how to tackle social inequalities. I argue that social mobility it too important a field of study to be deprived from the historical materialist perspective. Furthermore, I propound a renewed interest that can furnish the pertinent field with the perspective of class conflict and class struggle currently absent from mobility research.

Chapter 3 shows how the postwar political economy, social formation, occupational structure, and labor market of a late-industrialized country, namely Greece, were shaped by the Western orientation the country vehemently adopted after the war. The aim of the chapter is to contextualize the changes in all the aforementioned domains in the discussion on social mobility (chapter 2) and social stratification (chapter 1).

Chapter 4 highlights the key features, aspects, and trends with respect to education in liberal democracies, such as postwar Greece. It adds into the discussion of social formation, economic development, and social change, which were discussed in the previous chapters, and the impact of educational expansion. The aim of the chapter is to offer a critical account of how education in postwar Greece, and Western countries more generally, gained rapidly a prominent value as a mechanism of meritocratic allocation of occupational opportunities and a central avenue of (upward) social mobility. I argue that this meritocratic function was never successfully achieved, as it has been more of a programmatic political proclamation rather than a realistic expectation.

Part II

This part presents a case study in education and social mobility in North West Greece. Its aim is to instantiate the Greek development and modernization presented in the previous chapters through the in-depth study of a bounded community. Part II contextualizes the main issues discussed in the previous chapters, namely socioeconomic development, class formation and stratification, social mobility, and educational transformation. I start with the presentation of the case study and I move on to discuss some meso- and micro-aspects of social mobility that help us understand the role and class character of education in Greece in the last six decades or so.

Chapter 5 introduces the second part of the book by explicating the aims, scope, aspects, and key issues of the case study. Moreover, it presents the research design of the study and offers a brief account of its methodological foundations and methods of data collection and analysis. It presents the core dimensions of the locale where the research was conducted and it outlines the rationale for its selection followed by a brief presentation of its key socioeconomic, political, historical, and educational characteristics.

Chapter 6 discusses the patterns of absolute and relative, structural and exchange mobility and highlights the distributional aspects of change in Protopi. The aim of this chapter is to provide an overview of the general patterns and trends of social mobility, the relevance and importance of education in these processes for Protopi (meso-level), as well as to enhance the analytical connections between the two other levels of analysis: On the one hand, the changes that are discussed in Part I in relation to Greece (macro-level) and, on the other, the accounts of the research participants (micro-level) that are presented in chapters 7–9.

In order to explore the impact of education on the occupational movements of the research participants, I explore their experiences as well as the social, cultural, and political factors that impinged on their careers, movements within the social structure, and outcomes in life. In order to pay justice to the wealth, depth, and diversity of the research participants' experiences, I devoted chapters 7–9 to this exploration. Chapter 7 aims to build on evidence presented in chapter 6 by contributing to the exploration of the role of education in inter- and intragenerational mobility and the significance of educational qualifications in the life chances of the research participants. Furthermore, this chapter aims to provide an understanding of the significance of social class as a "subjective" category of analysis, that is to say as a way of understanding class consciousness and agency, which comprises a key parameter in my analysis of social-class movements.

Chapter 8 further elaborates and develops the themes that were advanced in chapter 7 regarding the occupational pathways of individuals and families. In particular, it expands on the inter- and intragenerational mobility experiences of residents in the research locale in the exploration of the role of education. It explores how education has shaped and transformed, in class terms, the careers, aspirations, employment pathways of individuals, and explains the varying impacts of education on individuals, families, and the community.

Chapter 9 discusses some alternative pathways to social mobility and sheds light on social, cultural, and political factors that impinge on the life chances of research participants, namely emigration, marriage, and the role of political patronage and clientelist relations. The role of chapter 9 in this book is to fill in the picture of processes that help us reach a better understanding of patterns of differential educational attainment and distribution of opportunities, as well as to provide a fuller account of the way social change has occurred in the community of Protopi.

In the concluding chapter, I return to the key themes of the book and discuss how they were addressed in the preceding chapters. More specifically, I evaluate the importance of education as part of the modernization project within the postwar political economy in late-industrialized countries, such as Greece. Subsequently, I discuss the emphasis that has been put on the association between education and social mobility and I critique the expectation attached to education as an expedient vehicle for occupational and social advancement. In addition, I question the role of the state and the political, socioeconomic system of organization that prevailed after the war, namely liberal capitalism, with its attendant emphasis on economic growth, competition, and the primacy of the markets, which allowed education to be unproblematically attached to the system of occupational and material rewards. The book closes with an assessment of its contribution to knowledge production and an exposition of the areas where its originality lies.

Part I

Part I aims to provide the reader with the necessary background for the understanding of the case study that is presented in Part II. This background consists of the core developments in the political economy, social structure, economy, labor market, and politics from the termination of the Second World War to the late 2000s. I first discuss some general issues in the study of social stratification and social inequalities in order to provide the historical context of the ideas pertinent to social mobility inquiry. I then explore how the field of social mobility has researched individuals' movements within modern social structures and I shed light on the political and epistemological significance of mobility research. Subsequently, I contextualize the discussion on class inequalities and attendant social mobility processes focusing on postwar Greece and the major transformations it has undergone in the last six decades or so. Finally, I relate the topic, ideas, theories, and research findings in the field of social mobility with educational accomplishments in Greece and more broadly. Part I focuses on the "big picture" ("macro-level" of analysis) of the main theme of this book, namely social change and education.

Chapter 1

Social Stratification and Class Analysis

Social mobility occupies a prominent position in *both* liberal and Marxist accounts, albeit they each approach it in different ways. The former, the liberal school, adopts a conventional stance whereby it explores and analyzes social movements in order to critique capitalism and offer tools for its improvement. By contrast, the Marxist school of thought reserves a marginal position to the study of social mobility and it invariably assigns it to the ideologically adversarial camp. In this book, I adopt an unfamiliar position as I intent to readjust that convention of social, analytical, and paradigmatic thinking on both counts. On the one hand, by moving away from the liberal theorizations that typically limit the potential of social mobility into a mechanism that has to be preserved, improved, and maximized, and viewing it as of universal value whose benefits ought to be distributed fairly to all members of society. As I argue in the remainder of this book, this interest stems from an unfounded optimism, which is predicated on the belief in the apropos of the capitalist system to provide a fair, equitable, and better future for all. On the other hand, I delineate from Marxist accounts that treat social mobility as a bourgeois preoccupation that precludes the formation of class consciousness and obfuscates the potential for transformative action. To this extent, I suggest that not only is it erroneous to ascribe the study of social mobility as a bourgeois fixation, but, in the contexts of social and economic crisis, like the ones we live in, social mobility or its lack thereof has the potential to instigate some of the radical transformations that Marxism is concerned with. This chapter offers an overview of the way social stratification and social class have been researched and theorized in the postwar years. In addition, it presents some key issues in the study of education and social mobility in the post–Second World War years, such as occupational and labor-market transformations, and it highlights significant factors in social mobility outcomes, such as gender, ethnicity, and social class. The aim of this chapter is to set out the framework for the study of social inequalities and social change that are discussed in the following chapters.

1.1 Social Stratification and Liberal Democracy

The study of social stratification has received substantial attention within sociology, especially since the second half of the twentieth century. This interest stems from the new world order that emerged after the Second World War, which is, chronologically, the starting point of this study. In order to contextualize this interest in social stratification it is paramount to provide a brief account of some key historical, political, and economic events that shaped the world as well as our understanding about it during the postwar years. The war was one of the most deadly events in human history, having claimed over 50 million lives, caused immense destruction in infrastructure and livelihood, and eradicated many years of progress hitherto achieved. Yet, it also became the savior of capitalism in the most remarkable fashion, as it "produced solutions, at least for decades. The dramatic social and economic problems of capitalism in its Age of Catastrophe [the inter-war years] seemed to disappear. The Western world economy entered its Golden Age; Western political democracy, backed by an extraordinary improvement in material life, was stable; war was banished to the Third World" (Hobsbawm, 1994, pp. 52–53). This historical paradox, namely, on the one hand, the desolation of human lives and civilization, and, on the other, the resurrection of the socioeconomic system in place, raised one of the most intriguing questions: Is capitalism the best system available or is there any scope to examine alternative ones? In order to safeguard humanity from another catastrophe similar to the Second World War, an improved version of capitalism was sought, one that would promote liberties of all kinds and would simultaneously support its citizens in various aspects of their lives. This gave rise to "liberal democracy," which emerged in late 1940s and was applied in Western countries of the world with several adaptations and local variations thereafter. But what is liberal democracy?

The restructuring of state forms and international relations after the war was deemed necessary in order to abort a threat to capitalism similar to the one that occurred in the 1920s and led to a deep economic crisis (the "Great Depression") and eventually to the emergence of Nazism and the Second World War. Hence, a class compromise was struck between labor and capital (Przeworski and Wallerstein, 1982; Wright, 2000; Harvey, 2010). This was predicated on the achievement of a fine balance among the state, the free market, and parliamentary democracy, which are the constituent elements of liberal democracy. This class compromise was largely achieved thanks to state intervention in the form of welfare for its citizens. This approach was espoused by Keynes (1936) and, among other things, it postulated fiscal and monetary policies in order to promote full employment and growth. In this way, the role of the state increased as attested to by its intervention in industrial policy and the establishment of the welfare system, through education, health, and other institutions. This interventionist approach rests upon a nexus of social and political constraints as well as other regulatory devices that harness market, corporate, and entrepreneurial activities and associated power. A cornerstone of this model of organization was the state management or ownership of key sectors of economic activity, such as the extraction and processing of raw materials (e.g., the steel or coal industry), key sectors in the export market, such as chemical or metallurgic industry, car manufacturing, and so on. This development is paramount in understanding how the political economy of postwar nation states, which espoused liberal democracy, was molded. Due to this active role played by the state, it was termed "embedded liberalism" (Harvey, 2010), that is to say the type of liberalism that is predicated upon the control of the state of key institutions and functions. For "the state in effect became a force field that internalized class relations. Working-class institutions such as labour unions and political parties of the left had a very real influence within the same apparatus" (Harvey, 2010, p. 11). This is the era of Keynesianism or "capitalism with a human face," which rested upon the expectation that if capitalism was appropriately regulated by the state, its negative aspects could be harnessed, and therefore, its benefits diffused to all stakeholders, namely individuals, businesses, and nation states. Keynesianism did indeed confer to the Western world some of its promised benefits, such as economic growth, increased wages, living standards and employment, as well as social provision. An example of the latter is that investment in education–the key institution in this book–rose significantly, which led to a concomitant rise in access and participation rates. It is within this context that social stratification became a core issue in social sciences, namely the need to measure whether the benefits of the postwar years were equally distributed or inequalities posed a threat to the attempt to achieve socioeconomic stability.

Despite the promising first years after the war, the so-called Golden Years of capitalism, the reign of embedded liberalism started to crumble, as unemployment and inflation sank many economies into the stage of stagflation. This was exacerbated by the two oil shocks in the 1970s, and after then capitalism started entering a new phase, that of neoliberalism. Against the dominant expectation of the time, investment in education was not sufficient to limit socioeconomic inequalities nor to ensure the equal distribution of material wealth. Instead, inequalities took various new forms and laid bare the flaws of the system. The need to understand the origins, historical development, types, causes, and forms of these inequalities gave impetus to the study of social stratification, whose content I shall discuss in the next section.

1.2 Class Structure and Analysis

Social stratification is concerned with the nature of hierarchically structured societies and the way inequalities are patterned within social systems. In some contexts, inequalities are perceived as preordained, hence, unaltered by any structures or processes humans might put into place. For example, the caste system in India is based on the belief that the division of society into castes is divinely ordained; therefore, it is accepted as natural and unaltered by human intervention. Despite differences in perceptions of social stratification, it always presupposes inequality. Analytically, inequality is claimed to have three dimensions: (a) differentiation, (b) ordering, and (c) evaluation (Hamilton and Hirzowicz, 1993). *Differentiation* refers to all these elements that make people diverse, ranging from inherited elements, such as skin color and height, to those acquired, such as social class, education, and income. However, these are all differences, which, on their own, are not enough to set people apart. Their importance varies in different contexts and points in time, depending on the social system within which they are developed and the value ascribed to each one of them by a specific social system. Hence, in some contexts, gender can be a defining factor of one's possible success or otherwise, while in others, it might be education. Usually, though, in modern societies, a combination of factors impinges on one's life outcomes. *Ordering* connotes the ranking of individuals, which is the outcome of some comparative process. That is to say, individuals are compared on the basis of one or more characteristics they possess and they are then ranked on a scale that orders these differential attributes they possess and their distance from the other people on the same scale, for example, income quantiles. Both differentiation and ordering presuppose the existence of a system of beliefs and values that makes any judgment meaningful. Hence, they require some form of evaluation, the third dimension of inequality. *Evaluation* is necessary for a framework of common understanding of differences and their ordering shared by members of the same social system (Hamilton and Hirzowicz, 1993). The notions, for example, of upward social mobility or educational underachievement, would be void of meaning if people did not share similar ideas about what constitutes mobility and achievement.

The discussion about social structure within modern academic disciplines, and especially within sociology, is riddled with confusion, tension, and ambiguity. The main point of contention is the deployment of appropriate epistemological framework. While some authors talk about class and stratification analysis interchangeably (cf. Kingsley and Moore (1970) [1945]), others insist on the importance of analytically and empirically distinguishing between these two and treating them as separate, though related, fields of study (Wright, 1994). A third approach argues for the diminishing importance of social class (Beck, 1992; Clark and Lipset, 1996) or for its disappearance altogether (Bauman, 1992; Crook *et al.*, 1992; Pakulski and Waters, 1996). Finally, another group of scholars propose that the best way to proceed is by accepting the different departure points and embracing the diversity of approaches as a sine qua non of the field (Crompton, 2008). As Crompton (2008) argued, "the way ahead in class and stratification analysis is to recognize the *de facto* plurality of conceptual frameworks and methodologies in the field ... What is required is a combination of different approaches to class and stratification ... even though the theoretical underpinnings of these different approaches might appear to be incompatible" (pp. vi–xii) (emphasis in the original). In this study, social class is treated as an analytically distinct concept in explaining social structure to stratification. Moreover, I shall argue that social-class analysis helps us understand both the way capitalist societies operate and can better elucidate the unequal arrangements in everyday life. However, I shall demonstrate how the empirical challenges of measuring social class have forced some researchers who adhere to a Marxist framework to adopt more conventional methods of operationalizing social class, which borrow elements from the social stratification mode of analysis.

Another problem with analyzing social structure is the problem of "exogenous transference" or simply "hegemony." This problem operates at the cross-country level of analysis and points to the borrowing of analytical and empirical elements or entire frameworks from the economically advanced societies for the exploration of less-affluent ones. In modern capitalism, though, economic advancement of some nations de facto implies direct or indirect influence and control of powerful over others, for the domination of the former can only be produced by the subordination of the latter. One of the most crucial forms this dialectical relationship between domination and subordination takes is created through reformulating labor–capital relations, which, in capitalism, always favor the ruling class at a country-specific level or the international ruling class at an international level. Hence, the dominant countries use cheap labor from subordinate countries in order to create the products the affluent world consumes; they exploit the services of workers within or across their borders (often through war, as in the case with the recent wars in Iraq or Afghanistan); they wield control over the conduct of international trade and exchange (e.g., through the General Agreement on Trade in Services [GATS]); they forge or reconstitute institutions and alliances structured to serve their own interests (e.g., the G8 summit, the World Bank, the International Monetary Fund [IMF], the creation of the Eurozone); they disproportionately influence the labor market, financial operations, and so on. This matrix of domination and subordination has also unequivocal cultural implications, for the economic is imbricated with the cultural (Kelsh and Hill 2006; Ebert and Zavarzadeh, 2008). This translates to ideological influences through the export of dominant nations' epistemological as well as analytical frames of reference that are now extensively used in subordinated countries. It is my contention, which I shall prove in the course of the book, that this transference of epistemic baggage from exogenous, dominant sources onto subordinate ones creates the conditions not only for the perpetuation of asymmetric cultural and ideological relations between dominant and subordinate countries (or core and peripheral ones), but also threatens the very independence of the latter. What is more, these relationships acquire holistic dimensions and implications insofar as they are coproduced by the material and ideological forces within the dominant capitalist mode of production. Their implications are all encompassing in relation to the institutional and structural domains they penetrate, though with varying degrees of success. A prime example is education, which, I shall argue, is a continuously shaped by-product of this relational unity-in-opposition between core and periphery. Such a relationship is underpinned by the continuous struggle and mutually exclusive interests of these two poles. To be precise, these are class interests and they are rooted in the antagonistic nature of modern capitalism. The increasing resemblance among the educational systems in disparate countries globally does not point to a process of growing communication and openness, but to one of mounting assimilation and subordination of the inferior to the dominant, as I show in the remaining chapters. For the moment, I shall turn my attention to the theoretical approaches proposed to explore the social structure of modern capitalist societies.

1.3 Studying Social Structure

It is important for this analysis to distinguish between class structure and class formation. Class structure, following Wright's (1987) definition, is understood here as "the structure of social relations into which individuals (or, in some cases, families) enter which determine their class interests" (p. 9). Hence, class structure "defines a set of empty places or positions filled by individuals or families... This implies that with respect to class structures we can talk about 'vacant' positions (positions which are not currently filled by actual people), about an 'absolute surplus population' (an excess of people with respect to the places within the class structure), and 'incumbents' of class positions (people actually located within a given class structure)" (Wright, 1987, pp. 9–10). While this definition takes into account the objective nature of class inequalities within capitalism, it is also sensitive to the changing form these inequalities take over time and in different contexts. Class formation, on the other hand, "refers to the formation of organized collectivities within the class structure on the basis of the interests shaped by that class structure. Class formation is a variable. A given type of class structure may be characterized by a range of possible types of class formation, varying in the extent and form of collective organization of classes" (Wright, 1987, p. 10). According to Poulantzas (1979), social formations could comprise several modes of production, for example, many European societies at the beginning of the twentieth century combined elements of the feudal mode of production, the simple commodity and manufacture, as well as the capitalist mode of production. This is an important point that I shall elaborate further in relation to the relations of production in early and mid-twentieth-century Greece in chapter 3.

Although ideas about the structure of modern social systems vary substantially, its significance as a topic of exploration has received nearly universal acceptance. As Ossowski (1963) argued, stratification is a very significant political issue within a society, since inequalities are potential sources of conflict and dissension. According to Cannadine (1999), there are three main ways of conceptualizing social structures within capitalism. The first one, influenced by Marx, approaches society as a division between two classes, the bourgeoisie and the proletariat. The second, Weberian one, perceives the social structure as divided into three classes, the upper, the middle, and the working classes. The third post-structuralist approach views classes as a web with more gradations and, hence, more fluid boundaries between the different classes.

In this study, only the Marxist and the Weberian approaches will be discussed, as they bear significance to the way the field of social mobility has explored social inequalities. Moreover, these two approaches are set apart from subsequent ones because of their potential to link the political with the analytical dimensions of social stratification that I am concerned with.

1.3.1 Marx

It has been argued that the ways we nowadays approach social inequalities emanates largely from the writings of the classics, especially Marx and Weber. Furthermore, as Weber was Marx's junior by approximately one generation, it was Marx's work that sparked off much of the ensuing discussion about the nature of capitalist societies. Hence, I shall devote more space to Marx's ideas, in order to contextualize both the discussion about inequalities in capitalist societies and also about different approaches that have been developed to understand them.

The distinctive characteristic of the Marxist approach to social structure is that it views social inequalities as undesirable and, therefore, their abolition as a historical necessity. For inequalities are a sine qua non of the capitalist system, one of its ontologically inextricable features. This is premised on the historical specificity of the relations of production, which for Marx entail that the working class, who sell their labor, are exploited by the bourgeoisie, who are the owners of the means of production. The means of production of each era seem as providing that era's dominant mode of production. Thus, to understand the way production occurs, *the mode of production*, we have to examine the way people produce, their *means of production* (Marx and Engels [1848] (1977)). The means of production, in turn, include the physical sites where production takes place, such as offices and factories, and also the labor done and the way it is organized in these sites. Moreover, a mode of production entails a broader mode of life (Marx and Engels [1845] (1970)) as Marx views production as a process that involves social relationships. Hence, productive activity has to be perceived in relation to other forms of activity. This can be achieved through the utilization of the concept of social class. The latter, social class, was perceived by Marx as the aggregates of people who are in the same relationship to the means of production (Marx [1867] (1990)). Marx emphasized the conflicting nature of the positions that the owners and nonowners of the means of production occupy. For him, understanding history meant understanding social classes and their struggles. Tellingly, in the opening of *The Communist Manifesto*, Marx and Engels [1848] (1977) state "The history of all hitherto existing society is the history of class struggles" (p. 3). History in Marx is viewed through the prism of class antagonisms, which have always existed. However, the capitalist phase in human history is conceived as distinctive from pervious ones because, among other things, it has ushered in a schism between the two main and antithetically positioned social classes, the bourgeoisie and the proletariat. As Giddens (1973) argued, "this most definitely does not mean that what constitutes a class is identical in each type of class society (although, of course, every class shares certain formal properties which define it as such), or that the process of the development of class conflict everywhere takes the same course" (p. 26). It simply means that although hierarchical social formations that resemble modern social classes existed previously, they cannot be characterized as social classes proper because the exploitative relations that underpin modern class systems owe their existence to the way production is organized within capitalism.

Despite the fact that Marx offered perhaps the most sophisticated account and critique of the capitalist system, his earlier analyses fell short of offering a coherent and systematic definition of social class (Allman, 2001; Rikowski, 2001). Hence, from the two-dimensional class system, that is bourgeoisie and proletariat, which Marx and Engels [1948] (1977) developed in *The Communist Manifesto*, Marx moved on to a three-dimensional understanding of social structure. The opening of the chapter titled "Classes" in Marx's seminal work, *Capital,* is informative: "The owners merely of labour-power, owners of capital, and land-owners, whose respective sources of income are wages, profit and ground-rent, in other words, wage-labourers, capitalists and landlords, constitute then three big classes of modern society based upon the capitalist mode of production" (Marx, 1894/1967, p. 885).

Marx's account leaves little doubt that the basis of the differentiation of social classes is their sources of income, that it to say social class is economically determined. However, he also indicated that social systems are not static entities but dynamic structures where more classes can be observed. With reference to England, in particular "the most highly and classically developed in economic structure" (Marx, 1865, p. 885), two more classes existed, namely the "middle" and "intermediate strata." However, Marx was aware that these were temporary formations within the capitalist mode of production as the intermediate strata had the tendency to move "into the camps of labour (especially) and capital as increasing tracts of social life come under the sway of the capitalist mode of production. In this process, labour is transformed into wage-labour on an incremental scale" (Rikowski, 2001). Similarly, landed property would likely be transformed to a group that would correspond to the capitalist mode of production. At any rate, one of the most important points that were made by Marx in relation to social classes is that they are closely related to the concept of "social relations of production." As Lenin ([1899] (1964), pp. 62–63) argued, "it is not with 'production' that political economy deals, but with the social relations of men in production. Once these social relations have been ascertained and thoroughly analysed, the place in production of every class, and, consequently, the share they get of the national consumption, are thereby defined." Thus, classes are conceived as social aggregates, collectivities that occupy common positions within the realm of social relations of production. Furthermore, classes are to be conceived as sets of social relations united by the antagonistic nature between each other. Their unity, therefore, rests on their oppositional character. In turn, as pointed out above, conflict exists as long as capitalism is the way production is organized. Put differently, classes are ontologically predicated upon the existence of capitalist social relations, which are permeated by antagonism. For the labor–capital relation "creates a social relation, and as this is generalised throughout the productive process it creates social classes" (Braverman, 1974, p. 413).

Marx importantly differentiates between what he called "class-in-itself" and "class-for-itself". Those with the same class position are a "class-in-itself," sharing the same objective conditions, though not necessarily a common sense of belonging or a cohesive course of action. By contrast, "class-for-itself" connotes the formation of class consciousness, which holds members of the same class together in order to achieve their common goals. This is one of the key ideas of Marx's political thinking, as he envisaged that the proletariat would transform itself from a "class-in-itself" to a "class-for-itself" in order to become a revolutionary social class and overthrow capitalism. As I discussed above, the antagonistic nature of the social relations in capitalism lends itself to an ongoing class struggle that will inescapably lead to the termination of capitalism. Capitalism will then be superseded by a mode of production associated with collective ownership of the means of production and absence of exploitation in the relations of production, namely communism. This will only be achieved if the key agent of this progressive change is the proletariat (Marx and Engels [1948] (1977)).

However, Marx's idea about the "natural progression" of society from an unequal and exploitative one, as it inescapably is under capitalism, to an equal and fair one, which will emerge with the advent of communism, has exposed Marxian theory to numerous criticisms. Modern Marxists do not adhere wholesale to this corpus of Marxian ideas, although they share some common understanding. The main bone of contention is that the abolition of capitalist relations and the transformation of society into a communist one has not yet occurred. Some insightful criticisms of Marxian ideas were developed by Max Weber. However, Weber did not only seek to challenge Marx but to advance his own theory about social structure and class relations. These ideas have been very influential in empirical sociology and the study of social mobility in particular and are worth discussing here.

1.3.2 Weber

Marx's materialist conception of history found a staunch critic in Max Weber. Weber rejected Marx's idea that the various forms of social inequalities stem from the relationship of people to the means of production and organization. Unlike Marx, Weber did not subscribe to the idea that economic position and political power were inextricably linked. Instead, Weber propounded a triptych based on social class, status, and political party. Moreover, he drew a further distinction between class interests and argued that the sociologist has to explore different class positions and the types of actions that result from them. Weber maintained that there is a multiplicity of social interests, which led him to develop a pluralistic approach to social stratification. This approach implies social fluidity within the social system and conceptualizes social stratification on the basis of the results actions have in the labor market for social agents. For Weber, there were two types of actions: communal, for example, solidaristic action, such as trade union membership, and societal action that seeks to change the distribution of life chances, such as those actions associated with membership in political parties. In this vein, class was perceived as a group of individuals with the same class opportunity to influence the market in order to provide privileges for a specific group in society (Moschonas, 1986, p. 25).

By the same token, to understand social class means to explore the market situation of individuals rather than their relationship to the means of production. In Weber's words [1924] (1978),

> we may speak of a "class" when (1) a number of people have in common a specific causal component of their life chances, insofar as (2) this component is represented exclusively by economic interests in the possession of goods and opportunities for income, and (3) is represented under the conditions of commodity labor or labor markets...It is the most elemental economic fact that the way in which the disposition over material property is distributed among a plurality of people, meeting competitively in the market for the purpose of exchange, in itself creates specific life chances...All this holds true within the

area in which pure market conditions prevail. "Property" and "lack of property" are, therefore, the basic categories of all class situations. Within these categories, however, class situations are further differentiated: on the one hand, according to the kind of property that is usable for returns; and, on the other hand, according to the kind of services that can be offered in the market...But always this is the generic connotation of the concept of class: that the kind of chance in the market is the decisive moment which presents a common condition for the individual's fate. Class situation is, in this sense, ultimately market situation. (pp. 927–928)

Hence, Weber was interested in class situation. Although he moved away from Marx's central idea about the relationship with the means of production, he still argued that owners have the advantage over nonowners. Hence, while the owners can use their access to economic resources to enhance their own benefits and economic position, the nonowners are reduced into service providers, that is, to their own labor. Although each of these two groups is further differentiated internally, for example, in terms of type of ownership or services provided, the underpinning of Weber's analysis is that the key feature of class differentiation is the position of individuals in the labor market. In other words, although the relations of the different classes to the production process matter both for Marx and Weber, for the latter, it is within the labor market where social-class relations are played out. This difference between the two thinkers, Marx and Weber, might appear as a simple case of dichotomous theorizing and conceptualizing social class: On the one hand, we have Marx who insisted on the significance of the relations of social-class position to the means of production, and, on the other hand, we have Weber, who stressed the way people exchange these relations in the market place. However, their difference is more nuanced than this. As Wright (1987, p. 107) argued, "both Marx and Weber adopt production-based definitions in that they define classes with respect to the effective ownership of production assets: capital, raw labour power and skills in Weber; capital and labour power (for the analysis of capitalism) in Marx."

However, the most salient point of departure between Marx and Weber lies in their perception of the production process. Wright (1987) articulated this point very eloquently: "The difference between them is that Weber views production from the vantage point of the market exchanges in which these assets are traded, whereas Marx views production from the vantage point of the exploitation it generates" (p. 107). This perspectival difference has been termed the "culturalist" and the "materialist" conceptions of society, respectively. This difference is fundamental for a number of reasons. First, it shapes the way social classes can be theorized and researched. If one adopts a Marxist framework, then social classes have an antagonistic underpinning. If there is no such underpinning, then the working class would be denied the opportunity of seeking to lead a liberation struggle against the exploitative forces of capitalism, and would become a class without a historical mission. Politically speaking, this (Weberian) approach reduces the most radical possibility of transforming capitalism, allowing only a mere succession of events with the working class compromising to a passive role. Second, Weber's culturalist analysis leaves little space to explore class struggle within the diverse institutional settings and terrains of capitalism. By contrast, though, the way social-class struggle is lived by the agents of social transformation and especially the proletariat is not self-righteously understood by a Marxist framework more than a Weberian one. Far from that, Weberian class analysis has shed light on micro-processes of oppression and class struggle and has enriched our understanding of class dynamics in modern capitalism in ways that the Marxist framework does not.

This aspect of Weberian theory has made its conceptualization of social class particularly influential for social mobility studies. This is due to a number of reasons that range from the ideological–political to the practical–empirical ones and I will discuss them in chapter 2. In what follows, I develop further some of the key ideas and concepts discussed by Marx and Weber and link them to the examination of social mobility that is central in thisb ook.

1.3.3 Social Mobility in Marx and Weber

Marx in particular and Marxism more generally have been criticized for having paid scant attention to the issue of social mobility. As I will show in chapter 2, this criticism is a misconception. Marx's contribution to social mobility lies in his emphasis on the relations of economic exploitation and political conflict. Marx developed a complex theory of the historical, political, and socioeconomic conditions that would make the egalitarian restructuring of society possible, through the exploited class usurping power from the ruling class. On the other hand, Weber developed an equally complex and pluralistic approach to social inequalities, whereby he delineated additional forms of social organization to that of social class, namely status and political party membership. Furthermore, Weber's contribution to mobility studies stems from his definition of social-class positions in relation to the way people fare within the labor market and his treatment of social class and status as two analytically distinct but interrelated categories (for more, see Mach and Wesolowski, 1986, pp. 25–27). Weber's analysis of capitalism and social structure, therefore, sought to improve, refine, and elaborate on Marx's work. Weber criticized Marx for generalizing from what is sometimes the case to what is necessarily the case. Thus, according to Weber, Marx's theory of class conflict and the inevitable collapse of capitalism was shaped predominantly by the conditions in England (where Marx was then living) and at that time was at a more advanced stage of capitalist development than the rest of Europe. For Weber [1924] (1978), working-class exploitation, the increasing conflict between capital and labor, and the potential for class conflict were idiosyncratic to mid- and late nineteenth century England, rather than emblematic of wider conditions of capitalism and the working class. In addition, although Weber accepted the possibility of class conflict, he argued that this could lead to the improvement of capitalism rather than its demise. Hence, conflict in Weber did not necessarily take the form of revolutionary transformation aiming to overthrow capitalism, but of social tension that could lead to improved working conditions, workforce security, and similar, short-term considerations. In stark contrast with Marx, Weber maintained that conflict does not necessarily lead to the collapse of capitalism but to its longevity, and as we will see in the next section, this view is also shared by functionalists.

Although Marxist social mobility studies are not common (see chapter 2), the analytical tools that Marx developed led to the creation of theories of social class and class boundaries that influenced social mobility analysis. Weber, on the other hand, seems to have had a stronger influence in the field of social mobility, both in terms of defining and operationalizing social classes. These influences will be discernible through some seminal studies that will be presented in chapter 2 (e.g. the Oxford Mobility Study). For the moment, I shall turn my attention to another influential theoretical strand in mobility studies, namely structural-functionalism or simply functionalism, which was advanced by Talcott Parsons.

1.3.4 Parsons

Structural-functionalism held sway in mainstream sociology from the mid-1940s to the late 1960s, but its influence waned after that. Nevertheless, functionalism's impact has influenced policy making as well as the field of social mobility, which is discussed below. For Talcott Parsons (1940), the founder and leading advocate of structural-functionalism, social stratification is the differential ranking of individuals in a given social system and their treatment as superior and inferior relative to one another in certain respects. Moreover, Parsons claimed that modern social systems are inherently hierarchical, leading to social stratification. Social stratification, in turn, involves the distribution and allocation of honor with which societal processes are integrated and ordered. In doing so, stratification serves integrative, rather than the socially corrosive purposes. Parsons further argued that ranking in a system of social stratification serves the purpose of moral evaluation and that "occupation and occupational accomplishment is the most important basis of evaluation and the main determinant of the individual's and his family's position in the stratification system" (Parsons, 1940, p. 94).

Parsons specifically, and functionalism more broadly, departed from the previous conflict theories of Marx and Weber, by arguing that inequalities might not only lead to conflict, but they are necessary to maintain the efficient operation of the system itself (Roberts, 2011). Even though conflict was not rejected as a possibility, Parsons (1940) nevertheless argued that social stratification serves to counteract such tendencies because society is inherently stable and power provides a resource for maintaining the system or guiding changes within it. What is interesting in Parson's theory for the purposes of my argument herein is his emphasis on stratification as an integrating aspect of modern societies. For functionalists, social practices serve societal purposes. Social inequalities, therefore, are perceived as serving functional purposes in that they motivate people possessing talents deemed as necessary for occupying the most important positions. Moreover, inequalities are viewed as helping "to integrate societies by affirming the importance of well-rewarded positions, and expressing the wider society's approval and gratitude to the incumbents" (Roberts, 2011, p. 8).

The general principles of functionalism, as expressed by Parsons, exerted a major influence on the mobility studies conducted by Lipset and Zetterberg (1959), Blau and Duncan (1967), as well in Glass's (1954) seminal study that is discussed in chapter 2. Modern applications of Parsonian functionalism adopt a view of society as stratified in multiple layers, though not necessarily connected with a hierarchical relationship between them. This has allowed researchers to study the way social inequality is transmitted but at the cost of neglecting the dynamics of social-class struggles.

1.4 Economism versus Culturalism and New Perspectives

Marx's and Weber's theories presented above have provided the basis for some of the most enduring debates in social sciences. From these debates, the most relevant for this book is that between the ways social structure has been theorized. First, analytical confusion engulfs the relevant field due to the separation, quite often more perceived than real, between structure and agency. Hence, on the one hand, Marxian ideas are depicted as emphasizing the role of structure over and against any consideration of agency within it. This is the "determinist" thesis (Molyneux, 1995) that has long tantalized social theorists and it refers to a perceived determinism of the cultural, political, and other spheres of activity, by the economic. The "base-superstructure" metaphor (Althusser and Balibar, 1970) has often been deployed as an exemplification of this determinism, which, according to its critics, was most evident in the works of Marx himself, and also in those of a number of so-called structural Marxists or neo-Marxists, such as Althusser (1971) and Poulantzas (1975). The emphasis, on the other hand, on the role of agency or action, has been associated with accounts that stress the subjective aspects of social class and its origins are attributed to the work of Weber. This approach stresses the importance of social actions, or, to be precise, meaningful social actions, their intentionality, and the role of values in forming judgments that lead to actions that matter socially. This division between "economistic"/"structuralist" versus "culturalist" explanations has created a split in theorizing social structure. In my view, this is a false and unwarranted dichotomy. This confusion has been exacerbated by some radical post-structuralist and postmodernist accounts in ascent from the 1980s onward. These accounts have placed little attention on issues of social inequalities and have relativized, marginalized, and misinterpreted the classical formulations concerning social structure. Moreover, drawing on the demise of the Eastern Block and the collapse of "existing socialism" in a big part of Central and Eastern Europe after 1989, a distrust or even scorn for the viability of Marx's ideas and their application in modern society started to also spread in social sciences. As Cannadine (1999) argued, "communism is dead, therefore Marxism is dead, therefore class is dead: thus runs the argument" (p. 14). In other words, class analysis was denigrated to the margins of sociological inquiry, because "doing" social class was perceived as a preoccupation of those who had a political interest in the transformation of society, and especially along radical egalitarian lines, often associated with socialism and communism. In this conjuncture, the study of social inequalities started receiving criticism or being ignored altogether. At the same time, the exploration of issues pertinent to the individual, such as the various forms of identities, subjectivities, and cultural differences, was gaining ground. This led many authors to proclaim the death of social class (cf. Pakulski and Waters, 1996), while others argued for its reduced significance (Beck, 1992; Clark and Lipset, 1996). I am contented that this rejection of social class as a topic of and for analysis is as analytically superfluous as it is epistemologically untenable. To begin with, the various forms of identity and issues surrounding subjectivity do not exist in a "floating" society nor in a superficial manner. They are aspects of life, or rather they form part of individuals' reality, which is lived in real families, groups, and societies (see Bourne, 1999; Kelly, 1999; Kelsh and Hill, 2006). In order for these subjectivities to be realized, a certain set of structural constraints operate, no matter how far one wants to go with their deconstruction. Social institutions, such as education that concerns this book, are a form of structure whose operation is shaped by the system of production in place, that is, capitalism. The identities of the participants in educational processes are important in reaching a fuller understanding of all aspects that make up the totality of the experience of these participants, whether such analysis is of a postmodernist form of "identitarianism," stressing particularity, complexity, and individuality, or whether the analysis of identity recognizes various/particular forms of group oppression, by paying attention to their non-class-based group identities such as those based on "race," gender, or sexuality. However, the usefulness of such approaches is seriously hampered by ignoring or paying little attention to dimensions outside the realm of the individual. The availability, for example, of educational opportunities, the recruitment patterns, the relationship of education with the labor market, the role and value of educational qualifications, and so on, are not discursive elements and cannot be approached through the lens of individual positionality alone. They are intertwined with the wider socioeconomic, cultural, and political arrangements that shape people's perceptions, aspirations, strategies, choices, and actions.

The conundrums exemplified above led to a reconceptualization of the way social structure and inequalities are approached and new, dynamic models were put forward. The most insightful and influential among them was that advanced by Pierre Bourdieu. Bourdieu attempted to transcend the problem between structure and agency, and economistic and culturalist explanations. In what is now widely acknowledged as an original contribution to social theory, Bourdieu added to the economic aspect of capital the social and the cultural, which he then further enriched with the symbolic capital. As Canaan (2013) argued, "Bourdieu (1984) began to redress the then developing class silence/confusion about class by opening up the concept of capital beyond its economic dimension, arguing that classes could not be adequately defined by economic capital; social and cultural capital also needed consideration—that is, those with the greatest economic capital were likely to respectively have the most powerful social networks and wield the greatest cultural and aesthetic knowledge and power." In other words, Bourdieu (1984) enriched our understanding of the forms and articulations of social inequalities in modern societies, where social agents occupy multiple roles and identities at the same time. This multiplicity of roles and identities, though, requires a dynamic analysis that takes seriously into account the structural location of individuals within the social structure. Bourdieu has offered us the analytical tools to achieve this within complex societies like the ones we live in. Especially, his use of the concept of cultural capital has found many followers as it allows for a nuanced explanation of class differentials and outcomes. Cultural capital according to Bourdieu implies that "Each family transmits to its children, more in an indirect than in a direct manner, a certain cultural capital and a certain ethos, a system of implicit and profoundly interiorized values, which contributes to define, among other things, the attitudes toward cultural capital and toward the school system. The cultural heritage that under these two aspects differs by social class is responsible for the initial inequality of children before the school selection, and thus, to a large degree, for their unequal rates of success" (Bourdieu, 1966, p. 388). As we will see in the remainder of this book, this theorization has enriched the ensuing discussions and improved our understanding of the underpinning processes and mechanisms, including those of social mobility. For example, I will show in Part II that in order to best understand the class struggle dynamics within the community I studied, it was paramount to also explore the social and cultural aspects of this community, such as marital practices and family values.

Bourdieu's analysis offered new directions in the analysis of social inequalities and social structures. Recently, scholars have developed some of his concepts further, in order to explore not only the concept of social class more fully than before, but also to articulate it dynamically to notions, such as gender, "race"/ethnicity, sexuality, disability, and so on (Skeggs, 1997; Reay, 1998; Reay et al., 2005, 2007; Lareau, 2003; Devine et al., 2004; Savage et al., 2005; Ball, 2007, 2008).

1.5 Summary

This chapter offered a brief overview of some key tenets of social theory pertinent to the examination of social stratification and social-class analysis. It argued for the centrality of the concept of social class in explaining structural inequalities in modern capitalist societies. In order to trace the history of associated ideas it offered a critical, yet brief discussion of the main analytical points developed by the classics of social theory, such as Marx and Weber, as well as by modern thinkers, such as Parsons and Bourdieu. This presentation aims to furnish the reader with the necessary background to the theoretical elaboration of concepts associated with social mobility that are discussed in chapter 2.

Chapter 2
Social Mobility: Issues, Trends, and Critique

Social mobility represents one of the most studied and least understood areas of sociological inquiry. (Dahrendorf, in Mach and Wesolowski, 1986,p.1 1)

2.1 Introduction

In chapter 1, I discussed some key ideas pertinent to the way social stratification has been theorized, in particular by some social theorists (e.g., Marx, Weber, and Parsons). I argued that these ideas have largely shaped our understanding of social inequalities and differential arrangements within capitalist societies. This is notably evident in the field of social mobility as I discuss in this chapter. Specifically, I argue that social mobility currently functions as the matrix of structural socioeconomic inequalities within modern societies, which explains the political and media attention it has been increasingly attracting in Britain and elsewhere.

The first part of this chapter discusses some key approaches, themes, and trends in the field of social mobility. The second part offers an appraisal of key postwar mobility studies and discusses some of their major theoretical and methodological shortcomings. The chapter concludes with a Marxist critique of mainstream mobility studies and a proposal for an enriched investigation of social mobility and attendant processes, for example, class formation and interchange. I argue that such an expanded investigation is necessary now more than ever as attested to by the global crisis in which capitalism has been immersed and the resultant stalling in upward social mobility.

2.2 Social Mobility Measurement (Occupational and Income-based)

From the mid-nineteenth century onward, the study of social structure of capitalist societies has received systematic attention. This attention is justified by the need to understand the nature of capitalism; the type and extent of hierarchal arrangements; and their impact on societies, families, and individuals. This interest led to the development of social mobility as a distinct field of inquiry that aims to explore the "openness" or "closure" of modern capitalist societies, the degree of social movement that occurs within them and the fair or otherwise distribution of opportunities. Put differently, social mobility study involves the examination of the degree of interchange between social classes, that is to say, whether people from any background can achieve the highest class positions. The reader might be aware that the relevant literature is permeated with different definitions and diverse approaches to the study of social mobility, depending on the unit of measurement (e.g., individuals, couples), focus of inquiry (social class, occupational, educational movement, and so on), and subfield of study (e.g., gender, feminist, or ethnic minorities studies). A definition that is more in line with the studies that will be presented in this chapter posits that social mobility is "the movement or opportunities for movement between different social classes or occupational groups, and the advantages and disadvantages that go with this in terms of income, security of employment, opportunities for advancement and so on" (Aldridge, 2003).

There are two main[1] approaches to the way social mobility is studied. The first one is based on occupation while the second on income. The former approach, the occupation-based, is mainly utilized by sociologists, while the second one is chiefly used by economists. According to the former, the occupational approach, the individuals' positions are derived from their "exchange capacity," that is to say their position in the labor market. Individuals are not aggregated in terms of their income as in the "economistic" approach discussed below, but, rather, on the basis of their occupational status. In turn, this is derived from their employment and market situation. This has been the most influential approach in the relevant field and has received extensive applications in contemporary studies of social stratification and mobility. It has been championed by the Nuffield study's lead proponent, namely John H. Goldthorpe (1980, 2000), and his collaborators. The occupation-based approach derives its theoretical influences from Weber's understanding of social class as discussed in chapter 1. However, the categories created for the measurement of mobility are not social classes proper, but, rather, conventionally accepted approximations of social classes. These groupings are determined by the necessities of empirical research: They owe their existence to the interest of social scientists to measure social mobility. The salience of this approach in the exploration of social mobility, despite its limitations, is explained by the need to measure the extent of social mobility as well as the interchange between social classes. As Monk put it (1970, in Reid, 1989, p. 6) "Occupation remained the backbone of social grading because no better methods have been found, and because it has still remained a powerful and useful stratification factor, even though the interpretation has become more complex." As some issues pertaining to occupation-based classification are discussed in some detail below, I shall now turn my attention to the second approach.

The second approach can be termed the "economistic" approach (cf. G. Duncan, 1984) and is based on income as the basis for allocating individuals into groupings. Although these groups are referred to as "classes," they are heuristic devices for the study of social mobility rather than real, social collectivities. For they only exist for as long as there is an interest in measuring the movement of people within a specific social structure in a way that is empirically feasible and easy to convey to diverse audiences. In Loury et al.'s (2005) words, "this approach tends to envision social classes defined basically in arbitrary terms (e.g. by income deciles), and to view the differences between individuals as incremental" (pp. 1–2). The advantage of this approach is that the measurement of the groups involved is reliable and easy to achieve and interpret. The main disadvantage[2] is that the linking of these groups to real social classes makes the discussion of social-class differentials and the concomitant theory generation or improvement practically impossible. Moreover, the basis of measurement, that is, income, routinely represents the monetary rewards granted to incumbents of different occupational positions. Other assets individuals might possess, for example, inherited wealth, land, financial products, such as bank deposits, shares, and so on, are not accounted for. Moreover, the economic rewards of individuals might vary considerably even within the same occupation. For example, an experienced doctor might be earning twice as much as a novice, which would consequently place the former on the top (or very near the top) of the grading scale, while the latter would be placed somewhere near the middle. Income differences and distances, therefore, conceal any relationship of these occupations not only to the means of production but also to the social system at large. Put differently, the fundamental dimension of occupations as social and cultural relations is replaced by numerical values with little relevance to the way social-class practices are lived, produced, reproduced, and interrelated. Most crucially, the potentially antagonistic relationship among social classes gives way to a simplistic representation of social structure, which consists of high-, middle-, and low-income earners. This approach has been criticized for paying scant attention to class antagonism and the possibility of class struggle. Although the basis of social class is economic and a higher pay might be a recurrent demand made by various collectivities in the labor market or other increasingly valuable asset holders or controllers to improve their living standards, critics argue that economic disparities stem from the nature of capitalism and the possibility allowed within it for one group of people to exploit another and/or use their position in the production and the capitalization processes to indirectly acquire capital through access to exploitation and commodification. This exploitation, the same argument goes, stems from the subordination of the working to the ruling class (rather than of one income group to another).

2.3 Postwar Mobility Studies

It could be argued that prewar mobility studies had a generic focus as they sought to explain the direction of change in society and to assess the possibility for the achievement of large-scale socioeconomic changes. In other words, these studies were interested in exploring social mobility as a factor of socioeconomic development and its relationship with macroeconomic and social transformations. Notable examples include Sorokin's (1927) work on mobility and the nature of social stratification and Pareto's (1935) study on social mobility and the elites. Both studies enhanced the shift from "a 'negative' interest in social mobility—that is, an interest in mobility as a phenomenon which complicates, impedes, or blocks the achievement of socialism via the labour movement—to a 'positive' liberal interest" (Goldthorpe, 1980, p. 13).

After the Second World War, the focus shifted to the exploration of the political potential of social mobility for liberal democracy. Consequently, mobility studies were now increasingly linked to the exploration of issues pertaining to equality of opportunities and outcome, the role of key institutions (e.g., education), the functioning of the welfare state, and so on. Moreover, according to Heath (1981, p. 30), there is another key difference that characterizes postwar mobility scholarship. This involves the technical and methodological advancements that were achieved and demonstrated through the development of methods of data collection and analysis. Some of these postwar mobility studies have given social mobility a prominent place within modern social sciences and social policy and are discussed next.

The interest in the political potential of liberal democracy and the exploration of the social fluidity of postwar societies is evident in three of the most highly acclaimed studies that were conducted in the 1950s and 1960s. As Glass's (1954) study is discussed separately, I shall briefly consider Lipset and Bendix's (1959) and Blau and Duncan's (1967) in the United States. Lipset and Bendix (1959) favored the idea of openness in society, albeit they pointed out the downside that high mobility might have on individuals and ultimately on social and political order. Their line of reasoning came from a conservative standpoint and was directed against the radical social policies associated with universalism, such as equality of opportunities, open access to education, and the like.

Blau and Duncan (1967), on the other hand, based their explanation of the preponderance of relatively high mobility rates (attested to in industrialized countries from the 1950s and until the late 1960s) on the underlying trend of universalism. That is to say, Blau and Duncan (1967) argued that in industrialized societies, there was a trend with nearly universal applicability whereby individuals in all aspects of their life base their decisions and judgments on considerations stemming from self-interest, rationality, and efficiency rather than on cultural (in terms of group membership, such as social class) values or norms.

At the same time, the field of social mobility was enmeshed in the exploration of three key theories, namely the Lipset and Zetterberg hypothesis (1959), the "Featherman Jones Hauser" (FJH) hypothesis (1975), and the "liberal theory of industrialism" (1960).

The Lipset and Zetterberg hypothesis holds that patterns in social fluidity will not vary across industrialized, European countries (Lipset and Zetterberg, 1959, p. 13). The FJH hypothesis postulates that all industrial societies "with a market economy and a nuclear family system" share some key similarities in relation to the social fluidity observed in their societies (Featherman et al., 1975, p. 340). Finally, the "liberal theory of industrialization" or "modernization theory" states that economic development will cause an increase in absolute mobility rates (Kerr et al., 1960; Kerr, 1983). Moreover, it expects educational qualifications to play an increasingly stronger role in job selection, because economic competition will force employers to appoint the most able candidates, that is, those with the highest qualifications (for a similar argument, see Treiman, 1970).

These hypotheses have been tested and discussed at length in numerous publications, which can be categorized into two groups: first, those that concurrently compared various countries. Pertinent examples are Ganzeboom et al. (1989), Erikson and Goldthorpe (1992), and Breen (2004). The second group of studies adopted a single-country focus. Some notable examples include the exploration of social mobility in France (Goldthorpe and Portocarero, 1981), Sweden (Erikson, 1983), the Netherlands (Luijkx and Ganzeboom, 1989), the Republic of Ireland (Breen et al., 1990), the United States (Hout, 1988; DiPrete and Grusky, 1990), Northern Ireland (Breen, 2000), and so on. The presentation of these works, albeit brief, was important in order to contextualize the recent and contemporary debates in the field of social mobility and present some of the major themes that have received attention of mobility researchers in the last 60 years or so. From these themes, two are central to this book. First, whether patterns of fluidity have any similarity among countries with similar characteristics (e.g., industrialized, late-industrialized). Second, if educational qualifications enhance occupational outcomes of individuals and assist in the economic growth of nations.

These themes were explored in depth in two prominent studies, both conducted in the United Kingdom, which I discuss in the following sections.

2.3.1 David Glass and the LSE[3] Study—Social Mobility and Large Social Inequalities: System Efficiency and Individual Advancement

David Glass (1954), who pioneered large-scale mobility research with a representative national sample of 10,000 individuals, sought to explore the role of social status in the social mobility of British people. Glass's study shifted the focus of mobility inquiries from the study of social structure and class formation that was dominant hitherto, to the investigation of "the extent of movement in social status or social position by individuals of diverse social origins" (Glass, 1954, p. 5) after then.

Glass's main findings, as "political arithmetic," indicated that there was overall neither a substantial change in social circulation in Britain until the Second World War nor any significant one in the period after the end of the war. Moreover, the type of individual mobility that was evident was within white- and blue-collar occupations rather than across this dividing line. In other words, there was a considerable amount of short-range mobility but an equally significant rigidity between the manual and nonmanual dividing lines. This rigidity was even more pronounced at the top of the social hierarchy where self-recruitment was quite high.

It is mainly this aspect of Glass's study that makes it considerably important: that is, the unravelling of the possibility within social systems (as in Britain of the immediate postwar years) to foster at the same time high social mobility rates and inequality of opportunities. This possibility raises serious questions about the nature of liberal capitalist societies and the effects of social fluidity on fair allocation of opportunities: If the social structure is open enough for some individuals to advance into higher social-class positions than their parents, is this very system legitimately hindering the social ascent of others? Could the putative openness be also unfair given that it is mainly those from the top of the class structure who have more chances of taking advantage of this "openness"?

For Glass (1954), high social fluidity within a system was desirable since it could increase its economic and social efficiency. Moreover, high rates of social fluidity could also confer benefits to the individuals, provided that the ablest among them would occupy the most suitable positions (according to their skills) and thus fulfill their potential. In other words, a meritocratic correspondence mechanism between occupants of high social positions and high ability would be established, premised upon the existence of a fluid social system. According to Glass (1954, p. 25), "even if there is little actual opportunity to rise in social status, the belief in a myth of opportunity may produce similar results" that is to say of personal actualization and social and economic efficiency. Glass, in a functionalist manner, saw in social mobility the key to ensuring social cohesion and tranquilizing against the disruptive potential of class divisions. For him, it was not the elimination of social inequalities that was of priority, but the unfair allocation of rewards and disadvantages: "We need to encourage mobility for the advantages it offers to individuals and to society; but we also need to avoid, as far as possible, such disadvantages as may follow from having a social structure in which status relationships between individuals in successive generations will be far less stable than at present or during the past half-century" (Glass, 1954, p. 25).

From a political perspective, Glass favored the preservation of capitalism as he believed that this was the best system for individual and social advancement. To be precise, Glass envisaged a meritocratic or fair capitalism, for this was the only way that both proliferation of occupational opportunities and economic growth could be realized. Class conflict was not seen as an agent of transformation of the system in toto, but as an opportunity for the improvement of capitalism or aspects of it (e.g., class antagonism could equip the system with the most able individuals and make the competing individuals better). Crucially, one of the mechanisms through which the system could enhance its efficiency and maximize its capacity was education. The role of education then was crucial in the distribution of occupational opportunities and it was to be largely entrusted with the maximization of system efficiency and allocation of rewards to individuals. As discussed in chapter 1, this has been one of the key ideological maxims of the postwar period and various governments with a commitment to liberalism have adhered to it.

2.3.2 John H. Goldthorpe and the Oxford Mobility Study—Unequal Rewards and the Educationally Mobile Generation

The person most closely associated with the Oxford Mobility Study (also known as the Nuffield Study) is John H. Goldthorpe. Goldthorpe's work is of special interest here as it has had great impact on subsequent mobility theorizing and has formed "the basis for much of our current knowledge and conceptualization of class mobility" (Payne and Roberts, 2002). The source of Goldthorpe's interest stems from a concern "with the extent to which characteristic features of the social structure of liberal democracy prevent individuals of certain social origin from realising their full potentialities as citizens, or indeed as human beings" (Goldthorpe, 1980, p. 27).

In other words, the way Goldthorpe views social mobility connotes an interest on the widening of occupational opportunities (openness) that are hierarchically placed in the division of labor. As a result, Goldthorpe maintained that mobility was the best vehicle toward greater openness in society that has to be pursued by all means. In his seminal work, *Social Mobility and Class Structure in Modern Britain* (1980), he drew on a representative, cross-sectional sample of all British males who were aged between 20 and 64 years, in 1972. His findings suggested that from the 1940s onward, there was substantial fluidity in British society. This was mainly upward intergenerational mobility rather than downward. Additionally, the observed patterns of movement pointed to short-range mobility, which implied movement between social positions that were regarded to be at a similar level (Heath, 1981, p. 54).

In addition, in the first three decades after the war, Britain experienced almost incessant economic growth and significant transformations in its occupational structure. This was also followed by educational expansion, which aimed to establish equality of opportunity. Nevertheless, the progress in educational provision did not suffice to qualify Britain of the early 1970s as an open society since the inherent inequalities in the social structure were left unchallenged. The reason for this was that the observed mobility rates were achieved thanks to structural changes Britain experienced after the war in its economy and labor market rather than due to the equalization of material rewards and opportunities for members of different social classes. Hence, these rates can be attributed to the " 'increasing room at the top' by the growth of professional, higher technical, administrative, and managerial positions… but without the members of any class having to become less advantaged than before in absolute terms" (Goldthorpe, 1980, p. 251).

What is crucial here is that a great amount of the ascending trajectories mentioned by Goldthorpe was achieved through the possession of educational qualifications. Therefore, many of those from working-class origins who made it to top positions were grammar-school graduates, unlike those who left school with no qualifications, who were more likely to stay in the working class. This reads as a triumph of liberal capitalism and the prevailing postwar "liberal consensus": capitalism, in its Golden Age, indeed conferred benefits to individuals, especially from lower-class positions to reach the top of the social structure and advance much more than their parents or grandparents did. As Westergaard and Resler (1975) put it, these findings "dispel any notion that Britain is a society in which the individual position in the hierarchy of inequality is fixed by birth. Capitalism here as elsewhere allows—indeed in some respects encourages—a fair degree of fluidity or circulation" (p. 298).

Nevertheless, the occurrence of fluidity or circulation does not preclude the existence of social inequalities or as Westergaard and Resler (1975) argued, "to say that circulation is fluid is not to say that it is free. Inequality of condition sets marked limits to individual opportunities and risks of ascent and descent" (p. 299).

2.3.3 Social Mobility and Politics

What is striking in both Glass's (1954) and Goldthorpe's (1980) studies is the common finding of high and historically persisting social-class inequality in the British social structure. According to Glass (1954), "there have been no major differences between successive generations in the overall intensity of the status association between fathers and sons" (p. 216). This finding was corroborated in the Oxford Mobility Study, which concluded that "even in the presumably very favourable context of a period of sustained economic growth and of major change in the form of occupational structure, the general underlying processes of intergenerational class mobility—or immobility— have apparently been little altered, and indeed have, if anything, tended in certain respects to generate still greater inequalities in class chances" (p. 85). The increase in unequally distributed opportunities pertaining to social class led Goldthorpe (1980) to conclude that "no greater degree of openness has been achieved in British society over recent decades" (p. 86).

Undoubtedly, these findings paint a picture of postwar Britain as fluid but unequal. That is to say, despite the relative existence of opportunities for social movement, the British social structure remains unequal and polarized along class lines. Opportunity for movement, therefore, is not coupled with reduction in class inequalities. By contrast, the latter seem to hold sway over adjacent generations and despite much policy activity, such as through the welfare system, educational expansion, and so on.

Goldthorpe and Payne (1986) obtained similar patterns through a more recent cohort, the examination of which led them to conclude that "relative mobility rates have remained essentially constant on the same pattern that they would appear to have displayed for most of the century" (p. 18). More recent examinations have asserted that there is a high degree of intergenerational class inequalities in the British social system and they have highlighted the relative stability in patterns of transmission of privilege and disadvantage onto the next generations along class lines (Breen and Goldthorpe, 2001). In other words, relative mobility rates (as distinct from absolute mobility rates), which demonstrate the degree of social-class inequalities or the extent to which rewards are fairly distributed (or otherwise), seem to hold sway in the British social structure. An even fresher wave of studies confirmed these trends (Goldthorpe and Mills, 2004; Goldthorpe and Jackson, 2007), while others (see, e.g., Erikson and Goldthorpe, 2009) unequivocally concluded that "the evidence points to a continuation of the essential stability that has been documented for several decades previously" (p. 3).

This line of thinking has been very influential in terms of how social mobility is understood in Britain and more broadly. As far as Britain is concerned, social mobility is an issue that attracts attention from media and political circles alike. Political parties from all persuasions have engaged with the attendant issues and, as Goldthorpe and Jackson (2007) argued, "in Britain in recent years social mobility has become a topic of central political concern" (p. 525). Especially, since the turn of the new millennium, it has become politically imperative to show a greater degree of commitment to social mobility than to many other areas of social policy. All major British parties have realized that social mobility makes the headlines in the national press because class inequalities in Britain have persisted over the years of putative affluence. In this vein, the New Labour government (1997–2010) showed an early interest in social mobility through the establishment of the Cabinet Office Performance and Innovation Unit and its concomitant publications (cf. Aldridge, 2001). One of the most widely discussed of these publications was the discussion paper *Getting On, Getting Ahead. A Discussion Paper Analysing the Trends and Drivers of Social Mobility* (Cabinet Office, 2008), which was commissioned directly by the then prime minister and identified various ways of enhancing social mobility. Subsequently, the New Labour government was galvanized into policy action with the White Paper, *New Opportunities: Fair Chances for the Future* (HM Government, 2009), which was shortly followed by the report *Fair Access: Good Practice; Phase 2 Report* (The Panel on Fair Access to the Professions, 2009). At the same time, social mobility received some interest from the Conservative Party with the publication of the document *Through the Glass Ceiling: A Conservative Agenda for Social Mobility* (Conservative Party, 2008). The Liberal Democrats followed suit with the establishment of an Independent Commission on Social Mobility. The Commission issued a *Report* (2009), which explored "how social mobility might be increased" (p. 3). This document seems to have had an impact on the incoming Coalition government as some of its findings and recommendations were followed up in one of the Coalition's flagship policy documents, namely *Opening Doors, Breaking Barriers: A Strategy for Social Mobility* (Cabinet Office, 2011). The latter brought afresh the target of increasing social mobility at the core of policy strategy by stating that "tackling the opportunity deficit—creating an open, socially mobile society—is our guiding purpose" (2011, p. 3) and going as far as to argue that "*improving social mobility is the principal goal of the Coalition Government's social policy*" (p. 3).

Despite the divergent policy responses developed by the three parties regarding how best to promote social mobility, the documents discussed above share Glass's view about the importance of social mobility in enhancing system efficiency and creating opportunities for individuals. Specifically, the three parties are in unison in their support for mechanisms that can promote social mobility, while at the same time they are equally evasive and obscure about how this can be achieved without the reduction of class inequalities.

2.3.4 Income Mobility and New Trends

Despite the broad acceptance the dominant approach (see sections 2.3.1 and 2.3.2) in social mobility has received and the widespread influence it has had on social policy, recent studies have challenged its main conclusions and propounded an alternative account of social mobility and associated trends. As far as the United Kingdom is concerned, researchers who used the same data sets as Goldthorpe and his associates (referring to their post-1980s studies in which Goldthorpe and his colleagues mainly used the 1958 cohort, that is the National Child Development Study, and the 1970 cohort, otherwise known as the British Cohort Study) came to substantially different conclusions. For example, Blanden et al. (2002) found that "the economic status of the 1970 cohort is much more strongly connected to parental economic status than the 1958 cohort" (p. 15). This finding points to increased association over the years between parents' and children's earnings and a concomitant decrease in intergenerational mobility. The authors of the study attributed this fall in mobility rates to the fact that "a greater share of the rapid upgrading of the British population has been focused on people with richer parents. This unequal increase in educational attainment is thus the factor that has acted to reinforce more strongly the link between earnings and income of children and parents" (Blanden et al., 2002, p. 16). Blanden and his associates produced a series of studies, in which similar patterns were observed (cf. Blanden and Machin, 2004, 2007; Blanden et al., 2004, 2008; Blanden, Gregg, and Machin, 2005; Blanden, Gregg, and Macmillan, 2007). These studies were distinctive because they challenged the hitherto dominant understating of mobility patterns and attendant results produced.[4] A renewed exploration of social mobility patterns in the United Kingdom (this time with new data sets, i.e., the Millennium Cohort Study) showed that the observed decrease in intergenerational mobility rates "appears to have been an episode caused by the particular circumstances of the time. Social mobility worsened and took a step change downwards, leaving the UK near the bottom of the intergenerational league table of mobility, and on a different trajectory relative to other countries in the world where there is less evidence of changes over time" (Blanden and Machin, 2007, p. 18). Blanden and Machin (2007) further argued that downward mobility was in this case matched by a rise in educational inequalities, which is explained by a big increase in the connection between educational attainment and family income as well as by the strong association among test scores, behavioral measures, and family income. The latter, namely the connection among educational attainment and test scores, behavioral measures, and family income, led Blanden and Machin (2007) to conclude that for more recent cohorts, there is "little evidence of change and thus it appears that *changes in social mobility may well have flattened out.* However, at the same time, they have not reversed nor started to improve" (p. 19) (my emphasis).

Despite the differences in conceptualization, measurement, and attendant findings in social mobility rates, the aforementioned studies lucidly demonstrate that the British postwar society has been characterized by stable patterns of unequal rewards and class allocation. This places the United Kingdom in one of the lowest positions internationally as far as openness and fairness are concerned. In this regard, the United Kingdom demonstrates similar rates to Germany and a few other countries but is set apart from a host of other countries with pronounced openness, such as Sweden (Erikson, 1983), the Netherlands (Bakker et al., 1984), France (Vallet, 2004), the United States (Hout, 1988), and so on.

2.4 Critique of the Mainstream Mobility Approach

The studies conducted after the war, and especially those led by Glass and Goldthorpe, have placed the examination of social mobility in a prominent position within modern sociology. In particular, Glass's and Goldthorpe's studies were significant in revealing the extent of the movements that occur between occupational and social classes and were very informative about the extent of the "openness" of the British social system. However, various elements of these works have attracted significant criticism. In the remainder of this section, I shall discuss some of the main shortcomings of these enquiries that are directly relevant to the argument of this book. The pertinent discussion started in the previous section with the presentation of some more general sociopolitical issues of contention. In this section, I explore some conceptual as well as technical criticisms of the mainstream approach in a more detailed manner.

In the first place, both in the LSE and the Oxford Mobility studies, the unit of analysis was the individual within a specific nation state. The repercussion of such a focus was that it restricted social mobility analysis to intergenerational, occupational mobility in a given nation state (Kelley, 1990). Moreover, the data these studies sought to collect were solely about men. This male bias has been associated by critics (Delphy, 1981; Crompton, 1990) with the "conventional," "traditional," or "dominant" approach in mobility studies, which admittedly has been engrossed in the study of a limited number of issues at the expense of other, equally important considerations. Thus, the occupational movements of women have been neglected because their intermittent careers created problems in the analysis of their mobility. Due to the fact that women were dependent upon men within marriage, and since husbands' occupational positions were not significantly influenced by their wives' occupation(s), classifying family units by the male head of the household appeared to be an appropriate and justified procedure of data collection and analysis in the traditional approach (Dex, 1987, p. 137). This led, though, feminist researchers to question this approach by arguing that patriarchal and capitalist relations are manifest and intersect (West, 1982). Therefore, renewed approaches were necessary in the study of social mobility that would adopt an expanded gender focus to also include women's social mobility. It was not before the 1980s that the hitherto male bias in mobility studies as well as the monolithic orientation in terms of the established methodological tradition were challenged. Britten and Heath (1983), for example, attempted to remedy this shortcoming by providing an alternative set of class categories based on both husbands' and wives' classes and by taking into account the changes in women's marital and employment statuses. This shift in theorizing and measuring social mobility came chiefly from a feminist perspective (e.g., West, 1982; Dex, 1987) and also from studies focused on the mobility of immigrants (Vermeulen and Perlmann, 2000) or ethnic minority groups (Heath and Ridge, 1983; Borjas, 1992; Loury et al., 2005).

In addition, there is another source of criticism directed at conventional studies that needs to be discussed here. The survey-method approach relies upon the use of large-scale data sets "that group together under a single label all the members of a population who have one or more common characteristics" (Mouzelis, 1978, p. 58). The problem that Mouzelis eludes is that of hypostatization. That is, the treatment of sociological artifacts and conceptual entities, such as that of social strata, as real ones. This kind of abstracted empiricism is problematic since it does not advance to the level of theorizing and thus explaining the sociocultural dynamics that constitute these groupings as social entities.

Furthermore, approaches that aggregate groups of people in order to create sociological categories, as is the case in conventional mobility research, do not examine the actual lived relationships between such groups nor do they take into account the experiences of individuals who form these categories. Hence, while the mainstream approach is useful in identifying distributional aspects of a social system, for example, how rewards are allocated, the distribution of income, and so on, it cannot be used adequately to explain them nor can it be informative about the reasons for their emergence and reproduction. In addition, what is often missing from conventional studies is an interest in individuals as the agents of such mobility processes and a theorizing of society not just as a "host body" of mobility processes, but also as a generator of them. As Ball (2003) argues, "class identities are not to be found within talk about categories, but in practices and accounts of practices" (p. 175). In other words, classifying (part of) the reality of the experiences of the survey respondents ignores these selfsame lived experiences.

What is also crucial for this book is that quantitative inquiries fail to see the intersections among social class, gender, and ethnicity, as they typically reduce them to a tally of parallel considerations that vary together or independently from each other and are subsequently plotted against an ideal type of social mobility (e.g., perfect mobility). Social class, gender, and ethnicity are not merely facets of one's identity, crude variables that contribute to an individual's social mobility and life chances, but they constitute "a dialectically mediated constellation of totality" (McLaren and Farahmandpur, 2005, p. 17). As the second part of the book demonstrates, these considerations were treated as central in the study of social mobility I conducted in Greece.

Following on from the previous point, the individualistic bias of the quantitative mobility approach (Crompton, 1990), which has tended to treat the randomly selected individuals as isolates, pays scant attention to their social embeddedness within specific contexts and is oblivious to the social, historical, and collective dimensions of people's identity, which influence their mobility processes. This wider context then has to be seen as the backdrop of any occupational and social mobility movement that gives meaning to strategies, struggles, alliances, pathways, and means that individuals utilize within the unequal arena of social stratification. In other words, while survey research offers a descriptive basis for invaluable insights in understanding the direction of change and in unravelling trends in the occupational milieu, it does not inform us about or explain how different class, gender, and ethnic practices relate to occupational positions nor how these practices change as one rises or falls through occupational categories (Crompton, 1990). From an epistemological viewpoint, mainstream mobility research has been criticized for its "hegemonic" position and for owing its preponderance to its relation to power (Goldthorpe, 2000, p. 66). That is to say, surveys require vast amounts of resources that only governments, major institutions, and businesses can provide, thus forming the agenda of the research conducted and limiting the autonomy of the researchers. Critics argue that this has an impact on the production of knowledge, which, in the case of survey methodology, is objectified as it comes from a superior position in relation to the realities of those studied and is ultimately aimed at their control (Burawoy, p. 66). On the other hand, ethnographers have put forward alternative explorations of social mobility that aim at the production of knowledge that does not seek to control but rather to provide empathetic understanding of those studied. In this manner, the researcher can also extend his or her interests to the study of powerless, marginalized, and subordinate groups, which are invariably not examined through the survey methodology.

Apart from the above criticisms leveled against conventional social mobility studies, there is a less-examined issue on which I want to shed light. This has to do with the ellipsis of the highest social classes in concomitant analyses and the partiality or even blindness of conventional mobility research to the complexities of capitalist social structures. The capitalist as well as the "upper class," that is the aristocracy[5] are nearly totally absent from mobility inquiries because the conventional tools for measurement of social-class situation are not sensitive to this type of information (more to follow in the next section). This creates a somewhat restricted and even distorted view of social structure and a significantly skewed idea of the social-class circulation and attendant opportunity for movement.

2.5 Marxist Critique and Social Mobility

It is often maintained (cf. Van Heek, 1956) that Marx himself, as well as historical materialism more broadly, paid lip service, at best, to the issue of social mobility or entirely ignored it. Indeed, some Marxists treated social mobility as an issue of secondary importance. Poulantzas (1973), for example, most famously dubbed it as "a problematique bourgeois." This assertion stems from the belief that social mobility does nothing more than measuring the extent of social inequalities among individuals or groups of individuals, when the point, for Marxists, is to abolish them in toto. Accordingly, social mobility is discounted by some Marxist authors as a counterrevolutionary field of study as it can uncritically legitimize social inequalities rather than provide the tools that could assist in challenging them. The social researcher, therefore, instead of offering his or her services to the emancipation of the working class from the capitalist domination, is complicit with the capitalist establishment by virtue of participating in research that is alleged to have limited or no transformative potential.

In a similar vein, the classification of occupations associated with mainstream mobility studies and the attendant derivation of social classes is dismissed by Marxist scholars as a mechanism that distracts attention from the existence and reproduction of class-based social inequalities, to the exploration of the distribution of opportunities for movement *within* the social structure (see, e.g., Hatcher, 2012). That is to say, the fact that these opportunities are hierarchically ordered and distributed in the first place is allegedly concealed from mobility research. It is further maintained by Marxist critics of social mobility studies that the classifications utilized typify society as consisting of multiple "classes" or strata, that is, layers that group individuals together according to their occupation, without attempting to make any connections with the ownership or not of the means of production of the incumbents of these positions. Any opportunity, therefore, for class struggle and attendant conflict, which, as we saw in chapter 1, is a sine qua non in the Marxist conception of history, is masked under the discussion of nonantagonistic movements within the social structure.

For Hill and Cole (2001, p. 30), this means that "consumption-based classifications of social class gloss over and hide, the fundamentally antagonistic relationship between the two main classes in society, the working class and the capitalist class. In Marxist analysis, the working class includes not only manual workers but also millions of white-collar workers...whose conditions of work are similar to those of manual workers." Hill and Cole (2001) further argue that, if it is to be consistent with a Marxist framework, the conception and operationalization of the working class need to be enriched in order to include occupations, such as bank clerks and check-out operators, who share the same working conditions and are exploited by the capitalist system of production in a similar fashion to the traditional working-class job holders, namely manual laborers.

The problem is as much an epistemological as an ideological/political one. On the one hand, the epistemological pitfalls rest with the knowledge produced through a nonantagonistic conception of social classes and the consequences this has in relation to the representation of the social world. That is to say, by collecting information in a manner familiar to conventional mobility research, society is depicted as if consisting of multiple occupational groups from which social classes are eventually derived. Indeed, these groupings are not ordered hierarchically, as has been argued by Goldthorpe (2000), one of the leading advocates of the mainstream mobility paradigm. Furthermore, Marxist critics argue that the capitalist class does not register in the class schemes typically utilized in mainstream mobility research; hence, the possibility of depicting society as conflict-ridden is de facto absent. In such a manner, the social scientist creates a representation of the world that does not resemble the one we inhabit for it lacks the potentially antagonistic element that is fundamental in any account of a capitalist society that comes from a Marxist perspective. The *episteme*, therefore, produced from conventional mobility research is closely aligned to the interests of the dominant class, namely the bourgeoisie, and, as such, is conflict-free.

On the other hand, this is an issue that also carries significant ideological and political implications that allude to the possibilities of the working class realizing its historical mission and, from a class in itself, becoming a class-for-itself (see chapter 1). Because "by segmenting the working class, they [the occupation-based derivations of social class] both hide the existence of a working class and they also serve the purpose of 'dividing and ruling' the working class—that, by segmenting different groups of workers, for example white collar and blue collar workers, and workers in work and the so-called 'underclass' workers... These subdivisions of the working class can be termed class fractions or segments (Ainley, 1993)" (Hill and Cole, 2001, p. 152).

The critics of conventional mobility studies, then, take issue with such classifications as they "hide and work to inhibit or disguise the common interests of these different groups comprising the working class. They serve, in various ways, to inhibit the development of a common (class) consciousness against the exploiting capitalist class" (Hill and Cole, 2001, p. 153). Rikowski (2001) develops this point further by inserting a political dimension in the critique of conventional classifications, which he perceives as "*basically ideological in nature*" (emphasis in original) and function to "mask and subvert attempts to analyse class from a critical social scientific perspective concerned with the constitution of capitalist society." For Rikowski (2001), such representations of social class "fail to capture it as a concept that expresses the deep antagonism within the heart of capitalist society."

Following this line of argument further, the connection between the epistemological and the ideological/political becomes inescapable. To be precise, this connection entails that the conventional classifications serve the interests of the ruling class, as Marx succinctly expressed it in the dictum "the ruling ideas of each age have ever been the ideas of its ruling class" (Marx [1848] (2004), p. 30). In this fashion, the inextricability of the two different forms of domination, the ideological and the political, becomes apparent. In other words, a form of ideological hegemony (Gramsci, 1971) is in play, thanks to the dominant position the conventional classifications occupy in the relevant body of literature and their shaping of our understanding of modern class-ridden societies. The knowledge generated, therefore, forms part of a hegemonic discourse, which serves the interests of the ruling class. Thus, the latter do not only dominate the working class in the real world of production, but also in the world of ideas and social representation. Furthermore, the danger with conventional analysis and research is that it "misreads the nature and significance of 'class', whilst capital oppresses us and human representatives of capital cheerfully (with their stock options, bonuses and public sector rip-offs) plot the extension of capital's rule over society. Mainstream analyses of class fail to engage this oppression" (Rikowski, 2001).

Here, I wish to develop and improve upon these accounts by outlining two analytically distinct but interrelated propositions. In doing so, I will follow the framework thus far developed by adhering to the epistemological and political/ideological tenets of the criticisms discussed above. First, from an epistemological perspective, I shall argue here that it would be erroneous to suggest that social mobility is completely overlooked or irrelevant to historical materialism. Rather, Marxism as a metatheory that is interested in explaining long-term historical change as well as in articulating a political and socioeconomic alternative puts emphasis on the formation of social classes and on the role the proletariat can play as the agent of transition from capitalism to socialism (and, eventually, to communism). Thus, social mobility is part of the economic and social transformation within the same process: the formation of social classes and (the formation of) class consciousness (Goldthorpe, 1980). The argument is that it seems to me more accurate to suggest that Marxists were primarily concerned with the theorization of mobility antecedents, such as social-class conflict, boundaries, and composition; the emergence, disappearance, and transformation of classes; and so on. In doing so, they did not systematically venture on the measurement of social mobility movement as such (perhaps with the conspicuous exception of Wright [1985]). Moreover, in line with an "orthodox"[6] conception of historical materialism, as developed by Marx [1859] (1977) in the Preface to the *A Contribution to the Critique of Political Economy*,[7] the discussion of social mobility was implicit within the study of capitalist development, and the attendant transformation within the social structure. It has been vigorously argued by some Marxists that the capitalist mode of production is but a temporary stage in human history and course of development. Following Marx, they argued that capitalism would be superseded by the next stage in socioeconomic development, namely socialism. This line of thinking, although now largely abandoned, was revived by some Western Marxists and it soon formed a "scientific" conception of historical materialism. This is furnished with an understanding of human history as a linear process that passes through stages, with the bourgeois mode of production being the current, though not the final one. In other words, history, like science, obeys universal laws of change and sooner or later the contradictions of capitalism will inevitably bring its own demise. Most prominent among those who developed an understanding of historical materialism as a "Marxist social science" (Levine and Wright, 1980, p. 49), or Marxist "science of history," are Althusser and Balibar (1970), as well as G. A. Cohen.[8] After the mid-1980s, more elaborate and sophisticated interpretations and reformulations of Marx's original thesis have been developed, which have accordingly led to more nuanced interpretations of historical materialism.

Be this as it may, it is palpable that this rekindled "scientific" Marxism has had an influence on contemporary Marxists who reject social mobility research as a counterrevolutionary and counterproductive pursuit to the emergence of socialism. Here, I want to argue that social mobility is an intrinsic feature of capitalist societies that needs to be taken as seriously as other topics more akin to traditional Marxist scholarship. Moreover, the study of social mobility is not a priori in opposition to Marxist thinking, or at least to some strands within it. A closer reading of Marx's (1894) [1999] own work reveals that not only did he not turn a blind eye to the issue of social mobility, but, by contrast, he devoted some space in one of his seminal economic writings, the *Capital*, which is worthwhile quoting here in some length:

> The circumstance that a man without fortune but possessing energy, solidity, ability and business acumen may become a capitalist in this manner [by receiving credit]—and the commercial value of each individual is pretty accurately estimated under the capitalist mode of production—is greatly admired by the apologists of the capitalist system. Although this circumstance continually brings an unwelcome number of new soldiers of fortune into the field and into competition with the already existing individual capitalists, it also reinforces the supremacy of capital itself, expands its base and enables it to recruit ever new forces for itself out of the sub-stratum of society. In a similar way, the circumstance that the Catholic Church in the Middle Ages formed its hierarchy out of the best brains in the land, regardless of their estate, birth or fortune, was one of the principal means of consolidating ecclesiastical rule and suppressing the laity. The more a ruling class is able to assimilate the foremost minds of a ruled class, the more stable and dangerous becomes its rule. (Marx, *Capital*, Vol. 3, part 5, ch. 36)

The last sentence of this excerpt is unambiguously revealing of how Marx perceived the functioning of social mobility. The resonance of these ideas in understanding social movement within contemporary capitalism has been pinpointed by Elster (1982) who argued that "various institutions of the capitalist era can be explained by their functions for capitalism, as in this analysis of social mobility" (p. 457). In other words, Marx suggests that social mobility and associated opportunities for upward movement, especially to the very top of the social structure, reinforce the capitalist edifice and safeguard its efficacious operation. Recruitment from the working to the capitalist class and the fostering of the belief in the possibility for doing so is indeed an indication of the success of the system, except that this success is defined so by the capitalist class. To put it differently, for Marx, social mobility carries the deceptive faculty of being perceived as a win–win situation: Upward social movement confers benefits to the individuals, while it also consists of a successful mechanism that secures the preservation of the capitalist system. Through social mobility, capitalism and its institutions, such as education, as will be shown in the remaining chapters, become the scriptwriters of success. Especially, in the case of a spectacular rise from rags to riches, the individuals adopt the dominant discourse, that is the capitalist discourse, and interpret their upward movement as personal success. At the same time, through the mechanism of social mobility, capitalism allows social agents to enact roles that are attached to a script that not only did they not write themselves, but, more disturbingly, functions against their best interests. This irony underpins life within capitalism. As Marx [1852] (1963) argued in one of the most oft-quoted lines from the *The Eighteenth Brumaire of Louis Bonaparte*, "Men make their own history, but they do not make it as they please; they do not make it under self-selected circumstances, but under circumstances existing already, given and transmitted from the past."

Focus on social mobility is not ipso facto in opposition to historical materialism, or at least an interpretation of it, by arguing that Marx himself paid some due attention, though not in a systematic manner. An interconnected source of criticism leveled against conventional mobility research is about social-class derivation. As argued above, mainstream classification schemes are subject to criticism for masking class conflict. Two questions arise from this proposition: first, why Marxists have not developed schemes that can measure social mobility in a manner consistent with historical materialism. That is to say, a scheme that measures the extent of movement within the social structure but also allows for the antagonistic relationship between social classes to be depicted. Second, in case conventional classifications fail to express the antagonistic relationship between the working and the capitalist classes, is this a sufficient reason to abandon the examination of social mobility from a Marxist perspective altogether?

Indeed, the difficulty presented in the measurement of social classes in a manner consonant with the fundamental distinction in Marxism between those who own the means of production and those who do not is a key operational obstacle that poses serious limitations in the empirical investigation of social mobility. Typically, in modern capitalist societies, those who own the means of production and possess most of the wealth and power (political and economic) are too small a group to be identified in conventional class measurements (Goldthorpe, 1980). This was acknowledged by Westergaard and Resler (1975), who were sympathetic to historical materialism but were also interested in the analysis of social mobility. For them (1975), to try "to trace the movement of people over time among categories of the population defined, for example, in terms of property ownership and the market earnings would be hardly feasible." Indeed, such an endeavor would run into practical problems, such as gaining access to this kind of information and determining the exact amount of assets people possess, especially for those people at the very top of the social hierarchy. Consequently, the social researcher has two options: either to abandon the study of social mobility altogether or to accept the limitations posed by the empirical challenges and proceed with the mobility analysis, in a manner, though, that deviates from traditional Marxist interpretations.

However, a construction of a social-class scheme that retains the Marxist principles is equally hard to create, given the lack of methodical conceptualization of social class in Marx's writings. As well-bemoaned and lamented by now, the point where Marx started to develop a systematic account of social class, in Vol. 3 of *Capital*, titled "Classes," is where the manuscript broke off. Nevertheless, Marx's work is replete with references to class and class analysis. The very opening of the *The Communist Manifesto* [1948] (1977) declares Marx's conceptualization of history as the history of class struggle. The nature of this struggle is always antagonistic, for there are two main opposing classes in each historical epoch: slave and master, patrician and plebeian, lord and serf, guild-master and journeyman, bourgeois and proletariat. This two-way depiction of society also appears in *Capital*, Marx's seminal economic work.

In spite of this polarized depiction of social relations by Marx, it would be erroneous to assume that his idea of social structure was simplistic. Once Marx offers his antagonistic version of history, he makes the following corrective statement "In the earlier epochs of history, we find almost everywhere a complicated arrangement of society into various orders, a manifold gradation of social rank... The bourgeois society that has sprouted from the ruins of feudal society has not done away with class antagonisms. It has established new classes, new conditions of oppression, new forms of struggle in place of the old ones" [1948] (2004, pp. 3–4). It is evident that Marx accepts in specific historical contexts the existence of social classes that correspond to the new conditions of oppression. However, as explained later in the *Communist Manifesto*, there is no doubt that capitalism "has simplified the class antagonisms" and that society is increasingly "splitting up into two great hostile camps, into two great classes directly facing each other: Bourgeoisie and Proletariat" [1948] (2004, p. 4). This should not confound the reader into believing that other classes, fractions, and strata are incompatible with the Marxian class analysis. In *The Communist Manifesto* and the *Eighteen Brumaire of Louis Bonaparte* [1852] (1963) alone, apart from the terms mentioned thus far, namely bourgeoisie and proletariat, all the following appear: industrial bourgeoisie, aristocracy, large landowners, aristocracy of finance, petty bourgeoisie, the middle class, peasants, and lumpen-proletariat. This makes Marx's account less monolithic and much more nuanced than critics have credited it for. Nevertheless, the critics are correct to highlight a major weakness in Marx's work, which stems from the fact that Marx failed to provide a systematic theory about the causal link between class structure and class formation, that is to say how positions within class structures form organized collectivities (Wright, 1985).

On the other hand, the second proposition I shall put forward deals with what I termed above as the *political/ideological level* of analysis. This proposition posits that it is not social mobility per se that is a bourgeois preoccupation, as Poulantzas (1973) disapprovingly exclaimed, but the use of social mobility findings for political expediency. Social mobility research is not de facto subservient to the bourgeois establishment or at least not more so than any other topic of social scientific inquiry. Social inequalities exist regardless of social scientists' willingness or ability to shed light on them. Furthermore, social movement is a generic feature of capitalist societies, for capitalism is a dynamic, ever-changing system sustained by the relationship between capital and labor and the contradictions intrinsic in this dialectical relationship (see Marx's *Capital* [1867] (1990), especially ch. 1). Although this falls beyond the scope of this book, suffice to say here, following the Marxian conception of capitalist development (see, e.g., Harman, 2009; Callinicos, 2010; Harvey, 2010), capital's insatiable demand for expansion creates new opportunities for individuals, groups of individuals, or even whole nation states for movement within the labor market, social structure, or world economy. The realization of this movement is only possible by the mobility of the "living stock" of capitalism, that is, the working people themselves. Pursuant to this line of thinking and, as already argued, it was Marx himself who gave rise to the discussion on social mobility. Following this, the rejection of the examination of social mobility on the basis of pro-bourgeois bias risks discarding the baby with the bath water.

However, not everything is on a par. That is to say, the exploration of movements within the social structure should not obfuscate or adumbrate the possibility for class struggle. I contend that plenty of mainstream mobility research has fallen victim to this tendency, largely due to its appeal to politicians and policy makers. In other words, research findings that stem from mainstream social mobility research, due to their potential for rise of multiple, even conflicting, interpretations are usurped by political agents, individual and collective ones alike, in an attempt to increase their share in the political market and gain concomitant rewards in terms of electoral power. Thus, rather than tackle the problem at its root, which is none other than the unequal nature of capitalist relations, the social mobility *problematique* becomes institutionalized and, therefore, enters the nexus of power relations embedded in the exigencies of parliamentary representation, which entails competition to win voters. This process, of course, is not unique to social mobility. Other issues, such as nationalism, religious tolerance, gender discrimination, and so on, once they enter the capitalist social relations, become potentially domesticated by one or more of capitalism's institutions. Never entirely, of course, as counter-hegemonic struggles also abound. Put differently, it would be destructive for the interests of mainstream bourgeois parties and threatening to their very existence if they tackled capitalism as a way of eliminating the inequalities that stem from it. Indeed, this would imply the disappearance of social mobility as a topic of and for research, for the abolition of capitalism would entail the end of social inequalities. Hence, operating in an area with high resonance with the mainstream electorate, such as social mobility, political parties of all persuasions appropriate it as an effective means for raising precious political capital while, at the same time, they help maintain the status quo. In other words, mainstream political parties need to be seen to be doing something about social mobility rather than actually tackling the serious issues that stem from it. In this vein, social mobility becomes one of the most effective anaesthetics of capitalism. As I will return to this issue in the final chapter, for the moment, it is essential to show how some of the ideas discussed above instantiated in a country that comprises a fascinating social mobility case, namely Greece.

2.6 Summary

In this chapter, I presented some major postwar mobility studies. I highlighted the importance of these works in the development of the pertinent field and discussed some key trends and patterns of intergenerational mobility, which showed a high degree of circulation but low rates of relative social mobility. I then linked the political potential of social mobility to reveal a key weakness within capitalism, namely the occurrence of high social movement, which can be accompanied by pronounced inequalities of opportunities. These trends were related to the United Kingdom albeit they also apply to other countries that adopted a liberal orientation.

In addition, I offered evidence that underpins Marx's consideration of social mobility issues and addressed some matters of conceptual and empirical nature facing the study of social mobility in modern societies. Finally, I argued against the dismissal of social mobility inquiry as a bourgeois preoccupation and in a somewhat unconventional manner I propounded the enrichment and improvement of the pertinent field with theoretical considerations from the Marxist corpus of ideas.

Chapter 3

The Political Economy, Social Stratification, and Class Formation in Postwar Greece

3.1 Introduction

While after the Second World War the (economically) advanced Western countries had to confront issues ranging from their deindustrialization to the restructuring of their labor markets and economies, late-industrialized countries, such as Greece, were faced with a plethora of different issues. These included their belated urbanization, their full participation in the global markets, the decline in agricultural production, and so on. Nevertheless, both these diverse sets of countries shared a renewed class formation with the concomitant expansion of the service sector, and especially the public sector, and a political economy more exposed than ever before to the forces of capitalism and, more recently, to global neoliberal capitalism.

By virtue of the magnitude of the aforementioned dimensions, my discussion in this chapter will be limited to some salient aspects. In doing so, I will adopt a single-country focus, namely Greece, and more specifically the features of the Greek political, economic and social life that are pertinent to the issues tackled in this book.

3.2 The Political Landscape

Given the inherent connection in modern social systems between the political and socioeconomic spheres of activity and their impact on education, in this section I shall outline the key political events that shaped postwar Greece. Although this is necessary background information, space limitations do not allow for a broader discussion. As a result, what follows is a synopsis rather than a detailed account.

The 1944–1949 Civil War that followed the Second World War is key to understanding postwar Greece as it created "a political, ideological and institutional polarisation that permeated all facets of activity" (Koliopoulos and Veremis, 2004, p. 99). The Civil War started in December 1944 in Athens as a fight among EAM/ELAS,[1] the communist resistance fighters ("*andartes*" in popular parlance), and the British who sought to gain control of Athens, which was liberated in October of the same year (Mazower, 2001). EMA/ELAS perceived the British involvement as an imperialist intervention and an extension to the German occupation. Indeed, the British took an active interest in the Greek affairs as they feared that that the country might go down the communist path, as many other Balkan and Eastern European countries had. The British, therefore, seized the opportunity, and with the "Percentages Agreement" between Churchill and Stalin, which sealed the Second World War, it was decided that they would hold 90 percent of share of the influence in Greece. EAM/ELAS, the communist resistance fighters, saw in this development a new fear emerging: The Greek government with the support of their local collaborators and the British were preparing a coup d'état and the restoration of the monarchy. Hence, EAM/ELAS were ready to fight again in order to abort a new order of imperialist rule. The conflict broke out in December 1944 and was largely between, on the one hand, EAM/ELAS and, on the other, the British and Greek loyalists and monarchists (Carabott and Sfikas, 2004). However, after 1946, the Americans also got involved through the administering of aid that was made possible with the Truman Doctrine (part of which was the "Marshall Plan," see this section). The conflict lasted for approximately five years and resulted in more than 50,000 casualties and 700,000 people being relocated (Voglis, 2004). It ended in October 1949 with the defeat of the EMA/ELAS fighters, many of whom were imprisoned or flew behind the Iron Curtain. Cheliotis and Xenakis (2010, p. 361) maintain that "leftist guerrillas who had fought for the liberation of occupied Greece in 1944 were swiftly subjected to systematic persecution, in stark contrast to Nazi collaborators." In one year alone, that is in 1945, approximately 10,000 communists or people broadly identified to be on the Left were imprisoned, while "at any given moment from 1947 to 1949, between 40,000 and 50,000 individuals were interned in prisons and camps" (Voglis, 2002, p. 63).

The Civil War sealed the political and social affairs of Greece for the years to come. The repercussions were multiple and palpable. The polarization between the Right and the Left, the two opposing camps, reflect the burgeoning schism in global politics of the time between capitalism and communism. As mentioned in chapter 1, the Second World War was of major significance for capitalism as a means of "reigniting" itself. In this context, the quest for new markets and the prevention of the communist threat from spreading into more countries were of consequential importance to the capitalist forces of Europe and more broadly. In the Greek case, this became manifest through the influence these forces exerted on Greek politics both during the Second World War and the Greek Civil War. Hence, once Greece entered the British "spheres of influence," the domestic communist forces took it upon themselves to defend the country from the threat of capitalism. This series of events created further polarization between the Right and the Left, leaving a lasting legacy (see chapter 9), which is paramount in understanding political, socioeconomic, and other developments in Greece in the last 60 years (appendix 1). In spite of the fact that, nominally, Greek parliamentary democracy was restored from the early 1950s, the former guerrilla fighters (*andartes*), their families, and anyone believed to be on the Left were persecuted, systematically victimized, excluded from political activities, and marginalized well into the 1960s. The split down the middle of Greek politics also affected labor market, economic and social arrangements. The conservative camp, which emerged victorious from the Civil War, imposed the conditions of post–Civil War peace, which lasted until 1967. During this period of time (i.e., 1949–1967), three main political actors were established: the monarchy, the army, and the parliament. The monarchy and the army were of conservative constitution, with ties with sovereigns in other European countries and with international underground networks of secret services and authoritarian regimes, respectively. The third actor, the parliament, although it maintained a modicum of institutional legitimacy, it was to a large extent a compromise of real democracy as it looked more like a playground of the ruling political forces of the time rather than the crucible of democracy that could be held accountable to the Greek people. Hence, the newly established democracy was fragile and "separatist" and was guarded through various anticommunist or "political-cleansing" acts, during the various coalition governments that were formed between 1949 and 1952 as well as throughout the single-party (conservative) rule and the various caretaker governments that interjected it in power between 1952 and 1963. This state of affairs lasted until 1967, with a short interlude between 1963 and 1967 when a Center–Left government with a liberal orientation assumed office. In 1967, the dictatorship of the colonels seized power through a coup d'état. During the reign of the colonels (1967–1974) the *andartes* were legally proclaimed as "enemies" of the Greek state (Mazower, 2001) and it was only after 1974 that the persecutions against them officially ceased. The restoration of democracy and the return to conservative rule from 1974 to 1981 saw some form of democratization taking place, which was further consolidated in 1981 with the advent into power of the Center–Left party (PASOK[2]), which sought to strengthen democratic institutions and civil liberties. However, if PASOK's legacy, on the one hand, in abating the polarization the Civil War bequeathed is to be exemplified, it has to be, on the other hand, weighted up against its critical contribution to the weakening of the radical left politics in Greece heretofore. PASOK sought to modernize the political system and the economy, and reconcile the social and political tensions that originated in the Civil War. In doing so, it adopted a modern rhetoric and a seemingly progressive outlook, which was different from the maverick, anti-Western (including anti-NATO[3] and anti–European Union [EU][4]) stance it championed while in opposition. In other words, PASOK popularized the capitalist discourse, while, at the same time, it was purporting to offer a radical alternative to the status quo. This shift from a radical to a liberal orientation, which offered the promise of "national reconciliation" and evolved around the principles of national independence, popular sovereignty, social emancipation, and democratization, appealed greatly to the electorate. Thanks to this strategy PASOK managed to penetrate the Left-wing camp, depriving it of the electoral influence it enjoyed hitherto. The anticapitalist proclamations that were often raised until the early 1980s by PASOK were now reduced to a few parliamentary squabbles. This reformed politics that PASOK adopted while in power entrenched Greek capitalism and facilitated further the penetration of international capital into the Greek economy and allowed the free-market model to become embedded in the Greek political economy. Moreover, it made any viable alternative to capitalism appear socially and politically unfeasible, a foregone possibility. In turn, PASOK's reformism ushered into Greek politics the era of "capitalism realism" (Fisher, 2009), that is to say the "contract with the people" was replaced by the contract with the markets. This reformism eventually led to a "political post-modernism," whereby the historical battlegrounds of the ideological wars of the past were abandoned and the terms "Left" and "Right," which used to connote communist versus conservative ideology and politics throughout Greece's postwar history, were buried for good. The new "realpolitik" of the time demanded compromises and radical abandonment of any ideological hurdles associated with the past. This new modus vivendi was embraced by the key political parties and was consolidated between 1989 and 1990 with various short-lived coalition governments between the Center–Right Nea Demokratia party, the Left-wing coalition party, Synaspismos, and the Communist Party of Greece, KKE.[5] This political development, namely the sharing of power between the Left and the Right, acted, symbolically and politically, as the anaesthetic of any old ideologically-riddled conflicts and suppressed the social and political tensions that stemmed from the Civil War. Furthermore, it was a move that further watered down the political divisions of the past and weaved them into the new social-class fabric that emerged after the wars, namely the expansion of the intermediate class, the shrinking of the peasantry and the embourgeoisement of large numbers of the population in swelling urban conurbations and more broadly. The increased social mobility rates that were attested to throughout this time (early 1950s–late 1980s) seem to have facilitated these political transitions or at least to have accommodated them. Increased social mobility is in itself one of the most effective tranquilizers of class divisions and legitimizers of capitalist inequalities (see chapters 1 and 2). Unfettered mobility in the Greek context meant relinquishing of the past restrictions and impediments to one's career and life chances, regardless of the political background. In other words, to become socially mobile meant either to denounce the leftist past one might have had, or for the whole system to become more open and democratic. It appears that both these processes occurred in Greece and they were influenced by internal and external factors. The most important external factor of the time was the entry into the EU. Entry into the EU and access into the international markets were two of the leading priorities of Greek governments until the 1980s, while, after that the consolidation and acceleration of market capitalism became the new priority. Despite the alternation in power between Center–Right (Nea Demokratia) and Center–Left (PASOK) parties, this priority remained unaltered. Nea Demokratia had a strong market-driven agenda, which they implemented during their two terms in power (first between 1990 and 1993, and then from 2004 to 2009). PASOK, in their first term (1996–2004), were occupied with the pursuit of modernization and liberalization policies, while in their second term (2009–2011) led the Greek economy to near bankruptcy and eventually handed over the administration of the country to a group of technocrats, the troika, which consisted of the IMF, the EU, and the European Central Bank (ECB). It seems that half a century after the Civil War and the attendant imposition of foreign rule in Greek politics—through the British intervention and the US involvement—Greece had become even more dependent on foreign powers, both politically and economically.

To sum up, the Civil War was the single most important event in the immediate postwar period in Greece. One of its most significant effects was the pro-Western commitment and orientation that Greece vehemently adopted after its termination (1949). This commitment involved the breaking of the communist ties Greece had had in the past and the adoption of the Western sociopolitical system of parliamentary democracy, which was linked, among other things, to the mixed-market economy. This pro-Western alignment was a strategic choice as it allowed Greece to become a member of various international organizations whose impacts were influential thereafter in political, economic, ideological, and social terms. The most important of these organizations were: in 1948, the Committee of the European Economic Cooperation (which was succeeded by the Organisation for Economic Co-operation and Development [OECD]); in 1949, the Council of Europe, and, in 1952, NATO. Greece also participated in the Bretton Woods Agreement (1944), which shaped the economic policies and priorities of all participating nation states thereafter. It is due to this involvement that Greece became one of the main recipients of the Marshall Aid Plan (see this section), which supported to a great extent its postwar development and economic growth (Zouboulakis, 2005). As I will show in the subsequent sections, this participation sealed the fate of Greece for the years to follow. All subsequent "choices" Greece made, such as to enter the EU and the European and Monetary Union (EMU), were shaped by the Westernization trajectory it followed in the early days after the Civil War.

3.3 The Greek Political Economy after the Second World War

It has been suggested that a nation's economic harmonization is predicated upon its political harmonization (Vergopoulos, 1986). As I discuss in this section, the ongoing economic adversities that have been facing Greece after the Civil War emanate to a large extent from the endurance of political and institutional tensions discussed in section 3.2. In other words, the outcome of the Civil War was a defining factor in the postwar economic development of Greece. Specifically, the defeat of the Left led to the defeat of the labor classes. This paved the way for a radical shift in practices within the labor market, which became more authoritarian and oppressive. At the same time, the labor costs throughout the 1950s and 1960s were very low, formal and informal barriers blocked trade union activity, while high unemployment rates led a big part of the workforce to emigrate. This set of factors bolstered Greek industrialization and development.

The underpinnings of the Greek postwar economic development can be traced to Keynesian economics, which emphasized the active role of the state in economic cycles and proclaimed "an enthusiastic belief in the primacy of economic growth and a strong preference for industrialisation as the driving force of growth" (Pagoulatos, 2003, p. 14). The Greek governments after the late 1940s and up until the 1970s made large investments in industry, which was in concert with the "developmentalist" or "Keynesianism for the underdeveloped" (Pagoulatos, 2003) approach that characterized this period. Subsequently, that is, from the mid-1970s to date, industrial investment declined while that of the service sector increased (Gekas, 2005). The main factors prevalent in postwar Greek development were the following:

a. state interventionism, which allowed the state to act as the main agent of development,
b. the interference of both Greek and foreign, political, and economic interest groups in the socioeconomic processes of the country, and
c. the rising connection between the Greek and the European economy.

I shall deal with each one of these factors in turn. First, as far as state interventionism is concerned, it has to be noted that this can take several forms. In the Greek case, the most salient type was financial interventionism, which has to be linked to the timing of Greek development. That is to say, the later an economy develops, the more active the role of the state is in engineering financial capital. In postwar Greece, this was achieved through the establishment of specialized institutions for industrial finance and the administering of credit in order to accelerate economic growth. The active role of the state was facilitated by the private sector, whose importance in the Greek development was secondary as it had limited potential to initiate industrialization due to the fact that it was overcapitalized and due to market failures (Zouboulakis, 2005). This vigorous interventionism rendered the state as the "main locus in which central economic actors can effectively promote their interests" (Tayfur, 2003, p. 39). In particular, the Greek state intervened through a set of policies in order to maintain the interests of financial and monopoly capital that were the main producers, at least in the 1950s and 1960s. As a result, the state itself maintained and protected the monopolistic and oligopolistic structures that operated in Greece at the time (Ellis, 1964).

The second crucial factor in the Greek postwar development was the interference of Greek and foreign interest groups. With regard to the former, Greek interest groups, the selfsame monopolistic and oligopolistic structures that were mentioned above, allowed the indigenous elite, that is, the Greek bourgeoisie, to gain in economic and political power. This power was evident through the close ties between financial and industrial capital, which despite the fact that it was hampering the economic dynamism and general development of the country, was actively fostered by the Greek state.[6] More specifically, the autochthonous bourgeoisie did not tie its interests to those of Greece as it did not take any initiatives to invest into these sectors of the economy that could support further the industrialization process of the country, such as manufacturing. For the Greek bourgeoisie, this was perceived as a high-risk investment that could result in huge capital and power loss (Mouzelis, 1978). Consequently, the lack of substantial investment by the Greek bourgeoisie was detrimental to Greece's future development, not least because it was offset by the large-scale penetration of foreign capital, mainly in the form of investment and foreign aid.[7] The main source of foreign aid was the Marshall Plan (1946–1950), which made Greece the beneficiary of more money, US$2.1 billion in total, than all foreign loans it had contracted nearly a century after its establishment as an independent state (i.e., from 1830 to 1921) (Koliopoulos and Veremis, 2004). The main reason that compelled the United States to channel such a voluminous amount of aid to Greece was in order to assist in the "preservation of a liberal ideology and the reconstruction of the Greek economy" (Tayfur, 2003, p. 44). To give the magnitude of reconstruction required, suffice to note that Greece only during the Second World War had lost nearly 70 percent of its national wealth, including public infrastructure such as roads and bridges. In 1947, the Greek gross domestic product (GDP) stood at 75 percent of what it was in 1938 and this was only exceeded in 1952. Hence, the foreign aid was mainly channeled to public investment, current budget deficits and also to military expenses (Psilos, 1968). However, this is to underplay the strategic motives of the United States, as a champion of capitalism wherever it could stretch its power. Hence, a more pragmatic account would have to acknowledge the fact that the then US government sought to prevent a possible ascent to power of communist forces by ameliorating the complete devastation of the war-stricken population. The downside was that the United States used this support as an opportunity to increase its influence in the Greek political economy. This penetration into Greek domestic affairs reached such high levels that the United States, arguably, controlled the fiscal and credit policies of Greece (Psilos, 1968). Gradually, the interventionism of foreign interest groups was matched by a steep rise in foreign investment, which increased as a percentage of overall investment from 3.4 percent in 1955 to 31.8 percent in 1965 (Koliopoulos and Veremis, 2004, p. 173), though it started to decline thereafter.

The third factor in Greek postwar development was its relationship with the European economy. According to Tayfur (2003), a massive influx of transfers from the EU to the Greek economy materialized throughout the 1980s and early 1990s and played a crucial role in offsetting Greece's balance of payment deficits. Throughout the 1990s, the Greek development was focused on the convergence of the Greek with the European economies, such as attaining the Maastricht criteria and entering the European Monetary Unification framework, a goal which was eventually attained in 2000. This attempt to converge with other economies in the EU was pursued largely through fiscal consolidation, tight economic policies, and an extensive privatization program that led to a drastic improvement of Greek economic indicators, especially after 1998. However, in 2008, real convergence with Greece's EU counterparts was far from accomplished and the Greek economy had still not overcome its structural impediments, such as the low level of technological advancement, poor infrastructure, and specialization in regressive industries (Tayfur, 2003, p. 99).

In sum, the postwar economic model that Greece adopted was heavily influenced by the "international ideological and policy context of its time, most prominently including the developmentalist economic orthodoxy" (Pagoulatos, 2003, p. 47). Economic policy was state-led, the market heavily protected (especially for an economy that championed the "free-market" model), while civil society and its institutions were still largely underdeveloped.

3.4 The Greek Economy and the Occupational Structure

The year that marked the beginning of the postwar Greek economic growth was 1953, which coincided with a series of steps taken by the Greek government to regulate the economy, such as currency devaluation, stabilization and market liberalization (Pagoulatos, 2003). Overall, the 1949–1974 period was characterized by rapid economic growth and accelerated industrialization achieved, mainly, thanks to foreign assistance and, partially, to domestic sources. Although per capita income at the time was still the lowest among 16 OECD countries, the GDP pace of growth between 1952 and 1972 was the highest in Europe, with an average rate of growth of 6.5 percent per annum (Kazakos, 2001). At the same time, American aid was reduced to one-third of what it stood in 1949 (Jouganatos, 1992). Yet, the spectacular early postwar growth was short lived: The global economic crisis that broke out in the early 1970s halted further economic growth and resulted in prolonged stagnation (Christodoulakis and Kalyvitis, 2001).

The next period, from 1974 to 1996, saw the Greek economy decelerating: Its annual GDP rate of growth not only started to slow down in relation to its European and OECD counterparts but also in comparison to its past growth. Indicatively, between 1979 and 1988, the Greek GDP was growing by 1.4 percent on average, while per capita income was still the lowest in OECD and the EU. This was exacerbated by two protracted periods of austerity (i.e., 1985–1987 and 1990–1992), which induced a drop in the share of wages in GDP and wider stagnation. The economic deceleration started being reversed in the mid-1990s when a fresh and steady wave of growth was pursued, a recovery in some economic indicators came about and wages, as a share of the GDP, increased.

In relation to the changing occupational landscape in postwar Greece, it is important to consider the changing demographic features throughout the postwar years. In particular, emphasis has to be placed on emigration as it was the factor with the most profound impact on the transformation of the occupational structure. There was voluminous emigration of the Greek workforce in the late 1950s and throughout the 1960s. This emigration movement was one of the main reasons for keeping employment rates high in Greece. In addition, emigration, mainly to Western Europe, contributed significantly to the fast pace of economic growth realized in the first phase of the Greek development, that is, 1950–1974, due to remittances and decreasing labor supply. Characteristically, between 1955 and 1977, net migration amounted to approximately 1 million people with over 1.2 million Greeks emigrating abroad mainly to West Germany, while only 237,000 repatriating (Damanakis, 1997). The majority of emigrants, approximately 900,000 people, were from rural areas, while another 600,000 people from the provinces moved into domestic urban city centers, such as Athens and Salonica (Doumanis, 1983). Apart from the substantial demographic transformations that resulted from emigration in a relatively short period of time there are two further issues I wish to highlight. The first issue points to the dependence of mainland Greece on capital raised abroad, which gave impetus to the Greek economic growth during the 1960s and 1970s. The second issue relates to the interdependence of rural and urban areas through the reliance of rural areas on remittance-derived capital that was raised in the urban centers.

In stark contrast with the above-mentioned trends, after the 1990s Greece was confronted with a new situation as the advent of a large volume of economic immigrants from Balkan and Eastern European countries turned it from a "sending" into a "hosting" country. It is estimated that, in 1951, the proportion of immigrants stood at less than 0.5 percent, whereas in the early 2000s, it accounted for 6–8 percent of the overall population and for 9–12 percent of those of working age (Kontis, 2001). Kontis (2001) claims that these numbers might be underestimates since they do not include the approximately 200,000 Greek Pontiacs and Greek-Albanians, that is "ethnic Greeks" who repatriated after the early 1990s, nor the undocumented economic immigrants.[8] According to the OECD (2005), economic immigrants in Greece invariably have found employment even in periods of high structural unemployment among the Greek workforce, thanks to their mobilization in the informal sector and the black market[9] economy (Papadimitriou, 2005). While economic immigrants have contributed in keeping the wages at low levels, they have also helped in increasing output production and profits as well as in allowing a large part of the Greek workforce to improve its own occupational situation. The majority of immigrants[10] have been employed in the service (47.7 percent) and in the secondary sectors (46.1 percent) (NSSG,[11] in Kollias et al., 2005, p. 485). Most of them have been concentrated in the two major urban centers, namely Athens and Salonica[12] (NSSG, in Kollias et al., 2005), though they can be found in all parts of the country, depending on labor demand and availability of resources, such as schools for their children.

In terms of unemployment rates, these were low throughout the 1950s and 1960s due to emigration of large numbers of the Greek workforce and the high reconstruction demands of the country. However, from the early 1970s onward, a range of factors has led to a substantial increase in labor supply and consequently to high unemployment rates, namely an increase in female participation in the labor market, accentuated internal migration from rural to urban areas, the regularization of immigrants from mainly Eastern European countries and the repatriation of co-ethnic Greeks from Western Europe and ex–Soviet Union countries (Christodoulakis and Kalyvitis, 2001).[13] Unemployment rates were particularly high throughout the 1990s, reaching 9.1 percent in 1995. Despite a temporary increase in employment in the early 2000s, unemployment was at even higher levels in the new millennium: 11.2 percent in 2000 and 9.9 percent in 2005 (Athanasiou, 2006). If this is linked with the relatively high growth that the Greek economy experienced from the mid-1990s onward, then the paradox of economic growth that was not accompanied by an increase in labor-force absorption emerges. The factors accounting for this "jobless growth" were the substantial increase in employment productivity between 1997 and 2002, the decline in employment in agriculture and modernization in industry, which involves the substitution of labor with capital (INE, 2005). In the 2000s and especially after the onset of the economic crisis that has engulfed Greece after 2008, unemployment has been increasing at an alarming pace. Characteristically, only in 2011 alone, unemployment rose by nearly 7 percentage points, from 14.7 percent in January 2011 to 21.7 percent in January 2012 (Eurostat, 2012). In addition, youth unemployment has been at strikingly high levels and it is examined separately in relation to education (section 4.1 [chapter 4]). Suffice to note here that despite a general increasing trend in unemployment both within the Eurozone economies and those of the EU, Greece has twice as high unemployment as the EU-27 group and the highest rate, 51.2 percent, in youth unemployment, that is in the age-group below 25 years[14] (Eurostat, 2012) (for more, see section 4.1 [chapter 4]). This points to a structural weakness of the Greek economy and labor market, and its wider political economy.

A related and equally alarming characteristic of the Greek labor market is the relatively low level of wages for those in employment and the higher poverty risk of the Greek workforce in comparison to their European counterparts (Cheliotis and Xenakis, 2010). In addition, the Greek labor market has traditionally been displaying high levels of flexibility, while, at the same time, keeping wages at very low levels, with median household incomes remaining much lower than the European average (Tikos, 2008).

As far as female participation in the labor market is concerned, concomitant rates were initially at very low levels, though they marked a steady increase over the years: from 20 percent in 1971 to 26 percent in 1985 (Vergopoulos, 1986). In 2009, female participation in the labor market rose to 48.9 percent though it was still much lower than that of males, which stood at 73.5 percent (OECD, 2010). Despite this continuous increase in female employment, there are still fewer women in the labor market compared to those of early-industrialized countries. Furthermore, women in Greece are traditionally affected more by unemployment: In 2012, 25.6 percent of females were out of work compared to 18.8 percent of males (Eurostat, 2012). This points to one of the most salient structural particularities of the Greek employment structure, namely its segmented labor market. This is further attested to by the higher rates of part-time female employment in comparison to males[15]; namely, in 2009, 14.4 percent of the female workforce was employed on a part-time basis versus 4.5 percent of the male workforce[16] (OECD, 2010). With reference to the 25- to 64-year-old age-group, in 2008, the female labor market participation rate was 54.4 percent, compared to the 84.3 percent rate of their male counterparts (amounting to an overall 29.9 percent gender difference) (OECD, 2008).[17] Education seems to be a good asset in increasing labor-market participation and narrowing the attendant gender gap. In particular, for women with university education the overall rate of employment for the 25- to 64-year-old age-group was substantially higher, 78.1 percent, while the respective rate for males was 87.6 percent (reducing the gender gap to 9.6 percent) (OECD, 2008).[18]

Another characteristic of the Greek labor market that demonstrates its structural particularities is the employment situation. In 1999, part-time employment in Greece accounted for only 5.8 percent of total employment (the EU average being 17.6 percent), while the Greek average rate for involuntary part-time employment (43.8 percent) was much higher than that of the EU member states (16.8 percent) (Papadimitriou, 2005). However, the deregulation of the labor market and the increase in unemployment have possibly led to a steady increase in part-time employment over the years, which accounted for 8.8 percent of overall employment in 2010, with the average OECD rate being more than double (16.6 percent) (OECD, 2011). Finally, a crucial feature of the Greek occupational structure after the 1950s has been the high proportion of self-employment, which in 1999 stood at 44.8 percent of the Greek workforce, the largest among all EU member states and almost three times higher than the EU average (Papadimitriou, 2005).

3.5 Sectoral Output and Employment: Some Key Postwar Trends

In order to contextualize the occupational and social mobility findings that are presented in chapters 5–8, I shall now turn my attention to the main labor-market characteristics and trends in the postwar period. This presentation illustrates the changes in output production and sectoral employment and aims to provide an integrated and holistic account of the pertinent themes.

From 1949 and until the early 1970s, the Greek economy and labor market underwent extensive restructuring. The growth in the industrial sector in the 1950s and 1960s was swift and sizable and it was matched by an equally rapid and considerable decline in agriculture as well as by a gradual but steady growth in the service sector. After the Civil War, the Greek agriculture lost its prominence as the motor of the Greek economy and, consequently, its capacity to retain the traditionally high labor force numbers (although they remained higher than those in any other EU country). Conversely, the service sector grew in volume and absorbed not only the "outflowing" labor force from agriculture but also that from the less-dramatic decline in industry. The disproportionate development of the three sectors and their subsectors reflects the pattern of development of dependent countries, such as Greece, and illustrates that "the larger the incommensurability of the development [of the different economic sectors], the lower is the level of development and, dynamically, the degree of development" (Photopoulos, 1985, p. 92). In a nutshell, Greece after the war was "portraying the 'classical' features of underdevelopment: a growing, highly parasitic tertiary sector, a weak and more or less stagnant manufacturing sector with a low labor absorption capacity, and a large but inefficient agricultural sector" (Mouzelis, 1978, p. 36).

3.5.1 Agriculture

For most part of its history, Greece was a predominantly agricultural country. However, after the 1950s, from the main pillar of the Greek economy,

Table 3.1 Primary-sector output in the Greek GDP, 1950–2008 (in %)

Year	Percent
1950	28.5
1960	22.8
1970	11.4
1980	11
2000	6.6
2008	3.7

Source: OECD (2010).

agriculture (and more broadly the primary sector) was now turned into a sector of secondary significance (Table 3.1). Volume output in agriculture from over a fourth of the Greek GDP in 1950 (28.5 percent) dropped to 11 percent in 1980, before it drastically diminished in 2008, down to 3.7 percent. Nevertheless, this was still higher than the European average,[19] which, in 2004, stood at 3 percent (Georgakopoulos, 1991). Despite this trend, a gradual net increase in the overall Greek GDP output production was registered in recent years, which indicates the rising contribution of the other two sectors of economic activity, namely manufacturing and the service sector (Gekas, 2005, p. 143).

Especially after the 1960s, some of the most prominent features of Greek agriculture were the aging population and the small size, family-run and, thus, fragmented, agricultural holdings. These factors impinged significantly on the cost of agricultural products, led to the low productivity of the sector (Karakioulafi, 2004), and imposed very hard conditions on its workforce, who invariably earned low income and were forced to survive on low living standards (Photopoulos, 1985). Moreover, farming was not sufficient to secure full-time employment and, as a result, most farmers had to do more than one job ("pluriactivity"[20]) at the same time or to shift to unrelated occupations.

In this way, agriculture, from being the main employment sector in the first half of the twentieth century, subsequently failed to retain the majority of its workforce. Hence, a dramatic outflow from agriculture occurred to the two other sectors of economic activity as well as through emigration. Indicatively, from over half of the economically active population that was employed in agriculture in 1961, within the next 40 years, less than one-fifth was left (Table 3.2).

A consequence of this "agricultural exodus" was a workforce shortage, especially in areas with substantial agricultural production. At the same time, the low-paid and hard working conditions were not appealing to younger workers and a significant renewal of the labor force was only achieved from the 1990s onward, thanks to "legal and illegal immigrants, who have undertaken a significant part of agricultural work" (Karakioulafi, 2004, p. 5).

Table 3.2 Primary-sector employment, 1961–2010 (in %)

Year	Percent
1961	52
1981	29.2
1991	22.7
2001	17
2010	11.5

Source: NSSG, Census (1951–2001); World Bank (2011).

3.5.2 Industry

The pattern of development in the secondary sector was the reverse of agriculture, though changes here were less dramatic. Industrial production output, as a percentage of GDP, grew from approximately one-fourth in 1960 to 28.1 percent in 1980 (OECD, 2010), although it subsequently started to decline and within the next two decades, dropped to its early postwar levels (19 percent in 2008) (Table 3.3).

Unlike in the advanced capitalist countries of Europe, the Greek industrial sector experienced an intense but very brief growth. This is in accordance with structural transformations within the sector, such as the high investments from Greek and multinational corporations in the 1960s and early 1970s and the shift from modern products to the production of more traditional ones, such as food, fur, tobacco, drinks, and others (Gekas, 2005). In relation to employment, suffice to note that, in 1981, after many years of continuous economic growth, the industrial sector employed approximately one-third (30.5 percent) of the overall working population, which was the lowest percentage in the EU (Gekas, 2005). By 2001, only 22.5 percent of the active population were still employed in the sector (the second lowest in EU), which is the outcome of the process of deindustrialization, which started unfolding in Greece after the late 1970s (Table 3.4).

Although industry played an important role in the general economic growth in the initial postwar years, it never managed to become the cutting edge of the Greek economy. Arguably, after it had facilitated and marked the transition from the simple commodity production to the capitalist mode of production, it started contracting and diminishing in importance, as the structure of the Greek economy and the developmental model that the country followed after that did not allow it to play a catalytic role (Mouzelis, 1978). The nature of employment in the sector offers some support to this proposition. Kouzis (2000) points out that 99 percent of businesses employed less than 20 members of staff, which accounts for more than 60 percent of total employment within the sector and it indicates its lack of dynamism. Moreover, in Greece, small firms occupy 58 percent of the labor market, while the average percentage of the rest of the EU-27 members

Table 3.3 Secondary-sector output in the Greek GDP, 1950–2008 (in %)

Year	Percent
1950	20.2
1960	25.7
1970	28.3
1980	28.1
2000	21
2008	19

Sources: NSSG, Census (1951–2001); OECD (2010).

Table 3.4 Secondary-sector employment, 1961–2010 (in %)

Year	Percent
1961	21
1971	26.8
1981	30.5
1991	27
2001	22.5
2010	22.5

Source: NSSG, Census (1951–2001); World Bank (2011).

is around 30 percent (Eurostat, 2011). Another particularity of the Greek industrial development was its concentration in the urban centers. Hence, in the early 1960s, Athens alone accounted for more than one-third of the total industrial workforce of the country.

Although in the 1990s some steps were taken to remedy weaknesses in the secondary sector, such as job creation, this was not enough to offset the expanding labor supply from the other sectors. Moreover, "defensive market rigidities prevented firms to restructure employment" (Christodoulakis and Kalyvitis, 2001, p. 3). These rigidities can be traced in the tradable sector (namely, mining and manufacturing), which, after a period of increase in total output in the 1960s and early 1970s, started contracting. These rigidities were further manifest in the small productive capacity of the sector, in the unaltered fixed capital investment throughout the 1980s and the 1990s and the lack of rise in competitiveness of the industrial sector (Christodoulakis and Kalyvitis, 2001).

3.5.3 Services

One of the main reasons for the major centrality and significance of the expanding public sector (Gekas, 2005), which accounts for most of the

Table 3.5 Service-sector output in the Greek GDP, 1950–2008 (in %).

Year	Percent
1950	51.3
1960	51.4
1970	59.4
1980	58.5
1990	63.4
2000	72.5
2008	77.3

Sources: NSSG, Census (1951–2001); OECD (2010).

service-sector employment in postwar Greece, has been its key role in the political and social arena, through its intimate relations with patronage and clientelist relationships (Table 3.5). In 1950, the service sector was responsible for more than half (51.3 percent) of the overall GDP output, whereas in 2008, it stood at over two-thirds (77.3 percent) (OECD, 2010). According to an OECD report (cited in Photopoulos, 1985), until 1975, the service sector was responsible for about 50 percent of the total increase in GDP, while after that, it accounted for approximately 75 percent. Nonetheless, this rise was not matched by a similar growth in productivity (Kollias et al., 2005, p. 97).

The "hypertrophy" and "parasitism" of the service sector is a common characteristic of many "peripheral" countries (Photopoulos, 1985, p. 94) and has had a profound influence on the relations of production and social arrangements in Greece. In contrast to the industrially developed countries, where the expansion of services is associated with the process of deindustrialization and the attendant higher concentration of capital in the service sector, for the peripheral (and semi-peripheral) countries, service-sector expansion is linked to their dependent pattern of industrialization. Therefore, in countries like Greece, the lack of growth and the small absorption capacity of the convertible sector were responsible for the inadequacy of the industry to absorb the outflowing workforce from the rural areas. Moreover, the contribution of agriculture and industry to the Greek economy has been diminishing, thus rendering the service sector (along with immigration) the main pillar of the Greek economy both in terms of output contribution and employment.

In respect of the latter, that is employment in the service sector, the drastic rise experienced in the sector compensated for rapid decline in agricultural and industrial employment. Characteristically, in 1961, the services absorbed 27 percent of the workforce (the second lowest percentage in EU), whereas in the subsequent years, service-sector employment has seen a steady and rapid expansion: from 43.6 percent in 1981 to 65.9 percent in 2010 (see Table 3.6).

To a large extent, this expansion is accounted for by the bigger size of the public sector in relation to the private sector. Especially between 1975

Table 3.6 Service-sector employment, 1961–2010 (in %)

Year	Percent
1961	27
1981	43.6
1991	50.3
2001	60.5
2010	65.9

Source: NSSG (2001); World Bank (2011).

and 1990, the public sector grew substantially, which is closely associated with clientelistic relationships, since substantial recruitment of public servants occurred close to the period of national elections (Tsoukalas, 1990). In addition, this enlargement was triggered by the repatriation of skilled workforce from the mid-1970s onward and the advent of economic migrants who entered Greece after the early 1990s. Finally, the area of economic activity with admittedly the most decisive contribution to the expansion of services in postwar Greece was that of travel and tourism. Indicatively, in 2005, tourism accounted for 18.2 percent of the overall GDP and 19 percent of the total employment (OECD, 2008).

Finally, the large urban centers, such as Salonica and chiefly Athens, absorbed most of the workforce in the public sector. For example, approximately 50 percent of public servants lived in Athens, which points to the acute regional disparities in the concentration of services and economic activities between urban and rural parts of Greece (Petrakos and Saratsis, 2000).

3.6 Social Structure and Class Formation

In this section, I discuss the social structure in contemporary Greece due to its centrality in the analysis of social mobility that ensues (see chapters 5–9). In the first part, I examine the social structure in the expanding urban centers, while in the second part, I present similar issues in smaller areas, such as provincial towns and villages, which is relevant to the second part of the book.

It has been suggested (Tsoukalas, 1977) that throughout the nineteenth century,[21] three main interconnected and interdependent social "groups," or embryonic classes, were identified as part of the Greek social structure. First, the demographically overwhelming but gradually declining peasantry.[22] Second, the rapidly increasing and heterogeneous, urban population; and, third, the powerful Greek diaspora. First, in relation to the peasantry,[23] an internal differentiation existed between large-scale landowners and small- or medium-scale agricultural production of a familial type. The distinction is significant since the first type of ownership is associated with property, which is the product of capital that comes from abroad, whereas the latter consists of small farmers and/or agricultural workers employed by big landlords. An important dimension in the development of these two subgroups is the so-called agricultural exodus (Tsoukalas, 1977, p. 68). That is to say, the sizable emigration to foreign metropoles as well as to domestic urban centers, such as Athens and Salonica, from the late-nineteenth century and throughout the twentieth century. Suffice to note that, in 1908, 67 percent of the overall population lived in villages with fewer than 2,000 people, while only 24 percent in towns with more than 10,000 people (Milonas, 1999). In 1920, the percentage of town dwellers increased to 30.2 percent of the total population.[24] Remarkably, with the intensification of urbanization, Greece experienced significant demographic shifts, especially from the mid-1940s to the early 1990s. In this period, the rural population declined from 52 percent in 1940 to 28 percent in 1991, while the urban population increased from 33 percent to 59 percent (Kotzamanis and Androulaki, 2004).

Second, the urban population consisted of diverse groups. One of the most populous among them was the former farmers. It is notable that a large proportion of them did not enter the ranks of the urban industrial proletariat, which was comprised of indigenous[25] and foreign (e.g., from Bulgaria) workers. On the contrary, many Greek migrants benefited from the expansion of the service sector and the respective decline in traditionally working working-class occupations[26] and acquired white-collar jobs.[27] This was eased by the mode of Greek urbanization, which was not attached to an extensive industrialization program. Hence, the industrial proletariat did not grow demographically to any significant extent. In other words, Greek urbanization did not lead to the "proletarianization" of the majority of the workforce but to its "embourgeoisement." Consequently, the middle and the intermediate classes expanded significantly, while the industrial working class and the peasantry contracted.

Third, the Greek diaspora played a leading role in the Greek socioeconomic developments and social-class formation processes. This group was dispersed from Egypt to Asia Minor and from Romania to Russia, and it benefited both economically and politically from the intensification and expansion of nineteenth-century capitalism. This diasporic elite was active in trade and financial services and invested considerable financial capital in Greece. This investment allowed the diaspora to play an active role in Greek internal affairs and to establish itself as a leading player in the socioeconomic processes of the country, although it was socially and geographically remote from the Greek social structure (Tsoukalas, 1977).

Thus far, I have outlined the late-nineteenth and early- to mid-twentieth-century Greek social formation with a focus on urban centers. However, this account does not cover rural parts of Greece, where there was neither industry nor any significant involvement of the Greek diaspora in the socioeconomic affairs. In order to reach an understanding of such areas, context-specific criteria are applied. In other words, the Greek social structure, at least until the Second World War, was not uniform but "dual." That is to say that a dual system of social stratification existed that reflected the urban—rural dichotomy (Mouzelis and Attalides, 1971; Lambiri-Dimaki, 1983). According to Mouzelis and Attalides (1971), this rural–urban dichotomy was based on education and property but a further differentiation based on power and prestige also operated. Thus, in the provincial towns and large villages, farmers were organized in a family and community system, though three main groups (or strata) could be identified:[28] the upper group, which consisted of the most prosperous peasants, such as large storekeepers or merchants, professionals, such as doctors, teachers, and governmental officials. The middle group, which was the most populous, was formed by the bulk of farm owners, small storekeepers, and a limited number of skilled workers. Finally, the lower group consisted of the landless agricultural laborers and the "outcasts" of the village.[29] This dual stratification system has to be examined in the context of the late advent of commodity capitalism in Greece, which did not occur at the same time in all areas. Furthermore, for some time, the existence of two modes of production, namely subsistence agriculture and commodity production, were in operation. Hence, in the urban centers of the immediate postwar years, which is, chronologically, the starting point of this study, commodity capitalism was the dominant mode of production, while in most rural areas, both modes were in operation, with subsistence agriculture being the dominant mode over commodity capitalism.

In terms of social-class formation, new social classes emerged while the existing ones were either abolished or transformed. For the purposes of this study, the most important of these new classes was the petty bourgeoisie, or intermediate class, because it absorbed a proportion of the former working class, some repatriating Greeks from abroad, and a large number of the exiting agricultural labor force. In terms of social mobility, for those peasants who entered the ranks of the intermediate class, this resulted in a significant upward trajectory. Apart from stable and typically higher income than that in agriculture, they also secured important symbolic rewards, such as recognition, prestige, and social status. The force that led to this development was the restructuring of the occupational structure and economy. More specifically, in the context of postwar reconstruction and state-service expansion, the demand for a highly qualified workforce was very high. Therefore, many individuals from rural parts of Greece acquired secondary and tertiary education credentials and the concomitant occupational positions. This new intermediate class was an important ally and source of power for the state itself as, to a great extent, it was a product of its own making. Indicatively, those employed directly or indirectly in the public sector had more than tripled within 20 years: from 130,000 in 1961 to 500,000 in 1981 (Tsoukalas, 2005).

3.7 The Study of Social Mobility in Greece

The study of social mobility in Greece has never been on the agenda of mainstream sociology. According to Tsoukalas (2005), its main aspects are "surrounded by deep darkness" (p. 56), while Kasimati (2004) claimed that social mobility in Greece has never been studied. What is more, there is a big deficit in systematic and consistent data and a conspicuous dearth of empirical studies with a clear focus on Greek social structure and social-class formation, thus hampering the possibility of a robust investigation of social mobility and attendant processes. This has resulted in Greece having been left outside the international social mobility debate and attendant knowledge production. Hence, the lack of history of ideas insofar as Greek social mobility is concerned is reflected in the lack of dynamism in the pertinent debate. In turn, this is mirrored in the manner of presentation in the remainder of this section, which focuses more on the key aspects of each study discussed than on their common themes and their development through time.

Existing studies have mainly focused on aspects of social-class formation in the nineteenth and early twentieth centuries (Moschov, 1972; Philias, 1974, 1999; Vergopoulos, 1975; Tsoukalas, 1977; Moschonas, 1986; Lytras, 1993) or on economic success of Greek migrants as a factor in their social mobility (Kouvertaris, 1971; Sandis, 1973; Vermeulen and Venema, 2000). An exception is Lambiri-Dimaki's study (1983), which was concerned with the educational mobility of 863 first-year university students in a specific department at the University of Athens. This study offered valuable insights into a number of issues that promoted or impeded the social mobility of individuals. However, its restricted focus limits the generalizability of its findings, while it precludes broader conclusions to be drawn about educational mobility in Greece. This is not to diminish the originality of the work, but rather to point to the absence of any similar ones that could give us a better idea of education and social mobility in the Greek postwar context.

Alexander (1964) had a similarly restricted focus, though this was on the social mobility of Greek industrialists in the first half of the twentieth century. Kasimati (1990), in a more systematic enquiry than the previous ones, examined the occupational mobility of industrial workers from a sample of 100 industrial units (including 1,017 individuals) in Athens. Kasimati (1990) was not concerned with economic inequalities measured by the success (outcomes) of individuals but rather with a number of factors, such as father's occupation, parent's family size, gender, age, educational level, and first occupation as determinants of the occupational status of the individual. The intra- and intergenerational social mobility rates of her sample were estimated through path models similar to those used by Blau and Duncan (1967), in order to shed light not only on the prevalent mobility patterns but also on the factors that generated occupational movements and the processes that impacted on the occupational status of the respondents. Kasimati's study (1990) was an important addition to the embryonic body of literature of mobility processes in Greece, though its restricted focus on a single occupational group, namely industrial workers, does not allow for broader conclusions to be drawn about the structure of Greek society, as other sectors of economic activity, different types of labor force, and other areas of Greece were not examined. Moreover, the period of time that Kasimati examined coincides with the growth and expansion of the industrial sector, when increased movements of labor force occurred and the opportunities for occupational and social mobility were substantially higher than those in subsequent years.

In a study that focused on the mechanisms of social-class reproduction, Petmezidou-Tsoulouvi (1987) estimated the occupational and educational mobility of 1,600 individuals in the area of Salonica, in the 1980s. Her sample consisted of middle-class and petty-bourgeois (intermediate) families, derived from the occupation of the male head of the household, his job position, educational level, and family income. In terms of occupational movement, the findings of the study suggested that middle-class children, that is those in managerial, professional, and higher administrative occupations, were the most immobile in relation to their fathers' occupations. Specifically, 72 percent of them remained in the same class as their fathers. The remaining 28 percent of middle-class children were intergenerationally mobile either into the secondary (industry) or to the tertiary (service) sector. With regard to the intermediate class, mobility here was more prevalent, between 45 percent and 57 percent in total, though movements were more common from the primary (agriculture) to the secondary (industry) sector. In respect of mobility according to educational background, both classes, that is, the middle class and the intermediate class, appear to have fared better in comparison to their fathers' educational statuses, although the middle class achieved higher educational status in comparison to the lower classes. The strength of this study is that it showed patterns of occupational mobility drawn from a relatively large sample. However, the exclusion of some occupational groups, such as the working class and the examination of a large urban center, which has its own characteristics and particularities, should be borne in mind. Most importantly, though, the lack of any linking of the findings with the structural characteristics and transformations of the labor market during the time the study covers, or in other words, the lack of distinction between structural and exchange mobility (Kasimati, 2004, p. 282) undermines the potential of this study.

Finally, the most recent study was conducted also by Kasimati (1998). Its aim was to examine the social characteristics of employment and the factors that affect job selection. The research was carried out in Athens and was based on a sample of 6,000 individuals. In terms of intergenerational educational mobility, 28 percent of the sample stayed at the same educational level as their fathers, 58 percent of whom were university graduates, while the remaining 72 percent were "educationally mobile." The vast majority of this movement, 86 percent, was of an upward kind, that is, movement to a higher educational level relative to their fathers. Furthermore, 44 percent of this same movement was structural, which means that it was absorbed by the division in the labor market.[30] In addition, upwardly mobile individuals stayed in education for over one school stage than their fathers. According to Kasimati (2004, p. 283), the findings demonstrate the great extent of educational mobility in postwar Greece and the widespread structural changes, which influenced the educational system and caused it to adjust to the demands of the changing division of labor. In terms of intergenerational mobility, higher education graduates were the most occupationally stable (64 percent of whom remained in their first job), followed by secondary-school graduates (58 percent) and those with primary-school certificates (52 percent of whom stayed in their first job). Indeed, this study revealed some thus-far unexplored trends in the educational movements of the labor force and it went beyond speculative and indirect estimates of their mobility movements. It is the only study that drew on a relatively large sample, albeit restricted to the workforce in Athens. Although its findings cannot be generalized to other areas with different demographic and labor-market characteristics, they still provide an understanding of aspects of social mobility in a somewhat consistentm anner.

3.8 Summary

If social mobility, or at least the belief in the idea of unfettered social fluidity, is the *seduction* of modern capitalism, then few countries can exemplify this in a more lucid manner than modern Greece. Through a series of political, economic, social, and historical transformations, I demonstrated how the Greek social system has sustained high levels of mobility in a social structure that was exemplarily fluid, yet remarkably unequal. From the utter devastation and annihilation the country experienced after two wars, the Second World War and the Civil War, it entered a prolonged, steep, and impressive reconstruction, democratization, and development processes. However, in this short postwar history, Greece must register as a case of "capitalism-gone-wrong," for it combines all the ingredients of a tragic failure of the market forces to keep the capitalist dream alive even for the sake of the capitalist system itself. A series of endogenous and exogenous factors made the Greek experience with liberal and neoliberal capitalism to resemble a bad experiment. Years of progress, growth, and prosperity are currently being reversed by the country's economic and financial problems, which are premised on weak institutional arrangements, unfair structures, and the penetration of foreign capital and interest groups in its financial, economic, and political functions.

Chapter 4

Education, Social Mobility, and the Question of Meritocracy

4.1 Introduction

As I pointed out in chapter 2, education in the postwar years was the main provider of the state apparatus with highly "credentialized" individuals. In the remainder of this chapter, I shall present the most salient features of Greek postwar education and the underpinnings for the substantial reforms and expansion it underwent over this period of time. Moreover, I shall discuss the theoretical tenets of the debate about the role and function of education as it was being developed at the time in advanced Western countries and "exported" to the European periphery, such as Greece.

4.2 Education in Postwar Greece: Reform and Expansion

In prewar Greece, education was to a large extent subjugated to the demands of the economy and, generally, to the prevailing political economy. To that extent, the state sought to use its legislative powers in order to align education with its overarching ideological principles. Hence, the oxymoron of overeducation went hand in hand with high illiteracy rates. The explanation of this paradox lies in the trenchant socioeconomic divisions between rural and urban areas, which were also reflected in education. Thus, high rates of school attendance in the cities and a dismal educational participation and attainment record in rural areas were part and parcel of the same educational system for the best part of the twentieth century (Milonas, 1999). For example, in 1911, only half of the nonurban areas had a secondary school, while the proportion of secondary-school students in Athens was by 250 percent higher than the national average. Given that, as mentioned in section 3.5 (chapter 3), the majority of the population lived in villages for most of the twentieth century, it seems plausible to suggest that educational inequalities mirrored wider, social ones.

The postwar years saw a significant increase in educational expansion and student participation in all economically advanced European countries and more generally. To be precise, this was the model favored in countries that adopted a liberal orientation, which, as discussed in chapter 1, entailed the implementation of a politics based on the pursuit of a fine balance between the centrifugal forces of free market, on the one hand, and parliamentary democracy and welfarism, on the other. This key role was enacted by the state, which adopted an active stance in intervening both for the smooth operation of the "free" market and for the protection of the interests of its citizens. This model has three main pillars or state priorities that are broadly shared among Western European states, though with varying degrees and in different versions: health, education, social protection, and security. In a nutshell, education was one of the cornerstones of the welfare state, which was financed through taxation. However, the increase in educational opportunities was not merely the effect of an ideological shift. According to Photopoulos (2005), "even more important was the post-war economic boom that required a vast expansion of the labour base, with women and, sometimes immigrants, filling the gaps. On top of this, the incessant increase in the division of labour, changes in production methods and organisation, as well as revolutionary changes in information technology required a growing number of highly skilled personnel, scientists, high-level professionals etc. As a result of these trends, the number of universities in many countries doubled or tripled between 1950 and 1970, whereas technical colleges, as well as part-time and evening courses, spread rapidly promoting adult education at all levels."

In Greece, this was achieved through state investment as well as educational reforms, which were the cornerstones of the ensuing transformations. Most of these changes sought to raise the educational standards of the population, to provide equal opportunities, to democratize education, as well as to provide the developing economy with skilled workforce in key positions (Milonas, 1999). Especially, democratization and equality of opportunities were particularly sought after due to the fact that the general educational standards of the population were very low and regional inequalities were, as mentioned above, quite stark. In particular, the reform of 1959 attempted to address this unequal educational provision by offering students from rural areas and all those with the potential to enter higher education (HE) with a second opportunity. Secondary education was now permeated by the ideal of humanism and, as in other European countries, it was reorganized so as to prepare those who could carry on into tertiary education and also to provide "terminal education" for those who would leave school and enter the labor market (Kazamias, 1960). Moreover, the 1959 reform sought to revamp technical and vocational education in order to link secondary education more tightly with the country's economic development (Saïti, 2000). Despite this attempt, the demand for education, which remained high in the city centers, was matched with increasing pressure from the rural population to access secondary education and HE[1] on equal terms. Indicatively, during the 1960s, it was estimated that only approximately 25 percent of all students completed secondary school, while in rural areas, a mere 15 percent of those enrolled in primary schools managed to advance into the secondary level and complete it (Katsikas and Kavadias, 2000). The core elements of this reform unequivocally underpin the market capitalist orientation that Greece had adopted after the wars (the Second World War and the Civil War). What is more, in attempting to solidify the capitalist edifice that was carved out of the ruins of the two wars, Greece seemed to be emulating educational models that had already been applied in economically advanced countries of the West, rather than attempting to develop a model that would suit its own historical, socioeconomic, and political particularities. This tendency of "policy-transposition" has been followed throughout the period examined here and has had discernible disadvantages. The division, for example, between general and technical/vocational education, is one that was demarcated in Western Europe long before it entered the Greek policy mainstream. In turn, this division was deemed imperative by the bourgeois forces in Western Europe in order to supply its burgeoning industry with technical expertise and its state apparatus with workers who possessed the appropriate knowledge to drive the growth of their economies forward.

The reform of 1964 set a milestone in Greek education, as it sought to establish for the first time nine-year compulsory education for all. Moreover, in order to improve student access, it made educational provision state-funded and, thus, free of charge for students and their families. The curriculum was enriched with new subjects that would prepare pupils for their role as citizens in a democratic society. Modernization and democratization elements were also inserted, such as the substitution of the archaic form of language as the language of instruction with modern Greek. Furthermore, the poor economic background of students from rural areas was recognized as an impediment to their access and attainment and was addressed with the provision of free school meals (Margaritis, 1964). This shows that Greek capitalism, as in Western countries with a longer capitalist tradition, was accommodating, or indeed encouraging of reformist attempts of a "democratizing" and inclusive type. In other words, it was in the best interests of the new economic requirements and new ways of organizing the production to equip the highly illiterate population with skills and knowledge so that they could fully participate in the economic activities of their country, both as workers and consumers.

Despite its progressive orientation, the reform of 1964 was short lived and soon it was substituted by the regressive reform of 1967, which was implemented by the military dictatorship that came into power the same year. As a result, all the democratic provisions that were accomplished hitherto were annulled and their most significant elements abolished. It seems that the political maturity of the Greek democracy was not strong enough to withhold the achievements of the immediate postwar years, even according to capitalist standards. The fragile political state of affairs that prevailed after, or because of the Civil War, gave rise to centrifugal forces that destabilized the trajectory thus far adhered to and the overall educational progress of the country. Hence, soon after the dictatorship of the colonels, the provision for nine-year compulsory education was replaced with six years' compulsory education, while all democratic and modernizing elements in the curriculum were suspended (Milonas, 1999). The archaic form of language instruction was reinstated as the official school language and rigid monitoring mechanisms for in- and out-of-school conduct were introduced, compromising education to the political establishment (Gouvias, 1998).

After the termination of the seven-year dictatorship in 1974, re-democratization of the educational system became a new priority of the reformist endeavors. In the reform of 1977, nine-year compulsory education was enshrined in as a constitutional right and upper-secondary education was revamped with the introduction of technical and vocational schools that could also provide access to tertiary education. However, it was in the reform of 1982 that the transition into postprimary education was eased and steps were taken toward its real democratization (in particular, in tertiary education). New, nonuniversity, tertiary institutions were created (Technological Educational Institutions) with the aim to establish further connections between the production of knowledge and the world of production (Kyriazis and Asderaki, 2008). As noted in chapter 3, despite the seemingly progressive rhetoric that characterized the newly elected Center-Leftist PASOK government, the promising elements of the reforms it implemented were not enough to mark a radical shift from a vehemently procapitalist education to one that prioritized wider social well-being and welfare.

The last sweeping reform was that of 1997, which sought to modernize, yet again, all educational levels (Grollios and Kaskaris, 2003) and to increase access to HE. Primary schools were reorganized, with longer tuition hours and an enriched curriculum in order to reflect the needs of the "knowledge economy." Furthermore, examinations were introduced in secondary education and university entry became easier as more places were created to absorb the very high demand and attendant social pressure. The reform coincided with the wider socioeconomic and political "modernization" project launched by PASOK, which returned to power in 1993, and it contained many contradictory elements. For example, under the rubric of "modernization," many disparate intentions lurked, such as the full subjugation of education to the needs of the economy, disguised, though under the rhetoric of flexibility, enhanced efficiency, and competitiveness of the workforce. More specifically, the orientation of the

Greek political economy at the time appears to have made a palpable turn toward embracing neoliberalism more fully than before, though the whole undertaking was glossed over in seemingly progressive mantras, such as "modernization." According to PASOK, in order for Greece to converge with the economically advanced countries of the Western block, Greek education needed to be aligned with the needs of the economy and labor market as fully as possible. Yet, this attempt was seriously compromised by its top-down manner of implementation, which alienated the relevant stakeholders and unleashed enormous tension. This tension, however, did not take the form of class conflict as it did not attach itself to the demands of a collective movement that represented the interests of the working class, but it was rather linked to a generalized anti-reformist movement that chiefly aimed to halt the reform itself. Hence, the reform was met with strong opposition from the teachers' unions and students and it accelerated private-school expansion (in the mid-1990s, 5–10 percent of all primary and secondary-school enrollments were accounted for by private schools) (Kanellopoulos and Psacharopoulos, 1997).

4.2.1 Private and Public Funding of Education

Although private schools in Greece may not be as widespread as in other European countries, private investment in education has been remarkably high and rising over the years. Recent studies estimated that the share of education expenditures in household budgets increased from 1.9 percent of the Greek GDP in 1955 (Saiti, 2000) to 2.15 percent in 1974 and 4.41 percent in 1999 (Kanellopoulos et al., 2004), which outnumbers by far the private expenditure for education in most other EU countries. On the other hand, public expenditure has traditionally been 4 percent or lower of the Greek GDP and significantly lower than that in other EU countries. If one takes into account the fact that public and private education spending in the mid-1990s stood at approximately 6.5 percent of Greek GDP (Kanellopoulos and Psacharopoulos, 1997), it becomes evident that private investment is likely to have been higher than public investment.[2] Thus, an extensive drive toward education that was manifest among many Greek families, especially after the 1970s, was not fully met by the state despite its pro-education agenda throughout the postwar era. This lacuna was filled in by the Greek family, which played a crucial role in planning and funding their offsprings' educational and concomitant occupational aspirations. This funding takes multiple forms. Perhaps, the most prominent among them is the so-called frontistiria, that is private evening schools, which are of two types. First, auxiliary to the state, day schools, which help with the learning of a second language, such as English or French, or the acquisition of Information and Communication Technology (ICT) knowledge and pertinent validation certificates. Second, preparatory evening classes to assist with school homework and mainly with the final examinations at the lower-secondary, gymnasium, level. For pupils in the upper-secondary school, lyceum, frontistiria play the role of a parallel form of schooling and are often considered if not of higher at least of equal importance to the mainstream, state school. Apart from frontistiria, private, one-to-one tuition (*idiaitera*) is also widespread. In addition to these forms of private funding, we should also add one that enjoys nearly universal acceptance, namely the direct financing of studying at university by the Greek families. Given the low numbers in student loans offered by Greek banks as well as the low uptake of such schemes, it is the families that are invariably burdened with financing their children's graduate or even postgraduate studies, by covering the living and/or accommodation expenses during the four or more years of studying. In the case of students who emigrate abroad, Greek families also have to cover the tuition fees[3] that apply in the host universities. The Centre for the Development of Education Policy of the General Confederation of Greek Workers (KANEP/GSEE[4]) (2011) recently estimated that private tuition expenses reached €952.6 million, which represents 18.6 percent of all household expenditures on education and 20.1 percent of the government expenditures on primary and secondary education. From this amount, €340.1 million was spent for private, home tutoring (*idiaitera*) and €612.5 million for private, evening classes (*frontistiria*). In monetary terms, the amount of money spent by Greek households on private tuition (idiaitera), evening classes (frontistiria), and any other form of educational services not covered by the state (including music lessons, sports, and so on) amounts to approximately €2 billion per year (KANEP/GSEE, 2011). If one adds the cost of private schooling, funding for HE studies abroad, and postgraduate studies, then this amount reaches €5.2 billion, a staggering amount for a country the size of Greece (KANEP/GSEE, 2011).

It is important to unpack some elements of the new reformist initiatives, especially after 1996, which is the year that marked the beginning of a concerted effort to further "modernize" the Greek political economy. In order to better understand the meaning of the concept of modernization, as applied in the Greek context, we should conceive it as the domestic version of Greek neoliberalism. This type of neoliberalism entails, among other things, the privatization of public assets, which include education. However, this was a "softer" version of neoliberalism than that implemented in other Western countries, such as the United Kingdom. Greek neoliberalism, at least in its initial stages, did not involve the direct privatization of education, for example, with the introduction of university tuition fees. Rather, it entailed the increase in private financing for education by the households and participants themselves through one or more of the forms discussed above.

What has to be also emphasized is a persistent feature of Greek society after the 1970s, namely its strong demand for education. Indicatively, between 1971 and 2001, the secondary-school population more than

Table 4.1 Number of students in Greek secondary education, 1971–2001

Year	Lower secondary (13–15 years old)	Upper secondary (16–18 years old)	Total
1971	263.499	172.995	436.494
1981	429.362	257.161	686.523
1991	442.815	361.016	803.831
2001*	360.248	400.241	760.489

Source: NSSG (2000), *KANEP (2003, p. 21).

doubled. In particular, the proportion of lower-secondary-school (gymnasium) graduates dropped between 1991 and 2001, while the respective percentage of upper-secondary-school (*lyceum*) students increased substantially. This indicates three associated tendencies; first, the majority of students stay on longer in education than previously; second, low attrition rates started to be established in the lower echelon of secondary education; and third, upper-secondary-school absorbs most of the outflow from the lower-secondary level (Table 4.1). In other words, the transition from lower- to upper-secondary tier is smooth and uninterrupted. This point is of some importance as it connotes that the amount of graduates who move from lower-secondary education to vocational/technical is far lower than that for pupils who move from lower- to upper-secondary education. In other words, five decades of reforms have established high literacy levels, increased rates of pupils who attend compulsory education as well as a clear preference for more academic rather than vocational routes.

4.2.2 Higher Education

Even more spectacular than the increase in primary and secondary education was that in HE. Greece was among a host of European countries where university education at the turn of the twentieth century was the privilege of the elites, that is to say reserved for less than 1 percent of the population of university age (Banks, 2001, in Schofer and Meyer, 2005). The expansion of HE in the interwar years was perceived in many countries as an issue of concern, as it was believed to do little more than produce a "sterile, educated proletariat…without a chance of gainful occupation while millions are wasted on its training" (*The New York Times*, 1931, p. 56). However, this attitude changed radically and after the Second World War. HE after that became one of the prime loci of investment for governments, in capitalist and noncapitalist countries alike. Globally, between 1950 and 1970, tertiary-education enlargement was much higher than primary and secondary, with a net increase of approximately 300 percent. This trend continued unabated in the next 30 years. In particular, between 1970 and 1997, the global increase

Table 4.2 Number of students in Greek tertiary education, 1956–2001

Year	Tertiary education
1956	19.864
1964	43.411
1977	84.718
1981	85.718
1996*	130.925
2001**	328.100

Source: Kerides (2003, p. 84), *Saïti (2000), **NSSG (2001).

in student population was close to 90 percent (Wolf, 2002). The relevant statistics for Greece are even more startling. Between 1956 and 2001, the number of tertiary-education students grew by nearly 16 times, while only between 1976 and 2001, the respective increase was fourfold[5] (KANEP, 2003) (Table 4.2). This rise, the second biggest among 31 European countries, makes Greece a remarkable case in Europe as far as educational expansion is concerned though not necessarily an exceptional one (HE participation between 1950 and 1965 more than doubled in almost every European country, with the exception of Spain and Portugal). In relation to Greece, the likely explanation for this astounding trend lies in the demands of the new economy, which as noted in chapter 3, manifestly entered its Keynesian phase after the end of the two wars. This Keynesian turn entailed an emphasis on growth, which necessitated the creation of highly skilled positions in the labor market. Three points emanate from this remark. First, prewar tertiary-education rates in Greece were very low; hence, any expansion after the war would expectantly lead to a steep increase in HE participation. Second, the postwar growth in household income and improvement in living conditions also led to higher consumption rates[6] and contributed to serious changes in lifestyle choices. One of them was the increased availability of leisure time, which helped the attendant sectors to flourish and led to new cultural expressions to develop, which aimed to improve the quality of life of the workforce. Such a change, with profound impact on the relations of production as well as on social relations was the expansion of tourism, which, in Greece, has to be viewed as an "industry" *amplo sensu*. Although employment in tourism and its associated occupations does not necessarily require high educational qualifications, the development of the sector itself contributed to the shift from agriculture into the service sector, which is largely associated with higher levels of education. Third, internal characteristics, endemic to Greece, are also to be taken into account. The small size of the Greek industry, the low-paying and hard-working conditions in agriculture, made the pursuit of service-sector occupations much more attractive than in the aforementioned sectors (i.e., agriculture and industry). In addition, a large proportion of new positions in the service sector were created by the Greek state, which underwent a prolonged period of recruitment as it sought to establish a public administration system that could support a highly bureaucratized apparatus and an increasingly intricate hierarchy of state functions that required more effective management, administration, and skilled workforce to operate within them. If one takes into account the added benefit of entering a high-status and relatively well-paid workforce, which could be secured with a university degree, then the appeal of HE becomes manifest for a country still characterized by severe social and regional inequalities between rural and urban areas. The latter, urban areas, offered more opportunities for occupational advancement and a better life, while the former, rural areas, were perceived to be loci of backwardness, where opportunities were few and far in between in comparison to the domestic or international metropoles.

Pursuant to the previous point, the growth in educational demand caught up in rural areas and it was soon pursued as the most expedient vehicle for exiting the peasantry and improving occupational conditions and low social-class positions. On the other hand, education in the urban centers was perceived as the key mechanism for entering the middle-class ranks. Findings from a number of studies offer support to this claim. For the academic year 1963–1964, 69 percent of those who entered tertiary education came from middle-class, 25 percent from intermediate-class, and 8 percent from working-class families, while the corresponding proportions of these classes in the Greek social structure were 5 percent, 20 percent, and 80 percent, respectively (Lambiri-Dimaki, 1983). Another study by Kontogianopoulou-Polidoridis (in Milonas, 1982) suggested that, in the mid-1970s, students whose fathers were in the "service class" (or middle class) were 2.3 times more likely to enter university than the children of manual workers and 4.3 times more likely than the children of farmers. Although this marked an improvement in relation to the 1950s (the respective chances for children with parents in the service class were 20 and 17.8 times higher than those for the children of manual workers and peasants, respectively), it is evident that educational inequality persisted even after the expansion of HE and the creation of attendant opportunities in the labor market.

Further findings from studies referring to the early and mid-1970s demonstrated that these inequalities were strongly correlated with place of residence. Thus, students who lived in the cities were more likely to complete secondary school than those who lived in some distance from a school, such as the majority of children in rural areas. Moreover, the further away students were from their school, the worse their performance was and the fewer chances they had to complete it (Milonas, 1982). Throughout the 1980s, no drastic challenge to these inequalities was mounted. On the contrary, those children who were born to highly educated fathers, that is to say children whose fathers were university graduates, had increased chances of entering university in comparison to children whose fathers were secondary-school graduates. Similar findings were obtained for the 1984–1998 period (Chryssakis and Soulis, 2001). University access was still positively associated with father's educational background, which, in turn, is determined by social-class background. Hence, children of blue-collar workers were somewhat underrepresented in the Greek universities, whereas children of white-collar families had twice as many chances as the national average to enter HE. In addition, children of farmers, the unemployed, and pensioners were less likely to access university and were considerably underrepresented in tertiary education. What is more, the higher the father's social origin, the more likely it was to find his offspring in faculties of high demand, such as medicine and engineering (Chryssakis and Soulis, 2001).

The aforementioned studies relate to students who attended education within Greece. However, a significant number of secondary-school graduates did not succeed the university entry examinations or chose not to take them and emigrated abroad. Between 1956 and 2007, student migration increased tenfold. In terms of country of destination, two patterns were established. On the one hand, many students who wanted to pursue a degree in the medical professions, such as medicine, dentistry, biology, and so on, emigrated chiefly to countries within the Eastern block, such as Bulgaria, Romania, and Hungary. One the other hand, for all other degrees and specializations, the emigration movement was chiefly absorbed by EU countries and, to some extent, by overseas destinations such as the United States. Symptomatic of the large volume of "brain-drain" was that in 1996 Greece had the highest rates of students in another EU member state. Specifically, 14 percent of students of university age with Greek origin studied abroad, while the respective average rate within the EU was at about 2 percent (Lianos et al., 2004). This trend took the characteristics of a social phenomenon as it continued to grow throughout the 2000s. In 2007, proportional to its size, Greece had the highest proportion of students studying abroad in comparison to any other country in the world (Table 4.3).

In terms of geographical origin, attendance rates, and gender, the general pattern for both men and women points to higher participation rates for those living in the cities than in provincial towns and villages, where the

Table 4.3 Greek students studying abroad, 1956–2007

Year	Number of students
1956	6.467
1963	7.421
1977	30.945
1981	32.111
2007*	51.138

Source: Kerides (2003), *OECD (2007).

attainment gap was still high. Throughout the 1950s and 1960s, women's education was lagging behind in relation to that of men in cities, provincial towns, and villages alike. A slight improvement was attested to in the early 1970s, which was mainly due to the increase in educational participation and improvement of completion rates for women in the cities. Furthermore, between 1961 and 1971, overall, more women than men entered primary education, which led to a substantial improvement in the respective literacy rates, although participation rates in secondary and tertiary education were improving faster for men than for women (Milonas, 1999, p. 97). Suffice to note that, in 1971, illiteracy rates in rural areas were still high for men, 38 percent, though much higher for women at 60 percent (Milonas, 1999). The respective rates of illiteracy in the cities, in 1971, were 21 percent for men and 34 percent for women (Milonas, 1999). According to an OECD (1999) report, the proportion of men aged 25–34 years with upper-secondary qualification (obtained at the age of 17 years) was more than double in comparison to the 55- to 64-year age-group. Similarly, the respective proportion of women with upper-secondary qualifications had tripled within 20 years and in 1999, it was higher than the OECD average (KANEP, 2003). Similar trends are evident also in relation to HE: between 1975 and 1996, the female tertiary-education population increased by 305 percent, while the male tertiary-education population rose by 155 percent (the overall increase in the student population in the same period was 210 percent) (KANEP, 2003).

It is clear that within four decades, notably from the mid-1960s to the mid-2000s, educational participation for both genders improved drastically, though the increase was even more pronounced for females. However, "educational 'openness' is not in itself a good indicator of social mobility, unless accompanied by an increasing capacity of the economy to absorb those who acquire this education" (Mouzelis and Attalides, 1971, p. 190). Indeed, Patrinos (1997) suggests that the phenomenon of overeducation[7] in Greece is the outcome of oversupply of graduates, who are hired in inappropriate fields. It is, therefore, essential to examine whether this steep rise in educational attainment was also reflected in the labor market. According to Tsakloglou and Cholezas (2005), "in 1974 only 7.3% of the labour market participants aged below 35 were tertiary education graduates while 62.2% had less than lower secondary education completed. By 1999 the corresponding percentages were 23.6% and 13.2%. Likewise, in 1974 only 5.3% of the labour market workforce aged over 50 were tertiary education graduates while 83.2% had not completed lower secondary education. Twenty-five years later the corresponding percentages were 14.1% and—the still high—63.8%" (p. 10).

In the early 2000s, the labor market was evidently more enriched with people with higher-educational credentials than in the previous decades. The improvement in educational participation was spread throughout all age-groups and both genders. Especially in relation to women, it was evident that in the new millennium, their rate of participation in the labor market was substantially improved than that in the previous decades. What is more, women were increasingly found in occupations that required high educational credentials, from which they were underrepresented hitherto (Kanellopoulos et al., 2004). However, women were still the victims of a considerable gender pay gap (Papapetrou, 2004).

Participation of qualified people in the labor market has to be considered in tandem with unemployment,[8] which has been increasingly affecting Greek graduates and has become, arguably, one of the most intricate features of the Greek labor market (Livanos, 2009). According to the European Commission (2003), the high unemployment rates of university graduates is explained by the fact that the Greek HE is not sufficiently linked to the labor market as it produces graduates with qualifications that are not relevant to the needs of employers. Indicatively, from a little over 5 percent in 1992, graduate unemployment increased to 8 percent in 1994 (OECD, 1995) and remained at such levels until the turn of the new millennium (OECD, 2005). These rates were the third highest among 27 EU member states, which indicates the inability of the Greek economy to absorb the very continuous supply of highly credentialed individuals. With the advent of the recent economic recession that has hit Greece since 2008, graduate unemployment increased to 14 percent, the highest rate among the 27 EU member states, and over two times higher than the EU average (Eurostat, 2011). Conversely, employment rates for Greek university graduates of all ages are consistent with the economic development of the country discussed in chapter 3. Hence, in 1992, 77.7 percent of university graduates were in employment, while ten years later, in 2002, the pertinent rate reached 80.7 percent (compared to 82.7 percent for the EU-27) (Eurostat, 2012). This increasing trend peaked in 2006 with 82.2 percent of Greek university graduates finding a job in the labor market (marginally lower than the EU-27 average at 83.2 percent) (Eurostat, 2012). Nevertheless, the occupational position of young graduates in the Greek labor market is very precarious. Karamesini (2010, p. 5) argues that this group displays "the highest unemployment and temporary employment rates among the 20–29 year-olds of all educational attainment levels. In 2008, their risk of unemployment in the 20–24, 25–29 and 30–34 age groups was respectively 29%, 16% and 7% while their rate of temporary work in the same age groups was respectively 33%, 26% and 17%. It follows that, even in the first half of their thirties, a significant proportion of Greek university graduates have no access to stable employment and thus not completed their transition from higher education to work." With the onset of the economic crisis from 2008 onward, the respective employment rates of this group went into decline, while unemployment followed the opposite trajectory. In particular, in 2012, the decrease in employment rates was dramatic and it reached 1980s levels (74.1 percent) (Eurostat, 2012). In other words, 40 years of university expansion and concomitant labor market transformations were abruptly bought to a halt. What is more, the current socioeconomic and political conditions indicate anything but a reversal of these trends. It is expected, therefore, that the low employment levels of university graduates will increase, escalating further the social pressure and limiting even more the ability of the Greek family to play the role of the safety net for its unemployed offspring.

In an ironic twist of history, educational expansion does not lead any more to better career prospects but to a precarious future. Remarkably, the ideological underpinnings and theoretical tenets of this tendency were highlighted more than a century ago in one of the most prophetic critiques of education that have ever been produced. It is this critique and the debate it generated I shall turn now my attention to.

4.3 Education and Social Mobility

In chapter 2, I discussed some central issues to the principal postwar field that seeks to explore and explain processes pertaining to equality of opportunities and outcomes. This field of study is commonly known as social mobility research and has a long tradition in the Anglophone world and also in other countries. As I argued in chapter 1 as well as in the first part of this chapter, the main institution that was assigned with the promotion of the key postwar goal of equality was education. Given then the prominence of education, I shall now examine its complex and crucial role after the Second World War. My primary aim is to link its functions to issues of social inequality and mobility in the context of modern social systems that adopted a liberal and, more recently, a neoliberal system of organization.

The central aim of postwar liberal democracy was the creation of an open society, which can be broadly identified as one permeated by the principles of equality of opportunity and participation in the various institutions and services, such as education. The latter, the institutions and services of liberal democracy, apart from a democratic ethos, have also to be characterized by the principle of fairness. In doing so, it was expected that education with its sorting, filtering, and ranking functions could also solve the twin problem of production of highly skilled graduates and the fair allocation of workforce into positions in the labor market. In other words, the expectation that education could deliver economic as well as social goods was the corollary of the postwar model of development that was shared by Western European countries, and more broadly by countries with liberal capitalist orientation. In order to assess the extent of "openness" of postwar liberal democracy, I devoted some space in chapter 2, where I presented findings from the field of social mobility, which are useful in explaining inequalities through time (Hout, 2003). In order to shed light on education's potential to facilitate the creation of an open society, I shall now turn my attention to the relationship between education (chiefly in the form of formal qualifications) and social mobility, and the way this relationship has developed throughout the postwar era. In doing so, I shall present the origins and evolution of the "meritocracy through education" debate and the role of ascription and achievement in the life chances of individuals.

4.3.1 The Emergence of Meritocracy through Education

An interest in meritocracy is justified by the attention it has attracted in the postwar period and also due to its social and political significance in modern societies. Although some concern for a fairer and more just society was evident in some Western countries throughout their industrialization, it was chiefly in the last six decades or so that the concept of meritocracy gained momentum and acquired added political significance. Postwar policy makers and politicians of all persuasions have maintained an ongoing interest in the organization of social systems and their institutions based on meritocratic principles. This interest remained, if anything, unscathed throughout these years and education came to be seen as the main mechanism for the fulfillment of the meritocratic ideal in modern societies.

The putative father of the term "meritocracy" was Michael Young. In his prophetic satire *The Rise of Meritocracy: 1870–2033* (1958), he aimed to warn about the consequences of the increasing importance of formal educational qualifications over all other considerations. Young (1958) defined meritocracy as the total amount of remunerations an individual can acquire thanks to their ability and effort. Put simply, in a meritocracy, IQ and effort are the ingredients of success rather than family background or other ascriptive traits. Analytically, Young (1958) linked merit with educational achievement, demonstrable through academic qualifications. The logic of this proposition is easy to follow: formally validated credentials stand the scrutiny of achievement that is based on fair and meritorious principles. Educational institutions are well placed to valorize and validate these traits, and, therefore, to become the sites of merit allocation. In other words, education can become the seal of approval of a society where achievement prevails over ascription. In turn, this process also benefits both education and the labor market, which become the pillars of the smooth, efficacious, and fair operation of capitalism.

With this work, Young (1958) intended to alert his contemporaries, not just in Britain, but also in other modern societies with similar characteristics (as we saw in chapters 2–4, Greece and the United Kingdom possess many such features) about the consequences of the increasing importance of formal educational qualifications in comparison to other factors. Thus, with the rise of meritocracy, Young (1958) maintained, those unable to make it through education, such as a large number of able working-class students, would be rejected from school. This rejection would curtail their opportunities for a better occupation than their parents. On the other hand, the rise of a new exclusive, highly educated social class could establish an equally discriminatory practice as older ones, such as those associated with social-class advantages that were dominant before the Second World War. Those families which possessed financial power and cultural capital, that is the middle class, could secure the rewards of increasing education and thus manage to reproduce the associated class privileges. On the other hand, Young feared that the working class would be locked into their position of subordination by failing to capitalize on education and associated social mobility opportunities. Hence, social inequalities could be passed in education, which could be thus rendered a site of reproduction of social inequalities rather than of meritocracy.

This belief was underpinned by the major transformations Young saw in postwar Britain (which were, by no means, restricted to Britain), namely the rapid expansion of the public sector, the restructuring of the occupational structure and the labor market. As a result, new occupations emerged that were largely suitable for university graduates. According to Young (2001), these graduates would be able to fit into this restructuring through their high educational credentials. Thus, they were in a privileged position to occupy the newly created positions, for example, in public administration. Of course, this was the first step in the established strategy of reproduction of class privileges, which, once secured, could then be passed down to the next generation. Such practices are endemic to any political system that is predicated upon the principles of freedom of choice, individual liberty, and self-determination, such as democracy. In particular, liberal capitalism was premised upon the democratic functioning of its institutions and especially education. Could it be then that democracy, as a system, is innately flawed as far as equality of opportunity is concerned? Weber's [1948] (2001, p. 240) ideas appended below were expressed a few decades before Young wrote his book and they reverberate Young's fears and a growing skepticism at that time about the potential of democracy to avoid unequal reward of merit: "Democracy takes an ambivalent stand in the face of specialized examinations, as it does in the face of all the phenomena of bureaucracy—although democracy itself promotes these developments. Special examinations, on the one hand, mean or appear to mean a 'selection' of those who qualify from all social strata rather than a rule by notables. On the other hand, democracy fears a merit system and educational certificates will result in a privileged caste."

In a similar vein, Young aimed to offer a critique of the foundations of the system that fostered institutionalization of selection and, in effect, the creation of the conditions for the exclusion from society of a large part of the population. The value of Young's remarks is significant both for the lucid manner in which the analytical and the political arguments are synthesized and for their originality. Young believed that the education-based occupations that he saw proliferating from the 1940s onward would bring closer education with the labor market. However, not in a desirable way.

This connection would have the potential to engineer deep social changes as it would influence the aspirations of pupils and their families. The latter, the families, would usurp education in order to promote their children's careers and, more broadly, to enhance their children's life chances. The metaphor of education as the "key" to a better life, a passport to the labor market, or even a royal way, an "avenue par excellence" for upward social mobility, could never have taken a stronger meaning. The momentum, however, of educational expansion and, indeed, its increasingly closer connection with the labor market, exactly what Young feared, soon became part and parcel of a social and economic divide between the rich and the poor that was never seen before. Meritocracy, therefore, "as it has been used in relation to education, could only serve the reproduction of this divide between the advantaged and the disadvantaged. Hence, this trend of justifying education as an underpinning (if not reinforcement) of 'meritocratic inequality,' gained in support" (Themelis, 2008, p. 429). Education, then, instead of acting to limit privileges associated with ascription, such as wealth and family background, has, in reality, augmented inequalities between those who can forge a successful pathway from the school to the labor market.

An array of functions and sub-institutions have been incorporated into the educational system over the years in order to safeguard this process. From examinations to the issuing of formal qualifications and from testing to the international accreditation of degrees, education has been engrossed in a process of distribution of rewards on the basis of putative meritocratic remuneration, that is achievement. However, nothing in education operates outside the wider political economy, which, in capitalism, is inherently unequal. In other words, merit in education is not necessarily allocated to those who are only able but also to those who know how to use it as a class-advancement mechanism, and climb up the "greasy pole of success" (Sennett, 2004). This is something I will examine in the following section.

4.3.2 Building Meritocratic Consensus

Subsequent to Young's (1958) work about the role of education, the notion of "meritocracy through education" attracted considerable popularity and became an expedient tool of policy making. Proponents of this approach maintain that selection in education and employment should be driven by principles based on "achievement" rather than on "ascription." Turner (1960), for example, claimed that all children should receive the same educational provision and that by testing and selecting them on the basis of their school performance, a meritocratic system of occupying positions in the labor market would emerge. This was termed by Goldthorpe (2003b) as "education-based meritocracy," which appears to be "a highly attractive 'progressive' goal to which center-left parties can commit themselves, while entailing no radically redistributive measures of a kind that might threaten the 'median voter' electoral strategies on which these parties typically rely" (Goldthorpe and Jackson, 2006, p. 4). The main assumption behind such a process is that improved access to education is sufficient to remove barriers related to social mobility. This created the "equality of opportunity" consensus, which upheld that all children should be receiving the same education and by testing and selecting them on their education performance, a meritocratic system of occupying social positions would be available (Turner, 1960). The supporters of this proposition argue that the school system should be "sponsoring" the academically able children. Thus, the inheritance of privilege would be avoided. This argument found expression in the policy initiatives implemented by countries with a liberal capitalist orientation and governments who believed in the importance of education in serving their economic exigencies. These exigencies, as discussed in the previous chapters, were underpinned by the pursuit of economic growth and saw state intervention for the benefit of the smooth operation of the markets as a sine qua non. Pursuant to this logic was the expectation that educational reforms and expansion could safeguard equality of opportunities, through enhanced occupational access. Various reforming initiatives undertaken in the postwar years, such as the Education Reform Act of 1944 in Britain, the educational reforms of the 1960s in Ireland, and the 1964 reform in Greece, come in support of this thesis. Ideologically, these efforts found recourse to human capital theory, which rests on the premise that individuals are "resources" within socioeconomic systems and, as such, they have to be exploited to the greatest degree, regardless of their position or ranking in the social hierarchy. As I argued elsewhere (Themelis, 2008, p. 430), "[t]his expectation, (that educational expansion and reforms are safeguards of the maximisation of human potential) carries the assumption that the ablest students are selected thus making irrelevant one's social origins and other family privileges, such as wealth or social networks. In other words, children from any social class background have in principle the opportunity to get as far in education as their abilities can take them and through the avenue of education to any occupation in the labor market."

As mentioned in chapter 2, this was the tenet of the "liberal theory of industrialism" or modernization, which held that economic development will increase absolute mobility rates (Kerr et al., 1960). In addition, economic competition was expected to promote those with the highest educational qualifications to enter the best jobs (Treiman, 1970). This position was further developed by Daniel Bell (1973) who argued that there was a shift in the economy after the Second World War from the production of goods to the production of services, which took various forms, such as financial, educational, health. This resulted in major transformations in the occupational structure, such as the decrease in blue-collar occupations and a concomitant increase in the professional and technical occupations.[9]

Furthermore, Bell (1973) argued that the common feature of the growing group of service-based labor force was high educational credentials. Among this group, there was a scientific and technical elite, who was considered by Bell (1973) as the driving force of much of the postwar economic growth and general prosperity.[10] This elite would replace "economizing" thinking with "theoretical knowledge" and "become the key source of innovation and policy orientation for both the economy and government" (Ross, 1974, p. 335).

Similarly, schooling would "sponsor" academically able children, thus limiting or even preventing the inheritance of privilege (ascription) and fostering a system whereby the allocation of occupational positions would be based on individual achievement (Bell, 1978). As a result, there "would be rewards that were gained within an increasingly 'open' form of society from which all unfair, ascriptive influences were being eliminated" (Goldthorpe and Jackson, 2006). In this way, education could secure the provision of equality of opportunities to all students and through the process of selection, only the most able could progress and occupy high educational credentials and top positions in the social structure. The pattern of social stratification that is thusly created "can claim legitimacy not only on the grounds of societal efficiency but on moral grounds also" (Breen and Goldthorpe, 2001). In a nutshell, Bell's (1973, 1978) understanding of meritocracy entails educational achievement and qualifications as the precondition for the recruitment to the best occupations and to the highest social positions. This type of thinking is discernible in our days and has infiltrated most (neo-)liberal societies, which invariably subscribe to the idea of "meritocracy through education" as a cornerstone for the efficacious function of their capitalist requirements.

4.3.3 "Education-Based Meritocracy"[11] and Social Mobility

Social mobility researchers have attempted to shed light on the existence or not of meritocracy through education from mainly two different perspectives: on the one hand, some adopted Young's definition of merit, as IQ plus individual effort, while others followed Bell's understanding, which puts emphasis on educational qualifications. For the former group of researchers, educational qualifications and their importance were customarily underplayed although not totally ignored. A prominent advocate of this approach is Saunders (1995, 1997), who examined the preponderance and extent of meritocracy in modern Britain. Saunders's (1997) findings suggested that a large proportion of his sample (52 percent) had been intergenerationally mobile and they have mainly experienced upward rather than downward mobility.[12] In terms of the causes of the observed mobility, Saunders argued that "ability is an important influence on occupational placement *over* and *above* any effect it might have through formal qualifications. Not only do brighter people tend to perform better in exams, but they also tend to continue performing better once they enter the labor market" (Saunders, 1997, pp. 276–277, emphasis in original).

Saunders (1996, 1997) further concluded that the British society has been, broadly speaking, a meritocratic one, where the intergenerational transmission of advantages and disadvantages are waning in comparison to the importance and influence they exerted in the past. In other words, achievement prevails in modern-day Britain, while the role of ascription is more limited than has been in the past. This has significant ramifications for the openness of the social structure and the attendant distribution of opportunities within it. For Saunders (1997), no ascriptive barriers would impede somebody's move from a low-class position into a higher one provided these individuals are able and motivated enough. As long as the system has secured equality of access, rewards will follow those who displayed the highest ability. As I argued before (Themelis, 2008, pp. 432–433),

> in this kind of theorisation, social class destinations are justified ex post facto, provided one has shown that they are obtained due to the ability and motivation that individuals possess (i.e. due to their IQ and effort). The focus is not on the reproduction of social class advantage and disadvantage, but rather on the justification or not of the system in place regarding the allocation of social positions. That is, for those who manage to secure the best-rewarded occupations for their children, thus reproducing their class advantage, this is of less significance. Instead we should be examining whether those who secure these positions are the ablest amongst all the participants in the competition system. Indeed, Saunders' findings confirm his hypothesis, therefore justifying the reproduction of social classes. The middle class manage to secure for their offspring the same class position because their children are equally able and motivated. Conversely, the working class lack in ability and motivation, and this is why they stay behind in the class advancement process. As a confirmation to this runs the finding that there are a few working-class children who enter into the best occupations and achieve middle-class positions: these children are the ablest and most laborious among their working-class counterparts, and for these virtues they are rewarded with upward mobility.

Saunders's position rests on weak foundations, both politically/ideologically and also theoretically/epistemologically. Apart from concerns that one could raise regarding the IQ tests upon which the assessment of ability is gauged, Saunders propounds a social-Darwinian justification to social-class inequalities and social mobility. Saunders's line of thinking implies that the "fittest" and ablest gets a bigger share of the resources available in the social system, hence leading to the "naturalization" of unequal rewards. This is in accordance with Saunders's functionalist view of society. As I showed in chapter 1, such an understanding is furnished with an expectation that the optimum functioning of society is predicated upon the creation of an open system of competition.

The second definition of merit is in line with the meaning Bell attached to it, whereby ability is indicated by the educational qualifications one holds. Authors who adopted this definition have attempted to assess the meritocratic hypothesis through analyses of academic qualifications and their use and value in the labor market. Machin (2003), for example, showed that the amount of intergenerational mobility decreased between an earlier cohort (respondents who were born in 1958) and a later one (respondents born in 1970). In addition, for the more recent cohort (those born in 1970), parental income was more closely associated with earnings and income of their children than for the earlier cohort (see chapter 2). A significant amount of this variation, Machin (2003) argued, can be accounted for by the role of education. That is to say, people from higher economic backgrounds benefited more from the sizable educational expansion that occurred during the lifespan of these cohorts. Crucially, this expansion resulted in a decrease in the degree of social mobility between the two cohorts. In other words, the movement (upwards and downwards) across the two cohorts had decreased, and education expansion "rather than acting to equalise the chances of people from lower income backgrounds, [it] has actually acted to reinforce and increase inequalities across generations" (Machin, 2003, p. 197).

A more elaborate variation of the achievement-versus-ascription argument was advanced by Jonsson (1992). Jonsson (1992) developed the "Increased Merit Selection" (IMS) thesis, which, apart from educational qualifications, also took into account other factors. Various researchers have put the thesis to empirical scrutiny (Marshall et al., 1997; Heath and Cheung, 1998). Notably, the analyses produced did not indicate much disparity between them and they reached similar conclusions regarding the role of education after the Second World War. That is, the significance of education in influencing employment prospects and promoting social mobility was high during the immediate postwar period, but it has decreased since then (Breen and Goldthorpe, 2001). Breen and Goldthorpe (2001), who conducted secondary analysis of Machin's data, included in their operational definition of merit, characteristics from both Young's and Bell's approaches, that is IQ plus effort as well as educational qualifications. Their findings suggested that the significance of merit, in all its forms, has declined over the years rather than increased, giving negligible support to the argument about the existence of meritocracy in Britain.

Similar findings were obtained by Goldthorpe and Mills (2004) for male and female respondents born in Britain in 1973 and 1992. Although educational attainment had a significant influence on relative mobility chances of men and women, the actual role of education in mobility processes has been decreasing in importance. This can be explained by other reasons that may mitigate against a strong effect of education on mobility rates, such as the increasingly changing criteria upon which employers make their choices in a free-market economy.

Likewise, studies of the rest of the United Kingdom and the Republic of Ireland offered little support to the IMS thesis. Two studies conducted in Northern Ireland (Breen, 2003; Layte and Whelan, 2004) suggested that although absolute social mobility has been high from the early 1970s to the mid-1990s, with upward offsetting downward mobility, this did lead to a more meritocratic social system.[13] Likewise, in the Republic of Ireland, people with the same educational qualifications experienced different occupational trajectories, suggesting that education alone does not suffice to improve one's class destination (Breen and Whelan, 1993). In Scotland, where education seems to have had some impact on upward social mobility, a closer look suggests that this was chiefly the outcome of a restructured labor market and structure of employment (Iannelli and Paterson, 2006). Furthermore, evidence suggests that the effect of educational qualifications on class destinations has decreased in more recent years as class strategies for intergenerational transmission of advantages have been reignited: "middle class parents must be finding other ways to give their children an advantage in life" (Iannelli and Paterson, 2006). Finally, studies from Britain (Breen and Golthorpe, 1999) and Sweden (Jonsson and Mills, 1993) have also led to similar conclusions, that is to say, educational qualifications have ceased to be the main promoter of upward social mobility.

The findings presented thus far indicate that there is currently less movement between social classes in Britain than in earlier periods. Moreover, the observed circulation in the British social system in the early postwar years was not the result of decreasing inequalities within the class structure but rather the product of the occupational restructuring that fostered high rates of structural mobility. At the same time, the importance of education on social mobility has weakened over the recent years (Cabinet Office, 2008; The Panel on Fair Access to the Professions, 2009), which is partly due to the proliferation of academic qualifications through the expansion of HE and the corresponding inability of the labor markets to absorb the rising educated workforce.

Although there is no consensus over the extent of meritocracy in contemporary British society, the existing evidence points to the fact that "merit," however one defines it, has a limited impact on determining class destinations of individuals. Put simply, achieved characteristics, such as educational qualifications, are important but not sufficient in securing access to high-class positions. As ascribed characteristics seem to play a decisive role in determining class destinations, regardless of attributes and assets that may be gained throughout one's life course, family practices seem to be in a position to shed light on this "meritocratic failure." As Brown and Tannock (2009, p. 389) argued, "the equality of opportunity that is promoted by meritocratic ideology is a poor substitute in progressive politics for previous commitments to equality of social and economic outcome."

4.4 Summary

In chapter 1, I argued that the pursuit of an open society has been a key target of liberal democracies after the war. More specifically, it was shown that, in many postwar countries with a liberal vision and orientation, such as Britain, education became an indexical site of meritocracy and the extent of social mobility an indicator of fairness of allocation of occupational rewards. However, I suggested that the failure of many postwar liberal countries to distribute occupational opportunities with fairness did not lie with education, but with the paradoxical commitment of capitalist systems to promote openness in their social structure and allow inequalities of various kinds to operate at the same time. Core elements of the "meritocracy through education" debate were critically discussed in order to link issues of ascription and achievement with the structure of opportunities and the system of allocation of occupational and social positions. It was argued that the "meritocratic failure" might be more appropriately understood as a manifestation of wider "system failure" rather than, strictly speaking, an educational one.

Part II

Part II presents a case study in education and social mobility that draws from a study that I carried out in North West Greece between 2004 and 2009. Its aim is to instantiate the discussion about Greek socioeconomic development and modernization presented in the previous chapters through a case study. Hence, Part II contextualizes the main issues discussed in theoretical, historical, and methodological terms in the previous chapters, namely socioeconomic development, social-class formation and stratification, social mobility, and educational transformation. I start with the presentation of the case study and I move on to the discussion of some meso- and micro-aspects of social mobility that help us understand the role and class character of education in Greece in the last six decades or so.

Chapter 5
Contextualizing the Case Study

5.1 The Research Setting: Protopi as an Atypical Case Study

Thus far, my analysis has focused on the macro-level. Initially, I explicated the ways social stratification has been theorized and then I shifted my focus onto some empirical applications and explorations of these macro-theories in the field of social mobility. Subsequently, I presented some major aspects of the Greek political economy, through a discussion of some key postwar socioeconomic, political, and labor-market trends. I then offered a "dissection" of education, which was described as a pivotal institution in the molding of the postwar consensus that emerged in liberal democracies in the Western world, including Greece. The Greek context that was discussed in the first part of the book has to be viewed as the springboard of my exploration, as the canvas upon which the stories of the participants (chapters 7, 8 and 9) will be projected. However, these stories were collected from a specific community whose most salient characteristics are presented in this chapter. This entails a shift in my level of analysis, from the macro- to the meso-level. This is important in order to allow the reader to connect the discussion about the characteristics of Greece that preceded to those of the empirical research I conducted and I present in the following chapters.

The research belongs to the tradition of case studies. However, this is not a study of a community, namely Protopi,[1] as it does not belong to the sociological tradition of "community case study" that stems from the mid-1950s onward, which aimed to explore the nature of relationships among members in various communities. Many studies that appeared after this period sought to explore the relationships among working men (Dennis et al., 1956); inquire into the kinship networks associated with working-class communities (Young and Willmott, 1957); examine the changing working relations and their impact on family life (Newson and Newson, 1963); describe the attitudes and behaviors of specific working groups in manual "communities"

(Goldthorpe et al., 1968); investigate "communities" formed through various group memberships, such as sports, religious, music, and other clubs (Jackson, 1968); and so on. By contrast, my aim here is to offer a sociological understanding of educational attainment and occupational movements, through the presentation, on the one hand, of patterns of change for a large number of individuals (chapter 6) and, on the other, of the impact of educational attainment on the pathways of a sample of individuals and their families in a bounded spatial community (chapter 7).

My interests, therefore, lie in the importance of a set of issues on individuals' lives, who are connected with each other through familial and social ties. This approach treats individuals as embedded within specific social, historical, political, and economic contexts. Furthermore, it conceives of people as related through interconnected institutions (such as family and education), which exert a significant influence on their decisions, strategies, opportunities, accomplishments, failures, and so on. In a nutshell, in this case study, the community is a bounded spatial, socioeconomic, and historical entity that helps us to understand and locate the research participants and the important processes in their lives rather than the subject matter itself. The single-case focus is justified by Protopi's social, political, economic, and other characteristics that make it an atypical case, which, though, can offer insights and raise implications about more typical ones.

The rationale for the selection of Protopi as my case study rests on manifold reasons. First, Protopi's socioeconomic development makes it an interesting case to explore, as it is markedly different from many other parts of Greece with an agricultural economic base and a belated advent of capitalist production. In particular, Protopi's postwar growth and development were not based solely on emigration as in most other rural areas in Greece. Instead of enduring a protracted demographic and economical contraction, as did the majority of provincial places after the war, Protopi expanded considerably. Its development stemmed from exogenous, that is to say emigration-derived remittances, and also endogenous sources, such as intensification of agricultural production and a concomitant exploitation of the benefits of commodity capitalism, such as proximity to the local markets and the flourishing of the service economy.

Second, the selection of Protopi was dictated by pragmatic reasons posed both by the resources available and the necessities of empirical research. Unlike many Western countries with a long history in record-keeping, systematic data collection for various aspects of life—such as employment and education, which were paramount in this study, and the establishment of a research tradition in the topics pertinent to this book—Greece lacks data and systematically archived information in most of these areas. Hence, the exploration of a larger community or more settings (cases) in order to enhance both the generalizability and the comparative dimension of the study was ruled out. Moreover, the dearth in social mobility literature and relevant research in Greece (see chapter 3) called for a research design sensitive to the realities of the research participants and the originality of the object of study. Hence, while Protopi is large enough an area geographically and demographically to allow the collection of rich and diverse material, it is also bounded so that it could be researched within a reasonable time line.

Third, Protopi possesses historical and socioeconomic characteristics that make it a fascinating case study. For example, knowing that in 1929 land was distributed equally to all its residents was an invaluable insight. This pointed to some equalization of opportunities and was a convenient starting point, given that other forms of property or income were nearly completely absent or they existed to a very small extent. Therefore, by and large, all residents shared the same material starting point and the same occupational situation, namely animal husbandry and farming for family consumption. This knowledge placed me, as a researcher, in a unique position: the measurement and understanding of social mobility appeared much more feasible there than in a place where occupational trajectories and social mobility careers were intertwined with ascriptive factors, such as long-standing transmission of family wealth, inheritance, and other forms of non-earned advantage. In other words, the reconstruction of occupational histories, which is a sine qua non to my intergenerational approach (chapters 7 and 8), could be easily accomplished in the case of Protopi due to the "common denominator," that is the land reform. That is to say, the equalization of material resources at a fixed point in time was expected to enhance the exploration of the distribution of opportunities and the estimation of inequalities in outcome at later points in life.

Additionally, I wanted to explore the educational experiences and the role of educational qualifications in relation to the social mobility of residents in this locale. Protopi, also in this regard offers to the researcher a comparative advantage. The local secondary school got established in 1964, which means that the introduction of mass, secondary education occurred at the same time for the vast majority of its residents. This, it was hoped, would make the estimation of differential educational outcomes on the life chances of respondents easier to achieve through the collection and reconstruction of the educational histories of my respondents.

However, apart from its unique features, Protopi also bears resemblance to other parts of Greece. In particular, its continuous demographic expansion after the war, the restructuring of its occupational base, the enrichment of the labor market, and the expansion of educational provision are common threads in the postwar fabric of large parts of Greece. Hence, many findings I will present and the ideas I will develop in the following chapters about education and social mobility are not idiosyncratic to Protopi but resonate also with other areas in Greece.

5.2 Protopi in Context

Protopi and its surrounding area were part of the New Provinces that were annexed to Greece in 1912–1913. At that time, most of its people were subjected to abject poverty, as they were landless with no alternative sources of income. Anecdotal evidence suggests that Protopi in the early twentieth century was inhabited by approximately 700 residents or 150 families, who were perceived to be autochthonous. Among them, it was estimated that roughly 10–15 percent were Roma. The family size was larger compared to contemporary standards and the household was invariably an extended version of the nuclear family, often including congenital relatives of the couple, such as parents, grandparents, and other relatives. Especially after the war, Protopi grew substantially in size and population, and people from other, mainly poorer and mountainous areas moved in. In 2008, it was estimated that at least 8,000 people lived in Protopi permanently, though a significant proportion of them was considered "heterochthonous," that is to say born and raised elsewhere and with no family roots in Protopi. However, this might be an underestimate as most of the Albanians or co-ethnic Greeks who came mainly from Albania after the early 1990s (they number a few hundreds) are not included in this estimate.

A milestone in the twentieth-century history of Protopi was marked with the Statutory Decree of 1929, which aimed to provide land to propertyless people. Approximately half of the land in the prefecture where Protopi is situated was subjected to the land reform (Petmezas, 1999).[2] The Decree stipulated that land ought to be equally distributed among the residents in the areas that were included in the scheme. In particular, it held that the head of each household was entitled to two types of land: arable and land for dwelling. Regarding Protopi, the reform fell short of its expectation to alleviate people from material deprivation as most of the arable land was flooded. This removed from the residents the possibility of increasing their income and improving their very low living standards, at least until the early 1950s, when some significant draining work was undertaken.

Before the war, the economy of Protopi was entirely based on farming and animal husbandry, and its mode of production was in a proto-capitalist stage. That is, the agricultural produce was rarely sold for profit and agricultural workers did not receive a regular wage, but a daily maintenance, which invariably consisted of their daily food intake. Working conditions in farming were exceptionally arduous and labor-intensive, with working hours stretching from dawn to dusk. The peasants were widely exposed to weather adversities and other unforeseen factors; for instance, the flooding of the plains resulted in very poor or no harvests, which at the time of the Italian invasion and the German occupation (1941–1945) further deteriorated the living conditions and claimed a high toll on the lives of the local population. Agricultural production, such as wheat, corn, oats, and barley, was mainly reserved for family use and in order to provide the means of subsistence though barter was not entirely absent. After the war, new crops with a higher market value, such as tobacco, began to be cultivated. This development coincided with the dominance of the commodity mode of production, which brought intensification of production, higher degree of interaction with other markets, and the systematic exchange of labor for money. This transition enriched the labor market with numerous occupations, such as in the house construction and the service sector. The latter saw a remarkable expansion in the postwar years, which was triggered by self-employment, largely sustained by small-scale and family-run businesses, and a proliferation in public-sector jobs.

The family and the local economy were tightly interconnected. Land was not only the means of subsistence, but also a mechanism of participation in the community's social life. The two major social events of the year that marked the beginning and the end of the agricultural season were attended by all residents and the same was the case with weddings (more in chapter 9). Kinship ties regulated and shaped social relations but ownership of land and livestock (the vast majority of residents in Protopi owned both) also qualified individuals to participate in networks of solidarity. This, though, does not suffice to portray the social structure of Protopi as internally undifferentiated. Viewing peasant societies as a vertically uniform, self-sufficient, consumer-labor group is erroneous.[3] As will be elucidated in chapters 7 and 8, differences among peasants grew fast throughout the 1930s and 1940s. For example, while some of them increased their share of property and hired land workers, others sold their land in order to alleviate the daily pressure in the pursuit of subsistence. After the war, the differentiation further increased both horizontally, through the enrichment of the division of labor with new occupations, and vertically, through the increase in socioeconomic inequalities.

Socially, Protopi comprises an atypical case as far as its demography is concerned and its ethnic mix, that is Roma and non-Roma population. This ethnic diversity has allowed an interesting relationship to develop between the two groups. Thus, despite the fact that the Roma group has coexisted with the dominant (non-Roma) one for many generations,[4] the persistence of the "othering" of the Roma people has continued. The processes underlying the labelling and marginalization of the Roma have less to do with their distinctiveness and more with a perceived need to protect the inner boundaries of the dominant group. For the non-Roma, this plays the role of a well-preserved strategy for achieving intergenerational homogeneity and maintaining resources and advantages, while for the Roma, it has been an unjust practice of social differentiation. This situation poses a challenge that needs a critical sociological investigation that can go beyond superficial explorations and synchronic considerations, such as those associated with identity politics and politics of representation that are usually employed to explain the situation of the Roma (for an example, see Stewart, 1997). At the same time, the coexistence of Roma and non-Roma people offers a unique opportunity to research some key processes, such as the occupational transitions, which both groups underwent and the differential outcomes of these processes. Additionally, Protopi offers the opportunity to explore some processes pertinent to racialization, its interrelatedness with the distribution of opportunities, and the mechanisms for merit allocation within a newly established capitalist economy. In this context, differential identities are perceived as underlaying access to and participation in institutional structures, social networks, community mechanisms and functions. Furthermore, these identities take the form of active ingredients in the molding of the emerging class structure, the reshaping and renegotiation of class boundaries, and the formation of class consciousness. In this sense, they are both forces of material and ideological significance, rather than issues of mere cultural differentiation, epiphenomena relegated to the sphere of individual or group expression of identity. In a nutshell, diverse identities of the residents in Protopi are not merely culturally differentiated forms of expression, but they are also rooted in the material circumstances of structurally mediated realities.

There is no more evidence of historical patterns of movement for the ancestors of today's Roma than of any other section of the local population. Invariably, the Roma live in neighborhoods where the non-Roma are underrepresented or absent altogether, although a recent trend has emerged for more mixed residential patterns than in the past (triggered after the 1990s by the presence of newcomers, such as economic migrants). At present, the proportion of the Roma is approximately 10 percent of the total population,[5] which is somewhat lower in comparison to the early and mid-twentieth century. The Roma are distinguished from the non-Roma residents on the basis of their skin color (they are perceived as having darker complexion), their area of residence (typically in the periphery of Protopi), their surnames, and other tacit markers. For the biggest part of Protopi's history, there was no intermarriage between the Roma and the non-Roma groups and very limited labor-market exchanges.

Politically, Protopi is closer to the Greek average nowadays than in the past. During the Civil War (1944–1949), it was divided as partisanship became a matter of life and death: one could either be in the guerrilla, Leftwing, or the conservative, Right-wing camp, a situation that often led members of the same family to opposing camps. The impact of this division has only started to diminish recently though some scars might still be visible. In the main, political tensions have yielded or have been transferred to other arenas. With regard to education, Protopi bears many similarities with other, former rural areas. Until the late 1950s, only primary school was available, while secondary, let alone tertiary, education was outside the remit of the vast majority of residents. Educational participation dramatically improved after the mid-1960s. Currently, university attendance is common among the offsprings of the average family (more in chapter 7).

5.3 Design of the Study

This study explores concurrently the complexity and richness of social class, ethnicity, and gender for participants in three adjacent generations. This approach is conceptually and epistemologically apropos for this study as it aims to furnish us with a fuller account of the realities of the research participants, while also highlighting the inseparability of the three key variables, namely social class, ethnicity, and gender, in the examination of social, institutional, and cultural processes pertinent to social mobility.

The research design of this study includes both dominant and marginalized groups, the non-Roma and the Roma, respectively. As a result, it breaks away from the study of minority groups in traditional ethnic, minority, or even "racial," studies and from prevailing, "othering" theorizations of the differential social mobility of minority groups, such as the Roma. By contrast, it examines both Roma and non-Roma groups as embedded in the same mode of socioeconomic organization and social relations of production and aims to promote a critical theorizing of the Roma people as an integral part of society rather than as the "others." My focus is equally on both genders since the social mobility of women can reveal the gender inequalities that exist within the family as well as in the labor market (Dex, 1987). This is another original element that characterizes this study and distinguishes it from conventional mobility studies and their typically male-centered approach.

At present, there is a conspicuous dearth of studies that have explored social mobility and its interrelated dimensions through the use of qualitative data, while there are probably no studies that have utilized a mixed-methods design. This study breaks new ground by treating qualitative and quantitative methodologies not as competing but complementary. In doing so, it adopts a mixed-methods design that uses elements from both the quantitative (Goldthorpe, 1980, 2000) and the qualitative traditions (Bertaux and Thomson, 1997) in the study of social mobility. This design aims to move beyond the positivist or post-positivist foundations of mainstream mobility research, which has arguably "narrowed its interest to hypotheses which a survey can test, at the price of cutting itself off from the observation of other dimensions of mobility processes and from the development of sociological and historical thinking as a whole" (Bertaux and Thomson, 1997, p. 5). To be precise, the experiences and "voices" of those studied, the power relationships that operate within communities, and the multiplicity of ways in which power is constructed and reproduced invariably falls outside the scope of such methodologies. Complex realities, where multiple aspects of one's identity are intertwined, cannot be conveyed through a reliance on such approaches, as the intersections of gender, ethnicity, and class "and other means of oppression cannot be reduced to a tally of competing claims" (Dei et al., 1997, p. 33). The struggle for resources, rewards, and equal participation in social institutions, the experiences of differential capitalization of opportunities, marginalization, and discrimination, the explanations and interpretations individuals provide about them need methods that allow for the richness and complexity of their stories to be revealed.

Finally, integral to this study is its transformative–emancipatory approach. The latter is permeated by a commitment to social justice and has been applied by feminists (Olesen, 1994; Truman et al., 2000), disability (Mertens, 2008a), and critical theorists (Kincheloe and McLaren, 2000). The transformative–emancipatory approach underlines the unequal distribution of opportunities and rewards and tries to reach an understanding of discriminatory processes and power differentials. At the same time, it recognizes that knowledge reflects power and social relationships in society without ignoring the subjectivities, social arrangements, values, and power differences between the researcher and the researched. A key overarching commitment to this approach is its search for a more egalitarian and equal society, which is embraced in this study. My focus on two groups that do not feature in mainstream mobility studies, namely Roma and women, is an attempt to address some of these imbalances mentioned above. Both groups are usually treated as of little relevance to the core mobility investigations and their inclusion in such studies is viewed as unlikely to produce any meaningful results and comparisons. I want to argue that a true commitment to issues of social justice is indissolubly linked to the research design adopted. Hence, the mobility careers and the educational and occupational experiences of women and the Roma cannot be inferred from those of men nor the dominant group.

From an ontological perspective, researchers within the transformative field consider the choice of methods to be contingent upon subjectivities, social arrangements, values, and power relations between the researchers and the researched (House and Howe, 1999). In addition, they hold that social realities can be viewed through many different viewpoints that can only be understood within their social, political, historical, and economic value systems (Mertens, 2008b). This has profound influence not only on the methods they chose and the "dosage" of each method in their study, but on the whole research design.

Throughout this research, I was interested in two dimensions, broadly termed as patterns and distributional aspects of education and social mobility, and the experiences of these mobility processes. As far as the first aspect is concerned, the distributional aspects and diachronic patterns, trends, and fluctuations of occupational and educational mobility, I considered suitable for this study that their exploration could be best served through the deployment of quantitative methods. This is explained by the apropos of such methods in establishing relationships between two or more characteristics, variables, in a comparable manner. Moreover, as I argued in chapter 2, given the established prominence of quantitative methodology in the field of social mobility research, the findings generated through quantitative methods, the inferences, and theoretical points that emanate from them could allow me to link them to previous studies and theories. This approach, it is hoped, can both enrich the field with new findings and insights and offer the possibility to those interested in social mobility and education, by scrutinizing this study, to further advance this area of research.

The specific method I utilized to collect quantitative data was a survey. The specific type of survey holds implications with "mixed-model" survey designs (de Leeuw, 2008) whereby both face-to-face and other methods (i.e., archival sources) were used. The aim of the survey was to collect information about a large number of individuals in order to identify patterns of intra- and intergenerational mobility change, while its scope was to collect representative data on the population of Protopi and the various groups that lived within its boundaries (i.e., for both genders and ethnic groups and for all social classes and age-groups). Given the lack of consistent and reliable data that could be obtained by national or local services, an alternative "directory" of key demographic characteristics had to be created in order to identify the features of the population that would allow me to construct a representative sample. This source was the Electoral Register (hereafter, the Register). The Register holds information about individuals and their families, such as their date of birth, family names, place of birth, place of residence, occupation, and family situation (for more information on the type of information obtained from the Register and how it was utilized, see appendix 2).

Once the cleaning of the data set was completed (for a step-by-step description of this process, see appendix 3), there were 1,248 cases left on the data set, which produced a representative sample in relation to most key areas of interest (Table 5.1). Specifically, the proportion of males and females in my sample was similar to that in Protopi (approximately 50 percent in each group). Although the Roma in my sample (22 percent) were overrepresented in comparison to Protopi (approximately 10 percent), the percentage of non-Roma people in my sample (78 percent) was similar to that in Protopi.[6] A proportion of the current population in Protopi (roughly 10 percent) consists of Greek ethnics from Albania or Albanian immigrants, who are not included in my sample.[7] Finally, 25 percent of the obtained sample belongs to the older age-group, 45 percent to the middle, and 30 percent to the

Table 5.1 Survey sample (by gender, generation, and ethnicity) ($N = 1,248$)

Gender	Older generation		Middle generation		Younger generation		Total
	Non-Roma	Roma	Non-Roma	Roma	Non-Roma	Roma	
Male	135	35	201	59	154	45	629
Female	118	25	234	71	137	34	619
Total	253	60	435	130	291	79	1.248

younger one. Although the middle age-group appears to be more represented than the other two, the latter were large enough to allow for limited sample bias to occur.

Second, I was interested in the experiences of people whose voices would otherwise be left unheard as well as in allowing their uniqueness and originality to come out as cogently and vigorously as possible. To this extent, I deployed critical ethnography which "can allow a degree of the activity, creativity and human agency within the object of study to come through into the analysis and the reader's experience" (Willis, 1977, p. 3). In other words, critical ethnography is rooted in the experiences and lives of the research participants, rather than solely in the researcher's "ivory tower" of knowledge construction.[8] From this remark, it follows that the critical ethnographer is engaged in a politics of transformation through raising questions about hierarchal and unequal relations he or she observes in society. Furthermore, the researcher is interested in offering his or her work as an opportunity to question the status quo and initiate a dialogue with the researched, especially with the oppressed and marginalized among them, about the conditions of their "disadvantage" and the possibilities of transformation. The social justice element that underpins my approach (Mertens, 2008a, 2008c) also informs the role of the researcher in an unequal world. Thus, the researcher is not merely seeking to obtain "data," but also has a commitment to unravel unearned privilege and expose hidden injustices sustained by the marginalized respondents (Mertens, 2008b, 2008c), an approach that is contingent upon the values the researcher brings with him or her. For Kincheloe and McLaren (1994), one of the most significant of these values is "research humility" (p. 151). This implies that researchers thoroughly interrogate their own fallibilities, locations, and investments in the notion of a privileged frame of reference. In the final assessment, however, the ethnographic inscription of human experience may indeed turn on tension and even ideological conflicts between scholars' and participants' readings. Of course, ethnographic enquiry, guided by its effort to grasp local experiences and situated practices, requires rigorous reflection and extended human interaction. Nevertheless, ethnographers must come to terms with how to justly and effectively engage individuals and groups that are living and (re-)producing the very spaces, structures, and relations of privilege that researchers seek to challenge.

For the qualitative part of this research, I conducted observations and interviews. The specific type of observation I conducted was participant observation, which involved an active attempt to become a member of the observed group, a process that extends beyond the physical presence of the researcher and the sharing of lived experiences with the participants to include "entry into their social and 'symbolic' world through learning their social conventions and habits, their use of language and non-verbal communication, and so on" (Robson, 2002, p. 314). My participation varied from "moderate" to "complete" (Mertens, 1998, p. 318). Moderate participation entails an attempt to "balance the insider and outsider roles by observing and participating in some but not all of the activities" (Mertens, 1998, p. 318), while "complete participation" involves the researcher naturally participating in what happens while observing it. The most common type of observation applied in this research was active participation, which involved following the participants and partaking in the same activities with them though without trying to blend in with them completely.

The second method of qualitative data collection I employed was interviews or, to be more precise, interviews located in the tradition of critical rather than conventional ethnography.[9] Interviewing is understood here as a social event that has a dynamic nature. As Bourdieu pointed out (1977), "the relationship between methodology and information collected and the determination of the eventual from the accounts of the interviewees can only be taken into account with the deployment of interviews." The interview method also holds implications for life histories as it can "provide valid and rich raw material for both social history and for the interpretation of social mobility" (Bertaux and Thomson, 1997, p. 34). At the same time, life history has the potential to offer insights into "objective" factual content as well as into "subjective" facets of people's lives. Semi-standardized (or semi-structured) interviews with 40 participants were undertaken in this study.

Transformative researchers, as I discussed above, place emphasis on the rootedness of their research in the social, political, economic, and historical context, and they are sensitive to the diversity of the participants and their realities. These principles, along with the research aims, guided the sampling procedures in this study. The adherence to these principles is demonstrated by my concerns to include both ethnic groups (Roma and non-Roma) in the research sample in order to allow the most marginalized and oppressed people among the participants to be given a voice, a process that could enable me to treat their accounts with due respect and sensitivity. Moreover, I included both men and women and ensured that the underrepresentation or absence of women in traditional mobility studies is remedied and that the influence of male power in knowledge production is redressed. In addition, people from all social classes were included and I tried to avoid letting the more powerful participants (in any terms) to overshadow those in a socially inferior position. Equally so, I included participants from diverse educational backgrounds and I did not allow the most educated to dominate or represent the less-educated ones. Finally, people from all age-groups, that is, from 25 to 86 years, were included in my sample as their mobility experiences and occupational pathways were expected to be considerably divergent.[10] All the participants in the qualitative part of the research were in the Electoral Register, which was used here as my sampling frame (for a similar approach,

Table 5.2 Interviews participants (by gender, generation, and ethnicity) (*N* = 40).

Gender	Older generation		Middle generation		Younger generation		Total
	Roma	Non-Roma	Roma	Non-Roma	Roma	Non-Roma	
Male	2	6	1	7	2	8	26
Female	3	4	0	3	1	3	14
Total	5	10	1	10	3	11	40

see Brannen et al., 2007), and they had to fit in with four criteria that were devised, namely:

a. ethnicity
b. age-group
c. gender
d. socialc lass

In order to meet the requirements of the intergenerational character of mobility research, the participants were further distributed into three age-groups:[11]

a. the younger ones (25–44 years old)
b. the middle-aged group (45–64 years old)
c. those older than 65 years

The majority of the respondents (26) were males (Table 5.2). Nine were Roma and the rest (31) non-Roma. Among the Roma, there was a balanced number of male (five) and female (four) respondents, whereas among the dominant group, the male respondents (21) made up a greater proportion of the sample (compared to ten females). While the proportion of the Roma respondents (22.5 percent) was higher than that in the general population (an estimated 10 percent), the percentage of women in my sample (35 percent) was lower than the general average (approximately 50 percent). In relation to age-group membership, 11 respondents belonged to the younger age-group, 14 to the middle age, and 15 to the older age. As I discussed above, inclusivity was a fundamental criterion in the sampling method I followed. Therefore, the proportions of interview participants in the sample were well within the desired range limits for including the different realities of members of the diverse social groups in Protopi. Any sampling imbalance, such as the lower number of women in comparison to men, was partially redressed by informal discussions and observations. Finally, the interviewees were spread in terms of social-class membership: five of them came from middle-class background, 14 from intermediate, 14 from working class, while seven were farmers.

Chapter 6

Quantitative Aspects of Social Mobility

6.1 Introduction

In this chapter, I discuss the quantitative aspects of social mobility (i.e., patterns of absolute, structural, and exchange mobility), and I explore the role of education in individuals' movement within the social structure in Protopi. The aim of this chapter is to provide the reader with an overview of the general mobility patterns and trends in Protopi (meso-level; chapter 5) and enhance the connections between the two other levels of analysis: on the one hand, with the country-specific changes that were discussed in relation to Greece (macro-level; chapters 3 and 4) and, on the other hand, with the accounts of mobility experiences of the research participants (micro-level) that will follow (chapters 7–9).

In the investigation of social mobility, multiple aspects can be examined depending on the focus of the study. The main aspects that concern this study are the following:

1. Absolute social mobility (horizontal, vertical, inflow, and outflow mobility rates).
2. The extent of social movements in time (inter- and intragenerational mobility).
3. The types of movements (structural and exchange/circulation mobility or relative mobility chances).

In the following sections, I deal with each one of these dimensions and explain their significance to this study.

6.2 The Extent of Social Movements: Absolute Social Mobility (Horizontal, Vertical, Inflow, and Outflow Mobility Rates)

The way social mobility is gauged is crucial as different types of measurement can produce different results about the "openness" or "closure" of a social system, and more generally about class formation and the composition of the social structure (IPPR, 2008), which, in turn, can lead to divergent conclusions about the extent of inequalities and the reproduction of advantages/disadvantages for incumbents of different social-class positions. De facto mobility rates or absolute mobility is the net amount of individuals' movements between different classes over a specific period of time (usually between two generations) (Goldthorpe, 1980, p. 29). The estimation of absolute mobility is based on a comparison between the social-class origins of individuals (usually determined by their parents' social-class position) and the social-class destinations these individuals achieve during their life course. Apart from the movement of individuals, absolute mobility is also used for the calculation of the movement of entire groups, such as families, kinship groups, or occupational groups. For the measurement of this kind of mobility, two types of data are collected. First, data about respondents' parents' social class (origin) and, second, about the social class of the respondents themselves in adulthood (destination). Absolute mobility rates are useful in unravelling the recruitment patterns within each social class, the destination of people according to their social-class origins, as well as the composition of each social class.

When mobility is measured according to the direction of the observed movements, talk is either about "vertical" or "horizontal" mobility. There are two types of vertical mobility. First, upward mobility, that is the movement from a lower into a higher social class, occupational group, stratum, educational level, and so on, and, second, downward mobility, which implies the reverse direction of movement, that is from a higher into a lower class (group and so on). Upward mobility is important in a social system as it connotes the potential for individuals or groups to move into a higher class, thus allowing for equality of opportunity to occur in a social system (Aldridge, 2003). However, a high incidence of upward mobility is not necessarily a positive feature of the relevant social structure, because it can be associated with unequal distribution of opportunities. For example, if some people or groups of people have better access to resources than others, it could entail differential dis/advantages. Furthermore, if all social classes move concurrently upward, then the inequalities between them remain uncontested. It is important, therefore, to bear in mind that when society undergoes significant economic, employment, or other structural changes, absolute mobility rates are typically higher than normal as more "space" is created at either poles of the social structure (Payne and Roberts, 2002). As a result, individuals have increased chances to occupy the emergent positions. As I discussed in chapter 2, this was to a large extent the case in many postwar societies, such as Britain, where the high upward mobility rates attested to, especially until the 1980s, were accompanied by chronic social inequalities. On the other hand, the occurrence of downward mobility is also of grave significance to a social system as it has the potential to challenge the reproduction of social inequalities. Nevertheless, downward mobility invariably receives less attention than upward mobility, largely due to the fact that it makes for unappealing political headlines. In either case, a high rate of vertical (upward or downward) mobility can have an adverse impact on people's lives as it may bring social instability, insecurity, individualism, and antagonism (Blau and Duncan, 1967).

According to Esping-Andersen (1993, p. 63), there is a further distinction to be drawn in respect of vertical (upward and downward) social mobility, depending on the extent of the observed movements. Thus, when the changes follow a long trajectory, as in the case, for example, of a non-skilled manual worker who enters the service class, this movement is termed "long-range mobility." On the other hand, when the movement covers a short distance, as in the case of an unskilled manual worker who gains some skills that she or he applies to perform a new job (thus becoming skilled manual worker), this is termed "short-range mobility."

Finally, horizontal mobility comprises of movements into different groups, be them social classes, socio-economic groups, and so on. If, for example, an unskilled manual worker moves into a sales job, this transition would imply a horizontal movement, because his or her relations to the market (and to the means of production) remain unaltered.

6.3 The Extent of Social Movements in Time: Intra- and Intergenerational Mobility

When social mobility is examined according to the extent of the observed changes in terms of time, it can take two forms. First, the form of intragenerational mobility, which is concerned with changes in the career history within the lifetime of individuals. Alternatively, the focus is on intergenerational or life-course mobility, which deals with the social-class movements between two or more adjacent generations. Usually, intergenerational mobility is explored more often than intragenerational mobility due to its usefulness in measuring the diachronic distribution of opportunities and inequalities.

6.4 The Types of Movements within the Social Structure: Structural and Exchange Mobility

One of the most important and, yet at the same time, less-explored aspects of social mobility involves the type of social movement, which can take two forms: structural or exchange mobility. Structural mobility (Goldthorpe, 2000) is characterized by movements within the social system that have resulted from structural rearrangements of this very system. Hence, changes in the labor market or in the structure of the economy may compel concomitant transformations in the occupational structure, which, in turn, are bound to alter the distribution of individuals in the social structure. The reorganization of production away from the manufacturing sector and into the service-based economy that occurred after the Second World War in many economically advanced countries of the West, such as Britain, is an example of how structural mobility can occur. In this case, some classes or occupational groups may contract while others will expand. According to Hout (2000), "structural mobility refers to all those factors that are independent of origins and destinations" (p. 294).

The second type of movement is termed relative mobility or relative mobility chances/rates. Relative mobility involves the net movement of individuals from one social position to another, that is the chances an individual (or a group) has to become mobile in relation to his or her original position. Relative rates, also known as exchange or circulation mobility, are held to be an appropriate indicator of the extent of openness in society. Unlike absolute mobility rates, relative rates do not provide mere aggregates of those who have been socially mobile. Instead, they offer the opportunity to draw comparisons among different social classes and to evaluate not only the extent of fluidity, but, more interestingly, the degree of rigidity of a social system. Thus, in a meritocratic society, it is anticipated that an individual's chances of attaining a better or worse social position than his or her parents will be independent of his or her parents' social class. Relative mobility rates, therefore, can inform us whether individuals' achievements or failures in social mobility terms have resulted from opportunities provided by the social system itself (achieved factors) or from other factors, such privileges inherited from their parents (ascribed factors).

The distinction between structural and relative mobility is crucial. The former, structural mobility, stems from the assumption that, in any measurement taken for two adjacent generations, some amount of mobility will be observed. That is to say, it is not possible for all children to assume their parents' occupations and, by extension, social classes. The latter, exchange mobility, is measured independently of any class movement between two different generations as it involves the estimation of "mutually offsetting instances of 'exchange' (or 'circulation') mobility" (Goldthorpe, 2000, p. 231). In other words, it refers to the amount of social positions that were "lost" or "gained" for each class in relation to another. Put differently, it is a measure that compares the chances between individuals from different social classes to end up in one class over another. In technical terminology, "exchange mobility is that part of the mobility process that produces equal flows between origin-destination pairs" (Hout, 2000, p. 294).

Relative rates have to be examined together with absolute mobility rates. Thus, high absolute mobility chances (which imply openness within the social structure) can coexist with high relative mobility rates, though, this combination does not necessarily lead to a fairer social system. Moreover, such a combined examination of structural and relative mobility rates can inform us about the success or otherwise of countries with a commitment to liberal orientation, such as postwar Britain and Greece, to achieve one of their key targets; namely, high rates of social fluidity, which are suggestive of a fair system whereby everyone has an opportunity to rise above his or her parents' social class.

6.5 Analytical Notes on the Classification of Occupations

Class is a very complex issue for any single researcher to be able to offer an all-encompassing definition. As I argued in chapter 1, despite attempts since Marx's time to offer a systematic explanatory framework for the examination of social class, there is still little consensus over what it means, how it works, and, crucially, how it should be treated in theoretical terms and in applied research (Mackintosh and Mooney, 2000). Numerous theoretical endeavors and research projects to clarify these issues have further exposed the unfathomable nature of social class as a concept, and also the incommensurability between, on the one hand, class theory and the treatment of social class as an abstract category, and, on the other hand, its operationalization as an empirical category, as a concrete entity that can be studied and investigated sociologically (Sayer, 2005). This intractable nature of social class is demonstrated by the various typologies for social-class allocation or classification schemes that have been generated over the years, and especially during the "golden years" of social mobility advancement, that is, from the 1950s onward.

Despite a plethora of tools for the measurement and classification of social class, to date, there is no device that is free of limitations. It is, therefore, no hyperbole to claim that the opaque character of social class as a conceptual category is one of its intrinsic and innermost features. As a result, any categorization created has to be treated with caution, given that the measurement of class is contingent upon researchers' ideas about it and the tools he or she utilized to empirically examine it. Moreover, class formation and boundaries continuously change as social inequalities take new forms and shapes over the years. In other words, while socioeconomic inequalities are inherent features of the capitalist mode of socioeconomic organization, its exact features (including class boundaries, flows in and out of classes, concomitant class expansion/contraction, creation of new classes or "strata," and so on) do not remain static over time. As a consequence, the empirical investigation of class and the tools employed to carry this out have to be periodically revisited and reviewed in order to capture transformations and new developments in the labor market, new occupational arrangements, changes in the structure of the economy, and so on.

Regarding this study, I considered the fundamental position in Marxist theory about the existence of class antagonisms and the concomitant notion of exploitation as a sine qua non in the construction of heuristic devices for the measurement of social mobility in Protopi. Similarly, the significance and centrality of the ownership of the means of production are understood as a fundamental condition within a capitalist society. However, it is also recognized that a number of technical difficulties emerge when operationalizing social class in these terms. For example, those who possess most of the wealth and power (political and economic) are too small a group to be identified in conventional class measurements (Westergaard and Resler, 1975; Goldthorpe, 1980). As a result, the occupational classifications are "serviceable as a rough and ready guide to overall differences in socio-economic position" (Westergaard and Resler, 1975, p. 288) for the majority of the rest of the population. In other words, the measurement of class based on ownership of the means of production, while retaining its theoretical validity (people continue to be divided along these lines), has to be enriched and updated in order to allow it to be also empirically measured. Modern systems of social stratification are rather too complex to be depicted by a two-class model.

Consequently, my main focus here will be upon occupational mobility. This is to keep in line with the social mobility tradition, which largely deals with movements between occupational groups. As Westergaard and Resler (1975) argued, to try "to trace the movement of people over time among categories of the population defined, for example, in terms of property ownership and the market earnings would be hardly feasible." Indeed, such an endeavor would run into practical problems, such as gaining access to this kind of information and how best to measure it. In addition, it would stumble upon operational difficulties, such as the estimation of wealth and power in the hands of this very small minority of people who possess the majority of material resources and assets. In relation to the social reality in Protopi, this group of people would be limited to a handful of individuals who, at any rate, could not stand alone as a social class. This does not mean that Protopi is free of exploitative relations nor that the means of production are publicly or collectively owned and no surplus value is generated from its workforce. Rather, it points to the existence of a nonnative ruling class, that is to say a capitalist class that is not based in Protopi and that owns (a big part of) the means of production.

The material distribution of assets and its relation to the means of production will be further elucidated as it is of some significance to this study. Hence, before the war, the main agricultural products, such as corn, maize, oats, and wheat, were sold mainly in local markets and were exchanged for other produce, services, or small sums of money. Additionally, dairy and other livestock produce, such as meat, were consumed within the family, exchanged for other foodstuffs and goods, or also sold in the local markets for money. As I mentioned in chapter 4, the dominance of capitalism, which gradually occurred after the war, transformed Protopi's relations of production and social structure. The function of land changed from serving as a means of subsistence agriculture before the war to becoming a means of commodity production after the war. On the other end of the social structure, big landowners in Protopi have never been in possession of vast hectares of land (see chapter 7, and in particular Phokion's account) as in other parts of Greece and, more broadly, in Europe. In addition, the lack of mechanization of production restricted the productive capacity of agricultural holdings, while production has been declining and is due to cease in the coming years.[1] As a result, the wealth, power, and surplus value big landowners amass are not enough to let them play the role of the ruling class. Interestingly, those who have been appropriating (after the war) the surplus value from agriculture are the big tobacco industries, none of which is based in Protopi.

In the secondary sector, those who own the means of production are the factory owners and the proprietors of various firms. This type of ownership is relatively new in the local social structure and it emerged from the mid-1950s onward (through small-scale, often family-run, firm and enterprise ownership). In Protopi, there are only a handful of company owners and they invariably employ between two and ten people (including own family members). The factory owners, where many locals find employment are by and large foreign to the social structure of Protopi and cannot be credited with ruling positions,[2] which points to the dependency of the economy of Protopi on that of the wider area and Greece more broadly.

6.6 The Occupational/Class Scheme Used in this Study

The discussion thus far has suggested that any classification model has to be adjusted to the characteristics of the social system it classifies (Westergaard and Resler, 1975, p. 289), given that different classification tools can produce divergent results. In a nutshell, classification issues are impossible to resolve once and for all nor in a universally accepted way (Savage, 1997).

With regard to this study, the class model I devised has to be treated as the most appropriate operational tool for the purposes of this enquiry (Table 6.1). In other words, it is a heuristic device, which does not claim universal applicability. Nonetheless, it has some key advantages. One of them is that it shares many characteristics with similar devices used in Greek (Petmezidou-Tsoulouvi, 1987; Kasimati, 1990) and in international studies (Goldthorpe, 1980; Breen, 2004b). In particular, this scheme is an adaptation of the major class schemes that have been utilized in mobility studies, such as the CASMIN[3] and less so the NS-SEC.[4] It is anticipated that in this way, the emergent findings can

Table 6.1 The class scheme

---
1. Higher- and lower-grade professional/ managerial occupations
2. Higher- and lower-grade, routine nonmanual/small proprietors/artisans
3. Skilled, semiskilled, and unskilled manual and lower-grade technicians (including farm workers)
4. Farmers (small-scale owners, family production)
---

be related to previous and future research. In addition, this scheme is sensitive both to the conceptual and theoretical issues concerning the classification of occupations and to the reality of those classified. That is to say, the scheme is not merely a theoretical artifact without resonance with the reality of the individuals who are categorized. The respondents themselves and their accounts of their own social mobility experiences informed the construction of the social-class scheme described below. For example, the allocation of the farmers into the working class (unlike the standard practice in mainstream mobility studies to assign them to the intermediate class) was a decision taken on the basis of the extensive ethnographic research I conducted (more to follow in chapters 7–9) and shed light on important differences in the division, nature of labor, and type of relations of production in Protopi.

Class 1 emerged by combining higher- and lower-grade professional and managerial occupations, respectively. The majority of these positions are education-based, such as doctors, teachers, and other higher-education graduates, whose employment, work situation, autonomy, and control completely differ from incumbents of occupations in other classes. Big landowners and owners of firms and enterprises are also included in this group. Class 1 will be referred to as the middle class or service class.

Class 2 is an amalgamation of four smaller occupational groups: higher- and lower-grade routine nonmanual occupations and small store owners. Some typical occupations in this group are those of office workers, small store owners, and various self-employed occupations. For these jobs, that is lower-grade routine nonmanual, some education is required but not necessarily of a higher level. The largest subgroup in this class consists of the self-employed store owners (with no more than one to two employees). For them, a higher-education degree was not necessary, albeit many self-employed people are at least secondary-education graduates. In this study, the term "intermediate" "or petty-bourgeoisie" will be used to refer to this class.

Classes 3 and 4 belong to the same social class, and, as I will show, they occupy similar position in relation to production. Class 3 consists of manual occupations as well as lower-grade technicians. In particular, it includes factory workers, agricultural workers (those who did not have land of their own), and anyone else who sold his or her labor power. This class also includes all manual laborers, such as employees working in garage stations, technicians (i.e., electricians and plumbers), builders, and so on.

The "agricultural class," Class 4, points to one of the key features of this model, namely, the allocation of farmers into a separate occupational group. Agricultural occupations were the most widespread in Protopi's recent history, and the class model I constructed had to be sensitive to this factor.[5] Nonetheless, as will be shown in chapter 7, this group was not undifferentiated but divisions within the farmers also existed. The reason that this distinction is not entirely captured in my class model is because the differences between more affluent and poorer farmers, while they were spoken about by the respondents in the qualitative interviews, were not explained by the key informants during the collection of the survey data. This is a crucial methodological point and is elaborated further in the next section and returned to in the final chapter.

6.7 Operationalizing Social Class

It is necessary to point out that this classification scheme is informed and devised drawing on existing models and also on notes, discussions, and observations I conducted with people in Protopi. In other words, it is not a model imposed "from above" and remote in relation to the reality of the residents in Protopi. By contrast, every effort was made to take into account the occupational complexity of the community. This approach is in line with the emancipatory–transformative approach and its emphasis on the individuals' contexts, experiences, ideas, and understandings as necessary criteria for the formation of the researcher's description and depiction of their reality.

For this reason, I ensured that once all occupations were classified, the resultant social classes were meaningful to the residents of Protopi. That is to say, they were depicting real occupational groups and not forcing occupations to be clustered with dissimilar ones. Thus, in order to avoid classification violation, that is, grouping together occupations with few common characteristics, the database was cross-examined. It appeared that the occupational group "land workers" was too small ($N = 30$) to stand separately. Since this is one of the most important aspects of the social differentiation in the prewar and immediate postwar years, namely the establishment of the size and qualitative characteristics of the land workers, the reasons for such a small size were further explored. It emerged that the instruments of data collection were not sensitive enough to capture the difference between landowners and landworkers. Moreover, the key informants in the survey (see appendix 2) were themselves reluctant to make this distinction for two main reasons. First, some of these informants did not perceive the distinction an important feature of social differentiation nor a determinant of social-class allocation. Second, very few key informants and survey participants could recollect with clarity and accuracy who belonged to either group, and, mainly, who was solely a landworker.

A further complication arose from the fact that some peasants were simultaneously landworkers and landowners. This can be partly explained by the fertility rates among different ethnic groups. A discernible pattern until commodity capitalism became the dominant mode of production was that the Roma families were more numerous than the non-Roma ones. This resulted in insufficient farm and livestock produce to cover the needs of the household. At the same time, these large families had a surplus of labor force. By contrast, non-Roma families were numerically smaller[6] and with bigger productive capacity. This imbalance of workforce and land availability led non-Roma families to hire Roma people as their landworkers. However, the distinction between landowners and landworkers was far from clear, because the vast majority of residents possessed some land, no matter how small the plot and the returns in output production. These considerations led to the decision to merge this group, namely the landworkers, with semi- and unskilled workers outside agriculture. The justification here comes from the perspective of the employment situation. Thus, both these groups include workers who experienced meager working conditions and had very little autonomy, skills, or capital to become self-employed and generally to improve their socioeconomic situation.

A separate issue that needs to be discussed here relates to the allocation of farmers in the working class. This goes against most existing classifications that derive from advanced countries, such the EGP[7] or the CASMIN schemes, which allocate farmers in the intermediate class. This is a matter of some significance and it is vital to explain the rationale for this decision. The explanation I provide is twofold.

First, peasants were, for the better part of Protopi's history (namely, until the early and mid-1950s), the only producing class. That is, before the domination of capitalism as a mode of production, the peasants of Protopi were engaged in petty commodity production as part of family farming.[8] During this period, the main mode of production in operation could be described as proto-capitalist or petty-commodity production (Cook and Binford, 1986). In other words, it is after the war that the penetration of the market into local economy becomes manifest and we can talk about "commoditization" of production (Kahn, 1982). Additionally, when the transition into capitalism was manifest, the class composition in Protopi also started to be transformed: from one dominated by agriculture to one with an exponentially growing service class. At the same time, the division of labor was enriched with more occupations and became more complex, a development that is reflected on the new class structure. Before this turning moment in the history of Protopi, the "agricultural class" was not linked to commodity production but to subsistence agriculture.[9] In other words, before the 1950s, land ownership in Protopi was linked to ownership of the means of subsistence rather than of production.

Second, before the years of free-market penetration and capitalist domination, there were hardly any formed classes in Protopi (see Figure 7.1 for a graphical depiction of the social structure of Protopi at this time). The main bulk of the population was working on the land. Among them, there were a few relatively larger-than-average landowners. Most crafts, such as tailoring, hairdressing, and so on, were performed by farmers in their spare time rather than by specialized professionals. A skills or credentials-based differentiation operated with the few educated individuals, such as doctors, priests, and teachers standing at the top of the relatively simple division of labor. Most of these highly skilled individuals, though, were external to the social structure of Protopi as they lived in the nearby city center and commuted to Protopi to perform their job. It would thus be difficult to sustain a classification of farmers as an intermediate class due to the very small productive capacity of the family farm and the similar situation of farmers in terms of ownership of the means of production to the working class. In this regard, the farmers maintained characteristics similar to the factory workers, to the proletariat, with the only difference being that the former (the farmers) were not wage workers. Nevertheless, they were exploited by the tobacco companies that expropriated their surplus value, which is consistent with the Marxist thesis on exploitation as the criterion for allocation of individuals into the working class. The decision not to allocate the farmers into the intermediate class was corroborated by the respondents in the qualitative interviews who spoke about "moving up" from peasantry.

Before I proceed, some caveats are necessary. First, the class scheme discussed here does not include the capitalist class. This, as already discussed, occurs for two main reasons. To begin with, the ruling class that appropriates the surplus value of the working men and women in Protopi is not native to the class structure of Protopi. Although the ruling class is internal to and fundamental in Protopi's division of labor, at the same time, it is external to Protopi's social structure. That is, the ruling class is based partly in the nearby city center and partly in the metropolitan centers of mainland Greece.[10] Second, the instrument for data collection, the class scheme I devised, was not sensitive to this type of differentiation (i.e., between capitalists and non-capitalists). This is not an omission or one-sidedness on my part. Rather, it was informed by knowledge I was furnished with from the ethnographic material and my understanding of the complexities and intricacies of the political economy of Protopi. If, however, the classification I devised might appear prima facie redolent with limitations, especially for an account that is interested in maintaining the conflicting aspect of class structure, it ought to be borne into mind that, as mentioned in chapter 2, all classification schemes are heuristic devices, therefore inherently limited in depicting, even with moderate accuracy, the complexities of modern class systems. Moreover, most classification schemes exclude by design the capitalist class. This ought to make no researcher, especially from a historical materialist persuasion, complacent or complicit. Rather, it begs for epistemic openness about the way they handle this important matter of analytical and empirical consideration. Hence, I would urge the reader to treat the class scheme presented here as an instrument for the depiction of a facet of the relations of production in question. This points to the arithmetical incommensurability of the ruling versus all other "classes." That is to say, while the ruling class is quantitatively very small, all other "classes," or occupational groupings to be more precise, are much more sizable. In this vein, if we are to follow Marx's thinking, despite the actual and eventual increase of the middle classes and the concomitant shrinking of the proletariat, the overall balance of forces would not threaten the capitalist equilibrium and power balance. In other words, the expansion of the middle classes is nothing but a characteristic of capitalist societies, which, though, is not enough to destabilize capitalism. This does not mean that the exploitative relationship between the capitalist and the working or the middle class ceases to exist at any point. The embourgeoized proletarian, the factory worker who became shop owner or army officer, has not entered a parallel universe where no exploitation exists. Rather, he or she has entered a qualitatively different form of exploitation that stems from her new employment situation and the way he or she exchanges his or her skills in the marketplace. What is more, his or her relation to the other classes, and mainly the working class, has changed. In turn, this caused a transformation in the social relations within production but not of production. That is to say, despite these changes within the division of labor and the occupational structure, the overall balance of forces within capitalism has remained unaltered. Not only is capitalism spared any harm from such fluctuations within its occupational and social structure, but it also becomes strengthened. This is something that Marx himself discussed in relation to the American social structure, which in the nineteeth century did not display any properties that would suggest a trend toward its proletarianization.[11] While these fluctuations are accurately depicted in the class scheme discussed here, as in most mobility studies, the conflicting nature of the social relationship that permeates the capitalist relations of production is not fully revealed. In keeping then with the Marxist tradition, the reader has to view all the "classes" discussed in this chapter as in opposition to the capitalist class. While mine and any similar class schemes do not portray this aspect of class struggle, namely between the capitalist and the working classes, they, however, help us to understand how the constantly changing class formations create new possibilities for class struggle within such a structure. Finally, what is lost in terms of class conflict from the quantitative part of the presentation is partially compensated for through the discussion of the exploitative and antagonistic relations of production in the qualitative part of the book (chapters 7–9).

6.8 Intergenerational Mobility Rates

6.8.1 *Absolute Mobility*

In chapter 3, I presented the changes in sectoral output and employment in the Greek labor market. I showed that throughout the postwar years, there was substantial movement out of agriculture and into the secondary and even more so into the service sector. I highlighted this feature as one of the key particularities of modern Greece and is worthwhile bearing this in mind as the general macro-analytical context of the ensuing presentation.

Table 6.2 is the core mobility table and illustrates the changes in class destinations according to individuals' social-class origins. This table is used throughout the following analysis as it epitomizes the absolute mobility rates of my survey sample.[12] The proportion of each class in the survey sample, which gave rise to the core mobility table, is hard to compare to the actual one in Protopi given that no data or class analysis exist (for Protopi). However, if we relate the rates presented below with the qualitative material discussed in chapters 7–9, the obtained sample in Table 6.2 appears to be a good reflection of the occupational structure of Protopi. For example, the voluminous proportion of people with origins in the agricultural class, specifically 63.5 percent of the overall sample, and the substantial shrinking of this class attested to from the destinations column (18.3 percent), correspond to the experiences of the respondents in the qualitative material, who were abandoning agriculture in large numbers.

Table 6.2 shows that a significant amount of movement occurred within the occupational and, by extension, class structure of Protopi. Hence, the overall mobility rate (62.1 percent) is rather high,[13] while vertical mobility exceeds horizontal mobility by far (Table 6.3). This means that more individuals moved into different (higher or lower) social classes than staying in the same one. It is also noticeable that this vertical movement is largely upward (43.2 percent) rather than downward (6.1 percent). The latter, downward movement, is rather negligible as the biggest flux occurred from the lower to the higher classes. This is represented by the large amount of individuals moving out from agriculture (Class 4) to the intermediate (Class 2) and middle classes (Class 1). Markedly, the findings confirm those discussed in relation to Greece (see chapter 3).

Table 6.2 The core mobility table (class origins and destinations) ($N = 1,248$)

Origins	Destinations				
	Class1	Class2	Class3	Class4	Total
Class 1	26	17	5	1	49
	53.1%	34.7%	10.2%	2.0%	100.0%
Class 2	59	172	51	2	284
	20.8%	60.6%	18.0%	0.7%	100.0%
Class 3	11	51	55	5	122
	9.0%	41.8%	45.1%	4.1%	100.0%
Class 4	78	340	155	220	793
	9.8%	42.9%	19.5%	27.7%	100.0%
Total	174	580	266	228	1248
	13.9%	46.5%	21.3%	18.3%	100.0%

Table 6.3 Absolute mobility rates[14]

Social mobility	Social immobility	Vertical mobility	Upward mobility	Downward mobility	Horizontal mobility
62.1	37.9	49.3	43.2	6.1	12.8

Table 6.4 Long- and short-range mobility

Mobility	Upward	Downward
Long-range mobility	7.1	0.5
Short-range mobility	36.1	5.6
Overall	43.2	6.1
Vertical mobility	49.3	

Although long-range[15] movement is not negligible (7.6 percent), it is short-range mobility that prevails (41.7 percent) (Table 6.4). In particular, approximately 84 percent of the overall upward movement is of a short-range type, which is explained by the peasants' exit from agriculture into self-employment and routine, nonmanual occupations. It also entails that service-class occupations, such as higher- and lower-grade professional and managerial jobs, were not equally open to the exiting farmers. This has crucial implications with regard to the life chances of people in Protopi and gives some insights into the role of education. In particular, it suggests that service-class occupations, which to a large extent were "educo-centric," were not as open to the majority of the peasants as the less "educo-centric" occupations (more to follow in the following sections).

Conversely, long-range downward movement from Class 1 into 3 and 4 is negligible and affects a small proportion of individuals. The overwhelming majority of downward mobility (91 percent of the total downward mobility) is short range, and it largely comprises of movement from Class 2 into 3, or out of routine, nonmanual to manual occupations. At any rate, downward mobility is very low and it could be influenced by the differences in the marginal distributions (see section 6.9).

The absorption of the extensive outflow of farmers across the social structure indicates that there were far-reaching structural rearrangements, such as the enrichment of the labor market with new occupations that came with the transition into capitalism. Overall, there is manifestly more room at the top of the class structure, which accommodated the biggest proportion of peasants who abandoned agriculture (indicatively, the service class and the intermediate class expanded more than three and two times, respectively, their original size). Put differently, there is no evidence of "proletarianization" of the peasants. Rather, we could talk about their "embourgeoisement": either *stricto sensu*, that is from farmers into the middle class, or *amplo sensu*, into the intermediate class, such as in the state bureaucracy, clerical jobs, and so on (which is in line with findings for Greece; see chapter 3). It is worthwhile pointing out that the findings presented in this section are in line with the experiences of the research participants that will be discussed in chapters 7–9. Moreover, they are in accordance with similar findings about European societies, though of an earlier time, that is of the 1960s and 1970s. Dahrendorf (1959, p. 250), for example, observed that "if any class bears witness to the comparative openness of European societies, it is the service class," which invariably recruits large numbers of working-class people. Similar findings were reported by Goldthorpe (1980) in his in-depth exploration of social mobility rates for British men (see chapter 2). This trend is also consistent with Marx's insights on social mobility, which are best gleaned through his discussion on class formation rather than social-class circulation per se. In a characteristic passage from the *Theories of Surplus Value*, in *Capital*, Vol. IV [1863] (1968, p. 573), Marx criticized Ricardo for overlooking in his analysis "the constantly growing number of middle classes, those who stand between the workman on the one hand and landlord on the other. The middle classes maintain themselves to an ever increasing extent directly out of revenue, they are a burden weighting heavily on the working base and increase the social security and power of the upper ten thousand."

However, the findings reported in this section have to be further examined against the ideal of an open society where all positions would be available to be occupied by anyone in the specific social system. In the case of Protopi, it can be safely argued that its structure appears to have been fairly "fluid." However, as was noted in relation to the British social structure in chapter 2, fluidity in social circulation is not in and of itself sufficient for the creation of a fair system of allocation of rewards that can allow or even promote the unrestricted movement to the highest social-class destinations of every individual and especially those in the lowest social positions.

6.8.2 Inflow Analysis

Inflow analysis (Table 6.5) is employed here in order to clarify the recruitment pattern into each class as well as class composition. In other words, inflow analysis is concerned with class origins. With regard to the middle class, most of its incumbents are recruited from the agricultural and the intermediate classes. However, this does not indicate yielding privileges for the middle class itself (section 6.7). Rather, it shows that farmers capitalized more than any other class upon the creation of more room at the upper end of the occupational structure. Moreover, the closer we look at the top of the structure, the less homogeneous the class composition is. On the other hand, the reverse occurs with regard to the lower end of the structure: Class 4 (peasants) is an exceptionally self-recruiting class with minimal entries into

Table 6.5 Inflow analysis table, in % (columns)

Origins	Destinations			
	Class 1	Class 2	Class 3	Class 4
Class 1	14.9	2.9	1.9	0.4
Class 2	33.9	29.7	19.2	0.9
Class 3	6.3	8.8	20.7	2.2
Class 4	44.8	58.6	58.3	96.5
Total	100	100	100	100

its ranks from the other three classes. Finally, Class 2 is more homogeneous than Classes 1 and 3, but still not as self-recruiting as Class 4. In other words, the middle class (Class 1) is the least self-recruiting and the agricultural the most.

It has been established by now that a substantial degree of openness occurred in Protopi, though the latter is by no means a social system characterized by perfect mobility. In fact, self-recruitment occurs to a good extent, which impedes some individuals' ability to access any other than their parents' class. As argued in chapter 3, a meritocratic society implies that no barriers ought to exist for talented or highly skilled (and/or credentialized) individuals to any class destination. Moreover, this was emphasized as a fundamental point of ideological and political departure of the liberal democratic order, insofar as Western capitalist countries were concerned, and the crux of the postwar consensus carved up through Keynesian-infused welfarist policies. This crucial dimension, that is to say the circulation or fluidity of each class, is partly explored in the next section.

6.8.3 Outflow Analysis

Notwithstanding the importance of the findings presented thus far, this account requires some further information about the destinations of members of each class. This is obtained through outflow analysis (Table 6.6), which is informative about the destination of people according to their class of origin. This analysis is pivotal in this study, as it will provide us with a comparative understanding of class outcomes. Crudely put, it will shed light into the question of who ended up where.

Table 6.6 shows that the majority (53.1 percent) of individuals with parents in the service class stayed in their class of origin. The remaining 46.9 percent experienced short-range downward mobility for they entered mainly the intermediate class (34.7 percent) and the working and agricultural classes (10.2 percent and 2 percent, respectively). Individuals with origins in Class 2 (intermediate class) were by far, 60.6 percent, the biggest "stayers." By contrast, peasants were the most mobile of all (only 27.7 percent of them stayed

Table 6.6 Outflow analysis, in % (rows)

Origins	Destinations			
	Class 1	Class 2	Class 3	Class 4
Class 1	53.1	34.7	10.2	2
Class 2	20.8	60.6	18	0.7
Class 3	9	41.8	45.1	4.1
Class 4	9.8	42.9	19.5	27.7
Total	13.9	46.5	21.3	18.3

in their parents' class). Additionally, there is a striking similarity in the class destinations of people from Classes 3 and 4: 9 percent and 9.8 percent ended up in Class 1, and 41.8 percent and 42.9 percent in Class 2, respectively. This points to similar chances among members of these classes (i.e., Classes 3 and 4) to reach the top levels of the social structure (which gives support to the class scheme, discussed in section 6.6). Thus, ascription, such as parents' social class, played some role in the social mobility movement of individuals in Protopi.

It could be further argued that despite the relatively fluid structure of Protopi, disadvantages seem to be passed down to the next generation, but so are advantages: proportionately, there are more people from Classes 1 and 2 who stayed in their parents' class than from Classes 3 and 4. Interestingly, the findings presented in this section find some support in the accounts of research participants (more to follow in chapters 7–9), who discussed similar patterns of occupational mobility through their experiences.

6.9 Structural and Exchange (Circulation) Mobility

In chapter 2, I argued that structural and exchange mobility are important as they provide information about the causes of social circulation. Thus, changes in the occupational structure and labor market are expected to inflict transformations in the social structure, which are depicted by the altered distribution of individuals in the mobility table. In this study, this estimation assisted in determining the intergenerational trends in Protopi, as an effect of the structural changes in its occupational structure and labor market.

Table 6.7 shows that the proportion of structural mobility, 45.2 percent, is high in relation to the overall mobility rates (62.1 percent). This means that nearly 73 percent of the overall mobility rate is due to transformations in the local labor market (new white-collar jobs, reconstruction requirements, and so on), rather than due to rearrangements in the structure of opportunities. This can be conceived as follows: more than three in four individuals who were mobile owed their movement to the structural rearrangements in the occupational structure and not as much to the elimination of inequalities

Table 6.7 Dissimilarity index (in %)

Class	Origins	Destinations	Difference
Class 1	3.9	13.9	−10.1
Class 2	22.7	46.5	−23.8
Class 3	9.7	21.3	−11.6
Class 4	63.5	18.3	45.2
Total	100	100	

Table 6.8 Structural and exchange mobility[16]

Overall mobility	Structural mobility	Exchange/circulation mobility
62.1	45.2	16.9

between social classes. However, high structural mobility[17] does not imply a higher degree of turnover among different classes. Plainly put, for every four people who occupied a different position (higher or lower), there was only one who lost his or her place. This is a striking finding as it implies that the new labor-market opportunities did not necessarily reverse existing inequalities in the social system of Protopi. Overall, the extensive restructuring of the occupational structure and labor market, which was consistent with the radical socioeconomic transformations that occurred after the war (see chapters 3 and 5), was not accompanied, as far as Protopi is concerned, with the weakening of the "distance" between the existing social classes.

On the other hand, the proportion of exchange mobility is rather small, 17 percent (Table 6.8). This is a useful indication in the evaluation of the degree of fluidity in the structure of Protopi. As I noted in chapter 2, exchange mobility can allow for comparisons to be drawn between destinations of individuals from different social classes relative to their class of origin (their parents' social class). In turn, the degree of exchange mobility can be linked to the ideal of a meritocratic society whereby one's class of origin is expected to be unrelated to his or her class destination. In order for this to occur, all positions have to be open to all individuals. The small rate of exchange mobility observed in Protopi (17 percent), though, indicates that approximately one in five individuals who were mobile moved "freely," while the remaining four moved due to changes in the social structure itself (structural mobility).

To summarize the key mobility findings presented thus far, I reported that a high degree of social mobility (62.1 percent) occurred in Protopi in the period examined. Most of this movement was short range, that is to say it pertained to the abandonment of agriculture in favor of self-employment and routine manual occupations. Individuals with parents in the service class had more chances to maintain their class position, whereas the agricultural class was the most self-recruiting social class (the peasants came from families with background in peasantry). At the same time, this class was the most mobile. However, their movement did not stem from a reduction in inequalities but from the creation of more room in the higher levels of the occupational structure of Protopi, mostly in middle- and intermediate-class positions. In other words, the peasants raised their social-class position by virtue of the upgrading of the occupational structure (the new occupations were to be found in the intermediate and the service classes) rather than due to the reduction of relative advantages between the social classes themselves. In other words, as peasants were improving their class position, so were individuals in other classes. This was highlighted in chapter 2 as an element of the dynamic nature of capitalism. To reiterate, there I argued that the possibility of fostering high rates of social mobility and inequality of opportunities has been one of the most salient postwar mobility trends in liberal capitalist countries, and it developed in parallel with the commitment of these countries to work toward the establishment of a meritocratic society.

6.10 Relative Mobility Chances and Odds Ratios

In section 6.9, I showed that, overall, there was a lot of circulation in the social structure of Protopi. Demonstrably, there was a lot more space at the top of the structure than at the bottom but it still remains unknown whether all classes benefited the same from the expansion of the labor market and the increase in white-collar jobs. In other words, what we need is a measure of relative mobility chances net of structural influences. In order to calculate these rates, I used the method of odds ratios, which are apropos in showing the chances of people from different classes entering a specific class (in this case, this was the service class).

The odds of people from Class 1 (service class) staying in the same class is 26, while the respective odds of individuals from Class 4 (farmers) entering Class 1 is less than 1 to 3 (1 : 2.8 to be precise) (Table 6.9). The ratio of the odds of Classes 1 and 4 is 73.3. This means that it was 73 times more likely for children from Class 1 (service class) to end up in their parents' class than it was for farmers' offsprings (Class 4).[18] It should be borne in mind, though, that some numbers are very small, that is only one person in my sample from

Table 6.9 Class 1 (service class) vs Class 4 (farmers)

Odds Class 1: (O/D): $\text{odds}_{1-4} = 26/1 = 26$	(A)
Odds Class 4: (O/D): $\text{odds}_{1-4} = 78/220 = 0.3545$ or $1 : 2.8$	(B)
Odds ratio 1/4: (A)/(B) = 26/0.35 = *73.3*	(C)

Class 1 ended in Class 4. This influenced significantly the obtained odds: for example, if two people from Class 1 had entered Class 4, the pertinent odds ratio would be substantially smaller (37.1).

The odds of people from Class 2 (intermediate) to enter Class 1 is 29.5 (as reported above, the odds for those from Class 4 [peasants] is less than 1 to 3) (Table 6.10). The ratio of their odds is 83.2. In other words, people from the intermediate class (Class 2) were extremely more likely to enter Class 1 in comparison to people from Class 4, that is, the farmers. It is striking that, in comparison to the chances of individuals in Class 4, the chances of people from Class 2 (83.2) to enter Class 1 were higher than the respective chances of people from Class 1 (73.3) to stay in their class (i.e., in Class 1) However, the small numbers in the cells of the core mobility table (Table 6.2) might again be accountable for this occurrence. At any event, this clearly demonstrates that both the service and the intermediate classes had better chances to maintain or improve their class situation in comparison to individuals from Class 4, that is, the peasants.

The odds for Class 3 (manual workers) entering Class 1 are 2.2 (compared to 1:2.8 for Class 4) (Table 6.11). The ratio of the odds of these two classes entering Class 1 (service class) is 6.2, which is substantially smaller than the odds that have been presented so far in relation to the other two classes (i.e., Classes 1 and 2). This demonstrates that the chances of manual workers and farmers were similar, which offers support to the class model I devised (sections 6.3 and 6.4), in which I classified the farmers in the same class with manual workers and lower-grade technicians.

It is evident that people from Classes 1 and 2 (service class and the intermediate) were more likely to stay at or enter into Class 1, respectively, in comparison to people from Classes 3 and 4. Hence, despite the high rates of absolute mobility that were discussed in section 6.8, the relative mobility chances in Protopi were unequally distributed and hierarchically structured. In other words, despite the high rates of new incumbents in Classes 1 and 2 with family background in Classes 3 and 4, it was still much easier for those

Table 6.10   Class 2 (intermediate class) vs Class 4 (farmers)

Odds Class 2: (O/D): $odds_{2-4} = 59/2 = 29.5$	(A)
Odds Class 4: (O/D): $odds_{2-4} = 78/220 = 1:2.8$	(D)
Odds ratio 2/4: (A)/(B) = 13.5/0.086 = *83.2*	(E)

Table 6.11   Class 3 (manual workers) vs Class 4 (farmers)

Odds Class 3: (O/D): $odds_{3-4} = 11/5 = 2.2$	(F)
Odds Class 4: (O/D): $odds_{3-4} = 78/220 = 1:2.8$	(G)
Odds ratio 3/4: (A)/(B) = 2.2/0.3545 = 6.2	(H)

in Classes 1 and 2 to end up in Class 1. In a nutshell, stark differences were observed between the chances at the top and the bottom of the class structure. Given the high rates of structural mobility (section 6.9) and the sizable expansion of Classes 1 and 2 (section 6.8), we can conclude that a general upgrade in the class structure occurred, which absorbed the exit of manual workers and peasants from their classes without, though, challenging the privileges of those at the top of the social structure. Differently put, even in conditions of occupational transition, socioeconomic restructuring, and labor-market transformations, the privileged classes retained, if not strengthened, their advantages.

6.11 Summary

This chapter presented evidence from mobility findings about Protopi, which suggested that a high amount of intergenerational mobility occurred during the postwar years. This was largely attributed to the sizable agricultural exit and the subsequent expansion in intermediate- and service-class occupations. The high incidence of structural mobility, though, operated concurrently with high social inequalities. That is, the high rates of movement within the social structure of Protopi did not stem from a reduction in inequalities but from the creation of more room in the higher levels of the occupational structure of Protopi, mostly in middle- and intermediate-class positions. Specifically, it was shown that the peasants raised their social-class position by virtue of the upgrading of the occupational structure (the new occupations were to be found in the intermediate and the service class) rather than due to the reduction of relative advantages between the social classes themselves. Protopi, therefore, seems to share some characteristics with social systems of early-industrialized countries such as Britain, which used to be permeated by high social fluidity but unequal distribution of opportunities for entering the top social classes. Whether this is the product of the type of measurement utilized here or an actual feature of Protopi's social structure is explored in the next three chapters.

Chapter 7

Occupational Trajectories and Experiences of Mobility

7.1 Introduction

In chapter 6, my focus was on some salient structural and compositional aspects of Protopi. The observed patterns of change indicated high rates of absolute mobility, which were largely attributed to the increased incidence of structural mobility, in line with the findings presented in chapter 3 regarding the intensity of transformations in the Greek economy and occupational structure. In this chapter, I shift the focus of my attention onto life-course mobility through the presentation of individuals' occupational and social mobility pathways.

In order to delve into the occupational movements of the research participants, the work experiences of their parents, partners, and children are presented as they form part of the same family strategy[1] to improve the occupational and social-class position of the household.

This chapter aims to build on the evidence presented in chapter 6 by offering an in-depth understanding of the social and cultural processes that impinge on patterns of differential educational attainment and distribution of life chances. The type of "depth" with which I am concerned is to be found in the "micro-dimensions" of social mobility, conceptualized here as the mobility trajectories of individuals, embedded within the family and the community, and the experiences and understanding of individuals of these processes.

The narrative order of the chapter is in accordance with the intergenerational character that has been adhered to thus far. Therefore, the chapter first follows the stories of the older male, non-Roma and Roma, respondents and then it moves on to the presentation of those in the middle and younger generation.[2] Subsequently, the findings on women's occupational experiences and pathways are presented in a different section as their participation in the labor market has distinct features in comparison to those of men.

A. The Occupational Pathways of Men

Agrarian communities in late-developed/underdeveloped countries have followed their own trajectories and entered the capitalist mode of production at different points in relation to agrarian communities in economically advanced European countries (Franklin, 1971). In 1830, the year when Greece gained independence from the Ottoman Empire, 60–70 percent of land was owned by the Ottoman Empire and 30–40 percent by private owners (Tsoukalas, 1977). The majority of the latter, privately owned land belonged to the Greek Orthodox monasteries, the Church, Ottoman officials, and wealthy Greeks (Doumanis, 1983). In 1917, land reform was introduced, which benefited the majority of Greek peasants whose contribution in terms of taxes accounted for over 50 percent of overall state revenues from taxation. Hence, "the peasant was de facto a landowner, since he payed [sic] no rent to the state or to any private individual" (Doumanis, 1983, pp. 119–120) but owned his or her own land. Moreover, it was not the individual who was taxable but the community and in case a peasant could not meet the tax demands set by the central administration, his or her dues were paid for by the community. This encouraged the peasants to develop networks of solidarity, which were significant forms of social organization in rural areas (Vergopoulos, 1975).

7.2 Older Generation

7.2.1 Non-Roma

As I pointed out in chapter 3, in 1928, 67 percent of the Greek population lived in villages and small provincial towns with fewer than 5,000 inhabitants, like Protopi. Moreover, 53.2 percent of the economically active population of Greece were employed in agriculture and animal husbandry (Seferiades, 1999) and the division of labor was relatively simple. While the overall patterns of change in the Greek economy and occupational structure identified in chapter 3 were largely reflected on Protopi's history, there is a feature that needs some special attention. This pertains to existence of a dual mode of production. The first mode bears proto-capitalist features and evolved around peasantry for non-trading purposes. The second one is closely associated with modern capitalism given that the labor market was enriched with new occupations and with the intensification of wage labor as a new form of organizing the relations of production. Moreover, the traditional products of peasantry, from livestock produce, such as meat, to dairy products started being transformed into commodities, which is another key characteristic of the entry into the capitalist mode of production.[3] These two features characterized the political economy of Protopi for the best part of the twentieth century.

As noted in chapter 5, the entire economic production of Protopi was based on peasantry, while employment outside of it was rare. The production unit was the household and there were two kinds of assets a family could possess: (a few acres of) land and livestock. Hence, the family was engaged in "petty commodity production," which, roughly until the 1960s, was a holistic system, a distinct mode of production. All members of the household were employed in peasantry, with a further division of labor operating across the gender divide (more of which is discussed in Part B, this chapter).

Euripides, 73 years, provides us with an idea of some of the intricacies of agrarian societies, such as Protopi:[4]

> *Euripides*: In 1929 the land was distributed in this area. They gave us land for dwelling; for each family to make their own house. Each resident who was married got a piece of land.
> *Q*: Were there any exceptions?
> *E*: None was exempted: everyone got equal size of land. There was this category that we used to call the "Yiftoi,"[5] well, they also got land.
> *Q*: Were there any people who used to work on the land as paid workers or was everyone a landowner?
> *E*: [All people were] landowners. There were only a few people [usually Roma[6]] who worked for somebody else for a small daily wage, which was a plate of food.
> *Q*: How about after the War? Were there still any paid land workers?
> *E*: Only some families who were very poor. When the daily wage started in the [the nearest] city, say in 1965, the local exploitation stopped.
> *Q*: Were the locals still heavily employed in agriculture in the 1950s?
> *E*: Of course, and if someone did not have enough land of his own, he would hire somebody else's who didn't know how to cultivate it.

Some key characteristics of the Greek peasantry in its proto-capitalist era were the family-based production and the small size of land. Although in Protopi land was distributed evenly in 1929, its fragmentation started occurring within a decade or so. Thus, some families sold part of or all their arable land to secure the necessary means of subsistence and worked subsequently on others' land for a daily wage. By contrast, other residents enhanced significantly their plot of land and the output capacity of their family unit. As a result of the increasing differentiation brought about by the accumulation of land and the intensification of labor activity, by the early 1950s, if not before then, a hierarchy was discernible (see Figure 7.1).[7]

Phokion, 58 years,[8] a white-collar worker, descends from a family of landowners. His grandfather's name was mentioned by other participants as an exemplar landlord who managed to transcend the small, family-based agricultural production from early on and to realize, when the transition into capitalism occurred, the importance of the new means of production. In the

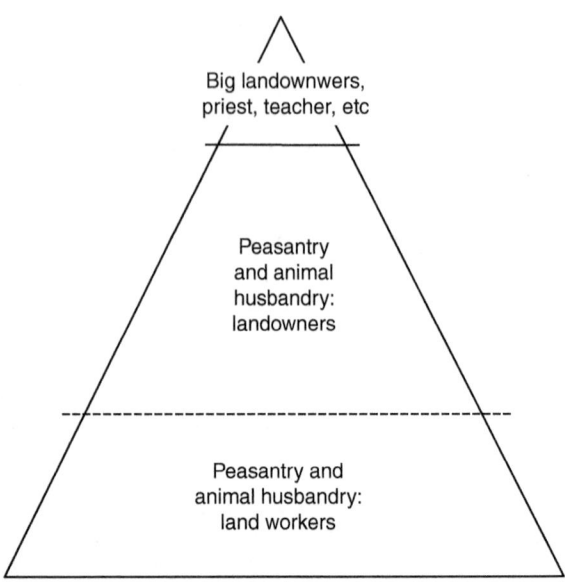

Figure 7.1 The proto-capitalist division of labor in Protopi.

following extract, Phokion talks about the early postwar years and the social differentiation within the ranks of the peasants:

> *Phokion*: Those who had land could secure the necessary means to get by. In these days, land had high value. Later on the value shifted to the means of production. Those who grasped it bought machinery, those who didn't [grasp it] bought land.
>
> *Q*: So, how come did some have and some others did not have land of their own [after the War]?
>
> *P*: Well, to begin with a family with many children had their land divided accordingly. Second, for some individuals it was in their nature, they transformed farming into business. My grandfather had workers in his farm who got paid when they sold the product [of their labor]. He [his grandfather] had the responsibility to give them a wage: a plate of food and some money... This was going on until '55–'60.

Adjustment to the changing economic conditions, such as that by Phokion's grandfather, offered a successful transformation of the small, family unit into a bigger and more profitable one with higher returns and a more secure income. On the other hand, small-scale owners and, even worse, paid workers either had to supplement their income from off-farm sources or switch into a different sector altogether. The low productive capacity of the family farm, the belated mechanization, and the fragmentation of land rendered the family farm a production unit characterized by low returns, insecure income, and uncertain prospects. In this context, one of the peculiarities of the peasant economy was the derivation of income, which did not stem solely from farm activities but also from off-farm ones. Philomenes, 78 years, always had more than one job throughout his career. The supplementation of income in his case was achieved through a plethora of temporary and seasonal jobs within and outside Protopi. For a son of peasants who was married to a woman with a similar background, the need to provide his family with the means of subsistence was a higher priority than any personal career aspirations:

> The main job I've had was peasantry but I did whatever else necessary to support my family. I even did sewage jobs if I needed the money, but mainly I've been working all my life as a peasant...These were very hard times. In 1951 I went to a small island to get trained as a blacksmith. I stayed there for a year. After this I came back here till I got married; I took, you see I forgot this, I took exams to become an [junior] army officer but I didn't like it and quit. Ah, I didn't tell you that I worked in Belgium, did I? I changed so many jobs, how can I remember them all? I worked there for four whole years as an economic migrant; in the coalmines...Then, I came back here and worked in a factory and at the same time on the farm. At the moment I do plumbing, electricity repairs and whatever else I can...Not easy, but there you go!

7.2.2 Roma

If Philomenes's life-course mobility involved many horizontal movements, that is from peasantry to unskilled and, at best, semiskilled, manual occupations, this trajectory demonstrates the existence of job opportunities. By contrast, for some other respondents, the opportunity to capitalize on a wide range of occupations was not available. This is evident in the accounts of those who worked on the land. Markedly, it was the Roma who sold their labor for "a plate of food," as Phokion put it, and/or very little money, reinforcing thus the reproduction of the unequal relations of production:

> Phokion: Yiftoi had large families so when land was given out, theirs soon got partitioned. Many of them were forced to sell it to get by because they were the poorest. In the 1950s, they were in inferior jobs; like shepherds, dustmen and other manual occupations...They worked on the land for very, very low [daily] wages. The others [the non-Roma] didn't; they had their own private land, so they worked on their own. Generally, it wasn't common here to work on the land for money.

The exploitative relations within the labor market alluded to by Euripides and Phokionin in section 7.2.1 allow us to take a better glimpse of the relations of production within Protopi. The "local exploitation," as Euripides referred to it, hints at one of the core principles of capitalist production: the appropriation of the product of one's labor by another person. Moreover, it points to the ethnic differentiation as a factor that enhances capitalist efficiency. In this way, the local Roma is legitimately exploited by the non-Roma, given that the capitalist organization of production is premised on exploitation. In other words, capitalism as a system of production has offered the conditions of possibility for the generation of divisions within the social structure.

Patroclos, 57 years, offers valuable insights into the division of labor in a place where, at least nominally, opportunities were equalized with the 1929 land reform. Researching this aspect, though, was difficult, not least because respondents' knowledge was often based on hearsay and speculation was mixed with facts. Thus, although large family size was often considered as the main reason for the common practice among Roma families of selling their land, other factors were also in operation, such as pressure by the non-Roma to expand their own land-share (at the expense of the Roma) and possibly the operation of parallel, Roma and non-Roma, support and solidarity networks in farming. The effect of these forces on the capitalization of opportunities and generally the life chances of the Roma people is hard to estimate. However, given that alternative routes out of peasantry, especially before the late 1950s, did not exist, it is safe for us to assume that their impact was big. For example, not having enough land of one's own removed one crucial possibility for the supplementation of income after the war when the labor market was enriched with new jobs and people maintained farming as a secondary occupation.

Hence, many unskilled or semiskilled jobs were not equally open to Roma people as to the non-Roma. The only job that was Roma-only was that of a musician, which was a supplementary source of income and conferred very little respect and certain risks:

> Bacchus: The locals perceived it as a second-rate job, as a "joke" so to speak, they used to say [with contempt]: "you are Yiftos and you play music, right"?...Back in the days the musicians were called "Yiftoi" and were dismissed. They were not respected.

Bacchus, 81 years, was mainly a peasant throughout his life, but in Protopi, he was known as "Bacchus the clarinet player." Playing the clarinet was a patrilineal skill, which Bacchus developed further in his Roma-only band that entertained audiences in open festivals, weddings, and other family or community gatherings:

> *Bacchus*: Well, sometimes you could get involved in a fight. Some people used to get drunk and make a fuss.
> *Q*: How were you treated as a musician?
> *B*: Well, generally ok, but we didn't dare go and play in some areas as a band. People were not used to these kind of things. There were fights: for example, once a [Roma] musician got shot!

Playing music, though, was turned from a hobby with no guaranteed material rewards into an established part-time job. The value of this parallel occupation in the supplementation of the family income was huge, given that no alternative occupational pathways were available either for Bacchus or his wife, who was working on the land and inside the household.

7.3 Middle Generation

7.3.1 Non-Roma

In chapter 3, I argued that in Greece, especially after the 1950s, the shift from agriculture to the other sectors of economic activity was drastic. Likewise, in Protopi, significant changes started being realized in its occupational structure and economy after the war. These transformations coincided with the emergence of two crucial factors: the entry of money or real capital into Protopi's economy and the expansion of the service sector. The former was heavily derived from remittances from the emigrant population (see section 9.2 [chapter 9]), while the latter from endogenous transformations in the local[9] labor market and economy.

With regard to new money that entered Protopi's economy, this occurred at the time of the dominance of the capitalist mode of production, which saw an array of new occupations being added to its hitherto simple division of labor. The sector that triggered these changes and assisted with the creation of the new jobs was house construction, a development that was mainly realized thanks to remittances from abroad (for more, see section 9.2). Apart from the cumulative advantages gained when remittances flowed into this hitherto undeveloped area, they also triggered changes in the division of labor, the relations of production, and the social character of the place. In agriculture, remittance-derived capital was often converted into "real capital" for the purchase of equipment and machinery that reduced production costs and improved and modernized production. More significantly, capital from remittances was invested directly in house construction, which galvanized the local economy. Hence, externally derived money allowed the locals to reconstruct their dwellings and gradually to replace the rudimentary prewar constructions, which were typically based on readily available local material and were built by the occupying family, with modern ones. Furthermore, the effects of the growth of the house-construction sector were multiplying in the local economy and labor market, and led to the proliferation in skilled and semiskilled workers (which was corroborated by the quantitative material; see core mobility table [Table 6.2] and inflow analysis [section 6.8.2], chapter 6). With the domination of the capitalist mode of production, many peasants became economic migrants (more in section 9.2 [chapter 9]). However, for those who stayed behind and could not or did not want to leave Protopi, other occupational pathways were available. In particular, the choices and strategies individuals pursued were shaped to a great extent by the capital and assets their families possessed or lacked. That is, some locals could reap the benefits of development that ensued after the war due to ascriptive factors, such as family property, as they were fortunate enough to have land in the right place and could open a shop or start up a small, usually family-run business.

For those who did not have access to such family assets, though, occupational transition was difficult as they had to meander through various conundrums. Adam, 49 years, for example, followed his parents to Germany where he got his first job as a factory worker. Eventually, he got married to a woman from Protopi and they both returned to Greece. Adam's second job was also as an unskilled factory worker in Athens where he stayed for about five years. Low wage, hard working conditions and low quality of life led him and his family to move back to Protopi where he set up a retail store. However, within nine years, Adam shut down the store and embarked on yet another career change: He became a driver in a local farm:

> *Q*: Who were the first ones to open a store here?
> *Adam*: Those who had land on the main road. They took advantage of their location and it was easier for them to open a store. I'd love to have opened a store here but I'd have to rent somebody else's. That was not easy, you know!...So I ended up working as a driver and, you know what, I kind of consider myself lucky that I got the job! If it was not for my wife's contacts, I wouldn't have even got it.

Although the investment capital required to open a store was not big, capital in the form of property inherited from one's family was crucial for those who opted for an entrepreneurial career. Hermes, 47 years, confirms the ascriptive element in the growing self-employment sector, which allowed many locals to abandon peasantry and secure a more prosperous future:

> Hermes: The old stores were normally passed down from the father to the son or to the children. Many shops are like that, you know, inherited.

After the 1960s and throughout the 1970s and 1980s, apart from the expansion of self-employment, other forms of service-sector employment flourished, such as public and state administration. The creation of a plethora of new jobs to furnish the state bureaucracy and support the concomitant apparatus with personnel to cope with the changing needs was crucial. At the same time, the benefits conferred to the individual were by no means negligible. A secure income and a high level of quality of life were safeguarded, which comprised an upward intergenerational movement for those from families with background in peasantry.

Although this will be further explored in relation to education (see chapter 8), here I shall underline a growing tendency in the middle generation to occupy these newly created, white-collar jobs. In the following extract, Sophron, 48 years, recounts his career choice to join the police force in the 1970s:

> Sophron: A career in the public sector was highly sought after at that time. Many locals aspired for such a career. The reason I chose to join the [police] force was because it was sort of a secure job. Pay was low. A waiter, for instance, in '76, when I entered the force was earning three times the money I was. I could have chosen to become a waiter or a builder but I wouldn't have made the [personal and social] progress I've made through my job.

7.3.2 Roma

Not all the residents benefited the same from the expansion of the labor market and the new employment opportunities. For the Roma residents, alternative occupational routes apart from music and unskilled labor were not equally available. The inferior treatment to which they were subjected to impeded their occupational careers and inhibited substantially their social mobility advancement:

> Euripides: There are no exchanges in the [labor] market [between Roma and non-Roma]. All the Roma are manual workers. Nowadays, at the best you can find a builder, a tiler and these kinds of [manual] jobs but there are no educated amongst them [the Roma]. Neither can you find them owning stores here. There's only one flower shop that belongs to a woman from this race. Nothing else. There was a guy who used to have a café/bar, but that's that and nothing else.

However, despite the generally inferior social position of the Roma in relation to the non-Roma, some of the former prospered and achieved substantive progress. A case in point is Euriklea, 53 years, who was evidently proud of her parents' socioeconomic situation and recalled with fondness the privileges of growing up in an affluent environment, thanks to her father's emigration to Germany. Her father had sensed that the construction sector would become the driving force in Protopi's economy but could not find a satisfactory job other than as a low-paid, unskilled manual worker. What is more, had he stayed in Protopi, he would most probably have had to work for a non-Roma employer. Although Roma-only building teams existed, it was harder for them to compete with their non-Roma counterparts:[10]

> Euriklea: When I was living with my parents we weren't working much on the land. That happened after I got married, because there was poverty [in the new household]. At my parents' we had lots of money. My father was earning a lot of money even before he left for Germany. While in Germany he was earning even more... That's how we achieved some things early on: we had a new house, like the new ones you see nowadays. Well, at my parents' I had these comforts. God forbid, I could even say we were rich!

The affluence that Euriklea discusses has to be viewed against the wider background. Although material conditions improved substantially for Euriklea's family, her father's occupational career did not progress as he expected. In fact, after he returned to Greece, he was unemployed for a while. Euriklea's father's story indicates that while the non-Roma were gradually improving their occupational and social positions, this was matched by commensurate, intragenerational mobility advancement. On the other hand, for many Roma, material improvement was also the case but, quite often, it was not accompanied by commensurate gains in life-course mobility.

7.4 Younger Generation

7.4.1 Non-Roma

In Greece, the declining significance of agriculture in the family economy, best exemplified by the accelerating pace of breakup of land holdings after 1950, was evidently accompanied by a growth in the secondary and tertiary sectors of economic activity (chapter 3). As far as Protopi is concerned, the abandonment of agriculture gathered momentum from the 1980s onward. Many families, especially those who entered the civil service, left agriculture completely. For other families, EU regulations and price competition with producers from other areas forced them into early retirement or to take employment in the secondary sector. Although the extent of the industrial employment in Protopi is hard to estimate, it is believed that it is not as salient as in other parts of Greece. From a household perspective, employment in industry (and more generally in the secondary sector) did not result in the complete abandonment of family farming. Usually, the males took employment in manufacturing or constructions and the other members of the household carried on with family farming, which became a secondary occupation. This pattern led many families to move from peasant–worker to worker–peasant type of employment pattern (Bull and Corner, 1993). This development coincides with the increasing exposure of Greece to the European and global markets. Incidentally, it was the EU itself that subsidized the abandonment of agriculture in Protopi, which was despised by a large number of participants. One of them, Yurkas, has always been a peasant just like his parents and grandparents as well as his wife's family. On one occasion, he pessimistically exclaimed "The youth has left agriculture: it is 'zero'. In five years' time it will completely disappear. We are in despair. There won't be many jobs in a few years' time." This development, although it was heralded as a victory of rationalization of production by EU officials and local politicians, by the locals it was perceived as the death of agriculture. From the perspective of family survival and social mobility advancement, the enforced abandonment of agriculture precluded many households from holding on to a supplementary source of income in case transition into another occupation was not successful. This is a remarkable case of foreign interventionism, in this case in the form of EU subsidies, not only in the Greek economy but in the relations of production. In the name of competition, the operation of the so-called free markets, unilaterally signaled the end of an occupation that was weaved in the economic, social, and historical fabric of Protopi. The peasants, in order to survive in the new status quo, had to reinvent themselves. At the macro-level, this change signifies the dominance of capitalism as a mode of production. The means of subsistence, hitherto provided by agriculture, were now replaced by EU subsidies. In other words, the participation of Greece in the EU removed from a largely agricultural country the possibility to sustain itself through the exploitation of its own means of production, the land. From now on, a large part of the Greek labor force would either have to move to the urban centers to find employment or rely on the EU subsidies. As shown by Tsoukalas (1977), the historical dependency of the Greek political economy on the capitalist metropoles outside Greece goes back to the onset of Greek capitalism. However, the conditions for the longevity of this dependency are secured through the participation of Greece in the international and supernational organizations that I mentioned in chapter 3, and especially the EU.

In chapter 3, I argued that education was becoming much more accessible to the wider population, rural and urban alike, especially from the 1970s onward. Insofar as respondents in the young generation are concerned, education was the main means for securing a job that would enable them to break away from the hardships associated with peasantry and the equally low-paid and strenuous semi- or unskilled labor in the industry. The needs of the new economy were now fully endorsed by families and the rise of the new, highly educated social group had marked the new era. Since I deal with this extensively in chapter 8, suffice it to note here that in the collective imagery of many respondents born after the 1950s, occupations were depicted in a dichotomous way: those that were education-related and those that were not, as Diomedes, 34 years, points out:

> Diomedes: When I graduated from [primary] school, my father let me choose my job. He told me "you are now free to do what you wanna do." Of course, in terms of financial support the option to carry on in school was out of the question for me, because I had to work. Thus, instead of staying on in school I went on to get a job.

From the mid-1990s onward, the occupational opportunities that the expansion of the labor market facilitated in the previous years was brought to a halt. In addition, demographic changes, such as decreased morbidity rates, advent of economic immigrants, population growth, and pressures from the wider (including the global) market, contributed to a decline in availability in occupational opportunities. Nestor, 44 years, was the son of a cobbler who, like many others in Protopi, migrated to Athens in the 1960s for better career opportunities. His main job was cobbling, and in his spare time, he worked with his brother as a plumber. After a 19-year career in cobbling, he opened a corner store with his wife. This allowed them to generate enough financial capital, which they invested in retailing business in Protopi. In the following extract, Nestor describes the pressures exerted on the self-employed, such as himself, and the impact of globalization. The latter, globalization, played out in terms of increased competition, which, though, threatened the interests of small-scale entrepreneurs for whom it was impossible to compete with global capital:

> Nestor: Both here and in Athens being a cobbler was a prosperous job. We were even exporting goods up until '95, '96. After Greece joined the EU, we started importing stuff and I started thinking that I should find another job. In Protopi, I know cobblers who are closing down their stores because there is no work. This job is dying out in Greece...We are flooded with Chinese products. It's the same situation also in other sectors, e.g. in retailing and in super markets: the likes of "Lidl" and "Dia" have knocked down the prices and we can't compete...Since agriculture has also died here, everyone has switched into something different. The place has now become urban.

7.4.2 Roma

Despite a growing perception among the non-Roma respondents that the labor-market participation of the Roma was improved, stereotyping and marginalization were not entirely removed as Vryon, 39 years, explains:

> *Vryon*: Things changed in the 1980s. Before then it was forbidden for the Roma to go to the local cafés.
> *Q*: Did this change the social relationships in the area?
> *V*: Yes, because gradually foreigners started coming into the area and they didn't know their origin [of the Roma]...Today there are about 15–16 carpentries here but I doubt that a single one belongs to a Yifto. It's also obvious from the cafeterias: there's one owned by one of them [Roma] but I don't think anyone else [non-Roma] goes there. It's only for Yiftoi and many of them don't even go themselves so they don't get ghettoized, especially the young people.

In the 2000s, the occupational insecurity had spread also into the secondary sector. Pericles, 42 years, started off working with his father as an apprentice electrician before he decided to take a factory job in order to secure a monthly wage as a semiskilled manual worker. For him, embarking on the specific career path was more of a forced choice:

> Pericles: Some people went to secondary school but some others, like myself, who didn't receive vocational training moved on to [the world of] work. Some

of my classmates became tilers, plumbers, carpenters and so on. I'm talking about those who weren't good enough at school to go to uni. Today one of them has a garage, another one owns a restaurant, another one is an entrepreneur, a teacher, an army officer, a captain and so on. But for me there was nothing else to do.

This lack of choices led Pericles to emigrate to Germany, where he stayed for six years, working in a factory as an unskilled laborer. During this period (mid-1990s), though, Germany was undergoing labor-market rigidities and high rates of unemployment, which were forcing many foreign workers to repatriate. This was the time that Greece was undergoing a "jobless growth," as noted in chapter 3. After returning to Greece, Pericles worked as self-employed electrician, but securing enough work to get by was hard. Although emigrating for a second time was not an easy option, this time it was triggered by his wife's unemployment and his own unstable employment situation. Pericles's second stay in Germany was shorter lived (two years) and his job was again as an unskilled factory worker. His subsequent return to Greece seems to have characteristics of longevity, as he is a full-time worker in a factory and self-employed electrician in his spare time. Although neither he nor his wife (upon repatriation, she found a part-time job as a cleaner) are satisfied with their financial rewards, they are content that they are at last both employed. It is evident that the occupational experiences of this generation (i.e., younger) have the characteristics of precariousness. Increased pressures for wage compression in order to increase the competitiveness of the Greek workforce is increasingly affecting the Greek youth,[11] who oscillate between difficult choices and impossibly tough conundrums: to accept a low-paying job or to emigrate abroad; to accept worse working conditions than before; or to venture out in the risky and vulnerable world of self-employment.

B. The Occupational Pathways of Women

In Protopi, women's employment was typically related to but not necessarily dependent on men's. A significant difference existed in the occupational and employment careers and experiences of men and women throughout the twentieth century. While females were typically involved in the family farm with full responsibilities, they also had the lion's share in the household workload. Hence, in the public sphere, insofar as employment participation was concerned, men and women were involved on equal terms. The hard working conditions, the long working hours, and the nature of work did not attest to a discernible differentiation across the gender divide. However, in the private sphere, women were the main laborers. Although men assisted with some domestic work, this was restricted to the "masculine" type of tasks and it hardly involved child rearing. Women were the main domestic workers under conditions that were generally poor and with little support from technological advancements that women in other countries were utilizing at the time (Reiger, 1985; Hoy, 1995). Although women played a crucial part in all aspects of occupational mobility of the family, their careers were more closely associated with the private sphere, that is to say, inside the house. Notably, many respondents did not perceive the employment of females within the household as a separate occupation but, rather, as a preordained duty in the sexual division of labor. In the following sections, the impact of female labor in improving the family's occupational and social-class position is highlighted in addition to their share in the general development and progress of the area.

7.5 Older Generation

7.5.1 Non-Roma

Although the distinction between the public and the private spheres and the distribution of responsibilities requires a critical sociological theorizing (Gamarnikow and Purvis, 1983), it is safe to say that in the private sphere, females were the main workers both in terms of housework and child rearing. Thetis, 81 years, stressed her equal contribution inside and outside the household. In her account, she did not make a distinction between the public and the private domains as they comprised her unified occupational realm. Instead, Thetis emphasized her domestic work as much as her other labor (i.e., farming). This points to the integral relationship between the two types of labor that women performed (Dex, 1987), a consideration that has been largely neglected by mainstream social mobility research:

> Thetis: My body aches from the pain I've endured. I had to look after four people; four men. Three were mine [her husband and her two sons] and the other one was my father-in-law. My youngest son used to come from the city once in a while and I had to wash his clothes, to iron them, to cook etc. Everything had to be done with my own hands...In my parents' house the situation was hard. All my family were peasants. That's what I used to do and am still doing. Now I'm a pensioner but I have my own garden, I grow everything you may think of. That's my job...and the domestic stuff.

Unlike Thetis, Acantha, 69 years, could be considered to be in a more advantageous position than most women of her age. Her parents were farmers who used to run their own livestock farm. Through marriage, Acantha's life and working conditions improved drastically, thanks to the property her parents-in-law possessed. She left peasantry and, together with her husband, opened a small store whose size could be adjusted according to the local labor-market requirements; in the beginning, it was very small due to limited availability in investment capital; in the 1980s and 1990s, it grew and after that it shrunk. In Acantha's case the existence of property and investment capital allowed for the transition from peasantry to self-employment to be less risky an endeavor and with promising returns. However, this transition did not free Acantha from housework responsibilities. Family capital (from her in-laws), though it offered Acantha better occupational prospects, did not reverse the sexual division of labor:

> Until '78–'79 we were growing tobacco, but we also had a café/convenience store. Then we knocked it down and made it bigger. Together with my husband we left peasantry. Initially we opened a super-market but, it wasn't very profitable and we shut it down in order to open this place [shows the current store]. When my husband died in '93, I kept it on my own. Ever since I have been working here; I managed to get my children married and whenever I can, I help them [financially]. But for many years, I raised my children with my mother in law. Half the day with the children, half the day on the land.

Housework and child-care duties, which were highlighted in Acantha's account, were important determinants of females' occupational careers. Although the distinction between these two different types of responsibilities needs to be borne in mind (Oakley, 1974a, 2005), both of them were almost solely performed by women.

7.5.2 Roma

In families of peasants there was no big differentiation in the division of labor between Roma and non-Roma women. Although Roma females were affected by the lower living standards in their households, they were an integral part of the same system of production and imbricated in the same social relations as the non-Roma women. Their labor in the crops and livestock farming was essential for supporting the family and securing the means of subsistence. In many cases, Roma women were concurrently pursuing a part-time craft, such as hairdressing. In most of their accounts, housework was treated as a different form of work, though equal to that performed in the public sphere, a situation that resembles that of women in other contexts (e.g., see Oakley, 1974b). Calliope, 68 years, contributed throughout her life to family farming, and in her limited "free time," she worked as a hairdresser in a makeshift studio at the back of her flat:

> *Calliope*: I was a peasant, just like my father. At the same time I was a part-time hairdresser; I was working really hard. I also used to work with my father in-law, in a very masculine and extremely tiring job [cutting stone bricks].
> *Q*: Is this all the jobs that you've ever had?
> *C*: Well, I did everything. Growing tobacco, wheat, corn; all was done by hand. There was no equipment. Firstly, I'd go to help my father in-law and

then I'd come back home to serve a lady who wanted to have her hair cut: there was no time to rest. In the evening I did all the domestic stuff.
Q: Did you choose any of these jobs, for example farming?
C: It was compulsory in order to get by. Everyone here did the same.
Q: Would you like to have had the chance to do something else?
C: I would but it didn't happen. I'd like not to have been all day long deep inside the water when going to the crops and doing all the heavy duty work. Yes, I would like to, but...

7.6 Middle Generation

7.6.1 Non-Roma

As already pointed out, the career choices of women born in the 1950s and early 1960s were influenced by their parents' occupations before marriage and by their husbands' thereafter. This was clearly evident in the accounts of women in the middle generation, such as Circe, who descends from a family of farmers with no high occupational expectations from and aspirations for their daughter. In the following account, Circe describes her occupational role as "assisting" her parents or her husband. What is more, her "second shift" (Hochschild, 1989), that in the household, was perceived as a "natural" component in the division of labor and was not even mentioned during the interview. While my observations suggested that Circe's participation in the house economy was crucial, all her work was unpaid, and was considered as integral to the "gender factory" of the home (Berk, 1985).

> *Circe*: Before I got married I was in agriculture and after that I was based here in the [husband's] store...Nothing else. I haven't done anything else, like my own job. I simply assist here.
> *Sophocles*:[12] In agriculture, my wife was only giving a hand.
> Q: Did your parents have any expectations from you, were they expecting you to do any specific job?
> C: No, no, no. What kind of expectations? They didn't have any.

Women's employment stories are more complex to explore because their accounts are often entangled with those of their parents and/or their husbands (see sections *4.4* [chapter 4] *and 2.3.2* [chapter 2]). During the course of this research, I was constantly on guard in order not to allow females' stories to be pushed under the males' own, which were perceived by many respondents as the most significant ones at least as far as income contribution and participation in the labor market were involved. Besides, if women's occupations and concomitant roles in the division of labor are taken on board, a more complete picture emerges about the occupational situation, the structure of opportunities and social relations in Protopi.

7.6.2 Roma

With regard to Roma women in the middle generation, they were predominately employed in the family farm and in the household, with very few exceptions. Opening a store was not an option, while the pursuit of a career in the public sector required education, which was in short supply. In a nutshell, the only pathway available for Roma women who abandoned farming was low-paid, unskilled manual employment in the nearby firms and factories. Philippa, 60 years, comes from a family of peasants. Her occupational career was typical of women of her age and it consisted of employment in the family farm and manual labor:

> *Philippa*: We were growing corn even from school age. After school time, we used to go to my dad's cattle. I was quite young, about 10 years old, but I still went to the cattle. I also went to school, on and off. I preferred to go to the cattle. Then, when I was 15, I went to a big timber factory for three years until I got married at 18. After then I went back to farming: tobacco, corn, vineyards, that kind of stuff. For a while I was a cleaner, I was going from place to place.
> *Q*: Would you like to have done a different job?
> *P*: Well, there was no chance! How? With no education or skills? It was not possible.

7.7 Younger Generation

7.7.1 Non-Roma

For women in the younger generation, access to secondary and tertiary education (for a detailed account, see chapter 8) and participation in the labor market improved drastically. Attitudes to female contribution to the household economy also changed and it was broadly acknowledged among participants of all age-groups that female employment was not only a positive development but also necessary. For the requirements of the new life and economy encouraged the participation of more women in the labor market even in sectors and positions that used to be traditionally male dominated. This is underlined by Aspasia, 50 years, a store owner:

> *Aspasia*: When I first came into this area [1970s] everyone was working on the land. There were no super markets, no skilled jobs and no crafts. These came later. At that time all women were inside.
> *Q*: When you say "inside," what do you mean?
> *A*: I mean in the house, with the kids and the other stuff they had to do at home.
> *Q*: Do you think that's changed now?
> *A*: Definitely, because they have to contribute [to the household]. Otherwise they can't make it [as a family]. There's no other way to make ends meet.

> You see, today we want more things in our lives. If just one partner is employed it's just impossible to survive.

Women's careers, or at least those who pursued one, did not have the same characteristics as those of men. Female employment was typically intermittent due to extensive involvement in the household, childbirth, and child-care commitments. Many participants reported that part-time employment was higher for women than for men and that women's pay was lower than that of their male counterparts. Venus's, 39 years, account is typical of many females who had to prioritize family over career in a way that was unknown to men of the same age. Venus's first occupational experience was as a short-term, part-time unskilled manual worker. Marriage and child-care responsibilities forced her out of employment for nearly 20 years. Upon reentry into the labor market, again in unskilled, manual labor, she had to confront a rigid labor market and a personal employment history that did not equip her with the necessary skills:

> Venus: I searched for a job in the past but, on one hand, I had the kids to look after and, on the other, some personal misfortunes, so I gave up. Now am back to work again thanks to good contacts who got me the job. But it was not easy getting one!

7.7.2 Roma

Roma women in the younger generation have also been increasingly contributing to the household economy and participating in the labor market. The jobs they hold are subject to the skills, experience, and qualifications they possess, as is the case with the non-Roma women. Although finding a job in Protopi is still harder for them than for non-Roma females, younger Roma women are much more mobile and active in seeking employment than their counterparts in the previous generations. For those with low educational qualifications, their main options are in semi- or unskilled employment, as was the case with regard to the two older age-groups. For those with higher qualifications, such as secondary school or university education, other opportunities have emerged mainly in the civil sector or in routine non-manual jobs. While this group (young, Roma women) was hard to reach[13] (see chapter 4), informal discussions and observations I carried out suggested that many of them move out of Protopi as soon as they complete secondary or tertiary education. For some families, traditional values that restrict the role of women outside the household still prevail, while others still encourage their daughters to get married at an early age (though, not as early as in the past).

It should be noted, though, that for many Roma families, the standards for their daughters' occupational careers have increased significantly in relation to the previous generations. Nowadays, many parents prefer their daughters to have no job at all rather than to fall prey to unscrupulous employers. The following extract is informative of this type of attitude through the account of a Roma woman whose daughter was unemployed for two years despite holding a university degree:

It's very difficult [for young people] to get a decent job these days but why should they do the shitty ones? After my daughter graduated from uni I told her: "Go get yourself a good, descent job or get none!" What's the point of spending all your day in a job that you hate and pays you peanuts? It's just insane, isn't it? Going through all the shit out there for €200–300 or 500 a month is not worth it! Not worth their effort and their youth!

The most radical changes in terms of mobility experiences and occupational pathways were observed with reference to women in the "700 Euro generation" (Kaskarelis and Tsilika, 2009). That is to say the generation that is hardly hired, easily fired, and strives for a basic salary of €700 a month, an amount of money totally insufficient for the requirements of current life.

7.8 Summary

Evidence showed that Protopi experienced rapid and substantial transformations in the organization of its employment, economy, and labor market, which allowed a great proportion of individuals to advance their socioeconomic positions. This resulted in some notable inter- and intragenerational social mobility movements, which were experienced, directly or indirectly, by the majority of respondents and their families. This chapter also shows that although a considerable amount of movement within the social structure of Protopi and a general improvement of the socioeconomic situation of many individuals and families was attested to, the occupational opportunities were not equally distributed to all the participants. Hence, in concert with findings presented in chapter 6, non-Roma men in the middle generation appeared to be the biggest winners of the occupational restructuring and the emergence of opportunities in the postwar labor market. Although female participation also increased dramatically, especially after the 1990s, the labor-market rigidities seem to have raised new barriers to their occupational advancement.[14]

Chapter 8

Educational Experiences and Pathways to Social Mobility

8.1 Introduction

In chapter 3, I showed that extended occupational and economic transformations occurred in Greece after the Second World War. A similar picture was also painted in relation to Protopi (chapters 6 and 7). Given that education has been regarded as *a*, if not *the*, *avenue par excellence* of social mobility in most economically advanced European societies after the war (chapter 2) and large investment has been directed into it ever since, its exploration is important for understanding the wider mobility processes with which this study is concerned. Chapter 8 expands on the inter- and intragenerational mobility experiences of residents in Protopi and furnishes us with an understanding of the role that education has played in shaping and transforming careers, aspirations, pathways, and employment experiences across the three generations. The argument I put forward is that education has played a significant role in the social mobility careers of individuals, although the relationship between education and social mobility is much more complex than that.

8.2 Educational Provision in Greece and Protopi

In chapter 3, I outlined the main educational transformations in Greece in the twentieth century. In this section, I shall revisit the most important of these developments in order to demonstrate how the Greek project of educational transformation was instantiated in Protopi. In prewar and immediate postwar Greece, big disparities in educational attainment existed between urban and rural areas. The former had very high attainment rates, and the majority of the urban population participated in primary and secondary education. Especially after 1964, schooling became more accessible and democratic; secondary education became compulsory, and new universities got established. Although some of these changes were suspended by the 1967–1974 military dictatorship, thereafter their impact on the educational provision of the country was profound. In recent years, that is, from the early 1990s onward, Greece has achieved remarkable rates of secondary and, even more so, university participation. Protopi benefited considerably from these reforms, especially after 1964 when a (lower and upper) secondary school was established there for the first time. This event, coupled with progressive social policy initiatives, contributed significantly to the improvement of the educational attainment of the community across all educational sectors and stages.

A. The Education of Men

8.3 Older Generation

8.3.1 Non-Roma

As I discussed in chapter 3, in prewar Greece, only primary education was free although access was not entirely unproblematic. Widespread poverty, large family size, and high mortality rates were among the factors that discouraged families from prioritizing their children's education. In Protopi, the majority of respondents in the first generation (born between 1913 and 1937) had gone to primary school though not all of them managed to complete it. Child labor was essential in the supplementation of family income and the years a child spent in education counted as foregone income for the household. Solon, 83 years, and Euthalia, 81 years, exemplify the common attitude toward education for respondents in their generation:

> *Q*: Did everyone go to school in the old days?
> *Euthalia*: Yes they did but only to primary. I finished it; my husband didn't.
>   His parents sent him to [herd] the sheep.
> *Q*: [Asking Solon] Did everyone in your year-group go to primary school?
> *Solon*: Nearly everyone.
> *E*: [Asking Solon] Did you go yourself?
> *S*: Id id.
> *E*: Did you finish it?
> *S*: No, [I went] up to fifth grade [11 years old].
> *Q*: And what did you do after then?
> *S*: I became a shepherd. My parents needed me there.

The time allocated to education-related activities, including attending school, was largely shaped by the division of labor in the household, which was the economic and decision-making unit. Going to primary school in the morning and returning to the cattle or the crops in the afternoon was not uncommon a practice for many children and young people in these early days. Enhancing the family production capacity and material gains took precedence in relation to attending school. In this way, a dichotomy was manufactured between, on the one hand, the productive activities of the family and, on the other, the unproductive activities of school. What is more, the traditional division between manual and mental labor was lived, enacted upon, and reproduced within a simple but coherent nexus of mutually reinforcing productive and social relations, as exemplified through Milena's account:

> Back then people didn't have their mind set to school. Let me give you an example: my brother's teacher told my father: "Your son is good. You should send him to secondary school." And my father replied: "What are you talking about? I've got such a large flock of sheep; who's gonna look after them? Are you crazy?" In this area there was not a single educated person, bar one or two.[1] All the rest were involved in the crops and animal breeding.

In such a context, primary-school completion rates were low, while secondary-school attainment was a distant reality for the peasants. However, this was not a universal condition in Protopi, for the differentiation in material and cultural assets allowed for a demarcation in attitudes in relation to education. That is to say, there was a minority of families who could afford the expenditure involved, both in terms of foregone income and direct expenditure, and who could pursue their offspring's education. These families invariably possessed high economic and academic capital and were part of the small and privileged middle class. In line with accounts from other parts of Greece (see, e.g., Lambiri-Dimaki, 1983), this was either the local "intelligentsia" or the economic elite, as Yurkas, 65 years, explains:

> Our place delayed in producing educated people. [Locals] worked on the land because it gave them enough to eat, whereas in other areas [of the country] they went to school because they didn't even have enough [gains from the land]. Here even when they finished [primary] school they'd say "I'm off to the crops," because they had this option. That's why no one was educated at the time.
> Q: And how about secondary school? Who used to go?
> A: First, those who had the money, because everything cost: books, rent, food etc. Second, those whose dads were educated.

8.3.2 Roma

In a context of desperate economic conditions and enormous pressure to secure the means of subsistence on a daily basis, there was no evident differentiation in respect of attitudes and practices vis-à-vis education between the Roma and the dominant group (i.e., the non-Roma). Bacchus's account below corroborates that of Solon in the previous section. Material deprivation was an equalizing factor and school attendance was perceived as a luxury, a middle-class privilege, which was outside the realm of the Roma.

In other words, poverty was an equalizing force that made the lines of ethnic differentiation less accentuated across the "have nots." Being a farmer was being working class and that was the single most decisive factor in one's social standing. Affluence and associated privileges, on the other hand, amplified the differences across the ethnic divide, given that by virtue of membership to the "haves," one could hardly be a Roma. However, the factor that disqualified people from belonging to the "haves," the local middle class, was not their ethnic identity. Ethnic differentiation was the *mechanism of justification* for the discrimination of the Roma from institutions, such as education, which could play the equalizing role that the redistribution of land had left unfinished. This process of unequal differentiation along ethnic lines was largely an *ideological mechanism* of ethical and moral justification of the social stratification. As such, it was a tool for the *justification of the subordination* not only of the Roma, but also of *the entire working class*.

Q: Did you go to school?
Bacchus: Up until fifth grade [11 years old]. Then I became a shepherd so school was over for me.
Q: Why? Did your parents tell you to do so?
B: No, there was no other option. We had to work.
Q: Who went to secondary school these days?
B: Those who had some money. Everyone else was starving. We had crops, animals and were trying to make ends meet. These were hard times.

8.4 Middle Generation

8.4.1 Non-Roma

As I argued in chapter 1 and demonstrated in chapter 4, in postwar Western Europe, a concerted effort started in order to stabilize capitalism and entrench democracy with the hope of avoiding another deadly war and a protracted capitalist crisis. This provided fertile ground for the Keynesian school of though that was to become the new paradigm in socioeconomic organization. State intervention in business, economic, and financial circles was one of its core principles. What concerns us here is the way this was instantiated in the realm of education. What was leading the attendant transformations was a belief in the association between education and the labor-market demands of capitalist economies. This was also the case in postwar Greece, where reforms sought to raise the educational standards of the population as well as to provide the developing economy with a skilled workforce for key positions. The majority of these positions were in the state and public services and they required educated workers to occupy them. Hence, education, especially after the mid-1960s, became the avenue *par excellence* for the new occupational opportunities and played a crucial role in class formation.

In relation to Protopi, the lack of secondary school required serious investment on behalf of the family who wanted their children to carry on in postprimary education. The cost of renting a house, buying the textbooks, commuting to the nearby city center, and all other associated expenses functioned for the majority of the population as a major deterrent. For most respondents in the middle generation, especially those born before the late 1940s, secondary-education completion rates were still very low. As was the case with the older generation, families could not afford the dual financial sacrifices that children's education required, that is, the school expenses and the foregone income due to the loss of the child/laborer. In other cases, it also involved the possibility of not passing down the land, craft, or the family store to the child (especially to the older son). This was more pronounced among informants who graduated from primary school before 1964 and had substantially different experiences to narrate than those who, albeit in the same generation, completed primary education after 1964 and benefited from the introduction of universal and free secondary education (chapter 3). Gorgias, 60 years, graduated from primary school before 1964. In his account, the similarities to respondents in the first generation are striking:

> Secondary school was for those whose fathers had some relationship with education. Those few children who became teachers and so on, their fathers were involved [in education]...but they also had the money. What could we do? I couldn't commute [to the nearest big city] because my father couldn't afford the rent, plus I didn't have a vehicle [to commute]. I was good at school but there was no time to prepare or study, because when I returned from school they'd tell me: "go and get the cows sorted" or "go to the tobacco crops." School was easier then; some of my peers who became teachers were not that much better in comparison to myself; had I spent a couple of hours every day studying, I could have become [educated] like them.

Gorgias is less remorseful about his own lack of advanced education than being critical about those who achieved it. In his eyes, there was no meritocracy established, at least if merit is conceptualized as talent + IQ. Instead, it was effort that determined educational success, which, in turn was contingent upon family background. This offers an insight into the intricacies of allocation of rewards in a system that appeared as a level playing field, at least in the immediate postwar years.

Although residents in Protopi did not start sending their children to school en masse after 1964, gradual changes in attitudes and practices were discernible after that. As I already pointed out, this was facilitated by the educational and welfare policy measures that were launched at the time, such as the provision of free and compulsory secondary education, which was followed by other supporting social policies, such as free school meals for all students. As educational costs decreased, the whole conception and measurement of "family economics of education" were reconfigured. Hence, from the straightforward equation, whereby one had to deduct the cost of education from the overall family income, in the years following 1964, the weight of education as an income-compression factor was reduced or totally removed. Furthermore, any short-term losses incurred from education were now seriously weighed up against promising long-term prospects. Crudely put, the social and economic returns that educational qualifications brought to their incumbents and their families converted them into valuable assets. In Bourdieuan terminology, one can see how cultural capital (e.g., educational qualifications) is converted into economic and possibly also social capital (e.g., social networks), but more importantly how all three forms of capital reinforce each other.

It is in this era that a certificate from upper-secondary school was increasingly required for positions in public administration and the public services more broadly. Higher educational credentials, such as a university degree, could secure their holders a job in the highest positions where they could enjoy all the accompanying benefits: higher income at least in comparison to agriculture, security of employment, good working conditions, and, not least, enhanced social status. The family of these highly educated individuals (especially at university level) could take pride from such an association, which was highly prestigious in the local community. For the *literati* themselves, passage into this group secured them membership into a newly formed social group—the intermediate class—or entry to the expanding middle class. In this vein, it can be safely argued that going to secondary school and, even more so, to university, was a secure means of upward social mobility. Life experiences from the first ones who "made it" through education, such as Phokion, a secondary school teacher, offer testimony to this:

> Everyone here was a farmer in those days. My parents sent me to the cattle and I saw what it was about and said to myself: "I need to get out of these dreadful conditions as soon as I can." That's why I went to university: out of necessity. I thought that going to university could be the easiest way for me to get a job and gain some money immediately [after graduation]. This is what urged many of us to go to university rather than our love for education...My family was pushing me to go to university also for reasons of social recognition. The prestige of the family was improved when the child went to school. That was the common attitude here back then, but only for those who had secured the necessary means to get by. Those who hadn't didn't think about it this way.
> *Q:* And who was in each group?
> *A:* Those who could get by were those who had [private] land. Those who didn't have land couldn't get by.

As lucidly elaborated in this excerpt, education conferred multiple benefits (or so it appeared anyway). First of all, one has to consider the benefits to the state itself. According to various liberal theories that proliferated after the war, such as human capital theory, a higher-educated workforce was linked to higher productivity and greater economic output, which would in turn lead to greater prosperity, both individual and social. Despite the flawed ideological undertones of these theories, the state was one of the greatest beneficiaries of this expansion. However, this was not due to the expected increase in productivity but due to the increased role of the state as an agent of social formation, control, and regulation of the workforce. The second area lies with the individuals and their families, as I already discussed. Finally, the benefits to the social system is a point that merits some elaboration. The sheer scale and velocity of educational and wider social policy reforms that were implemented in the first two decades after the Second World War, namely in the 1950s and 1960s, transformed the whole social fabric. While in Western Europe and other economically advanced countries, this was accompanied by the demise of industrial production and the de-proletarianization of a large part of the workforce, in Greece, this took a set of distinct characteristics, such as the abandonment of agriculture. Education fostered the expansion of the middle class and contributed to the creation of a new class or social group, namely the intermediate class. This was largely engineered by the Greek state, which sought to meet its expanding requirements through the recruitment of an educated workforce. The Greek state then became a catalyst in postwar mobility processes and the emergent restructuring of the Greek social system. This "state-sponsored mobility" had a profound ideological function as it proved to be a forceful mechanism of legitimization of the educational system as well as of individuals' strategies for social advancement through education. In a nutshell, the road to Greek modernization was chiefly paved through education. Furthermore, the blue-collar worker-turned-public servant—as was the case in economically advanced countries—and the peasant-turned-public servant or self-employed individual—as in the Greek case—required the reorganization of production along new lines. It could thus be argued that the deployment of education as a servant of this model of socioeconomic organization was a strategic choice as well as an instrument for the rearrangement of class formation and the reconfiguration of class power. Capitalism was only interested in creating educated workers insofar as it could serve its interests better. In other words, educational expansion was the *optimum means* for securing the conditions of reproduction of capitalism. Despite the evident improvement in working conditions for a large part of the workforce (either in comparison to agriculture or industry) and higher income gains, the embourgeoised worker had been converted into a serial "consuming machine." Any material gains[2] the workers experienced were the outcome of serious compromises between losses in terms of employment rights and the wider dismantling of the working-class organization, solidarity, and consciousness. However, every rearrangement within capitalist development needs more than the reorganization of production, if it is to enjoy longevity. The ideological transformation of social agents, especially those from the working class, is also paramount, if they are to be prevented from realizing class consciousness and acting as a class-for-themselves, which could threaten capitalism. It seems, then, that what my respondents have been eluding to is the genesis of this process in the microcosm of Protopi.

8.4.2 Roma

The high cost of educational participation was an extra burden for the generally poorer Roma families. Plato was in the same year group as Phokion, though his occupational pathway took a manifestly different course than Phokion's.

> The poorer kids didn't go to school. They just went for a daily wage or to learn their craft and nothing else. For instance, my father wanted to send me to [secondary] school but he couldn't afford it. A few years before my time, he had sent my elder brother to secondary [school] but he dropped out after a couple of years because my father couldn't afford the rent. Those kids who had the financial capacity, they went to secondary school and did great things [int heirl ives].

Plato's account illustrates how economic constraints shaped career aspirations and limited the range of job selection. What is striking is that in Protopi, manual labor was not accorded high social status (as was the case in economically advanced countries; see for an example Willis, 1977). By contrast, manual labor occupied in the collective consciousness of people in Protopi a position similar to agriculture as both fields involved high levels of insecurity and did not guarantee high returns. Moreover, the lack of a fully formed industrial proletariat, at least in its traditional form that could be observed either in advanced capitalist economies or in the existing socialist countries, did not allow for the solidification of a strong working-class consciousness among manual workers. The could-be-embourgeoisement of the peasants, which is apparent in Plato's account, serves here as an indication of the symbolic valuation of merit within Protopi's structure as well as a reminder of the internalization of the normative superiority of education as the most "virtuous" and desirable career pathway. At the same time, the material reality in Protopi leaves no room for the entertainment of any illusions: education was steeped in the ideas of the ruling class. As such, it was primarily the privilege of the ruling class. Although the vast majority of non-Roma people in Protopi, strictly speaking, are not part of the ruling class, they are nevertheless part of the dominant group, at least within the social relations of Protopi.

Different rates of attendance and dropout can only be explored in the postwar years as this is the time when participation increased and educational provision expanded. Cleanthes offers his explanation about the generally poor school attainment of Roma children, an explanation that rests on the stereotypical assumption that Roma parents did not care about their children's education:

> Not everyone in the 1960s completed school. How can I put it? The Yiftoi, for instance, didn't complete it. Their parents were not paying any attention to their children. They were worse than ours [the non-Roma]. They neglected their children and they still do so today. They don't send them to school. They don't care.

Hercules is a Roma man whose account about Roma attitudes to education contradicts Cleanthes's and those of the majority of the respondents in the dominant group. Although Hercules wanted to complete school and follow a related career path, lack of material means forced him to adjust his aspirations and occupational strategies. For Hercules, it was not lack of family interest that deterred him from making progress in education, but the brute force of material constraints:

> How did I choose my job? It was a time when very few children had the chance to study, it was the money [aspect], there were many things. I'm talking about '67, it was very hard; parents didn't have the money, so out of necessity we had to breed the cows and go to the crops; this is why we didn't manage to study. We were forced to choose a job and since it was a period of construction in the area and I had to choose a job too, I ended up in this one; my father was on the same job and that's how I chose to become a decorator.

The patrilinear transmission of the father's craft to the son was a common practice, probably even more so among the Roma. Due to a lack of alternative strategies for upward social mobility, such as education, dependency on the father's (or family's) occupation was strong. Euriklea talks about the selective function of education and the way she lived it through the schooling experiences of her two sons. None of them finished school despite the fact that she and her husband valued it highly and understood well its importance. Currently, in their mid-40s, her children have both moved a lot between jobs before they settled in their current ones; the elder one works with his father as a builder, while the younger one is a musician:

> In order to become teachers, the kids were selected, but if they didn't have aspirations they couldn't carry on. Those who had aspirations became educated back then. Those who had money carried on [in school] as well as those whose parents had studied themselves. As for myself, I couldn't even send my boys to primary school. Thankfully, they learned how to read and write, though they didn't go to secondary, we couldn't afford it. My brother could afford it and both his children finished secondary school. My children didn't wanna go, but to be honest with you, neither did we have the money.

Poor attendance among Roma children was one reason that impeded their school participation and completion rates. Other reasons have to be sought in the educational experiences and the unfavorable treatment they were subjected to by the non-Roma. Interestingly, it was the non-Roma respondents who provided insightful accounts in relation to this aspect. Patroclos and Aspasia both attended the local primary school, though they followed different trajectories after that. Aspasia migrated to Athens and Patroclos to the nearest urban center. Both completed secondary school. Patroclos attended university while Aspasia acquired further education. None of them had any recollections of studying next to a Roma person from secondary school onward:

> *Patroclos*: When I was going to [primary] school we had many Yiftoi in my class. Only one of them went to uni and, from the rest of them, none completed secondary school. They stopped earlier than us [the non-Roma]. They had no money…
> *Aspasia*: Nor the [appropriate] frame of mind.
> *P*: Yeah, well, if the family was not capable of encouraging their children to go to school I can't tell; I believe that poverty is a deterrent to everything. None of them graduated from high school in my days, but maybe after then they did.
> *A*: In my [school] days these children [Roma] were bullied and I believe that one of the reasons that they dropped out was because of this. I also think their parents were illiterate and were forced to withdraw them from school sooner rather than later. Poverty plus bullying and they dropped out.

8.5 Younger Generation

8.5.1 Non-Roma

Apart from self-employment or craft-based jobs that were bestowed by the parents, education was the main pathway for respondents in the younger generation. The requirements of the new economy were now largely endorsed by families, and the rise of a new, highly educated social group also marked the new trend. Moreover, the example of those in the middle generation, who capitalized on the demand for educational credentials started to be adopted by their offsprings. The immediate rewards these highly educated individuals enjoyed after graduation from upper-secondary, vocational school, and even more so from university set a good precedent for how to escape agriculture and secure a better future. Given that high credentials proved to be a successful avenue for promoting the occupational and social mobility of those in the middle generation, education was now widely perceived as the most-sought-after avenue into the labor market (reverberating Bell's forecast discussed in chapter 2). In Protopi, "education-based meritocracy" (Goldthorpe, 2003b) was to become the new ideal to which families rapidly subscribed. In other words, the residents expected the ablest students to attain the highest credentials and then to ascend to the best occupational positions. Kimon, 35 years, comes from a family of farmers. He and his siblings were the first ones in their family to finish secondary school and enter university. In the following extract, he illustrates the growing belief in education-based meritocracy, which, according to some of my respondents, had reached a near-universal acceptance in Protopi, especially from the 1970s until the late 1990s:

> I generally believe that having more children going to gymnasio [lower-secondary school] helped a lot in having more [children] going to upper-secondary and then to university regardless of the socio-economic status of the parents. The parents started to encourage their children, and nowadays they are even pushing them to carry on [to university]. Most of those in the older times were tormented by peasantry and wanted their children to move away from this—to get qualifications because they're a kind of passport. I believe that those with some credentials are preferred [in the labor market] over those without any…In general, there is a hierarchy created [due to credentials], which is a good thing.

Improved attitudes toward education contributed more broadly to an increase in the educational level of the general population in Greece and in Protopi more specifically. State support, with more schools and universities across the country and fewer barriers than for the previous generations, assisted considerably in the shift in collective practices to jobs that needed educational qualifications.

Vryon, 39 years, came from a poor family that emigrated to Germany in order to improve their living standards. During their stay there, his parents worked as factory workers, but after a few years, they repatriated only to continue their career as unskilled manual workers in local factories. The impact of Vryon's parents' occupational mobility on his own choices was strong, as it was the material constraints that made him choose his occupation rather than the availability of choices:

> I'm now employed in a hospital; I'm a technician, a plumber. Before I took this job I had spent 18 months in Germany. It was a forced choice. As soon as I graduated from gymnasio [lower-secondary school] I decided not to carry on in school and to go instead to vocational training. My family had no expectations regarding my job [selection] for as long as I could contribute to the [family] income. From an early age I had to cover not only my personal expenses but also theirs…I was completely taken aback when I found out that my application got accepted because you don't expect to get a job in the public sector with only a vocational qualification and some technical training, but I was lucky.

It is evident that the creation of opportunities was one issue; capitalizing on them was another. Luck was as crucial as motivation, especially for young people with little family support. In addition, Vryon's account is informative about the value of vocational education. The expansion of skilled services is in line with the increase in importance of the service sector from the late-1950s onward in Greece (see chapter 3). From my discussions with various research participants, it transpired that the collective consciousness in Protopi was remolded in order to accommodate this transition. This was expressed as a staunch belief in the primacy of employment in public services, which could guarantee a near-automatic social-class promotion.

However, the significance of education as a pathway to secure employment and a "royal avenue" to upward social mobility was short lived. Those participants who entered the labor market after the late-1990s are currently facing considerable difficulties securing a job. As Vryon observed: "When I got my job it was different; much easier. Now it's all changed. There are so many graduates that it's impossible to employ them all in the public sector." The returns of educational qualifications are no longer commensurate with the social and economic value that was traditionally associated with them. That is, a significant number of highly educated university graduates end up taking up jobs completely different from the ones they were trained for. Credentials no longer guarantee labor-market success as the economy has been further transformed in recent years. As a result, the occupational situation of people in the young generation can be described as very precarious, which is lucidly conveyed by Phaedon, 29 years, a recent university graduate. For him, aspiring to get a degree was part of his family upbringing: both his sister and father (rather unusual for his generation) went to university. In the seven years since his graduation from university, he has already moved a lot between jobs (throughout this time, he has had three full-time jobs and even more part-time ones). His views on occupational opportunities for university graduates are indicative of the insecurity the new economic conditions and the restructured labor market have brought about:

> For my peers it is hard to get a proper job although many of them have gone to university—one of them is a physical education teacher but works in a bar; another one is a Greek language teacher, but works as a waiter; everyone does something different, if not everyone, definitely most of them. They haven't selected these jobs; they were forced to do them in order to get by.

The weak association between educational qualifications and immediate labor-market absorption capacity has led many families and young people to turn to other pathways that they would have otherwise overlooked. In the following extract, Sophron, who entered the civil service as a lower-secondary-school graduate, explains the employment conundrums facing new graduates:

> So far so good, but the future is gloomy. Unemployment now hits university graduates. I believe it's up to 90%. Something's gotta change. My niece got top

grades but couldn't get a job: [with sarcasm] "she didn't have experience, she didn't have this and that"! Back in my days there were only a few children who went to university and that's why there were still jobs up for grabs. Whereas now there's a lot of kids going to university. Recently in my sector [the police force] there were 20,000 candidates for 200 places! Competition is now intense. In the past, there was none at all; employment came soon after graduation. Now there is saturation everywhere: among teachers, doctors, everywhere... Take my son as an example: I support him [financially] in order to cover his [university] expenses, but I have to wait until he graduates, and after that he has to do his military service; after that, he might get a job.

8.5.2 Roma

Access to secondary and tertiary education after the war improved drastically for people in Protopi, though not for the Roma. Poverty and unequal participation in the labor market impeded the educational attainment of first- and second-generation respondents. Moreover, bullying and discrimination in school acted as a further deterrent. This situation started improving for those in the younger generation, which coincides with the period of educational expansion, but also with the devaluation of educational qualifications. It could be argued that once the value of credentials started to decline, access became easier for the heretofore most disadvantaged groups, such as the Roma. Apart from forces external to school, we also have to examine internal factors that underpinned the increase in the educational participation of Roma children. More specifically, the treatment of the Roma pupils in school started improving and overt discrimination against them was not as widespread as in the past. Nestor discusses the education of his Roma peers and their school attendance from an intergenerational perspective:

Q: Did they [the Roma] go to school?
Nestor: In the past, they were the first ones to drop out during primary school. Nowadays, they all go to school without exception. I have relationships with many of them and I know this.
Q: When you say "in the past," how long ago?
N: During my school years, in the 1980s. Just a few of them completed primary school. Anyhow, today that's not the same and that's good.

Some covert forms of discrimination still might operate today while others may have become embedded in the school ethos. Many male Roma in the younger age group have graduated from university, though to a lesser extent than their non-Roma counterparts. Although some have pursued bright careers as senior public servants, self-employed individuals, merchants or entrepreneurs, military personnel, or academicians, only a few have stayed in Protopi because they usually emigrate to bigger urban centers or abroad (see chapter 9).

B. The Education of Women

8.6 Older Generation

8.6.1 Non-Roma

School attendance for women in the first generation was not very different from that of men. The same impediments and constraints, such as poverty, family size, and lack of positive association between educational qualifications and the labor market, were as much prohibiting factors for women as they were for men (section 8.3). It is not surprising, then, that there were probably no women in the older generation whose educational level exceeded that of primary school.

A female who stayed on in education was regarded by her family as a loss in a twofold manner. First, as foregone income that was required to cover her educational expenses, due to reduced labor power of the family unit. Second, the added significance of losing a female worker was not limited to her usefulness in family farming, but also extended to the domestic sphere of the household, for females carried out an important part of the household duties. The main source, though, of differentiation did not stem from economic factors but from cultural ones, as females were invariably impeded by stricter social and family control than their male counterparts. This is gleaned through the abstract from Naphsika and Adam's interview, a couple in their mid-40s who grew up in Protopi:

Naphsika: My mum finished [primary] school, my dad only went up to grade four [10 years old]. My mum wanted to carry on and become a teacher, but her mum didn't let her. It was difficult then.

Adam: Especially for women.

N: Yeah, you had to go to the city to attend school, but there were no busses and it was very hard. The teachers were telling her [Naphsika's grandmother]: "Let her study, she's good."

A: Women were restricted; it was very hard for them. We were very uneducated folk: "What will the neighbors say?" They were worried about their girls. It was a closed [mentality]. Whereas for the boys it was different, they could go [to secondary school].

N: There was no transportation like today. There was this thing between the city and the village. Although my grandma was a progressive person, I think she was heavily influenced by the majority [of her peers] on this.

Social values are more than a set of beliefs that carry symbolic significance. In the social context of Protopi, they were mechanisms of control, regulation, validation, or condemnation of what was perceived as consistent with or against the social norms of the area. In the days before commodity consumption turned members of the community into individuals who expressed their subjectivity through lifestyle choices and differential consumption, it was the collectively organized community that set the boundaries of individual expression. With the domination of capitalism as the mode of production, this subjectivity was now positively valorized by the spending capacity of the subject-consumer. The regulation of social relations included various forms of individual expression that would totally clash with today's definition of personal liberties and individual expression. Moreover, some of the issues raised by the participants, such as the formation of personal relationships, mating, and premarital sexual relationships, in the past fell quite naturally under the rubric of "the social protection of the girl" and was encroached on by the social obligations of the community. What is cherished in the present day as "individual liberty" has found an expression through some form of "human rights," which quite often plays the role of the institutionalization of formerly communally adjudicated issues. However, in the days of the pre-institutionalization of rights, such as the right to education, many females were denied this opportunity merely as a result of their gender:

> Well, women in the past were not meant to leave their home and go to study elsewhere, because their parents feared that a man could turn up and deceive them and they'd stop being good girls. That's why they didn't let the girls get educated. There were many girls who wanted to carry on in school but they were not supported [by their families].

Out of all the female respondents in the oldest generation, there was only one who had attended any form of postprimary education. This was Acantha, 69 years, who took pride in having attended a boarding training school. Although admission was not dependent on performance in primary school (nor on parents' financial capacity), it was still considered very prestigious for a female of this generation to carry on after primary school. The curriculum of the single-sex training school that Acantha attended included subjects that aimed to prepare young women for their role as housewives. Therefore, postprimary education for females in this age-group was strictly aimed at reproducing the existing social and economic relations:

> When I was at [primary] school I was not a very good student. I didn't even know how to do basic maths! In the training school, though, we took all sorts of courses, so when I came back here, after the training school, I knew lots of stuff, like how to do my cleaning, cooking and all sorts of other stuff that I then passed on to the girls here.

8.6.2 Roma

The Roma of the first generation were no exception to the lack of investment in females' education. Families saw it as a blessing to own land and livestock. by contrast, sending their children to school was perceived as a bad choice for all the reasons explained above in relation to non-Roma women, not least because it diminished the productive capacity of the household unit. Furthermore, Roma families were equally preoccupied with the maintenance of their daughters' moral standards and refused to send them to study in the big cities. Calliope, 68 years, elucidates this through her personal experience:

> In these days parents didn't send their children to school. Just primary school and that was enough. I wanted to go [to school] and I did go for a while but we couldn't escape from all the family work. We had cows, animals and we couldn't leave them behind [to go to school]. I also had to help at home [with housework].

Roxanne, 80 years, was not an atypical case with respect to poor school attendance due to lack of resources. Roma females assisted significantly in the household division of labor but it might have been the case that they were recruited from an earlier age than the non-Roma females on the family farm:

> *Q*: Did you go to school?
> *Roxanne*: I went for the same duration as my husband, up to fifth grade [11 years old].
> *Q*: Why did you stop?
> *R*: Out of necessity. My mum was taking me when I was 11 years old to go and dig [the crops] and the locals used to tell her: "Where are you taking her? She's too young," but others used to give up school too.
> *Q*: Who would go to secondary school?
> *R*: There were only a few who did; mainly those who had the money.

8.7 Middle Generation

8.7.1 Non-Roma

As already pointed out with regard to men's education, many women benefited from the postwar educational reforms and some important barriers to their postprimary education were removed. The year 1964 appears to have entered into popular parlance as a milestone in the provision of education to the country and Protopi. The reform that was implemented is believed to have had a wide-ranging impact on children's educational participation and attendance. Indeed, in Protopi, this coincided with the establishment of the secondary school, which had multiple positive effects: It facilitated the transition from primary to secondary school, it allowed girls to participate in greater numbers, it limited the educational dependence of this small town on the main city, and it also triggered the creation of many new jobs. Despite this development, which radically improved access to secondary school, it does not suffice to suggest that all other barriers were removed at a stroke. Females still had to overcome the restrictive mentality of the family (the nuclear or often the extended), as Naphsika, 46 years, explains:

> Even in the '80s many women didn't go to university; they stopped at primary school because their parents believed that a woman's future was to get married, to have a family.
> It was ok for a girl to get married as soon as she entered adulthood, say when she was 14 years old. Even in my years they used to say: "you don't need to go to uni." My mother was a special case because she was obsessed with sending me to university, but anyone else would have stopped me.

The experiences of women regarding their participation in higher education were distinct compared to those of men in the same generation. Aglaia's father was a manual worker who emigrated to Athens in order to take advantage of the emerging occupational opportunities there in the early 1950s. Her mother also found a job in a factory but she had to raise three children, which eventually forced her to leave paid labor for unpaid labor in the household. Even though Aglaia was the oldest of three children, her family did not have any aspirations for her to go to secondary school, let alone to university. This was an ambition reserved for their only son, an attitude not uncommon among many families in Protopi. Aglaia, 50 years, described the task of persuading her family that education was a worthier pathway than marriage as a "struggle" (more in chapter 9). Eventually, while she was employed part time to contribute to the family income, she pursued further education by attending college. Her first job was related to her degree though she did not hold it for long, as child-care responsibilities forced her out of the labor market. In the following extract, she reflects on the general situation for women of school age and the factors determining access to secondary school:

> Up until the time I went to high school [mid-1960s] it was difficult for girls to go to school. I don't think that there were any educated girls younger than me; maybe two or three who went to private schools. For children here [in Protopi] things were more difficult because there was not even a bus to go to the city. Some boys were allowed to stay in the city in order to attend school but girls weren't allowed. Things changed after 1964.

8.7.2 Roma

Roma women in the middle generation were still heavily involved in housework and family farming. Although some of their non-Roma counterparts (especially those who completed primary school after 1964) started entering secondary education, for Roma women, this was still out of reach. Philippa, 60 years, descends from a large Roma family. Her educational prospects were strongly influenced by her involvement in the family division of labor, while her aspirations were shaped by the availability of alternative pathways and her internal motivation:

> *Philippa*: I didn't have the experience and the qualifications to get a different job. I didn't study properly, so I stayed all my life in agriculture. I liked this job, the farming stuff. My brother wanted to study...he was crying: "I wanna go to secondary school" because my dad didn't have the money [to support him]; poverty was massive in these days. But I was getting a kick out of going to the crops. I liked it and I still like it.
>
> *Q*: Were your parents expecting you to do any specific job?
>
> *P*: My mum's expectation from me was to learn sewing, which I did. I took lessons and I learnt how to work the sewing machine. That's what my mum used to tell me and my sister since I was little: "I want you [girls] to become experts in housework."

Technical training for the future role that a female would occupy in the household was sought as the most relevant form of education a girl could receive at that time. For many Roma families, this might have been more pronounced a practice since a Roma woman first had to prove that she was worthy of getting married and having her own family (see discussion in chapter 9), and then of being able to secure a place in the labor market. As discussed above, school attainment of Roma pupils was influenced by practices such as bullying, stereotyping, and negative discrimination. No school mechanisms or government policies were in place to tackle these phenomena, and the inferior treatment of the Roma was not contested by the school or educational authorities. For a Roma woman, it was an enormous achievement to enter secondary school because she had to overcome factors that were outlined above, such as lack of financial means and parental mentality, and also widespread discrimination and stereotyping at school:

> This negative attitude [towards the Roma] and the overt discrimination against them was a massive thing in the past. It's only now has kind of drifted away, but the older folks can't get over it. It probably started shifting when they [the non-Roma] started going to school with the kids of Yiftoi. Once they started going to school together, they'd even go to university and even hang out together. But back in the old days, this was unheard of.

8.8 Younger Generation

8.8.1 Non-Roma

For respondents in the younger generation, the emphasis shifted from secondary to tertiary education. By and large access to and participation in secondary school eased after the mid-1960s and females were increasingly enrolling in secondary schools. From 1974, nine-year education was finally made compulsory, further enhancing access and participation. In most accounts of the respondents in the younger age-group, when asked about their educational level, they typically said "I have gone to school," which means lower-secondary school. The comparison with respondents in the old generation is palpable: When they used the same phrase, they meant primary school. Within less than two decades, the change was dramatic. Venus, 39 years, contrary to her own aspirations, did not progress into university because the secondary school she attended failed her. At the time of the interview, she had just started a manual, semiskilled job. In the following extract, she talks about her difficulties in finding employment and shares her thoughts about participation in education for people in her generation:

> For my peers it was easy to complete [secondary] school and even to go to university. Most of them carried on [in education]. I could have gone to university myself. I didn't go to frontistirio [evening, supporting classes] but...they [my peers] probably came from more affluent families, who paid for frontistirio and encouraged them to carry on. But nowadays women do go to university, because they want it for themselves and because they assist [financially] in the household. There's no other option.

Undoubtedly, females in the younger generation benefited from the transformations discussed thus far. Sappho, 44 years, a nursery nurse, is a characteristic example:

> *Sappho*: Women didn't study in the past. It was very hard.
> *Q*: Is it like this now or have things changed?
> *S*: Things have changed, because there was a general progress. Technology has assisted a lot too; like with the advent of television and all that stuff. They've made people change a lot.
> *Q*: Positively, in your opinion?
> *S*: Oh yes, definitely! Everything has changed for the better, in all aspects. We've made progress in all fronts. Woman's position has improved a lot. She's more involved in education and more active in the labor market. It started changing about 15 years ago. But now it's even easier for girls to go to school.
> *Q*: Do you think there is still a difference between girls and boys?
> *S*: No, not at all. It's as easy. A girl can study like a boy can. There's no difference any longer.

One is not surprised by the developments discussed by Sappho nor by their impact on the lives of ordinary people in Protopi. Rather, what is astounding is that greater access to schools and the advent of technology are considered as forces of similar value and significance in the lives of respondents. In other words, we are confronted with a cultural revolution, which ushered many new forces into what had been, up to this point, the simple lives of people living within an agrarian community.

The transition to mass education required not only serious government investment, but also the transformation of the mentality of the people in Protopi. At the same time, cultural processes were in motion that could offer an impetus toward this transition. This cultural transition conveniently mediated the passage from long-standing, traditional cultural values into modern ones, and it coincided with the creation of the new social formation. The expanded middle class, and the intermediate class found themselves with increased spending power and needed information about both new commodities and the reconfiguration of the value systems that underpinned the cultural revolution. While the former was largely facilitated by the advent of television as the main transmitter of the new cultural values, the latter was achieved through education. In other words, a new hegemony was being created that would bring the middle classes of Protopi closer to those in the rest of Greece and the international middle classes more broadly. This allowed and reinforced the transition of attitudes vis-à-vis education from a scarce resource—a luxury of the elites—to a sought-after necessity or even commodity.

8.8.2 Roma

A new educational environment and labor-market exigencies have led to an increase in participation of young Roma women in school. Moreover, it is not rare for females in the third generation, especially the younger ones, to enter university thanks to policies such as university expansion. Furthermore, the changing mentality about women's education is also evident in many Roma families. This is not to say that educational opportunities have been totally equalized for Roma females relative to their non-Roma peers. Rather, the complete lack of education for female Roma is quite rare. In addition, highly educated individuals are much more common than in the past. The major problem is that after the credential inflation attested to from the 1990s onward, educational qualifications are now being increasingly devalued, as discussed in relation to men. The association with the labor market is evidently weakening as the absorption capacity of sectors traditionally open to a qualified workforce, such as in public administration, is correspondingly decreasing. In the following extract, Hercules talks about his daughter's education and attendant career prospects:

> Unemployment is high for university graduates. My daughter is now taking a post-graduate diploma course, while my son works with me [as a painter and

decorator]. I've been taking him to work with me since he was little. He saw with his own eyes that unemployment is high for graduates and so he stayed with me...I was not expecting my children to do any specific job. I was only expecting the state to find them a job since they studied. But they are unemployed. I don't know what jobs I wouldn't want [my children] to do because my daughter is unemployed. She's got five certificates and she's unemployed; she often wonders, "why did I have to spend all these years in education?"

The same feeling was expressed by Heliad, Hercules's daughter. After graduating from university, she took up various part-time jobs, largely unrelated to her main degree. Postgraduate education did little to improve her employability. After three years in Protopi, she left for Athens where she attended further professional training and found a part-time job. When I last met her, she was 31 years old, with a new job as a routine nonmanual operator, which was full time and more fulfilling than her previous ones:

> It took me a long time to find this job. I'm satisfied because it's something that pays the bills and I'm doing things that are not that ridiculously irrelevant to my background! In my previous job I did all sorts of meaningless little things which I was never interested in.

Apart from the radical transformations in the labor market and the weakening association between educational credentials and employment, there are also other changes relevant to the schooling experiences of this age-group. For instance, discrimination against Roma pupils and bullying, which were widespread practices in the older and the middle generations, are not as prominent. There are many reasons for this positive change. Some of them are external, such as labor-market forces that impose rules according to the efficiency and productivity of workforce regardless of the ethnic origin. Other reasons are internal to education, such as improvement in the educational level of all the residents, and might have led to the combating of prejudices and stereotypes against the Roma. In addition to these reasons, we must briefly consider the advent of Albanian economic immigrants. Since the early 1990s, a large number of ethnic Albanians have immigrated to Greece (for more, see chapter 9) in search of employment and better living conditions. This has triggered significant demographic changes in most parts of Greece and has had a considerable effect on the ethnic composition of the student population in most schools (cf. Nikolaou, 2000). In Protopi, the number of Albanian students has also increased throughout the 1990s and the 2000s. In turn, it is possible that this has led to a shift in attention both at social and educational levels. That is to say, a new pattern has emerged, that is to say from scapegoating the Roma to scapegoating the Albanian pupils. Although the extent of this practice and the effects on school attainment and performance are yet to be explored, in the following extract, I quote a respondent's perception of how patterns of discrimination might have changed:

> *Phokion*: The differences between Yiftoi and non-Yiftoi have been diminishing. It used to be obvious everywhere, from education to anywhere else. But I think something similar is happening today between Greek kids and kids from other countries. I experience it every day at school [as a teacher] and every time I see it, my mind goes back to these days, I recall this picture from the old days. You can see it among children today. They call each other names like "you bloody Albanian," but I think children today will have to get disentangled from these traps since we live in multicultural society.
> *Q*: But where do you think these differences stem from?
> *P*: Well, class differences, economic differences, it matters what class you belong to. Because there are many locals who grabbed the opportunities and made it, really made very good progress.

Phokion's explanation about the origins of the stereotyping of and discrimination against Albanian and Roma pupils is disarming. Class and economic differences are, according to him, the true reasons behind this practice. Phokion was not alone in supporting this argument. In various informal discussions I had with Roma and non-Roma people in Protopi, the same view was expressed, often with resentment or even bitterness. Many respondents from both middle-class and working-class origins concurred that material differentiation had led to various types of hierarchical stratification, an issue I shall return to in the final chapter.

8.9 Summary

As I discussed in chapter 2, education was to become the "savior" of the meritocratic ideal that would prevail in postwar liberal democracies in Europe. In Greece, it was not only increased rates of participation and attendance that improved radically after the war, but also the expectation of individuals and families that this was the most expedient way to a better future, both occupationally and socially. In Protopi, the legitimization of structural inequalities in the name of universal and free access to education was remarkably pronounced for the best part of the postwar period. Evidence showed that education in Protopi indeed played a crucial role in promoting people's occupational and class positions and improving their life chances. Undoubtedly, it was one of the major forces of inter- and intragenerational social mobility. However, the function of education appears to be complex and far from enduring. The benefits conferred to many individuals in the older generation are not matched by similar ones in the younger generation. Moreover, other groups, such as women and the Roma, have secured higher rates of participation in education than in the past, but this did not correspond to better access to labor-market positions. In this chapter, I have implied that the explanation for this fluctuation in the relative significance of educational qualifications in respondents' lives might lie with the changing labor market and the new economic orthodoxy (Europeanization of the Greek economy, global pressures, and so on). In the following chapter, I shall consider alternative social mobility pathways (such as marriage and migration) and aspects of social, cultural, and political organization (such as patronage) that will enhance our understanding of the role of education and the concomitant mobility pathways of respondents in Protopi.

Chapter 9

Alternative Pathways to Social Mobility: The Role of Migration, Marriage, and Political Patronage

9.1 Introduction

Thus far, I have examined the occupational experiences of respondents and attendant mobility issues through the prism of two major institutions, namely labor market and education. For a more balanced consideration of the issues at hand, it is necessary to enrich my presentation with alternative pathways of social mobility and forces, arrangements, and mechanisms beyond the ones already discussed. In chapter 9, therefore, I will present some of the most important of these factors, namely emigration, marriage, and the role of patronage and clientelistic relations.

The first of these alternative pathways, emigration, expands the discussion about socioeconomic restructuring that was opened in chapter 7. By the same token, marriage is not reduced to a discussion about family and social reproduction, but is treated as a significant dimension in the socioeconomic organization and relations of production in Protopi. Finally, the exploration of patronage and clientelism are of significance to all mobility processes presented thus far, as they permeate social, political, economic, cultural, and other arrangements and explain differential access to social mobility pathways and outcomes.

9.2 Emigration

In the transition period from subsistence agriculture and petty commodity production to the dominance of free-market capitalism, that is, from the late 1950s to the 1970s, one of the main sources of occupational opportunities in Protopi and Greece was emigration (see section 3.4). Among the benefits of emigration were the diminishing population pressures on limited productive resources, the improvement of labor skills after repatriation, and the reduction in unemployment (Kavouriaris, 1974). Notwithstanding the decisive function of emigration as a "safety valve" in respect of employment demand, it is another dimension on which I shall focus in the next section. This involves the significance of remittances in the transformation of the political economy of Protopi and the general development of the area. For apart from the cumulative advantages gained when capital (in the form of remittances) flowed into this undeveloped area, its convertible capacity triggered changes in the relations of production, the division of labor, and social relations of production. Remittances, which in the case of Greece outnumbered in size other types of invisible receipts, namely of tourism and transportation[1] (Jouganatos, 1992). galvanized the local economy and allowed for a whole range of new occupations to be added into the thus-far simple division of labor.

9.2.1 Non-Roma

Only six respondents had no history of migration, domestic or abroad, in their family. One in four respondents had spent themselves some part of their life as economic emigrants abroad. Germany was the most frequent destination followed by Sweden and Belgium. In these countries, the emigrants either joined a family member (usually females joined their husbands and children their parents) or sought employment upon receipt of invitation, for example, as guest workers, "gastarbeiters." Only one respondent (in the younger generation) emigrated for postgraduate studies, but he also took employment abroad for some time after graduation. Seven respondents emigrated to a different part of Greece, usually Athens, in search of better career opportunities, while another four emigrated both abroad and to Athens (with internal emigration usually following repatriation). Some of these patterns are echoed in the emigration experiences of a couple in the middle age-group, Adam, Naphsika, as well as their parents:

> *Adam*: My parents were farmers. They were forced to emigrate, because there were no jobs here; there was severe poverty. My father left for Germany for the first time in 1962. Lots of people, especially from our area, left at that time because there were no jobs. So my father came back after five years, stayed here for two years and then took my mum with him [to Germany]. They both worked in factories. After seven-eight months my sister and I followed them...
> *Q*: How about your parents [asking Naphsika]?
> *Naphsika*: Well, my dad worked for 40 years in animal husbandry. When he was young he had gone to Germany, I think for two years, but he came back. Everyone was emigrating then.

It is clear from this account that many families were willing to emigrate rather than endure the hardships associated with farming. However, emigration was not an easy alternative as it involved substantial and long-term sacrifices and no secure financial returns. Initially, migration abroad was restricted to males, given that employment regulations for foreign workforce imposed strict rules on family emigration. Although this involved the separation of the family, people were so determined to escape farming and eager to open up alternative occupational pathways that they saw in emigration a unique opportunity of exiting poverty. In addition, there were families that had sold their land early on and were wage laborers. For them, emigration was not only a more appealing option but probably the only alternative to an improved occupational future. This was the case of Vryon and his parents who were among very few families that were not peasants. This meant, though, that they had to search for alternative pathways and different opportunities than the majority of the population, such as emigration:

> My parents were emigrants. My dad, soon after he finished primary school became a [daily] waged worker, a builder, because his family were not peasants like everyone else here. He worked anywhere he could. Then, after he did his military service, he went to Germany; he stayed there for a couple of years but he didn't like it and went to Belgium, where he stayed for about 15 years working in the coalmines. There, he met my mum and together they saved up some money. My mother only worked for a few years there because she had three children to look after. But my dad couldn't cope with his job and they returned to Greece. Initially, they opened a small brick-making plant, which they only kept a few years. Then, they started working as wage workers in factories, marble mines etc.

In Vryon's account, it is manifest that emigration was the only available career outlet for some individuals, especially with no or little agricultural holdings. At that time, that is in the late 1970s, the Greek economic recovery was gaining momentum while that of the industrially advanced European countries, such as Germany, was well underway. This meant that demand for unskilled and semiskilled labor in European industrial centers was high. The jobs these emigrants did were physically demanding and required long working hours. Despite this, many migrants were satisfied that they could secure a stable income and the advantages of the welfare system, such as health care, social benefits, and pensions, which were unknown to Greek farmers. In other words, the core elements of Western-style liberal democracy were perceived by the materially deprived members of the European periphery as panacea.

Apart from the positive effects that emigration had on the emigrants and their families, it also had multiple benefits on Protopi and the wider area. Theo, 68 years, worked throughout his lifetime in house construction. His parents were farmers, which made him explore alternative pathways from early on. Thus, he started off his occupational career as an apprentice-carpenter, but he soon got employed in a factory, as an unskilled shop-floor worker. Subsequently, he moved into a different manual, unskilled job in a small local firm that was producing and selling raw materials for house construction. This was the time when Theo realized that house construction was rapidly growing and foresaw that the first ones to switch into the sector would have a bright occupational future. In the extract below, he talks about aspects of labor-market restructuring which are evidently linked to wider themes, such as emigration. The role of remittances is also emphasized as it allowed those who emigrated to send money back home. In an area tied into a mode of production based on agriculture, this was the catalyst in its hitherto slowly developing economy:

> *Q:* When did the locals start having new jobs?
> *Theo:* In house construction after '65, when they started leaving for Germany. They were providing us with work but they were also building their own houses. We were trying to build up this area because there was nothing; only some very old houses. After that point there were more new houses, that's why I'm telling you we started making progress. But let's not fool ourselves: if it was not for those who left for Germany, we wouldn't have made these houses. While I was employed in house construction I was making good money, but I was also making somebody else's house.

The contribution of remittances was often regarded as the decisive component in the socioeconomic development of Protopi. As a participant put it, it was viewed as a "God-sent gift." Together with other factors linked to the development of Protopi, such as the changing occupational structure (chapter 7) and the expansion of the public sector (chapter 8), emigration and remittance-derived capital boosted the development of the community and instilled a much-needed dynamism to its economy. This dynamism was evident, especially after the late 1960s, when capital from remittances was progressively being invested on productive activities:

> Phokion: After the 1960s, the area started being industrialized. This is when the mechanization of production occurred; I'm talking about agricultural production. This is also when house construction started thriving. At some point, I don't remember when exactly but probably in the 1960s or 1970s, the proportion of house permissions [for Protopi] issued by the authorities was one of the highest in Greece! This was the time when capitalism arrived here. And, of course, the time when many locals emigrated abroad, because we needed the money they sent us. This money was used in all sorts of ways here; in agriculture, in building new houses etc.

9.2.2 Roma

While for most of the locals in the dominant group emigration was an opportunity to exit peasantry and improve their life standards, for the Roma, it was also an outlet for escaping discrimination in the labor market and,

ALTERNATIVE PATHWAYS TO SOCIAL MOBILITY 181

more broadly, in society. This was the case with regard to Euriklea's father who emigrated to Germany. Through remittances he sent to his family, they achieved substantial progress and thrived economically. Of course, this success was achieved also because of the hard work of the members of the family who stayed behind. In her interview, Euriklea emphasized her father's contribution in the success of the household as much as her mother's skills in managing their finances and investing carefully and strategically. Euriklea, 53 years, was evidently proud of this success and felt that her family achieved more in relation to others in Protopi:

> *Euriklea*: My dad left for Germany for a better future. He was a builder, but he was getting paid twice as much as someone [in the same job] here. He was sending us good money but we also had to work hard here in order to make something good, to "lift ourselves up." That's how we started up and managed to make the house, which was a big deal back then. That's how we "made it."
>
> *Q*: How many years did your dad stay in Germany?
>
> *E*: All in all 10 years. He was sending us money and we turned it into a house but my mum bought some land, saved up and took care of the money extremely skillfully. Were it not for her, we wouldn't have achieved this success. We were really well off these days. There was only a handful of families who had a new house and we were one of them: it was great! We counted the money with mum and put it in bundles and stacks because there was lots of it.

The impact of emigration is discernible in Euriklea's account. In order to understand its extent, especially in relation to the Roma people in Protopi, we only need to compare the occupational pathways of Roma residents who did not emigrate, such as Euriklea's husband, Theophilos, to the ones who did, such as Euriklea's father. Theophilos descended from a local Roma family, who were poor family landworkers. His family's situation could be improved through career advancement in the labor market or education. However, the former was not entirely open to the Roma people (chapter 7), while the latter was similarly not easily accessible (chapter 8). In other words, the only pathway available for occupational progress and upward social mobility was emigration, which, though, Theophilos's family did not pursue. As a result, after Euriklea married him, her socioeconomic position deteriorated substantially. Their sole source of income was Theophilos's job, which was never secure enough. Theophilos was the only respondent in the older age-group who was unemployed at the time of the interview and was demonstrably nervous about his own occupational situation.

Although emigration was a sought-after alternative to occupational mobility for some Roma in the middle age-group, the situation had changed regarding the younger generation. The immediate postwar economic growth was brought to a halt in the early 1970s due to the economic crisis.

The traditional hosting countries of Greek emigration, such as Germany, could not absorb any more workforce. Some of the participants tried to follow their parents' and relatives' footsteps but they confronted a different reality. Employment opportunities were limited in comparison to the recent past. As a consequence, emigration had lost its centrality as one of the main alternative pathways to social mobility, especially for those for whom the other two outlets—namely the local labor market and education—never materialized.

Pericles was one of those people in the younger age-group who were in an ambivalent position. As we saw in section 7.4.2. Pericles's occupational history involved two emigration attempts to Germany, which were both unsuccessful:

> Pericles: Things were not going well in Greece in terms of work and in particular in my job as an electrician. So I decided to go abroad to try my luck. I decided to go again to Germany because things seemed to be better over there but I soon found out that that this was not the case. Things had toughened up there too; factories were closing down, such as the ones I had worked in in the past. So after a couple of years I decided to take my family and come back here again.

Pericles's account exemplifies the changing impact of emigration on people's life chances and the adjusted strategies of individuals in response to this development. In particular, the erstwhile "pull" factors, such as job availability, secure income, and employment benefits, in the traditionally hosting European countries started losing their prominence. At the same time, the "push" factors, such as the poor living conditions in Greece, had also improved substantially. Given the complexity of these issues, I shall discuss them further in the next section.

9.2.3 Repatriation and Immigration

The economic progress of Protopi as well as its social and wider development that were achieved throughout the first postwar decades were largely based on emigration, which triggered transformations in the occupational structure and the labor market. The main emigration wave from Protopi occurred in the 1960s. In the 1970s, emigration had abated. At the same time, many of the first wave of emigrants started repatriating although net emigration was still at high levels. This pattern only started reversing in the 1980s, which is a period that saw Greece advancing in many aspects. It became a full member of the EU, the average standard of living increased, democracy was well consolidated, and political tensions dwindled down. These factors made Greece more appealing to indigenous and also to foreign workforce. This coincided with the collapse of the totalitarian regime in Albania in 1992, which spread disorder and drove large numbers of Albanian immigrants to Greece. The advent of Albanian immigrants lasted throughout the 1990s and the 2000s and had a considerable impact on the Greek society and economy. This period coincided with rapid socioeconomic transformations in Greece, such as increasing competition in the labor market, rising unemployment, and deceleration of economic growth. The continuous expansion of the service sector and the pursuit of white-collar, education-based occupations had left a plethora of manual jobs unfilled. These occupations were now marginal to the native labor force and were being taken by Albanian immigrants, who often worked under very poor conditions and at a lower pay rate than their Greek counterparts (Naxakis, 2001). This created in many cases resentment and even hostility from the Greek society to these workers who were often considered responsible for the rising unemployment (Amitsis and Lazaredi, 2001) and the sluggish growth of the Greek economy. Cleanthes reflects on the situation in relation to his job in the house construction:

> Cleanthes: I knew my job well and, thank God, I managed to support my family and lead a comfortable life. Nowadays, though, we're competing hard with the Albanians. I had employed a whole [Albanian] family for eight-nine years. As soon as they learnt the job they decided to leave and set up their own business. In order for them to get by they had to knock down the prices. We have to compete. The same happened with another group of Albanians who also left me, in a good way, we didn't fall out. I still help them out when I can, sending them work and stuff. You see, you have to [act in this way]. For the time being there's work [for me], but you never know what's gonna happen in the future. It's sad to say that the [Greek] youth don't fancy going to work. I wanted to employ a local, somebody from here but I couldn't find anyone. That's why the Albanians are taking all the jobs like mine: they [the Albanians] will soon hire our own children. They'll become bosses and our children their employees!

The transformations in the labor market of Protopi are further attested to by the types of jobs the locals abandoned. This alone created a new situation in the labor market, whereby the undesired occupations were left for the Albanian immigrants while some new ones have been added to the division of labor, thanks to the skills the "newcomers" brought with them. It is not hard, though, to find signs of rising xenophobia or, in the local context, "Albanophobia." The recent labor-market restructuring and the dominance of the neoliberal economic spirit, which supports flexibility at the cost of employment security, has resulted in relentless competition, especially in types of employment with high insecurity. Diomedes discusses this aspect further:

> Diomedes: In the past they used to make fun of somebody who was a builder. Nowadays, the Albanians have taken over. I believe that in 20 years time the Albanians will be ruling us. As I told you, some kids don't have skills and abilities, so when they'll be in need of a job, they'll just do anything, but the boss willb eA lbanian.

Invidious comparisons between the local workforce and immigrant laborers were quite common among skilled and semiskilled workers in a way that resembled comparisons that used to be drawn in the past between the Roma and the non-Roma. In contemporary Protopi, there is a widespread sense that the "moral panic" surrounding the Roma has now taken a new form. The Albanians seem to have replaced the Roma as the scapegoats to the collective consciousness of both the Roma and the dominant group, as demonstrated by Hermes's account:

> *Hermes*: Yiftoi could only get jobs that Albanians do nowadays.
> *Q*: What kind of jobs?
> *V*: [Unskilled] workers. The employers did not trust them to do other jobs, like crafts and skilled ones.
> *Q*: What period are you referring to?
> *H*: Before 1970. They [non-Roma employers] didn't train Yiftoi in skilled jobs perhaps because they were afraid they could make it, they could start moving up. Now the same is happening with the Albanians.

9.3 Marriage and Spouse-sponsored Mobility

As I argued in chapter 8, a woman's career was associated with and often dependent on others. Before marriage, women were essentially linked to their parents' employment and they were a basic component in the familial division of labor, while after marriage, their occupational career was tied to that of their husbands. In this section, I shall approach women's pathways from a different perspective, that of marriage. Marriage in Protopi cut across social relations and arrangements. Its importance spanned over social, personal, familial, economic, and other spheres. Apart from securing the reproduction of the family, which was vital at the time of ubiquitous poverty and child labor, marriage also acted as a mechanism of social "exchange," a leverage for economic transactions. As marriages were predominantly arranged by the parents (though rarely forced, especially after the 1940s), certain partnerships were allowed to develop while others could never materialize.

9.3.1 Non-Roma

From the woman's perspective, the guarantee for a good marital match was her dowry. The dowry invariably consisted of fabrics, linen, duvets, pillows, and other household essentials, but it could also include livestock, golden coins, and money. The dowry had many functions in the social universe of rural areas such as Protopi for the biggest part of the twentieth century. It carried symbolic as well as practical value. It was symbolic in the sense that it validated the bride-to-be's worth as a good housewife who was aware of the needs of the household. Moreover, having sizable dowry was a proof that the family was serious about their daughter's marriage, as preparation had started long before the wedding arrangements. The practical value of the dowry consisted in the practical utility of the items it included as well as the material value of some of the items. Livestock, for instance, was a valuable asset in the new household's planning and production capacity, while money could prove essential in meeting the first needs of the couple.

For the groom, a good dowry comprised of his skills and attitude, which was demonstrated by his love and commitment toward work, and his personal and familial reputation in the labor market and in the community. His pride was his "clean face," as the respondents said, that is to say the appreciation and high esteem the community granted him. It was the groom's side that needed reassurance that the bride possessed sufficient dowry. In case this expectation was not met, the "deal" could be cancelled. In the following account, Aglaia, 50 years, talks about the social and personal importance of dowry and the relevance of marriage in improving a woman's socioeconomic situation:

> *Aglaia*: From a very young age, probably from primary school, they [the females] started to prepare their dowry, like blankets, coverlets, bedspreads, embroidered stuff and all sorts of similar things. The girl with the biggest collection could get the best match. It was a privilege to have a good dowry.
> *Q*: Did they use to get husbands from within the area?
> *A*: Well, mainly from here but also from other places. Preferably from the main city because it was considered as a good fortune; [by leaving Protopi] a woman could have a better future and an easier life away from peasantry.

These economic considerations had a crucial role to play in marital arrangements. Differential strategies, choices, and expectations according to the family's socioeconomic standing were intrinsic to the organization and operation of the "marital market." Moreover, the location in the internal social stratification (see chapter 7) between landowners and landworkers was a strong determinant of spouse selection. In this way, the criteria for marital partner selection were threaded into the socioeconomic fabric of Protopi and positive "assortative mating"[2] (Becker, 1973) practices developed based on socioeconomic criteria.

Families anticipated that, with a good match, their children could secure a better future. Upon marriage, women usually lived with the groom's family, while men, and especially the older son, either stayed in the parental house or somewhere nearby. It could be argued that until the opening of the labor market and the emergence of the new occupational opportunities after the 1950s, marriage, along with emigration, were the key alternative routes to one's intragenerational mobility, as Plato elucidates:

> *Plato*: Girls didn't do any craft-based jobs [in the 1950s and 1960s]. At best they went for dressmaking, hairdressing and farming. Nothing else... and, er, marriage.
> *Q*: How was this done?

P: They were fixed. It was a bit tough then. There were only a few girls that were in love [with a man]. Say, out of 50 girls only four-five had selected their partners themselves. For all the rest, it [their marriage] was arranged.
Q: With a man from Protopi?
P: Of course, but also with someone out of here. If somebody attended a social gathering, a relative could say: "I've got you a match. She's a good girl." That's how the deal was done.
Q: And were there any preferences in case the match was from within Protopi?
P: Oh yes! There was this "exception," like: "why shall I give my daughter to a pauper? He's a good bloke but he's got too many siblings. My girl will be in trouble." The parents looked at things like jobs, land etc: "He's loaded. I'll send her there and if she works a bit she can make her own living." Whereas if someone didn't have any land, livestock, money etc it was not worthwhile.

Marriage was an alternative route to social mobility, as its outcome could seal the fate of the families involved: the groom's, the bride's, and the young couple's. With a careful selection arranged for their offspring, the latter could secure all that their parents lacked in the older generation: stable occupation, limited uncertainty, and possibly, also financial support from their parents. Therefore, the criteria for marital partner choice were mostly economic, but great value was also attached to the "ranking," the social status of the family in the microcosm of Protopi. That is to say, the selection criteria were both material and symbolic. In this way, the emergent social-class structure was shaped not only by arrangements in the labor market but also by important social arrangements, such as marriage. According to Milena, this could take the form of a direct discrimination against poorer families:

Milena: If, say, I had more money than you, more land or more livestock, then I wouldn't let my child get "demoted." Do you get me? I wouldn't let my child marry yours because for me this would be a disaster.
Q: What kind of disaster?
M: Well, multiple. It meant that my child would enter a lower category, a lower family. Why should I let my offspring have a hard life?

Invariably, in order to preclude the possibility of "marrying to a lower family," strategies of negative preferences and "mechanisms of avoidance" were developed, which equalled negative discrimination, as Hermes put it:

Q: Were there any preferences in terms of marital selection?
Hermes: Of course! People used to discriminate against some families or to prefer others. In the old times, money and property mattered a lot. For example, they would say: "X is poor; forget it. I'll go to Y who's better off." Issues such as personality matching were ignored. It was all about who's got more than the other and these kinds of things.

Spouse selection was also dictated by a differential "bargaining power" between the families of the bride and groom:

> *Q:* Did one side have more power over marital selection?
> *A:* Slightly the groom's side. The bride's side would try to find a good match for their daughter. That is, they wanted the groom to have some money, not to be completely poor, whereas the groom's side didn't care; he didn't mind getting married to a woman from a different background because he could work hard. The man could get married to a woman from any kind of background. However, parents didn't send their daughters to any family. They were careful who they chose, so their daughter could end up in a better [economic] category or at least in the same as her parents.

It has to be underlined that the groom's family did not have complete control over the marital arrangements and spouse selection process. The bride's family also played its part. Hence, in many cases, a prospective groom was rejected because he was not from an economically sound family or from one with good reputation. Although practices regarding arranged marriages have been rapidly changing in the recent years, the proactive role of the families is still discernible. Theo's daughter got married in the late 1980s. In the following extract, he outlines the criteria for granting his permission for his daughter's marriage:

> Theo: Parents were still involved [in the 1980s]. I will give you an example. My daughter got married through arranged marriage. The groom was a teacher. I thought that, since he's a teacher, that's fine with me. And since he was happy to come and live here I said "fine." He's a teacher and he's from a nearby place "let's do it," I said. If he was not a teacher why should we be looking to get a groom from that place? But that's all changed nowadays.

9.3.2 Roma

Roma parents took their offspring's partner selection as seriously as the non-Roma. Nevertheless, marriage was as closely guarded by the dominant group as any other social mobility route examined thus far. For landless Roma people and generally the poorer among them, marriage was a highly sought-after strategy for escaping poverty and providing a better future for their children. Especially in families where emigration was never pursued, occupational advancement did not materialize, and educational success not realized, marriage was probably the only pathway to social advancement. For the Roma, this could be achieved through exogamy, that is, through marriage with a non-Roma (either from Protopi or elsewhere). This was accompanied with social-status advancement for the Roma family and accordingly with social denigration for the non-Roma spouse and his or her family. In the eyes of the dominant group in Protopi, out-group marriage to a Romani family was not only undesirable but could also provoke expulsion from the family (in some cases also from the area) and loss of any inheritance rights. At any rate, mixed marriages were very contentious and they had community-wide dimensions. The social significance of marriage in Protopi was evident from practices of maintenance of the group boundaries between Roma and the non-Roma families. Interestingly, more than half of the respondents raised the lack of intermarriage as an issue that used to divide the community in the past. Sophocles discusses the reasons behind this division through the perspective of the majority group:

> *Q:* Apart from preferences and discrimination against families that did not have good financial standing, were there any other forms of discrimination when it came to marriage?
> *Sophocles:* Oh yeah. They [the non-Roma] shouldn't get married to a Yifto or a Vlacho.³
> *Q:* How about in relation to the Yiftoi? Why did they not want them?
> *S:* Racism! Thanks to my job I've been into many people's houses and I've seen many Yiftoi. They [the Yiftoi] are straight, only a few of them aren't decent, as there are some of us [non-Roma]. Seriously, I've been inside their houses and they are very clean, there's no trace of dust or anything!

In more recent years, that is to say after the 1990s, an improvement in marriage selection practices and an apparent increase in intermarriages have been attested to by many respondents. Many of them claimed that the rigid reproduction of selection patterns that the previous generations were accustomed to was now being eroded. Despite this assertion, a number of participants supported the opposite view. In other words, despite the fact that some mixed marriages had indeed occurred in the recent social history of Protopi, the widespread stereotyping and discrimination against the Roma still existed. It is worthwhile noting that many respondents preferred to talk about the topic in an informal rather than in a prearranged interview setting, which might demonstrate how much it still remains of a controversial issue. Venus for one became manifestly agitated when recounting her personal experience, which comes from a mixed marriage; her husband is from Roma origin while she is not:

> Oh God, where do I start? I'll tell you about the discrimination I experienced through my own marriage. To begin with, it still exists and it's very strong. The non-Yiftoi keep Yiftoi at distance, they still treat them as inferior beings. Society is divided and discrimination is well and alive. I'm really worried about my kids. I keep on telling my daughter to keep an eye open, so she doesn't go through what I went through. My mum didn't want me to get married to my husband. Living like this is very hard. People used to tell me stuff about my husband-to-become before we got married: "he's like this and that, and don't trust him." People keep on telling me stuff and it's not nice to hear the same things all the time. I don't know why they are so bothered. We've got to take it off our minds but people won't do it.

This discriminatory attitude against the Roma was also visible to non-Roma participants who lived in mixed neighborhoods, as Gregory asserts:

> *Gregory*: It was obvious that there was discrimination. For instance, in personal relationships. Society didn't tolerate many things.
> *Q*: What was the form of this discrimination?
> *G*: Well, it was an honor for a Yifto if his son or daughter got married to a non-Yifto. It exists. Regardless if we say it or not, it's still there. Probably not to the same extent, differences have diminished but it's still there. That's how I feel it.
> *Q*: Why do you think this is so?
> *G*: Prejudices; we grew up like that. Childhood experiences: "you shouldn't hang out with them," stuff like that was passed down to the children, it became lived experience. I believe though it's not as bad among our children as it used to be in the past. Our children have not experienced this in the same degree as we have and I believe that the next generation will have fewer prejudices than ours.

Even though in many aspects of life, overt discrimination may have given way to covert and tacit ways of excluding and stereotyping the Roma, the issue of marriage selection appears to be one of the remaining bastions of boundary maintenance and non-mixing practices. Discriminatory strategies and discourses have indeed changed regarding intermarriage, but this is not sufficient to wipe out non-mixing strategies completely. By contrast, new patterns have emerged with the advent of new groups. As in the case of employment, education, and emigration, the Albanian immigrants have, to some extent, replaced the Roma insofar as marital preferences are concerned. This does not mean, however, that attitudes toward mixed marriages between non-Roma and Roma have changed radically. By contrast, it means that some of the old barriers to marital selection have not been completely removed, while some new ones have emerged. Euriklea discusses some of these changes with reference to the last 20–30 years. She draws on experiences from her son's marriage and from people in her neighborhood, who are in their vast majority also Roma:

> *Euriklea*: There used to be a lot of discrimination: "You don't match with him, he's white, or he's black.[4] The black man will get the black woman and the white man the white woman." A lot of discrimination.
> *Q*: Was this big back then?
> *E*: Absolutely! And it still exists now though the parents can't overrule their children. But it's still strong. And it will stay like this until we die, it doesn't go away. It doesn't, no, no, no, no way! It's still here!
> *Q*: Why do you think it is like that?
> *E*: Racism! It is racism. It's only [happening] here. For example, elsewhere you can marry an Albanian woman; here, that's not possible. The parents will

step in and they won't let it happen. Or a Yiftisa [Roma woman]: the parents won't allow you to marry her. No way! Or you can marry her but you'll have to go and live elsewhere. I can still see this happening here, probably more often nowadays.
Q: Why is that?
E: Because people are racist!

If mixing in the labor market and in education has recently become more evident than in the past, then granting the "other," or for that matter the Roma or the Albanian, equal status has not caught up to the same extent. Non-Roma families continue to pursue strategies that aim to maintain the homogeneity of their group and avoid crossing the boundaries of the marginalized groups, namely the Albanians and the Roma. Although some mixed marriages were reported in more recent years, marital selection still remains an issue that is decided through mechanisms of early selection and prevention that operate within the majority group. The marital pathways of the two groups, the Roma and the non-Roma, are plotted in such a way as to allow for limited possibility of crossing each other.

Having said this, though, it is equally important to note that marital preferences also exist among the Roma. In the two oldest age groups, that is for participants born before 1963, the main criteria for marital selection were the socioeconomic standing and social status of the families. Hence, avoiding sliding down the social ladder was a crucial consideration in parents' decision-making process. In the younger generation, the same principle applies though there is an additional consideration that is taken into account: the avoidance of the Albanian families as their low social-class position and low social status make them undesirable for similar reasons that it used to be invidious for a member of the majority group to marry someone with a Roma background. Although the extent of this strategy (namely, Roma avoiding marriages with Albanians) is hard to establish, it seemed to be prevalent among better-off Roma families:

> The Albanians, are the ones with whom none wants to marry. It's easier for a Yifto to marry to an Albanian, but I think the Yiftoi also avoid the Albanians. Some Yiftoi, though, are penniless and destitute and they don't even have proper houses. People laugh at them and look down upon them because they are very poor and they got married to Albanians.

9.4 Patronage, Clientelism, and "Meson"

Thus far, my focus was on a specific institution, for example, education, on the reorganization of the occupational structure, and on mobility pathways, such as emigration and marriage. In this section, I turn my attention to a set of cultural, social, and political arrangements and their impacts on differential mobility strategies.

Since gaining independence from the Ottoman Empire in 1830, Greek political parties were formed on the basis of powerful local oligarchies. While the state was trying to consolidate its power, these oligarchies were enmeshed in a process that would allow them to get a foothold in the state (Mouzelis, 2005). This process led to the establishment of political factions with strong ties in rural areas. These factions thrived as agents of political patronage and control of the peasantry as they managed to link the peasants to the central government institutions and political parties (Mouzelis, 2005, p. 74). The vast majority of the Greek peasants in the prewar period were trapped within the clientelistic web of practices established by the mainstream political parties. These practices were orchestrated by local patrons, who were associated with the central political parties, but they enjoyed significant autonomy.

As I discussed in chapter 3, the Civil War, which terminated in 1949, bequeathed a political division between the Left and the Right. This situation created severe political tensions, which exerted enormous influence on the reorganization of the Greek state. The state used this social and political divide as a mechanism of ideological "refinement" of the population and a means of intervening in the Greek social-class formation (Tsoukalas, 2005). This was achieved initially through the distribution of the American aid and, chiefly, through the adoption of the role of the main employer by the state. In particular, the most crucial locus of state intervention was in the public sector, where most of the new jobs were created (see chapter 3). Markedly, between 1940 and 1970, the Greek population increased by 19 percent while the number of the civil servants by 140 percent (Koliopoulos and Veremis, 2004). Selection criteria for these civil-sector positions were often nontransparent in order to favor applicants who were sympathizers of the political establishment, hence, further deepening the authoritarianism of the Greek state and the entrenchment of clientelistic relations. With the rapid growth of the public sector and the gradual decline of family farming, the newly appointed workforce in the civil sector increased exponentially and started acquiring similar social characteristics. In other words, it formed a new social class, the intermediate class, which was continuously expanding and soon became state-dependent. To a large extent, the intermediate class was the by-product of clientelism. Nowadays, clientelistic patterns of political relations "still tend to see the state as the instrument for satisfying clientelistic demands; as a mechanism for allocating favours; as a collective patron to their active supporters who become clients of the state bureaucracy" (Ioakimidis, 1996, p. 45). The main agent of clientelism has been the political parties whose control and power over government and state functions are enormous. According to Charalambis (1989), modern Greece is a "political party democracy" given that the political parties, which operate on the basis of their clientelistic interests, are the main institutional agents.

9.4.1 Non-Roma

As I noted above, political instability and tensions were passed down to the post–Civil War epoch and the Greek society, polarized and politically divided between the Right and the Left Protopi, was deeply immersed in this situation. Political conflict has played a crucial role in the formation of labor-market partnerships and arrangements and in all aspects of social and economic relations, as Milena points out:

> Milena: Relationships between people here were different. People started to hate each other after the Civil War, when the state was divided. In our place we had a group of young men who got shot because they were guerrilla fighters, they were communists. After then, people started picking fights with each other: "You got them to shoot these lads" or they used to say: "I arranged for your father to get shot." They started accusing each other of all sorts of things that had happened in this [civil] war.

This deep-seated conflict had an indisputable impact on the daily life of the community, as demonstrated from this excerpt from a conversation with Hermes:

> *Hermes*: There used to be a lot of tension in this place. I was little, but I can clearly remember that there was a lot of tension. It split the place into two.
> *Q*: Was this tension strong?
> *H*: Of course! It deeply influenced us here. Given that the place was divided, especially after they shot these lads, the conflict was transferred across the entire area. People were careful about where they went shopping and where not; who to talk to and who not; who to do business with and who not etc.

In line with Greece's postwar development (see chapter 3), the state continued to play a pivotal role in allocating funding for emergent enterprises, regulating the "free" economy and trade, recruiting and retaining personnel, and making arrangements in the public sphere. For a young person who aspired to take advantage of the emergent opportunities, having skills, family support, determination, and financial and other assets (such as educational qualifications) was desirable but not sufficient to secure him or her a job in the labor market: knowing the right person in the right place was even more effective. In the years following the Civil War, this entailed the alignment of the candidate's beliefs with the prevailing ones in the state bureaucracy. Gregory explains the way that political affiliation was a determinant of occupational success:

> When I started my career, in order to take a loan as a farmer, it had to be approved by the bank's agronomist.[5] If you were on the Left, he was on the Right. So he'd find out where you belonged [politically] and could say: "whose

side were you on [in the Civil War]?" And if he found you were on the Left, he'd say: "Forget about him. Cross him out of the list." And the loan wouldn't be approved. Wherever this person would go to, all the doors would be shut. Just think about the loss in the economy: if this chap wanted to build a house with this loan, then consider how many jobs were affected. Or take another example; during the dictatorship [1967–1974], many enterprises, especially those in need of financial support, didn't get any money. It was again the "right" people and the dodgy ones who got it. That's what the system was like. The system has always been like that and it'll always be. It's still alive, though, it was harder in the old days.

As Gregory elucidated, being on the "right" side of the political divide was a big advantage. However, it appears that for some individuals, it was a prerequisite. For example, for Calliope's neighbor who sought to capitalize on his university degree and get a matching position in the growing public sector, it was a sine qua non. Calliope talks about the impact of political relations on employment opportunities and the effect of this process on social relations:

> *Calliope*: These days, they [state-sector bureaucrats] used to ask for a certificate of "social beliefs."
> *Q*: What's that?
> *C*: A proof of your political affiliation.
> *Q*: Was this important?
> *C*: Extremely! They could turn you down from a job if you didn't have it. And even if they didn't turn you down and you got the job, somebody could still say: "you know, that chap over there, put him aside; get rid of him."
> *Q*: Did they discriminate against certain people?
> *C*: Oh yeah, they did! There was a lot of discrimination. There was this neighbor of mine who was a lefty. He was forced to do all sorts of things to move on in his life, things you can't imagine. He took exams [for a job] and got rejected time after time after time. He went in through one door and out the other.

Political tensions were exacerbated during the seven-year dictatorship between 1967 and 1974. All the political and social divisions of the past became much more pronounced and many people were forced to quit their jobs, flee the country, or lie low. For some respondents in the middle generation, such as Aspasia, this curtailed their career choices considerably:

> *Aspasia*: When I applied for a job in Athens, the question I was asked [by employers] was not whether I had the relevant skills but whether I had the right [political] affiliation.
> *Q*: How could you prove this?
> *A*: Oh, they knew! They had the means to find out. They used to keep a file of your [political] acts, the "file." My father was marked as a communist, he had a file in the police so I knew that getting a job would be

hopeless. Eventually, I found a short-term job but they soon found out about my father and asked for an explanation: everything was on the line. I was scared. At the end, an uncle of mine "testified" to the authorities that I was of "good character" and I kept the job.

Q: How did your uncle make such a difference?
A: Because he was a policeman. A policeman back then was the law unto himself.

For participants in the younger generation (born after 1963), political patronage and clientelistic relationships are intrinsically linked to the labor-market relations and wider socioeconomic arrangements. The political, economic, cultural, educational, and all other institutions are interwoven in this state of affairs. Inescapably, individuals' and families' strategies to promote their occupational and social mobility careers are mediated by political patrons. In times of globalized economic pressures, clientelism regulates access to the limited occupational opportunities, rendering competition a tight race with unknown outcomes. However, clientelism is now increasingly viewed in an ambivalent way: on the one hand, as a savior of young people from unemployment and, on the other, as a socially corrosive and shameful practice, as Yurkas explains:

Yurkas: In the past you needed to have an MP to get a job. It didn't matter if you were educated or not: if you didn't know an MP your degree was only good enough to be put in a frame! Nowadays, it's even worse. You get a [university] degree: how much money will you earn from that [relevant] job? Nothing! Absolutely nothing. I've got a niece, she's graduated from university a few years ago with good grades, but she's still paid peanuts. That's 10–15 years after she graduated, ok? Everyday I see many young men and women with university degrees begging someone, who often is illiterate, to give them an unskilled job; without meson nothing can be done.

Yurkas's account highlights the two functions of political mediation, or "meson" in colloquial Greek. On the one hand, meson acts as a job-finding mechanism that can relieve someone from unemployment. On the other hand, meson acts as a corrosive social practice. The latter, the invidious aspect of meson, was emphasized by many people in the younger generation and was mentioned in more than 15 interviews and numerous informal discussions. Meson can be broadly defined as a mediator, an agent with some sort of political power and influence, who acts illicitly as a liaison for people they know in order to promote their interests. This mediation implies bending the rules and the conventions in place and undermining the equitable arrangements for exchange of more power and control over one's political territory. The huge significance of meson in the socioeconomic arrangements in modern Greece, generally, and Protopi in particular, is remarkable. The following excerpt comes from an informal discussion with a 30-year-old university graduate, who was very vocal about the insidious operation of meson:

> Meson is everywhere. It doesn't matter what you know or what you've done in your life: if you haven't got someone to put you through, to help you, you have no chance. It's pretty disgusting the way things are in Greece but what can you do?!

For many young people, political mediation seems to have weakened the expectation in the role of education that was dominant in respondents in the two previous generations. The normalization of meson acts as a counterweight to the ideal of "meritocracy-based education" that sustained the edifice of the Greek version of liberal democracy:

> Q: Are all jobs open to all people here?
> A: Not to everyone. There are some people who have a privileged position. If you have good contacts, you can go far. Getting a job depends more on who you know than on your education. Nowadays, good contacts can find you a job, whereas education can't.

The changing expectations about the role of education are noteworthy in a place where just 20 years ago educational qualifications were regarded as the optimum means of escaping poverty and securing a higher-class position. Furthermore, members of the younger age-group seem to be morally defeated by the omnipresence of meson. Pheadon is a university graduate who was initially unemployed, then worked in the private sector (as a skilled employee), and finally set up his own business. During our conversation, he was evidently exasperated because he works very long hours, receives very little state support and relies on personal networks for maintaining his place in the labor market:

> *Phaedon*: If I knew that I would have to go through all that [unemployment and under-employment], I'd have chosen something else, a different career path.
> Q: Such as?
> A: Well, I'd still go to university but I wouldn't have put much effort. At the end of the day no one cares! On the other hand, if you have money to set up your own business, everyone respects you. No one touches you.
> Q: And if you don't?
> A: Then at least you have to have some contacts, like politicians: they rule the game. They pull strings no matter if you have 50 [educational] qualifications or none. They can do much more than your degrees can do for you!

9.4.2 Roma

The consequences of political polarization and the effects of the extensive infiltration of meson in the social, political, and economic life of Protopi are far reaching. They cut across the social organization and have a profound impact on the outcomes of the Roma and the non-Roma people alike. Clientelistic relationships and patronage have exacerbated the unequal distribution of opportunities and the reproduction of class, gender, ethnic, educational, and other divisions.

In most accounts, participants looked back to the years of rife political polarization and condemned it regardless of their political affiliation. Philippa illustrates how party politics operated in Protopi from the perspective of a Roma woman:

> In the old times, it was hard to get a job. I'll give you an example of a local industry [gives name]. If you were not a member of the [right-wing] party you couldn't get a job. You had to get a "certificate" from your MP, as it happens nowadays. Let me give you another example: in our area if you didn't have meson you couldn't do anything. Even if you had a dispute with your neighbor and he harmed you, the court could acquit him. They had their means to influence the judges. People were illiterate these days. There was so much machismo and rousfeti.[6] The one with the meson was so macho, he could claim and take everything for himself: he had a "nobody-can-touch-me" sort of attitude.

The prevalence of political mediation and corruption in the form of "rousfeti," has been very extensive. While for those in the older generation, its role was crucial in occupational outcomes, for those in the middle and especially in the younger age-groups, it is even more pronounced. This was evident in the accounts of people who did not capitalize on the mobility pathways discussed thus far, such as the new occupational opportunities, education, emigration, and marriage. One of them is Pericles, 42 years, whose account of his occupational experiences is presented in section 9.2.2. There, he elucidated the reasons why emigration was not a successful mobility pathway for him and his family. In the following extract, he highlights how the different mobility pathways are fundamentally interlinked:

> *Q*: Are there some people who find it harder than others to get a job?
> *Pericles*: Rousfeti is big, very big: "why did your child get this job and not mine"? It exists. It's always been around. I saw it well when I stopped working with my dad [self-employed electrician]. When I started working in a factory, that is in the private sector, I saw lots of things I didn't like. There was a lot of rousfeti if they wanted to fire you.
> *Q*: Why especially when they wanted to fire you?
> *P*: Because someone could go up to the boss and slag you off in order to keep his position. In order to have good relationships with the boss he could harm you.

Pericles is illuminating about the distribution of opportunities. More specifically, his account sketches a rather non-meritocratic picture of the labor market and the nontransparent criteria with which it operates. This was largely attributed to the penetration of clientelistic relations in the workplace, which undermined the workers' trust and work ethos. For many respondents, such as Pericles, the existence of rousfeti and political mediation is an intimidating and discriminatory practice that runs against their core beliefs. The most common attitude advanced by participants was to denounce rousfeti and express their strong dislike against it. Regarding the mediators, it was acknowledged by respondents that their motives run against the common good, though, at the same time, their pursuits seemed to be well attuned to individual advancement. Arguably, if seen from a community perspective, meson and rousfeti could also have had a positive impact: They acted as a means of acknowledging the presence of the "other," the Roma, and thus granting them with recognition through their participation in the same political system as the dominant group.

This is not to say that patronage and clientelistic relations alone are enough to compensate for differential distribution of opportunities in the labor market (see chapters 6 and 7) or educational achievement (chapter 8) nor that they were sufficient to lift the barriers associated with social mobility of the Roma. It simply means that political mediation introduced the Roma to the unequal system of opportunities and outcomes and by doing so, it drew more "legitimacy" for itself. On the face of it, this is a "win–win" type of situation: The mediators were victorious by increasing their clientship and opening up the competition game. Simultaneously, the Roma also scored gains not least by being granted the right to participate in the same system of opportunities and rewards, as Diomedes asserts:

> *Diomedes*: In the past the Yiftoi were not allowed [by the non-Roma] to enter their shops, cafeterias etc.; you know, they were not allowed to climb up [the social ladder]. The Yiftoi didn't even appear in public festivities; if they turned up they could get shot.
> *Q*: Did they not have relations with the non-Yiftoi?
> *D*: No, but with the entry of politics they started [having relationships] in order [for the politicians] to get the votes [of the Yiftoi]. They realized that Yiftoi were not harmful to us [the non-Roma]; they did not take our jobs and they didn't do anything damaging, so there was no fear of allowing them [the Roma] into politics.

It is clear that by exercising their voting rights, the Roma people gained some political power. However, this was not enough to imperil the overall power balance in the local community. As Diomedes suggested, it was more about filling in the lacunae the dominant group left in the labor market rather than an opportunity to redistribute chances equally. In this way, the Roma could participate to a greater extent in the activities of the community and promote their own interests. The non-Roma were not threatened by this development, as long as their power was not contested. In other words, the increased participation of the Roma was welcome, provided that the non-Roma were in control of the allocation of opportunities and rewards.

9.5 Summary

The examination of the structural changes in the labor market (chapter 6), the impact of these transformations on occupational mobility of people in Protopi (chapter 7), and the role of education in mobility trajectories (chapter 8) raised some serious questions about the role of other interrelated mechanisms. Chapter 9 filled in this lacuna with the exploration of the role of emigration, marriage, and political patronage. I argued that the first two mechanisms, emigration and marriage, have had a wide-ranging impact on the social relations and organization in Protopi. Emigration's contribution was crucial in advancing the occupational careers of individuals and, more broadly, in the socioeconomic development of Protopi. Marriage acted as a mechanism for socioeconomic and ethnic boundary maintenance and also as an upward, intra- and intergenerational, social mobility pathway. Both practices conferred occupational and social benefits to individuals and their families and were approached in this chapter as alternative routes to social mobility. Their discussion therefore was important in order to present the full range of mobility pathways available to respondents in Protopi.

Regarding patronage and clientelistic relations, a "vignette" was offered here about the significance of this historically mediating force in the Greek socioeconomic, political, and cultural organization. I exemplified how political patronage and clientelism have gained enormous impetus that can suffice to militate against the principles of achieved factors, such as education. The exploration of the sociocultural processes underpinning patronage and clientelism revealed a paradox in the social reality of Protopi. That is, the coexistence of the belief in "education-based meritocracy" and participation in a profoundly non-meritocratic system of patronage and clientelistic relations. It is hoped that this chapter has enhanced the reader's understanding about the distribution of opportunities in Protopi and the alternative mobility pathways, and its has elucidated some important sociocultural processes that help us gain a holistic idea of the complex and multifaceted processes that impinge on social mobility.

Conclusion

Education in Protopi

In this section, I revisit the main findings presented in this book and demonstrate what role education has had in social mobility of different groups in Protopi, where the study was conducted. By specifically exploring intra- and intergenerational social mobility, I aim to show the impact of education on social change in a spatially and temporally specific context, namely in Protopi from the late 1940s to the late 2000s. For older-generation respondents (born from 1914 to 1937), evidence showed that the lack of education did not significantly impede their social mobility chances. Most of those respondents were either primary-school graduates or left school with no qualifications. Secondary and, in particular, tertiary education were restricted to a very small number of individuals. The reasons for such a low educational attainment were linked to the proto-capitalist mode of production prevalent until the late 1950s and the concomitant socioeconomic organization of production based on subsistence agriculture. As a result, education-based occupations were rare and time spent in education was perceived as foregone income.

The quantitative and qualitative evidence suggested that there was a more significant association between education and occupational mobility for middle-generation respondents (born from 1938 to 1962). This association was far from unidimensional. In particular, emergent occupational restructuring can be seen most clearly by the creation of new positions in the intermediate class (associated with self-employment and clerical occupations) and in the middle class (linked to professional and managerial occupations). These occupations, and in particular the ones leading to middle-class positions, invariably required high educational credentials. Attaining such credentials led to the high incidence of upward intergenerational mobility of the middle age-group. However, emergent occupational opportunities were ethnically structured, benefiting more non-Roma than Roma people. In addition, middle-generation non-Roma women did not capitalize on education-based occupational opportunities as much as their male peers as cultural barriers restricted their access to education. Roma women had still fewer education-based occupational opportunities than their non-Roma peers. Evidence from younger-generation participants (who entered the labor market after 1980) suggested that high educational qualifications are decreasingly associated with high labor-market outcomes and attendant social-class advancement. Although access to secondary and tertiary education improved dramatically for this age-group, the labor market has become more rigid for this generation than for previous ones. Members of the younger generation are better educated than their parents but they do not necessarily attract occupational opportunities and rewards commensurate with their skills and knowledge. Paradoxically, given their increasingly higher educational credentials relative to other generations, this group primarily experiences horizontal rather than vertical mobility, moving from service sector–based jobs to similar ones in retailing and routine, non-manual sectors of activity. In other words, within three decades, from the early 1960s to the mid-1990s, Protopi has shifted from being a highly illiterate society to one of overeducation due to "credentials inflation" (Collins, 1979). The powerful link between increased educational credentials and upward mobility that held sway from the 1950s until the mid-1980s has lost its strength. Nowadays, educational qualifications are increasingly devalued as they lead predominantly to low-income, insecure jobs or even to unemployment.

The Distribution of Opportunities: Who Got What

The synopsis offered in the previous section indicates the varying and complex role and significance of education for Protopi residents' social mobility. To appreciate the complexity of the processes discussed herein, I shall summarize how education impacts on the life chances of different groups of people. This will inform the reader about "who got what" in Protopi from the late 1940s up to 2008.

Evidence in previous chapters showed that Protopi residents' chances for upward social mobility were initially enhanced by the combination of educational expansion, increased occupational and socioeconomic transformations, as well as extensive labor-market restructuring in postwar Protopi. The qualitative material suggested that many of those individuals (especially in the middle age-group) who realized this achievement came from families with material and nonmaterial advantages, such as larger than average shares of land and/or educational capital. It could, thus, be argued that many who benefited from education came from privileged socioeconomic backgrounds. However, education-based occupational expansion up to the 1980s was so sizeable that those with a more privileged start in life could not fill in all vacant positions. Hence, many people from lower social classes benefited from the room at the top of the occupational structure and filled in these emergent positions. Characteristically, women, especially after the mid-1970s, started improving their educational credentials and participating in the labor market at higher rates than ever before. Similarly, many children from poor farming families, such as those from Roma origins, enhanced their occupational situation and social-class position mainly, though not exclusively, by obtaining high educational qualifications.

Overall, education provided an unequivocally positive impact on the life chances of people in Protopi from the late 1950s until the mid-1980s. However, its benefits were unevenly distributed. Despite the high levels of absolute mobility observed in the social structure of Protopi over the three generations studied, most social mobility movement (73 percent) was structural rather than exchange (chapter 6). Thus, three out of four socially mobile people occupied newly created positions and only one out of four people exchanged a lower-class position for a higher-class position. In other words, the relative distance between social classes in Protopi did not diminish over time. As a result, individuals in the younger generation find themselves in a situation characterized by polarization and rampant social inequalities despite the high educational credentials they hold.

However, education per se has never been able to accomplish such an equalizing mission. It was only the abundance of occupational opportunities, chiefly from the mid-1950s until the mid-1980s, which allowed education to strongly influence individuals' life chances. Once labor-market expansion filled all available educo-centric jobs, educational credentials failed to enable any further expansion in such jobs. Qualitative evidence largely confirmed these findings and shed further light on the concurrent incidence of high social mobility rates (for the middle generation) and inequality of opportunities (for some people in all three age-groups). For example, female graduates' (non-Roma and Roma alike) entry into the labor market did not reduce the occupational opportunities of their male counterparts although the gap in educational attainment and labor-market participation between men and women has decreased substantially since the 1970s. More women in the labor market has not meant fewer men, but more and different types of jobs, new employment patterns (such as part-time labor, a mode of employment largely associated with females), and the opening of traditional male, occupational bastions to women.

In addition, younger-generation Roma people have significantly improved their educational attainment and labor-market access, although this finding needs to be interpreted with some caution. Relative improvement compared to the previous, Roma-only, age-groups does not necessarily imply that inequalities between Roma and non-Roma were eliminated. Many Roma people benefited from the educational expansion, increased their concomitant attainments, and, therefore, secured better occupational and class positions than their parents. However, this needs to be seen in relation to their non-Roma counterparts who also achieved better educational attainment and higher social mobility than their own parents. In most cases, the latter surpassed the Roma people both educationally and socioeconomically. Plainly put, education-based mobility operated like the tide that lifts up all boats—but those previously in the highest classes retained their structurally superior position. All in the younger generation utilized this strategy, but as the middle-class workplace was glutted with graduates, class, gender, and ethnic privileges reared their ugly heads.

Thus, the examination of the relative mobility chances in prior chapters suggested that Protopi has not been as open as it might initially have appeared. As this suggests, the promise of meritocracy in postwar Protopi and Greece more broadly are illusory. Earlier chapters suggested that the educational openness and expansion realized in the first few postwar decades were tied to economic and occupational structuring demands rather than to the occupational promise that higher educational qualifications seemingly offered. This openness and expansion appealed to the rhetoric that higher educational attainment enhanced graduates' occupational opportunities. However, these opportunities were not distributed in a random or neutral manner nor spread evenly among all members of a society as if they simply fall from the sky. They are embedded in the socioeconomic and political arrangements intrinsic to the pertinent mode of production and accompanying social and cultural relations, to which I turn my attention next.

Educationi nG reece

In order to sharpen the focus of my exploration, my starting point was the Second World War. Because of the war, employment increased and economic growth was achieved. The war, therefore, represented capitalism as the savior that swept aside alternative ways to run a society. The capitalist system became entrenched, enduring, and dominant thanks to liberal democracy or "embedded liberalism" (Harvey, 2010), which required active state intervention in business and economic cycles and support for its citizens through developing the welfare state. This new approach introduced by the British economist Keynes argued that what was now needed was "to arrive at a set of scientific managerial strategies and state powers that would stabilize capitalism, while avoiding the evident repressions and irrationalities, all the warmongering and narrow nationalism that national socialist solutions implied. It is such a context of confusion that we have to understand the highly diversified attempts within different nation states to arrive at political, institutional and social arrangements that could accommodate the chronic incapacities of capitalism to regulate the essential conditions for its own reproduction" (Harvey, 1989, p. 129). Despite the diverse applications of the Keynesian model in different Western countries since the 1950s, one of its definitive characteristics was the importance placed on education as the means of realizing the potential that this new socioeconomic and political landscape offered. For example, increased (public and private) spending for education led to the universalization and extension of compulsory education and to the exponential growth in access, participation, and completion rates at all levels, but most impressively in higher education. Growth in university graduates was closely associated with public-sector expansion postulated by the new type of economic development, which required highly skilled people to occupy the emergent positions in the labor market and drive forward the economic growth that was hoped would be safeguarded thereafter. At the same time, while postwar reconstruction was gathering pace and new wealth was concomitantly being generated, income levels of the general population were rising, and employment security (especially in the public sector) and living standards were improving. Higher levels of socioeconomic progress enabled people to turn to education to fulfill their personal aspirations as well as to advance their careers and social positions. Education was promoted in liberal democracies as a win–win prospect: It was expected to confer socioeconomic benefits to individuals, and concomitantly to the state through increased economic growth and labor productivity. Liberal governments in Europe and elsewhere presented the association between high educational credentials and socioeconomic progress as a straightforward, long-lasting, and all-embracing one, as some sort of panacea for all social and economic ills of liberal capitalism.

At the same time, promoting the idea of unfettered movement within the social structure was adopted as a core value of liberal democratic capitalism. Social mobility gained social and moral value. Europe, for example, was seen as having just cast off the dark clouds of unemployment and lack of growth that led to the ascent of the Nazis and the Second World War itself. A new-found euphoria resided in the continent, living its apotheosis of the Keynesian model. The state thereby became an agent of social formation, control, and regulation of the workforce. More than that, the state through its active intervention in the labor market, economy, and production shaped the social relations *within* and *of* production.

With regard to Greece, a large part of the population entered a process of occupational transformation that did not involve transition from urban blue-collar to white-collar occupations, but from agriculture to white-collared ones. In particular, peasants became public servants or self-employed workers. This process required the reorganization of production away from rural agriculture and into the urban service sector. As I argued in chapters 3, 4 and 8, education was deployed to realize this new model of socioeconomic organization; it operated as both a strategic choice and a tool for the rearrangement of class formation and reconfiguration of class power. The steep increase in educated workforce numbers was conducive to the new political economy molded after the war. Educational expansion, therefore, was seen as the *optimum means* for securing the conditions of capitalism's reproduction. Capitalism had indeed managed to reinvent itself and to advance triumphantly not against its workers, but in harmony with what appeared to be beneficial to the workforce. The unequivocal improvement in working conditions for the majority of laborers and the higher income gains and attendant life quality improvement converted the newly embourgeoized worker into a product of the state. The significant material gains the Greek workers attained in the first few decades after the war were the outcome of serious compromises between losses of employment rights and the wider dismantling of working-class organization, solidarity, and consciousness, though, not without opposition from the workers themselves. This deep reconfiguration in the relations of production also required strong ideological supporting mechanisms, which were provided through the impregnation of the belief in a meritocratic system of allocation of opportunities. Such a system was premised upon the expectation that the best and ablest would occupy the top occupational and social positions. I critiqued mainly in chapters 4 and 8 the intentions of those who propounded such an ineffectual ideological construction that it proved expedient to the legitimization of unequal processes and practices, also attested to in the educational domain. The embourgeoisement of social agents, especially those from working class and peasant backgrounds, was completed with their ideological transformation. Not only did Greece enter Western liberal capitalism fully and irreversibly during the 1950s, but it also managed to create the necessary conditions for preventing its most radical forces from realizing class consciousness and acting as a class-for-themselves.

Furthermore, the proliferation of educational provision and attendant embourgeoisement of a large part of the population functioned as the ideological justification for the extensive embedding of inequalities within the Greek social structure. A new hegemony was in the making that would bring the middle classes of Greece (and Protopi in particular) closer to the international middle classes. This process allowed and reinforced the transition of attitudes vis-à-vis education from a scarce resource—a luxury of the elites—to a sought-after necessity or even commodity. Against this new consensus, I suggested how opportunities were neither equally distributed nor fairly allocated. For example, in chapter 7, I argued that ethnic differentiation was a crucial factor in the enhancement of capitalist efficiency as it allowed one group of people, namely the Roma, to be exploited by another group, the non-Roma. This account enhanced our understanding of the holistic nature of capitalist production. That is to say, the relations that permeate capitalist production are social relations, dividing groups asymmetrically based on associations: men versus women, Roma versus non-Roma, capitalist versus working class, and so on. Capitalism ushered division among people and created the ethnicized differentiation of Roma and non-Roma described by many of my respondents rather than ethnic difference per se. Insofar as the Roma play the role of the local "underclass," the non-Roma have the possibility of ameliorating their own social position and lessening their own exploitation. Ethnic differentiation was identified as another lever, *a mechanism of justification* so to speak, for the discrimination against the Roma people from institutions, such as education, which purportedly fulfilled the equalizing role land redistribution left incomplete a few decades earlier. I further argued that this process of ethnically based differentiation acted chiefly as an *ideological instrument* for the social and moral vindication of social-class structure rearrangements. Ethnic differentiation functioned for not just the *justification of the subordination* of the Roma, but of *the entire working class*. The differentiation of the Albanians and their inferior treatment by Roma and non-Roma people alike since the early 1990s offers support to this proposition. If this practice is enduring, it is because it is effective from a capitalist point of view. As Willis (1977, p. 152) argued more than 30 years ago, "racial division, helps, as with labour and gender divisions, to found the whole epistemological category and possibility of division. It also provides an evident underclass which is more heavily exploited than the white working class, and is therefore indirectly and partially exploited by the working class itself (at least lessening their exploitation); it also provides an ideological object for feelings about the degeneracy of others and the superiority of the self (thus reinforcing the dominant ideological terms which make the comparison possible). Racism therefore divides the working class both materially and ideologically." In contemporary European societies, one could observe various similar mutations and applications of the selfsame mechanism of ethnicized or racialized differentiation. It finds expression in the struggle between local white working-class groups against immigrants, especially in inner-city contexts (Hoggett et al., 2008; Garner et al., 2009; Hills et al., 2010; Pearce and Milne, 2010; Jones, 2011), anti-Gypsy discrimination (Hancock, 2000), and rising xenophobia in a plethora of contemporary contexts (Baumgartl and Favell, 1995; Hawley and Lindsey, 2012).

Education and the New Political Economy

Alison Wolf (2002) argued in *Does Education Matter?* that "governments that see rapid growth in higher education as a major tool for equalizing opportunity delude themselves...Pile more and more education on top of what is there already, and you end up with the same segmentation, the same positioning, and even greater problems of cost and quality" (p. 251). With respect to postwar Greece, a lot more education has indeed been "piled up" on top of the very little after the war. In spite of this quantitative increase in education, Greece is currently more polarized, inequitable, and inequality-riddled than before. It is worthwhile reminding ourselves how this book explored this set of issues.

In various places (e.g., in chapters 3, 4, 7, and 8), I argued that the scope, depth, and rapidity of educational transformations from the late 1940s until the mid-1980s went hand in hand with an array of transformations in the political, social, and economic spheres of activity. In fact, Greece was undergoing a massive program of reconstruction. First, in its war-wrecked infrastructure, which needed rebuilding, modernizing, and upgrading. Second, in its political, economic, financial, educational, and other institutions, which had to be attuned to the exigencies of liberal capitalism in its Keynesian phase. Third, in its social fabric. All these changes are interconnected and interdependent. One of the most intriguing of these transformations was the embourgeoisement of a large part of the rural population within a relatively short period of time. Specifically, throughout the postwar years, Greece has had a small industrial proletariat concentrated in urban centers, a declining peasantry, and conversely swelling intermediate and middle classes. Education propelled and partly created this amplification of intermediate and middle classes. To be precise, education was the most instrumental tool with which the Greek state engineered such an immense change in its social fabric. Thanks to the educational expansion and the concomitant restructuring of the labor market to absorb the educated workforce, postwar mobility rates remained high and Greek social structure appeared more open than it really was. I called this process of expansion in the state and public sector "state-sponsored mobility" as the state scaffolded many individuals' ascent to the highest echelons within the social structure.

This type of mobility would not have been achieved without education, which became the catalyst of the Greek postwar project of modernization. If this process, and especially the abandonment of previous forms of economic activity in the turn to the service sector, has similarities with other economically advanced European countries, it is because the transformations that Greece underwent were influenced to a large extent by external forces. For example, Greece was one of the biggest beneficiaries of US aid. This aid, in the form of reconstruction funds, allowed the US and to a smaller degree other Western countries (e.g., Britain) to play a pivotal role in determining the direction that Greece followed. To be precise, the specific type of Greek postwar development, the establishment of financial and economic structures that facilitated foreign capital penetration, the development of political actors who operated in alliance with foreign agents, and the socioeconomic developments I discussed thus far were largely shaped by the role foreign powers exerted on Greece. In a nutshell, together with the Greek ruling class and the state, foreign powers are responsible for the specific type of capitalist development that occurred throughout the postwar period. Much of the contradictions, though, of Greek capitalism have less to do with the state or the ruling classes being unable to follow an ideal-type development path, but to actual resistance from the subordinated classes (Sotiris, 2012).

These subordinated classes have a long history of resistance. Currently, this takes the form of resistance to globalization ushered with Greece's entrance into the EU. Although EU accession was originally celebrated as a national victory by virtue of offering Greece membership into the "holy alliance" of economically advanced, politically mature, and socially progressive countries, it soon started to crumble. Ordinary people in Protopi are as negatively predisposed to the EU as to the native elites. For them, the EU has meant short-lived affluence thanks to abundant EU subsidies and long-term immiseration. This became inextricably linked to the daily life of the Greek people, since the entry of Greece into the European Monetary Unification (EMU) in January 2001. According to Lapavitsas (2012), entry into EMU offered the native ruling classes in the European periphery access to the global capital markets. It was effectively an instrument for the acceleration of capital accumulation and the "unification" of the elites under the rubric of the unification of their nation states' monetary systems. This has exposed some of the inherent contradictions within the EU economy and more broadly the limits, flaws, and problems of global neoliberal capitalism. As Sotiris (2010) argued: "the Greek case brings forward the structural contradictions of the Eurozone and the whole financial and monetary architecture of the European Monetary Union. The introduction of the euro as a common currency accentuated the problems caused by the differences in competitiveness and productivity in European social formations. The traditional justification for this structure was the need to avoid inflationary pressures, in an attempt to guarantee the role of the euro as world money, but in terms of the social balance of forces it has mainly functioned as a constant pressure for capitalist restructuring." In other words, the foreign factor is yet again intervening in Greek social formation and class reorganization, thanks to the EU and its instruments, such as the Eurozone. This has brought about one of the worst crises Greece has ever faced, which has torn Greece asunder. The situation is increasingly converting highly educated young people into a reserve army of labor, who are locked in a position of "labor market passivity," that is, of reliance on unemployment benefits and their families for some income. For others, their situation suggests a form of "labor market captivity." The latter refers to the putative "700 Euro generation" (Kaskarelis and Tsilika, 2009). This group of "working poor" (Fraser, 2011), namely of people in employment with an income less than 60 percent of the national median, is growing at alarming rates. According to Lampousaki (2010, p. 1), "Greece has the highest proportion of working poor in the EU27. In-work poverty is directly associated with low wages, inability to find a full-time job and low skills. It is also associated with the existing system of taxation and the lack of an effective, well-planned social policy." At-risk-of poverty rates in Greece have been high since the early 1990s, while the respective poverty rate among those employed is at around 12–14 percent and is swiftly growing (Gazon, 2011). The 2011/2012 austerity measures have spread poverty also among the ranks of university graduates. With 45–60 percent of degrees awarded in the humanities and 60–80 percent of graduates finding employment in the public sector (OECD, 1995), it becomes clear that the problem of graduate unemployment does not lie solely with the rapid expansion of university education. The proliferation of university graduates is becoming a ticking social time bomb rather than a source of dynamism both in economic and social terms. The scale and duration of the crisis is a testament to the inappropriateness of the system of socioeconomic and political organization that Greece has followed since the war. Its highly skilled workforce is turning abroad in its quest for a better future. All indicators point to a renewed brain drain, while the country is unable to exit a crisis largely brought about by the "new global ruling class in the making" (Wacquant, 2009) and exacerbated by Greece's lenders, namely the "troika" of the IMF, the EU, and the ECB. In social terms, this points to a downward social movement and to the creation of a new social group, a new fraction, within the ranks of the working class: highly educated, underemployed, unemployed, or unemployable young people.

One of the most famous political mantras heard regularly during the heyday of modernization, and most regularly heard since the 1980s, was the so-called contract with the people. This seems to have been replaced with the contract with the markets, and more recently the troika, who hold sway over Greece's socioeconomic and political affairs and the country's future. In the days of liberal capitalism, Fordism was the biggest collective effort "to create, with unprecedented speed, and with a consciousness of purpose unmatched in history, a new type of worker and a new type of man," as Gramsci [1935] (1971) argued. Fordism created not only a system of mass production, but a new way of life. Currently, in the days of neoliberal global capitalism, these values are being eroded, reconfigured, and redefined. The new zeitgeist implies the abandonment of traditional Keynesian values, such as the right to employment, free education, and welfare state support, as the burden of responsibility shifts to the citizens themselves. As Wacquant argued (2009, pp. 306–307) "neoliberalism is a transnational political project aiming to remake the nexus of market, state, and citizenship from above. It entails not simply the reassertion of the prerogatives of capital and the promotion of the marketplace, but the close articulation of four institutional logics." These logics are "economic deregulation, welfare state devolution, retraction, and recomposition," the creation of an "expansive, intrusive, and proactive penal apparatus," and the "cultural trope of individual responsibility" (Wacquant, 2009, p. 307). From a holistic mode of production and organization, capitalism is swiftly turning into a "totalizing" one.

Social Mobility in Testing Times: Capitalism's Nemesis or Elixir?

This study examined the role of education in modern Greece. It dealt with differential rates of educational and social attainment, the key factors that affected them, and the consequences they have had on society and its institutions. This book took a different stance from common contentions that propounded a Greek "exceptionalism" regarding the significance and value of education. I argued that, in line with mobility findings from early-industrialized countries, a high incidence of education-sponsored mobility was achieved in Greece, especially in the immediate early postwar years and until the mid-1980s. However, substantial differences in the distribution of occupational opportunities and attendant outcomes across class, gender, and the ethnic divides have also persisted.

I suggested that education has not been a "free agent" of change. Far from that, it has been implicated in the mode of socioeconomic organization. In this vein, its function has varied widely at different points in time. It moved from an avenue *"par excellence"* of social mobility at times of labor-market openness, into a mechanism of social-class reproduction when education-based occupations were in relatively short supply. Furthermore, there is an emergent trend, which points to the role of education as a mechanism of social mobility stasis. Crucial to my approach is the connection I systematically pursued between, on the one hand, patterns of educational and social change and, on the other, the wider political economy. For example, I did not presume that education be subjugated to the economy, as has been the case with some Marxist accounts, which have been criticized for "reductionism" or "economism." Far from approaching the macro-trends in education (e.g., the expansion of higher education) or changes incurred from education (e.g., the increase in the educational standards in the Greek population) as epiphenomena, that is to say mere artifacts produced by changes in the economy and labor market, I seriously considered cultural, social, and political as well as community, family, and individual aspects. In chapter 9, for example, I explored different ways in which individuals reject, resist, reproduce, internalize, transcend, and reinforce their social-class positions or elements therewith. I achieved this through a discussion of an array of factors that extend beyond the considerations of traditional social mobility research. These factors included emigration, marriage, and political patronage and clientelist relations. Emigration, for example, expanded and extended the discussion on socioeconomic restructuring that I opened in chapters 7 and 8. By the same token, marriage was not reduced to a discussion on family and social reproduction strategies, but was treated as a significant dimension of socioeconomic relations and more broadly organization. Finally, I showed that political patronage and clientelism were significant in explaining differential occupational opportunities and social mobility outcomes because they permeated social, economic, cultural, and other arrangements.

Furthermore, I took a rather "unconventional" stance to social mobility as an area *for* research, which I justified on political/ideological and epistemological grounds. I argued against the widely held assertion among some Marxist scholars that social mobility is a priori bourgeois topic of study and I suggested that it deserves more systematic attention, especially from scholars holding a historical-materialist perspective. I then demonstrated how ideas originally developed by Karl Marx and Max Weber, and more recently by Talcott Parsons, have influenced our understanding of social inequalities and the way we explore them. In particular, I related this exploration to the field of social mobility research, dominated by scholars of either Parsonian or Weberian orientation. Both these approaches see social mobility as a positive mechanism within the capitalist system. Marxists, on the other hand, maintain that social mobility is counterproductive to the transformation of society. For them, the aim ought to be the abolition of social classes altogether not the preservation of movement among them. Although this would mark the end of social mobility as a practice, I argued that the exploration of social mobility is too important to be omitted from the perspective that historical materialism can offer and its attendant emphasis on class conflict.

If class conflict has been kept off the agenda of mainstream mobility research, it is not because conflict has ceased to exist. Rather, mobility research is concerned with the social movement of people and not the conditions under which this movement is achieved. However, for as long as social mobility exists both as a practice and lived experience, it acquires the capacity to ameliorate the polarization among potentially conflicting social classes. For this reason, I called social mobility the "anaesthetic" of class antagonisms. In other words, individuals' movement to, or close to, the top of the social structure allows them to ignore the distance that separates them from those they left behind. As far as those left behind are concerned, they accept their lower position, hoping one day they or their children can make it to the top too. This is the mechanism that makes social mobility the sweetener of the bitter pill of social inequalities. That is, the fact that it allows the ones who achieved a higher class position than their parents to focus on their effort to climb up the greasy pole, rather than on the consequences for those who did not. Instead of concentrating on the way inequalities are structurally patterned and strive to redress the social injustices that stem from them, Western (neo-)liberal governments inculcate into their citizens the expectation that everyone can "make it," incubating in this way a focus on the importance of personal accomplishments. In this way, social mobility becomes the celebration of individualism, as if social agents rise and fall outside society's structures and act independent of the way opportunities for social advancement are distributed. In other words, upward social mobility or even the possibility of its existence, that is to say the expectation that one can become socially mobile, serves to legitimize social inequalities that allocate, rank, differentiate, and separate people. This is what Marx and all Marxists after him feared the most. That is, capitalism's ingenuity to make class struggle wane and therefore to prolong the overthrowing of capitalism as the system organizing production and social life. In short, Marxists see social mobility as a counterweight to revolution. However, the mechanism of legitimization of social inequalities and the wide acceptance of social mobility as an aspiration to be realized by any means and at any cost is not as simple as it sounds. Societies are not theaters nor are individuals puppets whose strings are pulled into various directions by secret forces. Long-term historical processes cannot be reduced to a tally of variables that produce diverse outcomes depending on the way they interact with each other or the ways individuals manipulate them.

The reasons for the significance of social mobility and its widespread acceptance in modern Western societies have to be methodically explored. In this book, I addressed this through education in a historical perspective. One of the fundamental topics I explored was the role of education as a force of class struggle dynamics. In relation to modern Greece, for example, I discussed in chapter 3 how the creation of the new political economy that education assisted in creating supported the formation of new social classes, namely the intermediate and the middle classes. In doing so, the political conflicts between the Right and the Left subsided to make space for the a new ethos imposed by the new labor market conditions in accordance with the eroded political tensions and reduced class antagonisms. Social mobility seems to have become the shelter of liberal capitalism. However, as noted in the previous section of this chapter, the current times are characterized by downward mobility or mobility stasis (Reay, 2006). This means that people either move to lower social-class positions than their parents or stay static. Could this development exacerbate class conflicts and become the weakest link of the postwar system crafted so carefully all these years? Is this another crisis of capitalism or does it have the potential to become capitalism's nemesis? For younger people invariably inculcated into the dominant logic of unfettered movement to the top or preservation of class advantages they inherited, the lack of available occupational opportunities might seem an anathema to the maintenance of the status quo (though not necessarily to the overthrowing of the capitalist system itself). For example, in the current era of global capitalist crisis, the inherent dysfunctionality of neoliberal capitalism has been laid bare. Even the staunchest advocates of this system, such as the former US president George W. Bush (2008), declared that "the market is not functioning properly." Other apologists of capitalism came to similar conclusions. For example, Alan Greenspan (2008), chairman of the Federal Reserve Board, the American Central Bank, exclaimed that "a critical pillar to market competition and free markets, did break down...I still do not fully understand why it happened." This crisis has led to extensive spending cuts and attacks on the welfare state (where it still exists) and its key institutions, such as education, health care, social protection, and other key services. According to Panayotakis (2011), "brutal austerity policies are spreading throughout Europe, as the European Union more and more openly turns into a vehicle of neoliberal policies that deepen the economic crisis, while also dismantling welfare states and a social model that had supposedly tamed and humanized capitalism...Just as in the United States, European political and economic elites are clearly determined to 'solve' the crisis on the backs of those least responsible for it. Let teachers and firefighters, students and retirees, workers, and the unemployed pay!" (pp. 2–3). However, those who bear the brunt of the crisis seem to have started reacting to the stalling of occupational opportunities and to attendant social mobility stasis. Indeed, since 2008, a plethora of global movements attest to the quest for alternatives by disillusioned people across the globe. These movements have at their forefront highly educated individuals, who are denied the opportunity to maintain and/or improve their social-class position and fulfill their potential, according to the core dictum of liberal capitalism (see, e.g., Davis Glass's argument in relation to this in chapter 2). Those highly educated young people come from middle-class families or are part of the expanded intermediate class created in the aftermath of the war through education, self-employment, or emigration. In a reversal of the dominant postwar trend from the 1960s through the 1990s, the embourgeoisement of the peasants and the working class is now being brought to a halt. Conversely, it is the proletarianization of the middle and intermediate classes that is now occurring and with relative rapidity. The vulnerable situation of young people in the labor market earned them the term *precariat* (Standing, 2011), which is a new social formation, with seemingly common characteristics. Although these features are not sufficient to enable their incumbents to form a class-in-itself, they might assist in forging a coherent and unified class consciousness together with most of those disaffected by the failure of capitalism to provide solutions to their deteriorating working and living standards and the lack of opportunities to improve their lives. That is to say, the lack of social mobility these people experience might compel them to resist even further, and enter a process that might lead to the creation of a class-for-itself that could usher in an alternative and hopefully fair, just, equitable, and democratic form of organization. As Badiou (2010) reminds us, "Capitalism has always ensured that we pay the price for a few short decades of brutally inegalitarian prosperity: crises that swallow up astronomical quantities of value, bloody punitive expeditions to all zones it regards as threatening or strategic, and the world wars that allow it to recover its health" (p. 96).

However, every time capitalism enters a crisis, new social forces are unleashed. In May 1968, it was students and workers who resisted the then status quo and demanded a fairer and more equal world. Nowadays, it is students, the unemployed, the working poor, pensioners, and all those disenchanted with capitalism who express their anger at a failed system, from New York to Madrid, and from Athens to Tahrir Square. Today's movements are the expression of generalized disgruntlement about the previous compromises between labor and capital, which only delivered for the few and in short term, while they seized the opportunities from the new generations.

At the same time, this situation exemplifies the failure of capitalism to conquer its new territories as effectively as originally planned. A case is point is modern Greece, a country that entered the capitalist mode of production later than most other Western countries and had its "capitalist dream" turn into a nightmare sooner than anywhere else. Greece has become one of the prime loci at least in Europe where a real experiment has been conducted in

CONCLUSION 213

a very short period of time across its entire population. No other European country's economy has imploded so badly and so rapidly in the European history than modern Greece. Perhaps, there is a lesson to be learnt for countries ready to denounce socialist or other noncapitalist credentials they held in the past as they queue up in the corridors of Brussels to either enter the EU or take home recipes for economic and social development for their countries. They share the same desire to create a new middle class, to educate it at the best universities of the world and then have it send back home money, expertise, and make their capitalism work. When, though their capitalist dream will also turn into a nightmare, as it does so often these days, they might find the Greeks on the streets. As one of my respondents told me, "the best thing education has done for me is teach me ICT skills so I can link up with friends and find out about the next protest."

Contribution of the Book

In this section, I will highlight the elements of this enquiry that make it original and I will exemplify the areas where its contribution lies, both theoretically and methodologically.

While the intergenerational perspective of this inquiry offered a historical understanding of mobility processes and an exploration of the way they unfolded in a specific setting (Protopi), the parallel focus on gender and ethnicity allowed for the experiences of males and females, Roma and non-Roma to be included. More specifically, this book, without reinforcing and uncritically accepting the construction of a priori differences, integrated in the same research design both Roma and non-Roma. Hence, instead of looking at differences by delving into the ethnic, cultural, or "racial" terrain, it examined them in a symbiotic and dynamic way, as they naturally interact and play out in daily life. In other words, it moved beyond static and reifying ideas of difference and "otherness" in the exploration of issues that are anchored in material and symbolic differentials with social, political, economic, and ideological underpinnings.

In relation to gender, this inquiry went beyond male-centered approaches to social mobility and integrated the study of both men and women in the same design. While it argued that patriarchal and capitalist relations are manifest in society and that they intersect (West, 1982), the book avoided to the greatest possible extent the "intellectual sexism" of conventional studies and their male bias (Delphy, 1981; Allen, 1982). The class categories I used for the quantitative analysis of social mobility (chapter 6) were informed by male and female occupational realities, whereas the presentation of the mobility pathways of the research participants drew on the lived experiences of both women and men (chapters 7–9).

Moreover, my approach carefully avoided the reification of social classes and the trap of economic determinism, whereby social-class movements are interpreted as the outcome chiefly, if not solely, of economic forces (Stillman, 2005). By the same token, this approach did not treat groups, such as social classes, as the collection of individuals with no common characteristics apart from the pursuit of their individual goals in the same system of competition (Mouzelis, 1986, 1991; Sibeon, 1999). Rather, it gave due consideration to interconnected realms of social activity, such as the cultural, the economic, and the political, and drew attention to their impact on people's life chances and individuals' occupational trajectories.

Following on from the previous point, I conceptualized social mobility as a set of interconnected processes, which I tried to approach holistically as they were perceived as organically linked to the mode of production and social relations in Protopi. Holism here was pursued by drawing on the wider socioeconomic, political, cultural, historical, and educational contexts that fostered the mobility processes analyzed in the previous chapters. Hence, social mobility was not researched as a set of variables with varying degrees of interaction between each other but as the outcome of a plethora of developments with social, family, and individual significance. Put differently, the importance of factors examined in this book, such as ethnic origin, gender, age-group, and education, were not treated as categories of analysis remote from the social reality of the respondents but as being integral to the universe of individuals' experiences.

The scope and focus of the book aimed to go beyond conventional mobility studies, which routinely examine education within systems of social stratification merely as a factor in social mobility outcomes (Duncan and Hodge, 1963; Boudon, 1974; Shavit and Müller, 1997). Instead, while I retained the interest in "traditional" social mobility pathways, such as education and occupational advancement, I also gave due consideration to the impact of forces that underpin the system of competition, such as emigration, marriage, patronage and clientelism, and unequal power relationships. This was achieved thanks to the research design and scope of this study, which drew on a bounded community. More specifically, studying the case of a community made possible the examination of a number of different pathways, such as occupational, educational, political, and so on, which are interlinked and intertwined in the social history of Protopi.

Moreover, the particularities of Protopi, such as the attempted equalization of opportunities in 1929, the educational expansion after 1964, and its demographic composition (i.e., ethnically mixed and growing population) made it an atypical and unique community to explore. This atypicality, it is hoped, will also enhance the contribution of this study in a field dominated by large-scale explorations at the expense of depth and that mobility research of bounded communities will receive more due attention.

According to the evidence presented in the previous chapters, education was largely contingent upon wider social, cultural, political, economic, and historical forces. This finding can be of some value to those who periodically seek to adjust the function of education in order to serve the needs of specific groups and to those who simply view educational expansion as social policy panacea for problems, such as low productivity of the workforce, high unemployment, and so on. Although governments in many Western countries have renewed their commitment to expand higher-education participation to unprecedented levels, this study argued that the potential of educational qualifications in the social mobility of individuals is more complex than postwar governments have us believe and more episodic than popular wisdom may hold. This can offer new directions in the way education is treated in modern societies and can assist us in preventing it from becoming an expedient tool for promoting the political interests of the few at the cost of the many.

Another critical contribution of this study is its mixed-methods research design. By combining qualitative and quantitative methods, I explored into some depth the realities of the interviewees, while I shed light on the bigger picture, namely the community, in which these individuals are embedded. In particular, combining data from the survey enabled me to get an idea of patterns of intergenerational change and practices regarding education and then to associate them with the occupational trajectories of individuals. The statistical analysis allowed for the general patterns and trends of change to emerge with regard to the value of education in occupational and, by proxy, social-class outcomes of individuals and families. With the adoption of qualitative methods (such as interviews, observations, and informal discussions), I was able to explore individuals' subjective understanding of their lived experiences in relation to the social mobility processes I sought to explore. Moreover, I was able to reconstruct the life-course mobility and educational history of a large number of respondents and to relate them to other significant factors that underpinned their social mobility, such as emigration, marriage, and patronage and clientelist relations. In such a way, it is hoped, I managed to offer an adequate picture of structural processes and individuals' strategies, decisions, understanding, and experiences of them. I hope that the mixed-methods approach I adopted can offer a way out of the unproductive divide within the social mobility field between qualitative and quantitative approaches and can furnish us with an explanation of social phenomena that is not restricted to the structural or macro-aspects of change but is also sensitive to the micro-foundations that impinge on the same processes as well as their meso-context.

A further contribution of this study is its exploration of the impact of education on social mobility in Greece, as the country has a very limited tradition and small research output in this field. Through extensive ethnographic study of a specific community, namely Protopi, an important contribution was made for understanding the situation in Greece. It is hoped that this study will be utilized by future researchers as a stepping stone to the exploration of the role of education in social mobility in other settings. This study, then, could evoke some further interest in the role of education and the underlying processes in the postwar social mobility of communities and could assist in raising the profile of social mobility research in Greece.

Finally, it is anticipated that this study can also have a transformative potential and make a positive contribution to the researched community itself. Despite the fact that inequalities are prevalent and ascriptive forces are very powerful, this study might encourage people to explore strategies to improve their lives and reorganize some aspects in their community in a more fair and equitable manner.

Appendix 1: The Major Political, Economic, and Social Events in Greece, 1936–2011

Year	Government	Prime minister	Major events (political, economic, etc.)
1936–1941	Military dictatorship	I. Metaxas	
1941–1944	Italian–German occupation	Various, as acting heads of the state under Axis occupation	Widespread famine in urban centers
1944–1949	Civil War		1948: OECD entry
1949–1952*	Caretaker governments	Various alternating short-term governments	1949: Council of Europe entry
			1946–1951: Marshall Plan (American Aid)
1952–1955**	Greek Rally (Nationalist)	Al. Papagos	1952: NATO entry
1955–1963	National Radical Union (Right-wing)	C. G. Karamanlis	
1963–1965***	Centre Union (Centre–Left)	G. Papandreou	
1965–1967	5 Transitional Governments	Various [mainly Right-wing]	Political instability
1967–1974	Dictatorship	Army colonels	1973: Firstoil shock
			1974: Abolition of monarchy
1974–1980	New Democracy (Centre-Right)	C. G. Karamanlis (05.1980–10.1981:G. Rallis)	1974: Turkish invasion of Cyprus and crisis.
			1974/1975: Restoration of democracy
			1979: EEC Acceptance treaty signed
			1979: Secondoil shock
1981–1989	PASOK (Centre–Left)	A.G. Papandreou	1981: Entrance to the EEC
			1985–1988: Mediterranean Integrated Programmes
1989–1990	Right–Left Coalition	Various (Right-wing)	1989–1993: 1st Community Support Framework

Years	Party	Prime Minister	Key Events
1990–1993	New Democracy	C. Mitsotakis	1992: EEC becomes EU (Maastricht Treaty)
1993–1996	PASOK	A.G. Papandreou	1994–1999: 2nd Community Support Framework
1996–2000	PASOK	C. Simitis	2000: Lisbon Strategy
			1/1/2001: Entry to EMU
			2000–2006: 3rd Community Support Framework
2004–2007	New Democracy	C. A. Karamanlis	2004: Athens Olympic Games
2009–2011	PASOK	G. A. Papandreou	2009: Debt crisis
			2010: First bailout package from IMF, ECB, and EU
			2011: Second bailout package

*During this period, there were two caretaker governments that assumed office, each one lasting for a few months.

**Between 1952 and 1963, there were two caretaker governments. Karamanlis's term was followed by two caretaker governments until 1963 when G. Papandreou won the national election.

***One caretaker government interjected between Papandreou's term in office, which lasted for four months (December 1963 to February 1964).

Abbreviations: OECD, Organisation for Economic Co-operation and Development; NATO, North Atlantic Treaty Organization; EEC, European Economic Community; EMU, European Monetary Union; IMF, International Monetary Fund; ECB, European Central Bank.

Appendix 2: The Register

Each unit on the Register consists of a household. New entries are created only when a male becomes the head of a household, that is, upon marriage. Married females are registered in their husband's unit, while those individuals who emigrate remain on the Register for as long as they are registered to vote in the national and local elections in Protopi (instead of them registering in their new place of residence). Immigrants from other parts of Greece who do not vote in Protopi (that is to say, those who live in Protopi but vote in their place of origin) are not included in the Register. This is crucial as the size of the electorate determines the amount of money a municipality receives from the central government. Some of the immigrants from other countries, such as ethnic Greeks from Albania, were only granted voting rights in the mid- or late nineties; hence, they were not included in the Register at the time of data collection (except for a few females who were married to a man who lives and votes in Protopi). The first entries date back to the early twentieth century. As of 2007, an estimated 2,000–3,000 individuals lived permanently in Protopi but voted in other places. As such, they were not included in the Register, leaving approximately 5,000 individuals in its records. For most of the twentieth century, the Register was not regularly updated, and the information it contained was elementary and often imprecise. While the Register was more or less an accurate source of information about birth dates, family names, and size, it was less reliable in respect of occupations, as it only provided the occupation of the male, head of the household at the time of registration, which was fairly out of date. Moreover, information about geographical mobility was limited, and usually restricted to emigration abroad, leaving information on emigration to other parts of Greece an unknown. Multiple movements were not recorded and information about all members of the household was insufficient and outdated, compromising further the accuracy of the data set. Finally, educational attainment was not recorded nor was ethnic identity. While the information acquired from the Register was invaluable in forming a directory of the residents in Protopi, the shortcomings identified above, namely insufficient or inaccurate information on occupation, education, ethnic group membership, and migration, could seriously inhibit the conduct of the survey.

As a result, alternative sources were utilized in order to fill in these gaps. As is the case with most conventional surveys, the methods of data collection for this one were contingent upon the resources available. Unlike conventional surveys, though, this study relied for a large part of its data collection on "key informants" who are embedded in the local community. This somewhat "unconventional" approach was preferable to more traditional ones within the given context, for multiple reasons. First, because a small number of key informants, who knew the area and its people well, could provide more information than a much larger number of individuals. Second, my understanding of the cultural context of Protopi offered me insights into how best to approach respondents and collect data. In this vein, it would have been inappropriate to contact a large number of individuals in a traditional "survey-like" manner, which typically relies on the administering of questionnaires. This conventional approach does not allow for rapport to be established between researcher and participants and treats individuals as mere information providers. Such detachment clashes both with the values of the transformative–emancipatory approach and with the cultural context in Protopi. More specifically, the process of data collection for the survey was part of the overall research process, which invested a lot in establishing contacts and "learning" the local codes and values. Although, administering questionnaires could have been less time consuming than obtaining the essential information through the Register and key informants, it would have sat at odds with the local codes and values. Hence, in the local context, people are accustomed to one-to-one, personalized contacts in a way that collecting data through survey questionnaires on behalf of someone else does not allow. In addition, standardized questionnaires are easier to code and analyze, thus are more sensitive and effective to the needs of the researcher. By contrast, my approach needed to be more sensitive to the needs of the community and the informants. Third, giving to some selected individuals the role of the key informant was similar to granting them with some special role, with special recognition. This recognition derives from their role in the community and was not arbitrarily attributed by me. At the feasibility stage of the research, various residents pointed me to "important others," who were widely perceived as the most knowledgeable and suitable contacts for my research. This allowed them to talk to me about many community issues, with the "unspoken" albeit warranted consent of the community. Given the large interplay between the private and public sphere in such communities, I was fully aware that my interactions with key informants could become known to other locals. Hence, in order to preclude any possibility of upsetting any individuals by unauthorized disclosure of their personal information by someone else, I adhered to two further principles. First, key informants were only asked about people with whom they had a close relationship, especially about their family members and people they had close ties with in their residential communities. Given the key role of family, generally, in Greece and, specifically, in Protopi (see chapters 7–9), providing information on one's relatives is not perceived as a violation of data protection, but a legitimate practice in contexts where "dense networks" and personalized relations prevail. Second, I asked key informants to provide information that was in the "public domain," that is to say about occupation, education, and emigration, rather than strictly personal information. In particular, I made it clear to them that I was interested in the occupations their relatives had and not in the reasons for changing them. Similarly, I left as little room for ambiguity as possible about my interests. For example, that I was interested in the level of education of people they knew and not their educational performance, and so on.

Despite this reciprocal trust between me and the key informants, the accuracy of the information obtained and potential bias in the data collected (either with the aim to distort or to conceal information from the researcher) had yet to be determined. Hence, although different key informants approached the issues at hand in a different manner, the responses they gave could not suffice to classify any of them as unreliable or biased. In other words, while all of them engaged with the research process in different ways, the overall "pattern" of their responses was consistent, thus not raising issues of reliability of the information obtained. It was thus noticed that where information was missing, this had to do with the informants' lack of knowledge rather than any intention on their part to misinform me. In other words, there was no evidence of distortion of the data collected nor any systematic bias.

Each time new data were collected, existing information was cross-checked again in order to identify any inconsistencies or bias from the information collected from the key informants. It emerged that inconsistencies, inaccuracies, and gaps were no more frequent or important than one would expect. Thus, key informants in the older age-group were not always able to recollect information about people in the youngest generation as the latter had entered different occupational and social groups and were very mobile (both occupationally and geographically). In this way (through the combined use of the Register and the information obtained from the key informants), the educational and occupational information concerning a large number of households was acquired. In the majority of cases, the main occupation was recorded at the age of 35 years. However, for many participants, their secondary, parallel, and supplementary occupations were also recorded. Regarding education, the latest qualification obtained or the completed formal education stage was recorded separately. In terms of geographical movements, it was important to know the duration and the place of emigration (e.g., abroad or within Greece, and, if known, the exact destination). In case individuals did not return to Protopi, they were removed from the data set.

While this strategy allowed me to obtain crucial information without risking my relationship with the participants or imperiling the subsequent phases of the research, there was still the issue of ethnic group membership to be resolved.

This type of information was obtained through three key informants with whom a long, faithful relationship preceded the research. Though most of the locals, especially the older ones, knew all the Roma by their surnames and the areas where they lived, it was essential for me to verify that those broadly identified as Roma were indeed members of this group. Therefore, the three key informants were contacted separately, and they all provided the same information. However, this approach is not entirely unproblematic. As Mertens warned (1998, p. 88), "bias can result when the method of determining racial or ethnic identity does not adequately address the complexities of the situation." This is also echoed in Stanfield's (1993) query: "How do we conceptualize identity issues in race and ethnicity research that go beyond reified, simplistic stereotyping?"

Although this research did not aim to delve into issues of construction of difference, it nevertheless took pertinent issues to classifying different ethnic identities seriously as they could result in sampling and interpretation bias, and ultimately weaken the research outcome. Thus, I also spoke to Roma informants about the identification of the different ethnic groups. In addition, the qualitative interviews offered testimony to ethnic identification. It is recognized that issues of "hetero-" or "self-" designation are hard to resolve once and for all, in particular with reference to Roma groups, chiefly because they are entrenched in the mode of socioeconomic organization, which produces the prevailing power relations and determines the value, context, and importance of these differences. Nevertheless, "[d]iscontinuing such research based on the rationale that our understanding of race, gender, and disability is limited needs to be weighed against the benefit associated with revealing inequalities in resources and outcomes in education, psychology, and the broader society" (Mertens, 1998, p. 90).

After all the information from the Registry and other sources had been recorded, I sought to verify as much of it as possible. This was achieved through the use of the material obtained from the qualitative interviews given that they elicited information about the main areas of interest of the survey research (e.g., education, occupation, geographical movements). Apart from data validation, this procedure led to a further improvement in the accuracy and breadth of the information obtained from the Electoral Register and the key informants.

Appendix 3: Quantitative Data Analysis

After all necessary information was copied from the Register and it was updated, complemented, and expanded with the assistance of the key informants, I transferred it onto SPSS software for quantitative data analysis (stage one of the data analysis). Initially, I created 15 variables and I input all the cases, 2,318 from a population of approximately 5,000, onto the database. Subsequently, a large number of these cases were removed, which left 1,358 cases.

Once this stage (stage one) of the data analysis was completed I proceeded to the next one, which involved the cleaning of the database (stage two). All cases that did not contain information for a large number of variables were dropped. Furthermore, I checked a large number of cases against the data set to make sure that no error entries were input and, if so, that there was no systematic error during the data entry. This resulted in a further elimination of approximately 50 cases.

The next stage, stage three, consisted of running frequencies and crosstabulations to determine the characteristics of the sample and to obtain distributions that mattered to the exploration of the research questions (such as, the gender, ethnicity, and age-group distribution) (Table A1).

These 1,248 cases produced a representative sample of Protopi in relation to most key areas of interests. Hence, the proportion of males and females in my sample was similar to that in Protopi (approximately 50 percent in each group). Roma people were overrepresented in my sample (22 percent)

Table A1 Survey sample (by gender, generation, and ethnicity) ($N = 1,248$)

	Older generation		Middle generation		Younger generation		Total
	Non-Roma	Roma	Non-Roma	Roma	Non-Roma	Roma	
Male	135	35	201	59	154	45	629
Female	118	25	234	71	137	34	619
Total	253	60	435	130	291	79	1,248

in comparison with their actual proportion in Protopi (approximately 10 percent). However, the proportion of the non-Roma people in my sample (78 percent) was similar to that in Protopi, given that other groups, such as Albanian immigrants, were not included in my sample. Finally, 25 percent of the obtained sample were in the older age-group, 45 percent in the middle, and 30 percent in the younger. Although, the middle age-group appears to be more represented than the other two, the latter were large enough to allow for limited sample bias to occur.

Notes

2 Social Mobility: Issues, Trends, and Critique

1. These are not the only ways of exploring social mobility. Loury et al. (2005) delineate two further approaches both of which come from the field of ethnic minorities studies. The first one "sees social mobility in terms of 'recognition' and social citizenship—that is, in the degree to which individuals are affirmed by others as being equal partners in the community" (Loury et al., 2005, p. 2). This approach pays emphasis, on the one hand, to the gap between labor market success and, on the other, social equality. Hence, while the former might be achieved by a specific minority group, the latter might not follow suit. This approach then sees social mobility "less in terms of classes moving in a labor market hierarchy, and more in terms of racially and ethnically defined groups operating within a hierarchical system of social statuses" (Loury et al., 2005, p. 2). The second approach is termed as the "political" school of social mobility study (Loury et al., 2005). Here the focus is on "the capacity of groups to organize for collective action and to significantly influence the institutions that affect them" (Loury et al., 2005, p. 2). Individuals from minority groups are viewed as outsiders to social institutions that are significant in enhancing social mobility and as having inferior status and bargaining power to mobilize resources for their social advancement. "Mobility in this understanding is the process by which groups attain sufficient internal coherence to legitimately threaten existing social institutions with the loss of power, and thus to obtain a fair (or more than fair) slice of the collective pie" (Loury et al., 2005, p. 3). In other words, this school of thought conceives social mobility as the set of processes within which racial and ethnic minorities are embroiled in order to improve their social position. The main exponents of this approach are Glazer and Moynihan (1963) and Rex and Moore (1967).
2. The shortcomings of the occupation-based approach are discussed separately in section 2.4 in connection with Glass's and Goldthorpe's works, which both used occupations for the derivation of social classes in their analyses.
3. LSE stands for the London School of Economics, the institution that hosted Glass and his team who worked on the social mobility study discussed here.
4. The originality of these studies also lies with the fact that the researchers who produced them used income groups as the unit of their analysis rather than social classes that were predominantly used hitherto.

5. Although the existence of a capitalist or ruling class is a sine qua non for every capitalist society, the existence of an aristocracy or upper class is not. Britain is an interesting country, which hosts both a formidable capitalist class and a traditional aristocracy. The latter, aristocracy, is a medieval relic that has survived the transition into the capitalist mode of production and enjoys significant symbolic and material privileges.
6. I am using the term "orthodox" here to refer to those who adopted the assertions made by Marx in the *Preface* (1859) to the *Critique of the Political Economy* about historical materialism, as a new "theory" of history. Although Marx never elaborated on the ideas laid out in the *Preface*, these ideas were later adopted by the members of the Second and Third Internationals and were "frozen into dogma, immune from the often facile but sometimes trenchant criticisms levelled against it, and impervious to theoretical elaboration or even clarification" (Levine and Wright, 1980, p. 47).
7. It is worth quoting here the main passage from which this "orthodox" position stems. Although space limitations do not allow me to delve into depth, I wish to stress that it is the interpretation of this passage that has led to a lot of debate and tension within Marxist circles, both academic and activist/political ones, in relation to the conception of historical development: "In studying such transformations it is always necessary to distinguish between the material transformation of the economic conditions of production, which can be determined with the precision of natural science, and the legal, political, religious, artistic or philosophic—in short, ideological forms in which men become conscious of this conflict and fight it out. Just as one does not judge an individual by what he thinks about himself, so one cannot judge such a period of transformation by its consciousness, but, on the contrary, this consciousness must be explained from the contradictions of material life, from the conflict existing between the social forces of production and the relations of production. No social order is ever destroyed before all the productive forces for which it is sufficient have been developed, and new superior relations of production never replace older ones before the material conditions for their existence have matured within the framework of the old society. Mankind thus inevitably sets itself only such tasks as it is able to solve, since closer examination will always show that the problem itself arises only when the material conditions for its solution are already present or at least in the course of formation. In broad outline, the Asiatic, ancient, feudal and modern bourgeois modes of production may be designated as epochs marking progress in the economic development of society. The bourgeois mode of production is the last antagonistic form of the social process of production – antagonistic not in the sense of individual antagonism but of an antagonism that emanates from the individuals' social conditions of existence – but the productive forces developing within bourgeois society create also the material conditions for a solution of this antagonism. The prehistory of human society accordingly closes with this social formation" (Marx, 1977).
8. Especially, Cohen's (1978) book, *Karl Marx's Theory of History: A Defence*, exerted a major influence in the rearticulation of Marx's original idea of socioeconomic development. This was expressed in Cohen's (1978) "Primacy Thesis," which upholds "that the nature of a set of production relations is explained by

the level of development of the productive forces embraced by it" (1978, p. 134). As Levine and Wright (1980) argued, "The overall argument can be decomposed into five relatively independent theses: A given level of development of productive forces is compatible with only a limited range of relations of production (Thesis 1). Since the forces of production tend to develop over time (Thesis 2), these forces eventually reach a level at which they are no longer compatible with existing relations of production (Thesis 3). When this occurs, the relations are said to "fetter" the productive forces. Because rational human beings will not in the long run tolerate the fettering of productive forces, they will transform these relations of production (Thesis 4), and substitute new relations that are optimal for the further development of productive forces (Thesis 5)" (pp. 51–52). This interpretation of Marx's original thesis, however, has since been abandoned as it has led to a plethora of problems and theoretical conundrums. For a detailed discussion of some major problems within Marxist thinking, see Mészáros (1995), especially pp. 917–936.

3   The Political Economy, Social Stratification, and Class Formation in Postwar Greece

1. EAM stands for Ethniko Apeleftherotiko Metopo (National Liberation Front) and it was the main political and social force of organized resistance against the occupation of the Axis forces during the Second World War. ELAS stands for Ellinikós Laïkós Apeleftherotikós Stratós (Greek People's Liberation Army or ELAS). Although initially autonomous, ELAS soon became EAM's military branch.
2. PASOK stands for Panellinio Sosialistiko Kinima (Panhellenic Socialist Movement).
3. North Atlantic Treaty Organization.
4. The European Economic Community (EEC) was superseded by the EU, in 1996. Hereafter, for the sake of consistency, I shall be using the term EU in order to refer to both entities.
5. KKE stands for Kouministiko Komma Ellados (Communist Party of Greece).
6. For a discussion of the role of the Greek state in administering and facilitating financial capital, see Ellis (1964) and Psilos (1968). For a discussion of the close ties between the Greek state and the shipping sector, the other significant source of capital during the same period, see Serafetinides (1979).
7. Mouzelis (1978) maintains that the indigenous Greek capital operated in the more profitable and less-risky nonmanufacturing sectors, mainly on borrowed money. In turn, a big share of the profits of the Greek capitalists was shifted into foreign banks or into shipping, making therefore unavoidable the reliance of the Greek economy on foreign capital, which started taking place in the early 1960s and it "had serious impact on the structure of the economy" (p. 37).
8. For difficulties in the estimation of this type of immigrants, see Papadimitriou (2005); Petronoti and Triandafyllidou (2003).
9. Although it is very difficult to offer an accurate estimate of the size of tax evasion and black market economy, expert guesstimates posit the former, that

is, tax evasion, in the area of 10–13 billion Euros, that is 5–6 percent of the overall Greek GDP (as it stood in 2008). The black market activity is estimated to be between 25 and 28 percent of the GDP, that is, 54 and 61 billion Euros. In case these indicators, namely tax evasion and black market activity, are accurate, then Greece occupies the top position among its OECD counterparts. Finally, it has been further estimated that the "secret income," that is to say income that is evaded from the tax authorities, is around 10–15 percent for those in the top decile of the income structure and around 24 percent for the top 1 percent (Matsaganis, in Kostarelou, 2011). In other words, the highest an individual's income is, the greatest the amount of money evaded from taxation. For more on the black market economy, see Vavouras and Manolas (2005).

10. Data refer to 2003, a year that Greece was intensively preparing for the 2004 Olympic Games. As a result, a large number of immigrants were on short-term contracts in sectors with increased demand, such as in constructions (indicatively, 29.3 percent of those immigrants in the secondary sector were employed in constructions).
11. NSSG stands for National Statistical Services of Greece. The acronym is direct translation of Elliniki Statistiki Ypiresia Ellados (ESYE) and is preferred here to ESYE for issues of consistency with the international literature, where it appears as NSSG.
12. In 2003, 66.1 percent of them lived in Attica—the area surrounding Athens—and 8.4 percent in Central Macedonia, the prefecture of the second biggest urban center, Salonika.
13. According to Christodoulakis and Kalyvitis (2001), the repatriated co-ethnics and foreign immigrants who were added to the labor force by 2000 were estimated to be more than 500,000 people.
14. Data refer to January 2012. It is likely that the rate of youth unemployment in Spain has increased faster than in Greece, which might have led to a concomitant change in the relevant rate of youth unemployment. Nevertheless, this does not suffice to change the overall picture, with Greece as one of the "champions" of youth unemployment in the EU. It is expected that the effects of the severe austerity measures and the strict terms of the bail-out packages that Greece signed from 2010 onward will exacerbate this situation and implode the social, financial, and economic position of the country in the forthcoming years.
15. In spite of the high rates of female part-time employment in Greece, overall part-time employment has been traditionally low. For example, 20.3 percent of women and 6.5 percent of men in the EU-27 were in part-time employment, while countries with a more aggressive neoliberal model and a more deregulated labor market, such the United Kingdom, displayed much higher rates of part-time employment: 38.8 percent for women and 8.9 percent for men (OECD, 2010).
16. This means that for every 100 women in the labor market, approximately 14 are employed part time and the rest (i.e., 86) are employed full time. In terms of men, approximately 4 in every 100 are part-time employed, with the remaining 96 in full-time work (OECD, 2010).

17. The rate of females in the 25- to 64-year-old group in the labor market in the EU-27 was slightly higher than that for Greece, that is, 64.4 percent, with a much narrower gender gap, that is, 15.7 percent (OECD, 2008).
18. Indicative of the structural determinants of the gender gap is that Greece has one of the lowest rates in terms of women in managerial positions among all OECD countries: In 2007, the concomitant rate stood at 27.9 percent for Greek females compared to 32.1 percent in the OECD countries (ELSF, 2007).
19. For the advanced capitalist economies, the exit from agriculture occurred at a much earlier stage than in Greece. In England, for example, 80 percent of the population was employed in agriculture in 1500, compared to only 20 percent in 1850 (and approximately 40 percent in industry) (Overton, 1996). Other European countries, such as France, Germany, and Italy, reached a low level of agricultural employment after the Second World War (Crafts, 1985).
20. "Pluriactivity" here is used to connote "the willingness of the individual or the family as a unit, to engage in more than one activity across sectors in order to integrate relatively low income level" (Bull and Corner, 1993, p. 10).
21. This is the period after Greece gained independence from the Ottoman Empire, which starts with the fight for liberation, in 1821, and the establishment of the independent Greek Kingdom in 1830.
22. The existence or not of an agricultural class as a distinctive one with its own characteristics, particularities, and relations with the other social classes is an issue of special consideration. While some authors (Vergopoulos, 1975) accept it as a different class, others (Mouzelis, 1976) are more skeptical about the value of this concept, given the difficulty it posits in demonstrating how it is implicated in the capitalist mode of production and what its relationships with the other classes are.
23. During this period, the dominant mode of production was agriculture, which was very heterogeneous and multilayered (comprised of various structures). This transition period from the protocapitalist mode of production to the capitalist one was followed by the massive influx of the defining mechanisms of the global market (Tsoukalas, 1977).
24. In the same year, namely 1920, 17.6 percent of the population lived in cities with more than 20,000 people and 12.6 percent in large cities with more than 100,000 people (Mouzelis, 2005).
25. This included more than one million refugees from Asia Minor who were expelled to Greece in 1921 (Voutira, 1997).
26. Toward the end of the nineteenth century, the service-employed part of the population was estimated to be more than 60 percent of the nonagricultural population. Moreover, in 1928, 35 percent of the overall urban population were indigenous, that is born in an urban center, 32 percent refugees, and about 33 percent immigrants from another part of Greece (Tsoukalas, 1977, p.2 05).
27. To this end, it has also to be acknowledged that emigration from the urban population abroad, chiefly to the United States and Australia, allowed the refugees and those who emigrated from the villages to the cities to fill in the positions that were left vacant.

28. "Groups" is preferred here instead of social classes, because the dominant mode of production in these rural areas, at least until the war, was still pre-capitalist with some proto-capitalist features.
29. These "outcasts" consisted of entire ethnic groups, such as people of Romani origin ("Yiftoi" in Greek), or people with marginal position in the local division of labor.
30. In other words, occupational changes, such as the creation of new jobs, absorbed this movement. This means that, while the absolute number of socially mobile individuals may have been high, inequalities in the social structure might also have remained unchallenged.

4 Education, Social Mobility, and the Question of Meritocracy

1. Primary education was free from 1836.
2. In 2007, the share of private funding as a proportion of overall educational expenditure was 36.5 percent compared to 52.2 percent that was expended by the state. The remaining 11.2 percent was contributed by EU funds (KANEP/GSEE, 2012).
3. Greek universities, apart from the Open Greek University, do not charge tuition fees for undergraduate courses. Fees for postgraduate studies have increasingly been applied by many Greek universities, but they vary across institutions and subject of study.
4. The Centre for the Development of Education Policy (Kentro Anaptiksis Ekpaideytikis Politikis) of the General Confederation of Greek Workers (Yeniki Sinomospondia Ergaton Elladas) appears hereafter with the initials that relate to its acronym in Greek, that is, KANEP/GSEE, in order to allow for consistency with relevant publications in the Anglophone literature.
5. Since 2000, university entry rates saw a steep increase: from 30 percent of the corresponding age-group in 2000 to 43 percent in 2007 (OECD, 2010). Nevertheless, the graduation rates have traditionally been at very low levels: at 14.5 percent in 2000, Greece had the fourth lowest graduation rate among 24 OECD countries and in 2007, the worst rate, 17.7 percent, among 22 OECD countries (OECD, 2010).
6. Household consumption rose sharply from the 1990s onward. NSSG (2010) data indicate that between 1993/1994 and 1998/1999, it rose by 22 percent and by 12.1 percent during the 1998/1999 to 2004/2005 period. According to Cheliotis and Xenakis (2010, p. 366), "[t]his was facilitated by the deregulation of both consumer and housing credit, which in turn produced a steep rise in household indebtedness."
7. Notably, according to an OECD (2006) study, in Greece, there were more physicians per capita than in any other OECD country (OECD, 2006). Katsanevas (2003) drew similar conclusions in relation to dentists and lawyers.
8. Graduate unemployment has to be examined at the backdrop of youth unemployment. In the EU-27, youth unemployment stood at 21.4 percent, which is over twice as high as the total unemployment rate in 2011. In Greece, in 2011, the youth unemployment rate was 44.4 percent, more than double the EU-27 average (Eurostat, 2011).

9. This lies at the heart of the "post-industrialization" thesis, whose major tenet was that as long as the blue-collar workers outnumber white-collar ones, a society can be characterized as "industrial"; if, however, the white-collar labor force overtakes arithmetically the blue-collar labor force, then this signifies the emergence of the "post-industrial" society.
10. Since the American society was perceived by Bell (1973) as the vanguard of social and economic changes in the world, other countries, he speculated, would soon follow suit.
11. Goldthorpe (2003b).
12. To be precise, the type of social mobility that was evident was "short distance movement" (Westergaard and Resler, 1975), that is, within white- or blue-collar occupations rather than across these groups.
13. It should be borne in mind that educational qualifications operate differently for men and women. For the latter, there seems to be a stronger effect of educational qualifications on class destinations.

5 Contextualizingt he CaseS tudy

1. The name of the locale and of all the respondents were replaced with pseudonyms for issues pertaining to protection of the anonymity of the participants and the confidentiality of issues discussed with them.
2. Apart from the poor landless people in areas that had recently joined Greece, there were approximately 1.2 million refugees (Voutira, 1997), who fled from Minor Asia to Greece after 1921. Although the Decree was also concerned with their settlement, this did not affect Protopi because the main bulk of these refugees settled in East and North Eastern Greece.
3. For an analysis of differentiations within peasant societies, see Chayanov (in Thorner et al., 1986).
4. No officially recorded date exists for the establishment of Protopi. According to anecdotal sources, it dates back to the early thirteenth century. Its first inhabitants, according to the same sources, were non-Roma with the Roma appearing toward the end of the same century.
5. This raises issues pertinent to fertility and morbidity rates of the Roma and the general population. As the investigation of this aspect is still ongoing, tentative findings suggest that Roma families have tended to be larger than the non-Roma for the best part of the twentieth century.
6. It is estimated that the non-Roma group consists of approximately 80 percent of the overall population in Protopi, the Roma approximately 10 percent and the newly arrived immigrants from Albania also 10 percent.
7. These groups moved into Protopi after the early 1990s. Consequently, the estimation of their intra- and intergenerational social mobility could not be achieved given that they were not native to Protopi's social structure, labor market, and social relations for the main part of their educational and occupational lives.
8. This does not negate the possibility that much of the power of interpretation still lies with the researcher. In other words, the researcher is not turned into an "objective operator" of the research she or he conducts. She or he still carries a lot of the burden of responsibility as far as knowledge construction

is concerned. The difference, though, is that in critical ethnography, the researcher is aware of this process and actively tries to limit his or her power and interpretative bias.

9. This study extends beyond the interest of conventional ethnography, which typically entails focusing exclusively on everyday-life situations in order to understand and describe a culture from the "native" point of view. While, on the one hand, I was interested in unpacking social inequalities and injustices embedded in Protopi, on the other hand, I was also concerned with maintaining a commitment toward positive social change. As Wainwright (1997, p. 5) contended, "the objective is still to access the subjective beliefs of the people being studied, but rather than accepting such beliefs at face value they are examined critically in the context of a broader historical and structural analysis."

10. Although these criteria (ethnicity, gender, age, class, educational level) possibly also guide much conventional ethnographic research, the main originality of this study is the way they were deployed. Thus, these criteria did not comprise a list of variables to be taken into account. Instead, for each of these aspects (ethnicity, gender, and so on), I sought to include people whose voice was less "heard," who belonged to the most-oppressed and least-powerful groups. I managed, to the best of my ability and to the optimum the circumstances allowed, to achieve this through a number of ways. For example, I spent a lot of time familiarizing myself with the research locale. I also acquired as extensive knowledge as possible of the historical, social, political, economic, and educational context of Protopi so that my knowledge was up to date and my sampling criteria aligned with the principles of the transformative approach.

11. The need to identify these three age-groups is justified by their diverse experiences in respect of the labor market (chapter 7) educational participation (chapter 8), marital selection, and social differentiation (chapter 9). It was anticipated that their stories would be different as they belonged to three adjacent generations who experienced different struggles, choices, opportunities, and pursued different strategies to advance their careers, and personal and family well-being.

6 Quantitative Aspects of Social Mobility

1. It mainly, though not exclusively, refers to tobacco growth, the most widely cultivated and commercially exploited product by farmers in Protopi.
2. For a similar approach, see Lambiri-Dimaki (1983).
3. CASMIN stands for Comparative Analysis of Social Mobility in Industrial Nations.
4. NS-SEC stands for National Statistics Socio-Economic Classification.
5. Admittedly, this is a very different approach to the most widely used schemes, such as the seven-class CASMIN scheme, in which the agricultural class is absent. While this is consistent with the shrinking of British agriculture—in 2006, approximately 1.8 percent of the UK workforce was employed in agriculture (Defra, 2006)—such an approach would be historically, socially, and culturally inaccurate in relation to Protopi.

6. Although more systematic data collection needs to prove this point, it could be argued that in current days, the size of the Roma and non-Roma families is not as disparate as it used to be.
7. EGP stands for the Erikson, Goldthorpe, and Portocarero, who created the relevant (i.e., EGP) class scheme.
8. The family as the production unit might resemble the "domestic" or "cottage industry" in Britain in the eighteenth and early nineteenth century (Timmins, 2005) or the development of the family industry (Marx and Engels [1888], 1977; Thompson, 1963).
9. Commodity production in Protopi emerged mainly after the Second World War, when the farmers started trading the products of agriculture and their labor power gained in exchange value.
10. This externality of the ruling class to the class structure of Protopi is neither an anomaly nor a feature limited to Protopi. As I discussed in relation to ninetieth-century Greece, the Greek diaspora was the leading and for a long time the main capitalist class, which was, though, in social and geographic terms, remote to Greece.
11. If anything, Marx (1969, p. 444) observed that "Capital may there try its utmost. It cannot prevent the labour market from being continuously emptied by the continuous conversion of wages labourers into independent, self-sustaining peasants. The position of a wages labourer is for a very large part of the American people but a probational state, which they are sure to leave within a longer or shorter term."
12. In the remainder of this chapter, my unit of analysis is the individual and, when applicable, partners living together. It is individual and "couple" mobility that this chapter is concerned with and not mobility of entire (occupational) groups.
13. A rate of 100 percent would indicate perfect mobility, meaning that all social positions are open to everyone. In other words, no class, and especially the top one(s), is self-recruiting.
14. In order to obtain the results that are discussed in section 6.8, the following calculations were conducted:
Total mobility rate = vertical + horizontal mobility = 49.3 + 12.8 = 62.1% (1)
Total immobility rate = sum on diagonal/total = 473/1,248 = 37.9%   (2)
Vertical mobility = upward + downward = 43.2 + 6.1 = 49.3%   (3)
Upward mobility = cells below the diagonal – horizontal mobility
cells/total = 539/1,248 = 43.2%   (4)
Downward mobility = cells above the diagonal – horizontal mobility
cells/ total = 76/1,248 = 6.1%   (5)
Horizontal mobility = total mobility – vertical mobility = 12.8%   (6)
15. Long-range mobility is the movement between the two ends of Table 6.1 (any movement that crosses both intermittent lines). That is movement out of Class 3 or 4 into Class 1 pertains to long-range, upward mobility. The reverse, namely movement from Class 1 into 3 or 4, indicates long-range, downward mobility. Movements above or below one of the two virtual lines (i.e., out of Class 2 into Class 1 and vice versa, or out of Class 3 or 4 into Class 2 and vice versa) represent short-range mobility.
16. Exchange mobility = total – structural mobility = 62.1 – 45.2 = 16.9%   (7)

17. A degree of caution is necessary in the interpretation of these findings. According to Heath (1981), structural and circulation mobility are artifacts due to the asymmetry in the mobility tables. In other words, structural mobility can never be appropriately depicted in a typical mobility table (such as Table 6.2) because some observed movement is due to differences in class distributions between two adjacent generations.
18. If the odds ratio was 1, then individuals from both classes would have the same likelihood of entering Class 1. In other words, it would be as easy for peasants' children to enter the middle class as it would be for the offsprings of the middle class itself. The bigger the odds are than 1, the higher is the amount of inequality in the relative mobility chances and between respective classes.

7 Occupational Trajectories and Experiences of Mobility

1. The "family mobility strategy" was also followed in chapter 6 in order to account for the occupational trajectories of women, which are typically ignored in mainstream mobility studies. The appropriateness of examining together the social mobility of partners is also dictated by factors entrenched in the socioeconomic history of Protopi. For example, even when women stayed at home, their contribution to the family economy was multiple as it is demonstrated in the remainder of the chapter.
2. As I mentioned in chapter 5, the three generations were as follows: younger generation, 25–44 years old; middle generation, 45–64 years old; and older generation, 65 years and older.
3. This is depicted in the accounts of the participants in the older generation, especially those whose occupational experiences drew on the immediate post-war years, which is the time when this transition from subsistence agriculture to commodity capitalism was more pronounced.
4. In the following lines, where "Q" appears at the beginning of an extract, it refers to the question posed by the interviewer. When an extract is taken from a two-to-one interview (e.g., with a couple), first the name(s) and then the initials of the respondents are used in order to connote the person who spoke each time.
5. "Yiftoi" in the context of Protopi is typically a derogatory exonym used by the non-Roma to designate the Roma.
6. The insinuation that the Roma people were less likely to be landowners came from informal discussions with Euripides that preceded the more "formal" interview.
7. While this aspect was depicted only to a small extent in the quantitative material (see section 6.7), the richness and versatility of the qualitative material allow for this important aspect to be explored in more depth in this chapter.
8. It will be noticed that the age of some of the respondents does not correspond to the age-group discussed in each section. For example, Phokion belongs to the middle age-group, but his account is included in the discussion about the older generation. Wherever this occurs, it is due to the themes recounted by the respondents, such as Phokion, which relate not strictly to their own generation, but to other ones.

9. "Local" refers here to the wider area surrounding Protopi. This includes all nearby villages and towns as well as the main city, which was the administrative and economic center in the wider area.
10. Evidence on the ethnic composition of the clients of Roma professionals in the early postwar years is inconclusive. However, in the last 10–15 years, Roma builders have been frequently commissioned jobs by non-Roma and with similar pay rates to the non-Roma builders.
11. As I am writing these lines, this precariousness has taken the characteristics of a crisis not only in the labor market but also in the relations of production. The latter are being radically transformed not only in Greece, but globally (Harman, 2009; Harvey, 2010).
12. Interestingly, Circe's husband, Sophocles, 55 years, often interjected to offer his views on issues relevant to Circe's working experiences and filled in her account when he judged that his contribution could enhance the clarity of Circe's narration.
13. It can be suggested that two main factors might have impinged on this difficulty to access young Roma women. First, as a male researcher, it was generally more difficult for me to gain access to females. Second, young Roma women move out of Protopi in much larger volumes than in the past.
14. A caveat here is necessary: in the material presented in chapter 6, accounts from male and/or non-Roma participants were more extensive than for women and/or Roma. Although this reflects the sample of the ethnographic research (see chapter 4), the main reason for such an approach lies with the fact that most of the new jobs that were created after the 1950s were "male-centered"; hence, it was invariably men who made the most of the new opportunities. The non-Roma imbalance has to be seen as a reflection of the domination of the more powerful group, the non-Roma, in the labor market and its disproportionate share in the capitalization of the new occupational opportunities that emerged in the postwar years. This unevenness will be redressed in chapters 8 and 9.

8 EducationalE xperiences and Pathways to Social Mobility

1. For a similar argument, see chapter 6, especially the class-scheme construction.
2. These gains were not restricted to white-collar workforce. A number of studies that appeared at that time also shed light on the relative affluence of blue-collar workers. For example, Burawoy's (1982) book *Manufacturing Consent: Changes in the Labor Process under Monopoly Capitalism* and Goldthorpe et al.'s (1968a, 1968b, 1969) series of studies titled *The Affluent Worker* showed some of the intricacies of the reorganized labor processes on the working and social lives of manual workers in traditional blue-collar sectors, such as car manufacturing. Crucially, though, the relative improvement in material standing of these workers did not translate into concomitant social mobility advancement, that is to their embourgeoisement. Consistent with the argument I am propounding here, the affluence of these workers was the result of a postwar focus on increased production and consumption. Policy initiatives, such as the New Deal in the United States, aimed at exactly this: the empowerment of the worker as a consumer, for it was believed that

by receiving increased wages, workers would have more expendable income and thus sustain the capitalist need for expansion. The remedy, in other words, for avoiding another disastrous economic crisis, such as the one that preceded the Second World War, was the creation of a consumption-driven economy, which required the reorganization of production.

9 Alternative Pathways to Social Mobility: The Role of Migration, Marriage, and Political Patronage

1. Referring to the 1952–1966 period.
2. Assortative mating connotes the matching of traits between spouses. Positive assortative mating refers to pairing practices between partners who possess the same degree or type of a specific characteristic. For example, in my study, I use positive assortative to refer to the pairing of partners with the same socioeconomic background. If there are socioeconomic differences between the spouses, for example, if one partner comes from a family of landowners and the other from a family of landworkers, this would be negative assortative mating.
3. Groups of people who used to live on the mountains, typically involved in livestock farming. In Protopi, there are a number of families with a Vlachic origin who, according to anecdotal evidence, range between 20 and 30 families.
4. For many locals in the majority group, "black" is a reference to the darker skin color of the Roma people, as this has been perceived as a major marker of differentiation between Roma and non-Roma.
5. A member of staff in a bank, who was specialized in agricultural issues.
6. Loosely translated, it means a "gift," usually related to securing a position, such as in the civil service. More broadly, rousfeti implies achieving a goal thanks to political mediation.

Bibliography

Adorno, Th. W. (1974) *Minima Moralia. Reflections from Damaged Life*. (First published in German in 1951.) London: NLB.
Ainley, P. (1993) *Class and Skill: Changing Divisions of Knowledge and Labour*. London: Cassell.
Aldridge, S. (2001) *Social Mobility: A Discussion Paper*. London: Performance and Innovation Unit.
———. (2003) "The facts about social mobility," *New Economy*, 10(4): 189–193.
Alexander, A. (1964) *Greek Industrialists*. Athens: Centre of Planning and Economic Research.
Allen, S. (1982) "Gender Inequality and Class Formation," in A. Giddens and G. Makenzie (eds), *Social Class and the Division of Labour*. Cambridge: Cambridge University Press.
Allman, P. (2001) *Critical Education against Global Capitalism: Karl Marx and Revolutionary Critical Education*. Westport, CT: Bergin & Garvey.
Althusser, L. (1971) *Lenin and Philosophy and Other Essays*. London: Monthly Review Press.
Althusser, L. and Balibar, E. (1970) *Reading Capital*. London: New Left Books.
Amitsis, G. and Lazaredi, G. (eds) (2001) *Legal and Sociopolitical Dimensions of Immigration in Greece* (in Greek). Athens: Papazesi.
Armstrong, K. (2008) "Ethnography and Audience," in P. Alasuutari, L. Bickman, and J. Brannen (eds), *The Sage Handbook of Social Research Methods*. London: Sage.
Arnot, M. (2004) "Male Working Class Identities and Social Justice: A Reconsideration of Paul Willis's Learning to Labour in Light of Contemporary Research," in N. Dolby, G. Dimitriadis, and P. Willis (eds), *Learning to Labor in New Times*. New York: Routledge Falmer.
Athanasiou, L. (2006) "Collective Employment Contracts and the Function of the Labour Market" (in Greek), in *Economic Developments, Centre for Planning and Economic Research* (KEPE), Issue 11, pp. 37–47.
Badiou, A. (2010) *The Communist Hypothesis*. London: Verso.
Bakker, B. F. M., Dronkers, J., and Ganzeboom, H. B. G. (1984) *Social Stratification and Mobility in the Netherlands*. Amsterdam: Siswo.
Ball, S. (2003) *The More Things Change: Educational Research, Social Class and "Interlocking" Inequalities*. London: Institute of Education, University of London.

Ball, S. (2007) *Education plc: Private Sector Participation in Public Sector Education*. London: Routledge.
——. (2008) *The Education Debate: Policy and Politics in the 21st Century*. Bristol: Policy Press.
Banks, A. S. (2001) *Cross-national time-series data archive [dataset]*. Binghamton, NY: Computer Systems Unlimited.
Bauman, Z. (1992) *Intimations of Postmodernity*. London: Routledge.
Baumgartl, B. and Favell, A. (1995) *New Xenophobia in Europe*. London: Kluwer Law International.
Beck, U. (1992) *Risk Society: Towards a New Modernity*. London: Sage.
Becker, G. S. (1973) "A Theory of Marriage: Part I," *Journal of Political Economy*, 81(4): 813–846.
Bell, D. (1973) *The Coming of Post-Industrial Society*. London: Heinemann.
——. (1978) "On Meritocracy and Equality," in J. Karabel and A. H. Halsey (eds), *Power and Ideology in Education*. New York: Oxford University Press.
Berk, S. E. (1985) *The Gender Factory: The Apportionment of Work in American Households*. New York and London: Plenum Press.
Bertaux, D. and Thomson, P. (1997) *Pathways to Social Class: A Qualitative Approach to Social Mobility*. New Brunswick and London: Transaction Publishers.
Bhatti, G. (2003) "Social Justice and Non-traditional Participants in Higher Education: A Tale of 'Border Crossing' and Instrumental Drift," in C. Vincent (ed.), *Social Justice, Education and Identity*. London: Routledge Falmer.
Blanden, J., Goodman, A., Gregg, P., and Machin, S. (2002) "Changes in Intergenerational Mobility in Britain," Centre for the Economics of Education Discussion Paper No. 26, London School of Economics, forthcoming in M. Corak (ed.), *Generational Income Mobility in North America and Europe*. Cambridge: Cambridge University Press.
Blanden, J. and Machin, S. (2004) "Educational inequality and the expansion of higher education," *Scottish Journal of Political Economy*, 51: 230–249.
Blanden, J., Goodman, A., Gregg, P., and Machin, S. (2004) "Changes in Intergenerational Mobility in Britain," in M. Corak (ed.), *Generational Income Mobility in North America and Europe*. Cambridge: Cambridge University Press.
Blanden, J., Gregg, P., and Machin, S. (2005) "Educational Inequality and Intergenerational Mobility," in S. Machin and A. Vignoles (eds), *What's the Good of Education?* Princeton, NJ: Princeton University Press.
Blanden, J. and Machin, S. (2007) *Recent Changes in Intergenerational Mobility in Britain*. London: Sutton Trust.
Blanden, J., Gregg, P., and Macmillan, L. (2007) "Accounting for intergenerational income persistence: noncognitive skills, ability and education," *Economic Journal*, 117: 43–60.
Blanden, J., Gregg, P., and Macmillan, L. (2008) *Intergenerational Persistence in Income and Social Class: The Impact of Increased Inequality*. Centre for Market and Public Organisation Working Paper 08/195.
Blau, P. M. and Duncan, O. D. (1967) *The American Occupational Structure*. New York: Wiley.
Blaxter, L., Hughes, C., and Tight, M. (2001) (2nd ed.) *How to Research*. Buckingham: Open University Press.
Borjas, G. (1992) "Ethnic capital and intergenerational mobility," *Quarterly Journal of Economics*, 107(1): 123–150.

Boudon, R. (1974) *Education, Opportunity, and Social Inequality.* New York: John Wiley.
Bourdieu, P. (1966) "Champ Intellectuel et Projet Créatur." *Les temps modernes,* pp. 865–906. Translated by Sian France (1969) and printed as "Intellectual Field and Creative Project," *Social Science Information,* 8(2): 89–119.
———. (1977) *Towards a Theory of Practice.* Cambridge: Cambridge University Press.
———. (1984) *Distinction: A Social Critique of the Judgement of Taste.* Cambridge, MA: Harvard University Press.
———. (1991) *Language and Symbolic Power.* Polity: Cambridge.
Bourne, J. (1999) "Racism, Postmodernism and the Flight from Class," in D. Hill, P. McLaren, M. Cole, and G. Rikowski (eds), *Postmodernism in Educational Theory: Education and the Politics of Human Resistance.* London: Tufnell Press.
Bowles, S. (1972) "Unequal Education and the Reproduction of the Social Division of Labor," in A. P. Coxon and C. L. Jones (eds) (1975), *Social Mobility.* Ringwood: Penguin Education.
Brannen, J. (1988) "The study of sensitive subjects," *Sociological Review,* 36(3): 552–563.
———. (2008) *Mixed Methods Research: Rationalities, Risks and Realities.* Keynote presentation given at the "Fourth Mixed Methods Conference and Workshops," Fitzwilliam College, University of Cambridge, July 21–24, 2008, Cambridge, UK.
Brannen, J., Statham, J., Mooney, A., and Brockmann, M. (2007) *Coming to Care: The Work and Family Lives of Workers Caring for Vulnerable Children.* Bristol: Policy Press.
Braun, M. and Müller, W. (1997) "Measurement of Education in Comparative Perspective," in L. Mjoset, F. Engelstad, A. Leira, R. Kalleberg, and G. Brochmann (eds), *Methodological Issues in Comparative Social Science.* Greenwich: JAI Press, pp. 163–201.
Braverman, H. (1974) *Labor and Monopoly Capital.* New York: Free Press.
Breen, R. (2000) "Class inequality and social mobility in Northern Ireland, 1973–1996," *American Sociological Review,* 65(3): 392–406.
———. (2003) "Is Northern Ireland and educational meritocracy?" *Sociology,* 37(4): 657–675.
———. (2004a) (ed.) *Social Mobility in Europe.* Oxford: Oxford University Press.
———. (2004b) "The Comparative Study of Social Mobility: A Review," in C. T. Whelan, *Changequal: Economic Change, Unequal Life Chances and Quality of Life, European.* Luxembourg: Office for Official Publications of the European Communities.
Breen, R. and Goldthorpe, J. H. (1999) "Class Inequality and Meritocracy: A Critique of Saunders and an Alternative Analysis," *British Journal of Sociology,* 50(1): 1–27.
———. (2001) "Class, mobility and merit: the experience of two British birth cohorts," *European Sociological Review,* 17(2): 81–101.
Breen, R. and Whelan, C. T. (1993) "From ascription to achievement? Origins, education and entry to the labour force in Ireland," *Acta Sociologica,* 36(1): 3–18.
Breen, R., Hannan, F., Rottman, D. B., and Whelan, C. T. (1990) *Understanding Contemporary Ireland.* London: Gill and Macmillan.

Bridges, D. (2001) "The ethics of outsider research," *Journal of Philosophy of Education*, 35(3): 371–386.
Britten, N. and Heath, A. (1983) "Women, Men and Social Class," in E. Gamarnikow (ed.), *Gender, Class and Work*. London: Heinemann, pp. 46–60.
Brown, P. and Tannock, S. (2009) "Education, meritocracy and the global war for talent," *Journal of Education Policy*, 24(4): 377–392.
Bryman, A. (1989) *Research Methods and Organisation Studies*. London: Unwin Hyman.
———. (2001) *Social Research Methods*. Oxford: Oxford University Press.
———. (2008) "The End of the Paradigm Wars?" in P. Alasuutari, L. Bickman, and J. Brannen (eds), *The Sage Handbook of Social Research Methods*. London: Sage.
Bull, A. and Corner, P. (1993) *From Peasant to Entrepreneur: The Survival of the Family Economy*. Oxford: BERG.
Bulmer, M. (2001) "The Ethics of Social Research," in N. Gilbert (ed.), *Researching Social Life*. London: Sage Publications.
Burawoy, M. B. (1982) *Manufacturing Consent: Changes in the Labor Process under Monopoly Capitalism*. Chicago, CA: The University of Chicago Press.
———. (2000) *Global Ethnography*. Berkeley, CA: University of California Press.
Burgess, E. W. (1927) "Statistics and Case Studies as Methods of Sociological Research," *Sociology and Social Research*, 12: 103–120.
Bush, G. W. (2008) Speech, Economic Crisis. Available at: http://uspolitics.about.com/od/gwbush/a/bush_economy.htm (Accessed: March 2012).
Cabinet Office (2008) *Getting On, Getting Ahead. A Discussion Paper Analysing the Trends and Drivers of Social Mobility*. London: Cabinet Office. The Strategy Unit.
———(2011) *Opening Doors, Breaking Barriers: A Strategy for Social Mobility*. London: Cabinet Office. Available at: www.dpm.cabinetoffice.gov.uk/resource-library/opening-doors-breaking-barriers-strategy-social-mobility-update-progress-april-2011 (Accessed: June 2012).
Callinicos, A. (2010) *Bonfire of Illusions: The Twin Crises of the Liberal World*. Cambridge: Polity Press.
Cannadine, D. (1999) *The Rise and Fall of Class in Britain*. New York: Columbia University Press.
Carabott, P. and Sfikas, Th. D. (2004) *The Greek Civil War: Essays on a Conflict of Exceptionalism and Silences*. London: Ashgate Publishing, Ltd.
Carspecken, P. F. (1996) *Critical Ethnography in Educational Research: A Theoretical and Practical Guide*. London and New York: Routledge.
Charalambis, D. (1989) *Clientelist Relations and Populism: The Illegitimate Consensus in the Greece Political System* (in Greek). Athens: Exantas.
Cheliotis, L. K. and Xenakis, S. (2010) "What's neoliberalism got to do with it? Towards a political economy of punishment in Greece," *Criminology and Criminal Justice*, 10: 353.
Chletsos, M. (2005) "Labour Market—Unemployment and Employment Policies," in C. Kollias, C. Naxakis, and M. Chletsos (eds), *Modern Approaches to the Greek Economy* (in Greek). Athens: Patakis.
Christodoulakis, N. and Kalyvitis, S. (2001) *Structural Funds: Growth, Employment and the Environment. Modelling and Forecasting the Greek Economy*. London: Kluwer Academic Publishing.

Chryssakis, M. and Soulis, S. (2001) "Inequalities in access to university education: an approach to the official data" (in Greek). *Panepistimio*, 3: 31–65.

Clark, T. and Lipset, S. (1996) "Are Social Classes Dying?" in D. Lee and B. Turner (eds), *Conflicts about Class: Debating Inequality in Late Industrialism*. London: Longman.

Clark, J., Modgil, C., and Modgil, S. (eds) (1990) *John H. Goldthorpe: Consensus and Controversy*. London: The Falmer Press.

Clogg, R. (1992) *A Concise History of Greece*. Cambridge: Cambridge University Press.

Cohen, G. A. (1978) *Karl Marx's Theory of History: A Defence*. Oxford: Clarendon Press.

Collins, R. (1979) *The Credential Society: An Historical Sociology of Education and Stratification*. London: Academic Press.

Conservative Party (2008) *A Conservative Agenda for Social Mobility*. London: Conservative Party.

Cook, S. and Binford, L. (1986) "Petty commodity production, capital accumulation, and peasant differentiation: Lenin vs. Chayanov in rural Mexico," *Review of Radical Political Economics*, 18(4): 1–31.

Coulby, D. (2005) "The Knowledge Economy: Institutions," in D. Coulby and E. Zambeta (eds), *Globalization and Nationalism in Education*. London: Routledge, pp. 37–56.

Crafts, N. (1985) *British Economic Growth during the Industrial Revolution*. Oxford: Clarendon Press.

Crompton, R. (1990) "Goldthorpe and Marxist Theories of Historical Development," in J. Clark, C. Modgil, and S. Modgil (eds), *John H. Goldthorpe: Consensus and Controversy*. London: The Falmer Press.

——. (2008) (3rd ed.) *Class and Stratification*. Cambridge: Polity Press.

Crook, S., Pakulski, J., and Waters, M. (1992) *Postmodernization*. London: Sage.

Crul, M. (2000) "Breaking the Circle of Disadvantage. Social Mobility of Second-Generation Moroccans and Turks in the Netherlands," in H. Vermeulen and J. Perlmann (eds), *Immigration, Schooling and Social Mobility*. London: MacMillan Press.

Dahrendorf, R. (1959) *Class and Class Conflict in Industrial Society*. Stanford: Stanford University Press

Damanakis, M. (1997) *Educating Repatriated Greek and Alien Students in Greece. A Multicultural Approach* (in Greek). Athens: Gutenberg.

Dei, J. S., Mazzuca, J., McIsaac, E., and Zine, J. (1997) *Reconstructing "Drop-Out": A Critical Ethnography of the Dynamics of Black Students' Disengagement from School*. Toronto: University of Toronto Press.

De Leeuw, E. (2008) "Self-administered Questionnaires and Standardised Interviews," in P. Alasuutari, L. Bickman, and J. Brannen (eds), *The Sage Handbook of Social Research Methods*. London: Sage.

Delphy, C. (1981) "Women in Stratification Studies," in H. Roberts (ed.), *Doing Feminist Research*. London: Routledge and Kegan Paul, pp. 114–128.

Dennis, N., Henriques P., and Slaughter, C. (1956) *Coal is Our Life*. London: Routledge and Kegan Paul.

Denzin, N. and Lincoln, Y. (1994) (eds) *Handbook of Qualitative Research*. London: Sage.

Department for Environment, Food, and Rural Affairs (DEFRA) (2006) *Agriculture in the United Kingdom 2005*. London: Department for Environment, Food, and Rural Affairs.

Devine, F., Savage, M., Crompton, R., and Scott, J. (2004) (eds) *Rethinking Class, Identities, Cultures and Lifestyles*. Basingstoke: Palgrave.

Dex, S. (1987) *Women's Occupational Mobility*. London: Macmillan Press.

DiPrete, T. A. and Grusky, D. B. (1990) "Structure and trend in the process of stratification for American men and women," *American Journal of Sociology*, 96: 107–143.

Doucet, P. and Mauthner, N. (2008) "Qualitative Interviewing and Feminist Research," in P. Alasuutari, L. Bickman, and J. Brannen (eds), *The Sage Handbook of Social Research Methods*. London: Sage.

Douglas, J. D. (1976) *Investigative Social Research*. Beverly Hills, CA: Sage.

Doumanis, M. (1983) *Mothering in Greece: From Collectivism to Individualism*. London: Academic Press.

Dousas, D. (1997) *Rom and Racial Discriminations* (in Greek). Athens: Gutenberg.

Duncan, G. (1984) *Year of Poverty, Years of Plenty: The Changing Economic Fortunes of American Workers and Families*. Ann Arbor, MI: Institute for Social Research.

Duncan, O. D. and Hodge, R. W. (1963) "Education and occupational mobility: a regression analysis," *American Journal of Sociology*, 68(6): 629–649.

Ellis, H. (1964) *Industrial Capital in Greek Development* (in Greek). Athens: Center of Economic Research.

Erikson, R. (1983) "Changes in social mobility in industrial nations: the case of Sweden," *Research in Social Stratification and Mobility*, 2: 165–195.

Erikson, R. and Goldthorpe, J. H. (1992) *The Constant Flux. A Study of Class Mobility in Industrial Societies*. Oxford: Clarendon Press.

Esping-Andersen, G. (1993) *Changing Classes. Stratification and Mobility in Post-Industrial Societies*. London: Sage.

European Commission (2003) "European Education Production Functions: What Makes a Difference for Student Achievement in Europe" (European Commission Munich).

Eurostat (2012) Harmonised unemployment rate by sex. Available at: http://epp.eurostat.ec.europa.eu/portal/page/portal/eurostat/home/ (Accessed: June 2012).

Featherman, D. L. and Hauser, H. M. (1978) *Opportunity and Change*. New York: Academic Press.

Featherman, D. L., Jones, F. L., and Hauser, M. L. (1975) "Assumptions of mobility research in the United States: the case of occupational status. *Social Science Research*, 4: 329–360.

Fielding, J. (2001) (2nd ed.) "Coding and Managing Data," in N. Gilbert (ed.), *Researching Social Life*. London: Sage Publications, pp. 227–251.

Fielding, N. and Thomas, H. (2001) (2nd ed.) "Qualitative Interviewing," in N. Gilbert (ed.), *Researching Social Life*. London: Sage Publications, pp. 123–144.

Fisher, M. (2009) *Capitalist Realism: Is There No Alternative?* Winchester: Zero Books.

Fragoudaki, A. and Dragona, T. (1997) (eds) *What is Our Country? Ethnocentrism in Education* (in Greek). Athens: Alexandria.

Franklin, H. (1971) "The Worker Peasant in Europe," in T. Shanin (ed.), *Peasants and Peasant Societies*. Harmondsworth: Penguin.

Fraser, N., Gutierrez, R. and Pena-Casas, R. (eds) (2011) *Working Poverty in Europe*. Basingstoke: Palgrave Macmillan.

BIBLIOGRAPHY

Gamarnikow, E. and Purvis, J. (1983) "Introduction," in E. Gamarnikow, D. Morgan, J. Purvis, and D. Taylorson (eds), *The Public and the Private*. London: Heinemann.
Ganzeboom, B. G., Luijkx, R., and Treiman, D. J. (1989) "Intergenerational Class Mobility in Comparative Perspective," *Research in Social Stratification and Mobility*, 8, Greenwich, CT: JAI Press, pp. 3–84.
Garner, S., Cowles, J., Lung, B., and Stott, M. (2009) *Sources of Resentment, and Perceptions of Ethnic Minorities among Poor White People in England*. London: National Community Forum/Department for Communities and Local Government.
Gazon, E. (2011) "Which tools to fight in-work poverty?" *Peer Review*, 31 March–1 April 2011.
Gekas, R. (2005) "Sectors of the Greek Economy: Structural Problems and Prospects," in C. Kollias, C. Naxakis, and M. Chletsos (eds), *Modern Approaches to the Greek Economy* (in Greek). Athens: Patakis.
Georgakopoulos, T. (1991) *The Greek Economy in the EEC*. Athens: Greek Agricultural Bank.
Giddens, A. (1973) *The Class Structure of the Advanced Societies*. London: Hutchinson.
Giddens, A. and Held, A. (1982) *Classes, Power, and Conflict: Classical and Contemporary Debates*. Berkeley, CA: University of California Press.
Gilbert, N. (2001) (ed.) (2nd ed.) *Researching Social Life*. London: Sage.
Gillborn, D. and Youdell, D. (2000) *Rationing Education: Policy, Practice, Reform and Equity*. Buckingham: Open University Press.
Glass, D. V. (ed.) (1954) *Social Mobility in Great Britain*. London: Routledge and Kegan Paul.
Glazer, N. and Moynihan, D. P. (1963) *Beyond the Melting Pot*. Cambridge, MA: MIT Press.
Glesne, C. and Peshkin, A. (1992) *Becoming Qualitative Researchers: An Introduction*. New York: Longman.
Gobo, G. (2008) "Re-conceptualizing Generalisation: Old Issues in a New Frame," in P. Alasuutari, L. Bickman, and J. Brannen (eds), *The Sage Handbook of Social Research Methods*. London: Sage, pp. 193–213.
Goldthorpe, J. H. (1980) *Social Mobility and Class Structure in Modern Britain*. Oxford: Clarendon Press.
———. (2000) *On Sociology: Numbers, Narratives and the Integration of Research and Theory*. Oxford: Oxford University Press.
———. (2003a) "Problems of 'Meritocracy', " in R. Erikson and J. O. Jonsson (eds), *Can Education be Equalized? The Swedish Case in Comparative Perspective*. Boulder, CO: Westview Press.
———. (2003b) "The myth of education-based meritocracy: why the theory isn't working," *New Economy*, 10(4): 189–193.
Goldthorpe, J. H. and Portocarero, L. (1981) "La Mobilite Social en France, 1953–1970: Nouvel examen," *Revue Francaise de Sociologie*, 22.
Goldthorpe, J. H. and Mills, C. (2004) "Trends in Intergenerational Class Mobility in Britain in the late Twentieth century," in R. Breen (ed.), *Social Mobility in Europe*. Oxford: Oxford University Press.
Goldthorpe, J. H. and Jackson, M. (2006) "Education Based Meritocracy: The Barriers to its Realisation," Paper presented at the EQUALSOC conference. Mannheim, December 2–3, 2005.

Goldthorpe, J. H. and Jackson, M. (2007) "Intergenerational class mobility in contemporary Britain: political concerns and empirical findings," *British Journal of Sociology*, 58(4): 525–546.

Goldthorpe, J. H., Lockwood, D., Bechhofer, and Platt, J. (1968a) *The Affluent Worker: Industrial Attitudes and Behaviour*. Cambridge: Cambridge University Press.

Goldthorpe, J. H., Lockwood, D., Bechhofer, F., and Platt, J. (1968b) *The Affluent Worker: Political Attitudes and Behaviour*. Cambridge: Cambridge University Press.

———. (1969) *The Affluent Worker in the Class Structure*. Cambridge: Cambridge University Press.

Goodhart, D. (2008) "We are more mobile than we think," *Prospect* (153), 20.12.2008. Available at: www.prospectmagazine.co.uk/2008/12/moremobilethanwethink/ (Accessed: January 2012).

Goodman, A., Blundell, R., Dearden, L., and Reed, H. (1997) *Higher Education, Employment and Earnings in Britain*. London: London Institute for Fiscal Studies.

Gotovos, A. (2002) *Education and Diversity: Issues of Intercultural Education* (in Greek). Athens: Metechmio.

Gouvias, D. (1998) "Comparative issues of selection in Europe: the case of Greece," *Education Policy Analysis Archives*, 6(4). Available at: http://epaa.asu.edu/epaa/v6n4.html (Accessed: June 2009).

Gramsci, A. (1971) [1935] *Selections from the Prison Notebooks of Antonio Gramsci*. New York: International Publishers.

Grbich, C. (2007) *Qualitative Data Analysis: An Introduction*. London: Sage.

Greenspan, A. (2008) Testimony in the House Committee on Oversight and Government Reform. Available at: http://www.clipsandcomment.com/2008/10/23/text-alan-greenspan-testimony-congress-october-23/ (Accessed: July 2012).

Grollios, G. and Kaskaris, I. (2003) "From socialist–democratic to 'Third Way' politics and rhetoric in Greek education (1997–2002)," *Journal for Critical Education Policy Studies*, 1(1). Available at: www.jceps.com/index.php?pageID=article&articleID=4 (Accessed: June 2008).

Hamilton, M. and Hirzowicz, M. (1993) *Class and Inequality: In Pre-Industrial, Capitalist and Communist Societies*. New York: Harvester Wheatsheaf.

Hammersley, M. (1990) *Reading Ethnographic Research: A Critical Guide*. London: Longman.

———. (1992) *What's Wrong with Ethnography?* London: Routledge.

Hammersley, M. and Atkinson, P. (1983) *Ethnography: Principles in Practice*. London: Tavistock.

Hancock, I. (2000) "The consequences of anti-gypsy racism in Europe. *Other Voices*, 2(1). Available at: www.othervoices.org/2.1/hancock/roma.php#4b (Accessed: July 2012).

Harman, C. (2009) *Zombie Capitalism: Global Crisis and the Relevance of Marx*. London: Bookmarks Publications.

Harvey, D. (1989) *The Condition of Postmodernity*. Oxford: Basil Blackwell.

———. (2010) *A brief History of Neoliberalism*. New York: Oxford University Press.

Hatcher, R. (2012) "Social Class and Schooling: Differentiation or Democracy?" in M. C. Cole (ed.), *Education, Equality and Human Rights: Issues of Gender,'Race', Sexuality, Disability and Social Class*. London: Routledge.

Hawley, C. and Lindsey, D. (2012) "Racism and Xenophobia Still Prevalent in Germany." Der spiegel, Available at: www.spiegel.de/international/germany/xenophobia-still-prevalent-in-germany-20-years-after-neo-nazi-attacks-a-851972.html (Accessed: July 2012).
Heath, A. (1981) *Social Mobility*. Glasgow: Fontana.
Heath, A. F. and Cheung, S. Y. (1998) "Education and Occupation in Britain," in Y. Shavit and W. Muller (eds), *From School to Work*. Oxford: Clarendon Press.
Heath, A. and Ridge, J. (1983) "Social mobility of ethnic minorities," *Journal of Biosocial Science Supplement*, 8: 169–184.
Hill, D. and Cole, M. (2001) *Schooling and Equality: Fact, Concept and Policy*. London: Kogan Page.
Hills, J., Brewer, M., Jenkins, S., Lister, R., Lupton, R., Machin, S., Mills, C., Modood, T., Rees, T., and Riddell, S. (2010) *An Anatomy of Economic Inequality in the UK: Report of the National Equality Panel*. London: Government Equalities Office.
Hirschman, A.O. (1970) *A Bias for Hope. Essays on Development and Latin America*. New Haven: Yale University Press.
HM Government (2009) *New Opportunities: Fair Chances for the Future*. London: The Stationary Office.
Hobsbawm, E. (1994) *The Age of Extremes: 1914–1991*. London: Abacus.
Hochschild, A. R. (1989) *The Second Shift: Working Parents and the Revolution at Home*. New York: Viking.
Hoggett, P., Garner, S., Wilkinson, H., Cowles, J., Lung, B., and Beedell, P. (2008) *Race, Class and Cohesion: A Community Profile of Hillfields, Bristol*. Bristol: Bristol City Council/UWE, Centre for Psychosocial Studies.
House, E. and Howe, K. (1999) *Values in Evaluation and Social Research*. Thousand Oaks, CA: Sage.
Hout, M. (1988) "More universalism, less structural mobility: the American occupational structure in the 1980s," *American Journal of Sociology*, 93: 1358–1400.
———. (2000) "The Politics of Mobility," in A. Kerckhoff (ed.), *Generating Social Stratification*. Oxford: Westview Press.
———. (2003) "The inequality-mobility paradox: the lack of correlation between social mobility and equality," *New Economy*, 10(4): 205–207.
Hoy, S. (1995) *Chasing Dirt: The American Pursuit of Cleanliness*. New York: Oxford University Press.
Iannelli, C. and Paterson, L. (2006) "Education Systems Have Little Impact on Social Mobility." Available at: www.esrcsocietytoday.ac.uk/ESRCInfoCentre/PO/releases/2006/february/social_mobility.aspx?ComponentId=13915&SourcePageId=5433 (Accessed: July 2008).
Institute for Employment (INE) (2005) *The Greek Economy and Employment: Annual Report*. Athens: INE/GCGL.
Institute for Public Policy Research (IPPR) (2008) *Social Mobility: A Background Review*. London: Institute for Public Policy Research.
Ioakimidis, P. (1996) "Contradictions in the Europeanisation Process," in K. Featherstone and K. Yfantis (eds), *Greece in a Changing Europe*. Manchester: Manchester University Press.
Jackson, B. (1968) *Working Class Community: Some General Notions Raised by a Series of Studies in Northern England*. London: Routledge and Kegan Paul.
Jary, D. and Jary, J. (1991) *Collins Dictionary of Sociology*. Glasgow: HarperCollins.

Jones, O. (2011) *Chavs: The Demonization of the Working Class*. London: Verso.
Jonsson, J. O. (1992) *Towards the Merit-Selective Society?* Stockholm: Swedish Institute for Social Research, University of Stockholm.
Jonsson, J. O. and Mills, C. (1993) "Social class and educational attainment in historical perspective: a Swedish-English comparison," *British Journal of Sociology*, 44(3): 403–428.
Jordan, S. (2002) "Critical Ethnography and the Sociology of Education," in C. A. Torres and A. Antikainen (eds), *The International Handbook of the Sociology of Education: An International Assessment of New Research and Theory*. Oxford: Rowman and Littlefield.
Jouganatos, G. (1992) *The Development of the Greek Economy, 1950–1991: An Historical, Empirical, and Econometric Analysis*. Westport, CT: Greenwood Press.
Kahn, S. (1982) "From peasants to petty commodity production in Southeast Asia," *Bulletin of Concerned Asian Scholars*, 14(1): 3–15.
Kanellopoulos, C. N. and Psacharopoulos, G. (1997) "Private education expenditure in a 'free education' country: the case of Greece," *International Journal of Educational Development* 17: 73–81.
Kanellopoulos, C. N., Mayromaras, K. Y., and Mitrakos T. (2004) *Education and Labour Market* (in Greek). Athens: Center of Planning and Economic Research, Scientific Studies No 50.
KANEP/GSEE (Center for Development of Education Policy—Greek General Confederation of Labour) (2003) *The Greek Educational System: A Brief Overview in Numbers* (in Greek). Athens: KANEP/GSEE.
Karakioulafi, C. (2004) *Demographic Changes, Labour Market and Pensions in Greece and the EU* (in Greek). Athens: INE/GCGL.
Karamesini, M. (2010) Transition Strategies and Labour Market Integration of Greek University Graduates. GreeSE Paper No 32. London: LSE. The European Institute. Hellenic Observatory Papers on Greece and Southeast Europe.
Kasimati, K. (1990) *Research on the Social Characteristics of Employment Study I: Occupational Choice* (in Greek). Athens: EKKE.
———. (1998) *Research on the Social Characteristics of Employment Study II: The Form of Second Employment* (in Greek). Athens: EKKE.
———. (2004) *Structures and Flows: The Phenomenon of Social and Occupational Mobility (in Greek)*. Athens: Gutenberg.
Kaskarelis, I. A. and Tsilika, K. (2009) "Early retirement for mothers in Greece," *International Journal of Social Economic*, 36(5): 566–579.
Katsanevas, T. (2003) *Professions of the future and the past*. Athens: Patakis (in Greek).
Katsikas, C. and Kavvadias, Y. K. (2000) (2nd ed.) *Inequality in Greek Education: The Development of Equalities of Access to Greek Education (1960–2000) (in Greek)*. Athens: Gutenberg.
Kavouriaris, M. (1974) "Some Thoughts about the Causes and Consequences of Immigration," in M. Nikolinakos (ed.), *Economic Development and Immigration in Greece*. Athens: Kalvos.
Kazakos, P. (2001) *Between State and Market: The Economy and Economic Policy in post-war Greece, 1944–2000* (in Greek). Athens: Patakis.
Kazamias, A. (1960) "The 'Renaissance' of Greek secondary education," *Comparative Education Review*, 3(3): 22–27.

BIBLIOGRAPHY

Kelley, J. (1990) "The Failure of a Paradigm: Log-Linear Models of Social Mobility," in J. Clark, C. Modgil, and S. Modgil (eds), *John H. Goldthorpe: Consensus and Controversy*. London: The Falmer Press.

Kelly, J. (1999) "Postmodernism and Feminism: The Road to Nowhere," in D. Hill, P. McLaren, M. Cole, and G. Rikowski (eds), *Postmodernism in Educational Theory: Education and the Politics of Human Resistance*. London: Tufnell Press.

Kelsh, D. and Hill, D. (2006) "The culturalization of class and the occluding of class consciousness: the knowledge industry in/of education," *Journal for Critical Education Policy Studies*, 4(1). Available at: http://www.jceps.com/index.php?pageID=article&articleID=59 (Accessed: July 2012).

Kenway, J. and Kraak, A. (2004) "Reordering Work and Destabilizing Masculinity," in N. Dolby, G. Dimitriadis, and P. Willis (eds), *Learning to Labor in New Times*. New York: Routledge Falmer.

Keynes, J. M. (1936) *The General Theory of Employment, Interest and Money*. New York: Harcourt, Brace and Co.

National Centre for Employment Orientation (KEPE) (2009) *Tertiary Education* (in Greek). Athens: National Centre for Employment Orientation (KEPE).

Kerides, A. (2003) *Inequality in Greek Education and University Access (1955–1985)* (in Greek). Athens: Gutenberg.

Kerr, C. (1983) *The Future of Industrial Societies*. Cambridge, MA: Harvard University Press.

Kerr, C., Dunlop, J. T., Harbison, F. H., and Myers, C. A. (1960) *Industrialism and Industrial Man*. Cambridge, MA: Harvard University Press.

Kincheloe, J. and McLarean, P. (1994a) (1st ed.) "Rethinking Critical Theory and Qualitative Research," in N. Denzin and Y. Lincoln (eds), *Handbook of Qualitative Research*. London: Sage.

———. (1994b) (2nd ed.) "Rethinking Critical Theory and Qualitative Research," in N. Denzin and Y. Lincoln (eds), *Handbook of Qualitative Research*. London: Sage.

Kingsley, D. and Moore, W. E. (1970 [1945]) "Some principles of stratification," *American Sociological Review*, 10(2): 242–249.

Koliopoulos, J. and Veremis, T. (2004) *Greece, the Modern Sequel. From 1821 to the Present*. London: C. Hurst & Co.

Kollias, C., Manolas, G., and Palaiologou, S. M. (2005) "The Greek Economy: Comparative Position and Progress of Basic Indicators," in C. Kollias, C. Naxakis, and M. Chletsos (eds), *Modern Approaches to the Greek Economy* (in Greek). Athens: Patakis.

Kontis, A. (2001) "Economic and Social Integration of Immigrants in the Host Country," in G. Amitsis and G. Lazaredi (eds), *Legal and Sociopolitical Dimensions of Immigration in Greece* (in Greek). Athens: Papazesi.

Kostarelou, E. (2011) "40% of the tax and the fine goes into the taxman's pocket," *Eleftherotypia*, December 14, p. 23.

Kotzamanis, B. and Androulaki, E. (2004) *Spatial Dimensions of Demographic Evolutions in Greece, 1981–1991, a First Approach* (in Greek). Thessaly: University of Thessaly.

Kouvertaris, G. (1971) *First and Second Generation Greeks in Chicago* (in Greek). Athens: EKKE.

Kouzis G. (2000) "Labour Relations and Social Dialogue," in G. Kouzis and S. Robolis (eds), *Issues of Social Dialogue* (in Greek). Athens: Gutenberg.
Kvale, S. (1996) *Interviews: An Introduction to Qualitative Research Interviewing*. London: Sage.
Kyriazis, A. and Asderaki, F. (2008) *Higher Education in Greece*. Bucharest: CEPES/UNESCO.
Lacey, A. and Luff, D. (2001) *Trent Focus for Research and Development in Primary Care Health*. London: Trent Focus.
Lambiri-Dimaki, J. (1983) *Social Stratification in Greece: 1962–1982*. Athens: Sakkoulas.
Lampousaki, S. (2010) *Working Poor in Europe: Greece*. INE/GSEE submission to a comparative study by the European Working Conditions Observatory (EWCO). Available at: www.eurofound.europa.eu/ewco/studies/tn0910026s/index.htm (Accessed: May 2012).
Lapavitsas K. (2012) "Default and Exit from the Eurozone: A Radical Left Strategy," *Socialist Register* 48: 288–297.
Lareau, A. (2003) *Unequal Childhoods*. Berkeley, CA: University of California Press.
Layte, R. and Whelan, C. T. (2004) "Class Transformation and Trends in Social Fluidity in the Republic of Ireland 1973–94," in R. Breen (ed.) *Social Mobility in Europe*. Oxford: Oxford University Press.
Leacock, E. B. (1971) *Culture of Poverty: A Critique*. New York: Simon and Schuster.
Lee, R. (1993) *Doing Research on Sensitive Topics*. London: Sage.
Lenin, V. I. (1964/1899) *Collected Works* (4th ed.). Moscow: Progress Publishers.
Levine, A. and Wright, E. O. (1980) "Rationality and the Class Struggle," *New Left Review* 123: 47–68.
Lewis, L. (2007) "Epistemic authority and the gender lens," *The Sociological Review*, 55(2): 273–292.
Lewis, O. (1959) *Five Families: Mexican Case Studies in the Culture of Poverty*. New York: Basic Books.
Lianos, T., Asteriou, D., and Agiomirgianakis, G. (2004) "Foreign university graduates in the Greek labour market: employment, salaries and overeducation," *International Journal of Finance and Economics*, 9: 151–164.
Liégeois, J-P. (1999) *Roma, Tsiganes, Voyageurs* (in Greek). Athens: Kastaniotis.
Lincoln, Y. (1995) "Emerging criteria for quality in qualitative research," *Qualitative Inquiry*, 1(3): 275–289.
Lipset, S. M. and Bendix, R. (1959) (eds), *Social Mobility in Industrial Society*. Berkeley, CA: University of California Press.
Lipset, S. M. and Zetterberg, H. (1959) "Social Mobility in Industrial Societies," in S. M. Lipset and R. Bendix (eds), *Social Mobility in Industrial Society*. Berkeley, CA: University of California Press.
Livanos, I. (2009) "The Relationship between Higher Education and Labour Market in Greece: The Weakest Link?" Munich: Munich Personal RePEc Archive (MPRA). Available at: http://mpra.ub.uni-muenchen.de/16239/ (Accessed: May 2012).
Lofland, J. and Lofland, L. (1996) (3rd ed.) *Analyzing Social Settings: A Guide to Qualitative Observation and Analysis*. London: Wadsworth.
Loury, G. C., Modood, T., and Teles, S. M. (2005), *Ethnicity, Social Mobility and Public Policy: Comparing the US and UK*. Cambridge: Cambridge University Press.

Luijkx, R. and Ganzeboom, H. B. G (1989) "Intergenerational Class Mobility between 1970 and 1986," in W. Jansen, J. Dronkers, and K. Verrips (eds), *Similar or Different?* Amsterdam: SISWO.
Lytras, A. (1993) *Introduction to the Theory of Greek Social Structure* (in Greek). Athens: Nea Sinora.
Mach and Wesolowski (1986) *Social Mobility and Social Structure*. New York: Routledge.
Machin, P. (2003) "Higher Education, Family Income and Changes in Intergenerational Mobility," in R. Dickens, P. Gregg, and J. Wadsworth (eds), *The Labour Market under New Labour*. Basingstoke: Palgrave MacMillan.
Mackintosh, M. and Mooney, G. (2000) "Identity, Inequality and Social Class," in K. Woodward (ed.), *Questioning Identity: Gender, Class and Ethnicity*. London: Routledge.
Madison, S. D. (2005) *Critical Ethnography: Method, Ethics, and Performance*. Thousand Oaks, CA: Sage.
Marcus, G. and Cushman, D. (1982) "Ethnographies as texts," *Annual Review of Anthropology*, 11: 25–69.
Margaritis, S. C. (1964) "Higher education in Greece," *International Review of Education*, 10(3): 297–311.
Markou, G. (1997) *Introduction to Intercultural Education* (in Greek). Athens: Elektronikes Tehnes.
Marsden, T. K. (1999) "Rural futures: the consumption countryside and its regulation," *Sociologia Ruralis*, 39: 501–520.
Marsh, D. (1958) *The Changing Social Structure of England and Wales 1871 to 1951*. New York: Routledge and Kegan Paul.
Marshall, G. (1990) "John Goldthorpe and Class Analysis," in J. Clark, C. Modgil, and S. Modgil (eds), *John H. Goldthorpe: Consensus and Controversy*. London: The Falmer Press.
Marshall, G., Swift, A., and Roberts, S. (1997) *Against the Odds? Social Class and Social Justice in Industrial Societies*. Oxford: Oxford University Press.
Marx, K. (1963/1852) *The Eighteenth Brumaire of Louis Bonaparte*. New York: International Publishers.
———. (1968/1863) *Theories of Surplus Value*. Moscow: Progress Publishers.
———. (1977/1859) *A Contribution to the Critique of Political Economy*. Moscow: Progress Publishers.
———. (1990/1867) *Capital, Volume I*. London: Penguin Books.
———. (1967/1894) *Capital, Volume 3*. New York: International Publishers.
Marx, K. and Engels, F. (1970/1845) *The German Ideology*. Norfolk: Bibbles Ltd.
———. (1977/1848) *The Communist Manifesto*. London: Penguin.
May, T. (1997) (2nd ed.) *Social Research: Issues, Methods and Process*. Buckingham: Open University Press.
Mazower, M. (2000) *Salonica, City of Ghosts: Christians, Muslims and Jews, 1430–1950*. London: Harper Collins.
———. (2001) *Inside Hitler's Greece: The Experience of Occupation, 1941–44*. London: Yale University Press.
McLaren, P. and Farahmandpur, R. (2005) "Marx after Post-Marxism: Reclaiming Critical Pedagogy for the Left," in P. McLaren (ed.), *Red Seminars: Radical Excursions into Educational Theory, Cultural Politics, and Pedagogy*. Cresskill, NJ: Hampton Press Inc.

Mertens, D. (1998) *Research Methods in Education and Psychology: Integrating Diversity within Quantitative and Qualitative Approaches.* Thousand Oaks, CA: Sage.
———. (1999) "Inclusive evaluation: implications of transformative theory for evaluation," *American Journal of Evaluation,* 20(1): 1–14.
———. (2008a) "Mixed Methods and the Politics of Human Research: The Transformative-Emancipatory Perspective," in V. L. Plano Clark and J. W. Creswell (eds), *The Mixed Methods Reader.* London: Sage, pp. 68–104.
———. (2008b) "Mixed Methods Research Ethics." Plenary speech given at the "Fourth Mixed Methods Conference and Workshops," Fitzwilliam College, University of Cambridge, July 21–24, 2008, Cambridge, UK.
———. (2008c) "Transformative Mixed Methods: Implications for Social Justice Research." Paper presented at the Annual Conference of the American Educational Research Associations (AERA), March 24–28, 2008, New York, USA.
Mészáros, I. (1995) *Beyond Capital: Toward a Theory of Transition.* London: Merlin Press.
Miles and Huberman (1994) (2nd ed.) *Qualitative Data Analysis.* London: Sage.
Miller, J. and Glassner, B. (1997) "The 'Inside' and the 'Outside': Finding Realities in Interviews," in D. Silverman (ed.), *Qualitative Research: Theory, Method and Practice.* London: Sage.
Milonas, T. (1982) *Social Reproduction in School* (in Greek). Athens: Armos.
———. (1999) *Social Class Reproduction through Schooling; Secondary Education in the Village and in the City* (in Greek). Athens: Gutenberg.
Molyneux, J. (1995) "Is Marxism Deterministic?" *International Socialism Journal,* 68. Available at: http://pubs.socialistreviewindex.org.uk/isj68/molyneux.htm. (Accessed: June 2010).
Moschonas, A. (1986) *Traditional Petty-bourgeoisie Strata. The Case of Greece* (in Greek). Athens: Institute for Mediterranean Studies.
Moschov, K. (1972) *National and Social Consciousness in Greece, 1830–1909* (in Greek). Salonica: Nea Poria.
Mouzelis, N. (1976) "Capitalism and development of agriculture," *Journal of Peasant Studies,* 3(4): 483–492.
———. (1978) *Modern Greece: Facets of Underdevelopment.* London: Macmillan.
———. (1986) "Types of reductionism in Marxist theory," *Telos,* Fall issue.
———. (1991) *Back to Sociological Theory.* London: Macmillan.
———. (2005) *Politics in the Semi-periphery. Early Parliamentarism and Late Industrialisation in the Balkans and Latin America* (in Greek). Athens: Themelio.
Mouzelis, N. and Attalides, M. (1971) "Greece," in M. S. Archer and S. Giner (eds), *Contemporary Europe: Class, Status and Power.* London: Weidenfeld and Nicholson.
National Statistical Service of Greece (2001) *National Accounts.* Athens: NSSG.
Naxakis, Ch. (2001) *Immigrants and Immigration: Economic, Political and Social Aspects* (in Greek). Athens: Patakis.
The New York Times (1931) "Warns Germany on overeducation: sees economic waste," November 1, p. 56.
Newson, J. and Newson, E. (1963) *Infant Care in an Urban Community.* London: Allen and Unwin.

Nikolaou, G. (2000) *Inclusion and Education of Foreign Students in Primary School: From "Hemogeneity" to Multiculturalism* (in Greek). Athens: Ellinika Grammata.

Oakley, A. (1974a) *Housewife*. London: Allen Lane.

———. (1974b) *The Sociology of Housework*. London: Martin Robertson.

Okely, J. (1983) *The Traveller-Gypsies*. Cambridge: Cambridge University Press.

Olesen, V. (1994) "Feminism and Models of Qualitative Research," in N. K. Denzin and Y. S. Lincoln (eds), *Handbook of Qualitative Research*. Thousand Oaks, CA: Sage, pp. 158–174.

Oakley, A. (2005) *The Ann Oakley Reader: Gender, Women and Social Science*. Bristol: The Policy Press.

Organisation for Economic Co-operation and Development OECD (1995) *Educational Policy Review of Greece*. Athens: OECD.

——— (1999) (ed.) *Classifying Educational Programmes: Manual for ISCED–97 Implementation in OECD Countries*. Paris: OECD.

——— (2005) *Economic Surveys, Greece. The Economic Impact of Migration*, 12: 126–154. Paris: OECD.

———(2007) *Education at a Glance*. Paris: OECD.

———(2008) *Tourism in OECD Countries 2008: Trends and Policies*. Paris: OECD.

———(2010) *Employment Outlook*. Paris: OECD.

Ossowski, S. (1963) *Class Structure in the Social Consciousness*. New York: The Free Press.

Overton, M. (1996) (2nd ed.) *Agricultural Revolution in England: The Transformation of the Agrarian Economy 1500–1850*. Cambridge: Cambridge University Press.

Pagoulatos, G. (2003) *Greece's New Political Economy: State, Finance, and Growth from Postwar to EMU*. New York: Palgrave Macmillan.

Pakulski, J., and Waters, M. (1996) *The Death of Class*. London: Sage.

Panayotakis, C. (2011) *Remaking Scarcity: From Capitalist Inefficiency to Economic Democracy*. London: Pluto Press.

Papadimitriou, D. (2005), "The Limits of Engineering Collective Escape: The 2000 Reform of the Greek Labour Market," in K. Featherstone (ed.), *Greece: the Challenge of Modernisation*. London: Routledge.

Papapetrou, E. (2004), "Gender wage differentials in Greece," *Bank of Greece Economic Bulletin*, 23: 47–64.

Pareto, V. (1935) *The Mind and Society [Trattato Di Sociologia Generale]*. Harcourt: Brace.

Parsons, T. (1940) *Essays in Sociological Theory*. New York: Free Press.

Patrinos, H. (1997) "Overeducation in Greece," *International Review of Education*, 43(2): 203–223.

Payne, G. (1987) *Mobility and Change in Modern Society*. London: Macmillan.

Payne, G. and Roberts, J. (2002) "Opening and closing the gates: recent developments in male social mobility in Britain," *Sociological Research Online*, 6(4).

Payne, G. and Williams, M. (2005) "Generalization in qualitative research," *Sociology*, 39(2): 295–314.

Pearce, J. and Milne, E. (2010) *Participation and Community on Bradford's Traditionally White Estates: A Community Research Project*. York: JRF.

Petmezas, S. (1999) "Rural Economy," in C. Chatziiossif (ed.), *History of Greece in the 20th Century. The Beginning*, Vol. A (1). Athens: Vivliorama, pp. 53–85.

Petmezidou-Tsoulouvi, M. (1987) *Social Classes and Mechanisms of Social Reproduction.* Athens: Exantas.
Petrakos, G. and Saratsis, Y. (2000) "Regional Inequalities in Greece," *Papers in Regional Science,* 79: 57–74.
Petronoti, M. and Triandafyllidou A. (2003) *Recent Immigration Flows to Greece* (in Greek). Athens: National Centre of Social Research.
Philias, V. (1974) *Society and Power in Greece* (in Greek). Athens: Makriniotis.
———. (1999) (2nd ed.) *Sociology of Underdevelopment* (in Greek). Athens: Sighroni Epochi.
Photopoulos, T. (1985) *Dependent Development: The Greek case* (in Greek). Athens: Exantas.
———. (2005) "From mis(education) to Paideia," *The Journal of Inclusive Democracy,* 2(1). www.inclusivedemocracy.org/journal/vol2/vol2_no1_miseducation_paideia_takis_PRINTABLE.htm (Accessed: March 2012).
Poulantzas, N. (1973) "On social classes," *New Left Review* 78: 27–50.
———. (1975) *Classes in Contemporary Capitalism.* London: New Left Books.
Power, S., Whitty, G., and Wigfall, V. (2003) *Education and the Middle Class.* Buckingham: Open University Press.
Przeworski, A. and Wallerstein. M. (1982) "The structure of class conflict in democratic capitalist societies," *American Political Science Review,* 76(2): 215–238.
Psilos, D. (1968) *Economic Development Issues: Greece, Israel, Taiwan and Thailand.* Committee for Economic Development. New York: Praeger.
Reay, D. (1998) "Rethinking Social Class: Qualitative Perspectives on Gender and Social Class," *Sociology* 32(2): 259–75.
Reay, D., David, M. E., and Ball, S. J. (eds) (2005) *Degrees of Choice: Social Class, Race and Gender in Higher Education.* Stoke on Trent: Trentham Books.
Reay, D., Hollingworth, S., Williams, K., Crozier, G., Jamieson, F., James, D., and Beedell, P. (2007) " 'A darker shade of pale?' Whiteness, the middle classes and multi-ethnic inner city schooling," *Sociology,* 41(6): 1041–1060.
Reichardt, C. and Rallis, S. (1994) "Qualitative and Quantitative Inquiries are not Incompatible: A Call for a New Partnership," in C. Reichardt and S. Rallis (eds), *The Qualitative-Quantitative Debate: New Perspectives.* San Francisco: Jossey-Bass.
Reid, I. (1989) (3rd ed.) *Social Class Differences in Britain.* London: Fontana Press.
Reiger, K. M. (1985) *The Disenchantment of the Home: Modernizing the Australian Family 1880–1940.* Melbourne: Oxford University Press.
Rex, J. and Moore, R. (1967) *Race, Conflict and Community: A Study of Sparkbrook.* New York: Oxford University Press for the Institute of Race Relations.
Rikowski, G. (2001) *After the Manuscript Broke off: Thoughts on Marx, Social Class and Education.* Available at: www.leeds.ac.uk/educol/documents/00001931.htm (Accessed: October 2008).
Roberts, H. (1981) (1st ed.) *Doing Feminist Research.* London: Routledge.
Roberts, K. (2011) (2nd ed.) *Class in Contemporary Britain.* New York: Palgrave Macmillan.
Robson, C. (2002) (2nd ed.) *Real World Research: A Resource for Social Scientists and Practitioner-Researchers.* Oxford: Blackwell.
Rose, D. and O'Reilly, K. (1998) *The ESRC Review of Government Social Classifications.* London: ESRC and ONS.

Ross, G. (1974) "The Second Coming of Daniel Bell," *The Socialist Register*, 11: 331–348.
Rothon, C. (2007) "Can achievement differentials be explained by social class alone? An examination of minority ethnic educational performance in England and Wales at the end of compulsory schooling," *Ethnicities*, 7(3): 306–322.
Rubin, H. and Rubin, I. (1995) *Qualitative Interviewing: The Art of Hearing Data.* London: Sage.
Saïti, A. (2000) *Education and Economic Development* (in Greek). Athens: Tipothito.
Sandis, E. (1973) *Refugees and Economic Migrants in Greater Athens* (in Greek). Athens: EKKE.
Saunders, P. (1995) "Might Britain be a meritocracy?" *Sociology*, 29(1): 23–41.
———. (1996) *Unequal but Fair? A Study of Class Barriers in Britain.* London: Institute for Economic Affairs.
———. (1997) "Social Mobility in Britain: An Empirical Evaluation of Two Competing Theories," *Sociology*, 31(2): 261–288.
Savage, M. (1997) "Social Mobility and the Survey Method: A Critical Analysis," in D. Bertaux and P. Thomson (eds), *Pathways to Social Class: A Qualitative Approach to Social Mobility.* New Brunswick and London: Transaction Publishers.
Savage, M., Bagnall, G., and Longhurst, B. (2005) *Theory, Culture & Society: Globalization and Belonging.* London: Sage.
Sayer, A. (2005) *The Moral Significance of Class.* Cambridge: Cambridge University Press.
Schofer, E. and Meyer, J. W. (2005) "The World-Wide Expansion of Higher Education in the Twentieth Century." Center on Democracy, Development, and the Rule of Law. Stanford: Stanford Institute on International Studies. Available at: http://cddrl.stanford.edu/publications/20801/ (Accessed: May 2012).
Seferiades, S. (1999) "Small rural ownership, subsistence agriculture, and peasant protest in interwar Greece: The agrarian question recast," *Journal of Modern Greek Studies*, 17(2): 277–323. Available at: http://muse.jhu.edu/journals/journal_of_modern_greek_studies/toc/mgs17.2.html (Accessed: June 2008).
Sennett, R. (2004) *Respect: The Formation of Character in an Age of Inequality.* London: Penguin.
Serafetinidis, M. (1979) *The Breakdown of Parliamentary Democracy in Greece, 1947–1967.* London: Department of Government, London School of Economics and Political Science (unpublished thesis).
Shavit, Y. and Muller, W. (1997) *From School to Work—Comparative Educational Qualifications and Occupational Destinations.* Oxford: Clarendon Press.
Sibeon, R. (1999) "Anti-reductionist sociology," *Sociology*, 33(2): 317–334.
Sibley, D. (1981) *Outsiders in Urban Societies.* Oxford: Blackwell.
Silverman, D. (1997) (ed.) *Qualitative Research: Theory, Method and Practice.* London: Sage.
Skeggs, B. (1997) *Becoming Respectable: Formations of Class and Gender.* London: Sage.
Sorokin, P. (1927) *Social and Cultural Mobility.* New York: Free Press.
Sotiris, P. (2012) "Greece: From Despair to Resistance." *The Bullet*, E-Bulletin No. 598, February 14, 2012. Available at www.socialistproject.ca/bullet/598.php (Accessed: June 2012).
———. (2012) Greek social structure (private correspondence with the author via email). June 2012.

———. (2010) "Greece: The EU-ECB-IMF austerity package and the challenge for the Left," http://greekleftreview.wordpress.com/2010/07/15/greece-the-eu-ecb-imf-austerity-package-and-the-challenge-for-the-left/ (Accessed: June 2012).
Standing, G. (2011) *The Precariat: The New Dangerous Class.* London: Bloomsbury Academic.
Stanfield, J. H. (1993) "Epistemological Considerations," in J. H. Stanfield and R. M. Dennis (eds), *Race and Ethnicity in Research Methods.* Newbury Park, CA: Sage, pp. 16–36.
Stake, E. (1995) *The Art of Case Study.* London; Thousand Oaks, CA: Sage.
Stewart, M. (1997) *The Time of the Gypsies. Studies in Ethnographic Imagination.* Boulder, CO; Oxford: Westview Press.
Stillman, G. (2005) "The Myth of Marx's Economic Reductionism, in Marx Myths and Legends." Available at: www.marxmyths.org/peter-stillman/index.php (Accessed: June 2009).
Sullivan, A. (2001) "Cultural capital and educational attainment," *Sociology*, 35(4): 893–912.
Swift, A. (2004) "Would perfect mobility be perfect?" *European Sociological Review*, 20(1): 1–11.
Tashakkori, A. and Teddlie, C. (1998) *Mixed Methodology: Combining Qualitative and Quantitative Approaches.* London: Sage.
———. (2003) (eds) *Handbook of Mixed Methods in Social and Behavioral Research.* London: Sage.
Tayfur, M. F. (2003) *Semiperipheral Development and Foreign Policy: The Cases of Greece and Spain.* Aldershot; Burlington, VT: Ashgate.
The Panel on Fair Access to the Professions (2009) *Fair Access: Good Practice; Phase 2 Report.* The Strategy Unit: London: Cabinet Office. Available at: www.cabinetoffice.gov.uk/resource-library/fair-access-professional-careers-progress-report (Accessed: April 2012).
Themelis, S. (2005) *A Qualitative Study of Education and Social Mobility.* London: Institute of Education, University of London (unpublished Master's dissertation).
———. (2008a) "Labour market restructuring and employment pathways: the case of a mixed community (Roma, non-Roma) in North-West Greece," *Romani Studies Journal*, 18(2): 123–154.
———. (2008b) "Meritocracy through education and social mobility in post-war Britain: a critical examination," *British Journal of Sociology of Education*, 29(5): 427–438.
———. (2008c) "Some Theoretical and Methodological Issues in the Study of Social Mobility and Education from a Mixed Methods Perspective." Paper presented at the "Fourth Mixed Methods Conference and Workshops," Fitzwilliam College, University of Cambridge, July 21–24, 2008, Cambridge, UK.
———. (2009) "Questioning Inclusion. The education of Roma/traveller students and young people in Europe and the UK: a critical examination," *Research in Comparative and International Education Journal* 4(3): 262–275.
The New Oxford English Dictionary (2001) (1st ed.) Oxford: Oxford University Press.
Thompson, E. P. (1963) *The Making of the English Working Class.* London: Penguin.
Thompson, P. (2004) "Researching family and social mobility with two eyes: some experiences of the interaction between qualitative and quantitative data,"

International Journal of Social Research Methodology, Theory and Practice, 7(3): 237–257.
Thorner, D., Kerblay, B., and Smith, R. E. F. (1986) *A.V. Chayanov on the Theory of Peasant Economy*. Manchester: Manchester University Press.
Tikos, S. (2008) *Social Partners and Opposition Parties Oppose Government Reforms of the Pension System*. Submission by INE/GSEE to the European Industrial Relations Observatory (EIRO). Available at: www.eurofound.europa.eu/eiro/2008/05 /articles/gr0805029i.htm.
Timmins, G. (2005) "Domestic industry in Britain during the 18th and 19th centuries: field evidence and the research agenda," *Industrial Archaeology Review*, 27(1): 67–75.
Treiman, D. J. (1970) "Industrialization and social stratification," *Sociological Inquiry Special Issue: Stratification Theory and Research*, 40(2): 207–234.
Truman, C., Mertens, D., and Humphries, B. (2000) (eds) *Research and Inequality*. London: Taylor and Francis.
Tsakloglou, P. and Cholezas, I. (2005) "Education and Inequality in Greece." IZA Discussion Paper No. 1582. Available at: http://ssrn.com/abstract=719924 (Accessed: June 2008).
Tsoukalas K. (1977) *Dependence and Reproduction: The Social Role of Education Mechanisms in Greece, 1830–1922* (in Greek). Athens: Themelio.
———. (1990) "On the Characteristics of the Greek Society," in K. Tsoukalas, Th. Maloutas, S. Pesmatzoglou, N. Routzounis, and Agourakis (eds), *Approaches: Social Structure and the Left: Changes in the 1980s and 1990s* (in Greek). Athens: Sighroni Epochi.
———. (2005) (3rd ed.) *State, Society, Employment in Postwar Greece* (in Greek). Athens: Themelio.
Tsouparopoulos, K. and Stamou, P. (2008) "The Numbers Don't Match" (in Greek). Available at: www.enet.gr/online/online_text/c=114,id=77356872 (Accessed: October 2008).
Turner, R. H. (1960) "Modes of Social Ascent through Education," in P. Worsley (ed.) (1970), *Modern Sociology*. Harmondsworth: Penguin Education.
Vaïtsos, K. and Yiannitsis, T. (2005) "Post-war Economic Growth," in Sakellaropoulos, Th. (ed.), *Economy and Politics in Modern Greece*, Vol. A. Athens: Dionikos.
Valentine, C. A. (1968) *Culture and Poverty: Critique and Counter-proposals*. London: University of Chicago Press.
Vallet, L.-A. 2004. "Change in Intergenerational Class Mobility in France from the 1970s to the 1990s and its Explanation: An Analysis Following the CASMIN Approach," in R. Breen (ed.), *Social Mobility in Europe*. Oxford: Oxford University Press.
Van Heek, F. (1956) "Some Introductory Remarks on Social Mobility and Class Structure," in "Class Transactions of the Third World Congress of Sociology," London, International Sociological Association, vol. III, p. 131.
Vavouras, I. and Manolas, G. (2005) "Black-market Economy: The Observed and Non-registered Activity and Its Relationships with Corruption," in C. Kollias, C. Naxakis, and M. Chletsos (eds), *Modern Approaches to the Greek Economy* (in Greek). Athens: Patakis.
Vergopoulos, K. (1975) *The Agricultural Issue in Greece. The Problem of Social Integration of Agriculture* (in Greek). Athens: Exantas.

———. (1986) *Underdevelopment Today?* (in Greek). Athens: Exantas.
Vermeulen, H. and Perlmann, J. (eds) (2000) *Immigration, Schooling and Social Mobility*. London: MacMillan Press.
Vermeulen, H. and Venema, T. (2000) "Peasantry and Trading Diaspora. Differential Social Mobility of Italians and Greeks in the United States," in H. Vermeulen and J. Perlmann (eds), *Immigration, Schooling and Social Mobility*. London: MacMillan Press.
Vincent, C. and Warren, S. (2001) " 'This won't take long'...interviewing, ethics and diversity," *Qualitative Studies in Education*, 14(1): 39–53.
Voglis, P. (2002) *Becoming a Subject: Political Prisoners during the Greek Civil War*. New York and Oxford: Berghahn Books.
———. (2004) "Becoming Communist: Political Prisoners as a Subject during the Greek Civil War," in P. Carabott and Th. D. Sfikas (eds), *The Greek Civil War: Essays on a Conflict of Exceptionalism and Silences*. London: Ashgate Publishing, Ltd.
Voutira, E. (1997) "Population Transfers and Resettlement Policies in Inter-war Europe: The Case of Asia Minor Refugees in Macedonia from an International and National Perspective," in P. Mackridge and E. Yiannakakis (eds), *Ourselves and Others: The Development of a Greek Macedonian Cultural identity Since 1912*. Oxford: BERG.
Wacquant, L. J. D. (2009) *Punishing the Poor: The Neoliberal Government of Social Insecurity*. Durham, NC: Duke University Press.
Wainwright, D. (1997) "Can sociological research be qualitative, critical *and* valid?" *The Qualitative Report*, 3(2). Available at: www.nova.edu/ssss/QR/QR3–2/wain.html. (Accessed: December 2008).
Walby, S. (1986) *Patriarchy at Work*. Cambridge: Cambridge, Polity Press.
Wallerstein, I. (1974) *The Modern World-System: Capitalist Agriculture and the Origins of the European World-Economy in the Sixteenth Century*. London: Academic Press.
Weber, M. (1948) *From Max Weber: Essays in Sociology: International Library of Sociology A: Social Theory and Methodology*. London: Routledge and Kegan Paul.
———. (1978) *Economy and Society: An Outline of Interpretive Sociology*, Vols. 1 and 2, Los Angeles, CA, and London: University of California Press.
West, J. (1982) (ed.) *Work, Women and the Labour Market*. London: Routledge and Kegan Paul.
Westergaard, J. and Resler, H. (1975) *Class in a Capitalist Society; A Study of Contemporary Britain*. Harmondsworth: Penguin.
Wexler, P. (2000) *Mystical Society: An Emerging Social Vision*. Boulder, CO/Oxford: Westview Press.
Williams, B. F. (1989) "A class act: anthropology and the race to nation across ethnic terrain," *Annual Review of Anthropology*, 18: 401–444.
Willis, P. (1977) *Learning to Labour: Why Working Class Kids Get Working Class Jobs*. Farnborough: Saxon House.
Wolf, A. (2002) *Does Education Matter? Myths about Education and Economic Growth*. London: Penguin.
Wright, E. O. (1985) *Classes*. London: Verso Books.
———. (1985) "Working-Class Power, Capitalist-Class Interests, and Class Compromise," *The American Journal of Sociology*, 105(4): 957–1002.
———. (1994) *Interrogating* Inequality. London: Verso.

Young, M. (1958) *The Rise of the Meritocracy: 1870–2023*. Harmondsworth: Penguin.
———. (2001) "Down with meritocracy," *The Guardian*, June 29, 2001.
Young, M. and Willmott, P. (1957) *Family and Kinship in East London*. London: Routledge and Kegan Paul.
Zouboulakis (2005) "Institutions and Changes in the Greek Economy," in C. Kollias, C. Naxakis, and M. Chletsos (eds), *Modern Approaches to the Greek Economy* (in Greek). Athens: Patakis.

Index

*Note: Appendix pages are in **bold italics;** tables pages are in **bold;** figures pages are in **bold and underlined**

Achievement, 96, 127
 and ascription, 5, 88, 90, 92, 93, 94
 in/and education *see* Educational achievement
Action
 communal, 22
 social, 26-7
 solidaristic, 22
Advancement
 class, 90, 93
 economic, 17
 individual, 35, 37, 197
 occupational, 10, 151, 187
 social, 10, 115, 159, 187, 210
 social mobility, 141-2, 237
Affluence, 142, 156, 207, 237
Age group, 63, 85-6, 107-10, 149-50, 165, 167, 171, 173, 178, 181-2, 190, 195-6, 199-201, 214, 223-6, 232, 234, 236
Agrarian communities, 134
Agricultural exodus, 65, 70
Agriculturalproduction, 69, 102, 180
 see also Production
Agriculture, 64-5, 68, 73, 122, 123, 124, 142-3, 148, 159, 180, 203, 231
 employment in, 62
 subsistence, 71, 117, 177, 199, 236
Aid
 American, 54, 57, 61, 191, 206, 218
  see also American aid
 foreign, *59 see also* Foreign aid
Ainley, Patrick, 46
Albania, 102, 107, 182, 221, 233
Albanians, 62, 102, 173-4, 182-4, 189-90, 205
Aldridge, Richard, 32, 39, 112
Allocation of opportunities and rewards, 198
Alternative mobility pathways, 5, 198
 see also under Social mobility
Althusser, Louis and Balibar, Etienne, 26, 47
American aid, 54, 57, 61, 191, 206, 218
Andartes, 54, 55 *see also* EAM/ELAS fighters; Resistance fighters
Animal husbandry, 101, 102, 134, 136
Antagonistic
 conception of social classes, 45
 relationship(s), 33, 45, 49
Antagonism, 46, 113, 228
 Class, 33, 37, 50, 116
Asia Minor, 231
Ascription, 5, 88, 90, 92, 93, 94, 96, 127
Assortative mating, 185, 238
Athens, 54, 61, 62, 67, 69, 70, 73, 215, 230
Atypicalcasestudy, 99-101
 see also Methodology
Austerity, 61, 207, 211, 230
Autonomy, 118, 120, 191
Avenue par excellence of social mobility, 153 *see also* Education

INDEX

Badiou, Alain, 212
Ball, Stephen, 29, 43
Base-superstructure, 26
Beck, Ulrich, 16, 27, 185
Belgium, 3, 137, 178, 179
Bell, Daniel, 91, 92, 94, 162, 233
Bendix, Reinhard, 34
Bertaux, Daniel and Thomson, Paul, 6, 105, 109
Blanden, Jo, 40, 41
Blau, Peter and Duncan, Otis, 26, 34, 72, 113
Boudon, Raymond, 214
Bourdieu, Pierre, 28, 29, 109, 158
Brain-drain, 84, 208
Braverman, Harry, 21
Breen, Richard, 35, 39, 92, 94, 95, 117
Bretton Woods, 57
British political parties
  see under Political parties, British
Brown, Phillip and Tannock, Stuart, 95
Builder(s) see Occupations
Bullying, 165, 170, 173
Bush, George W., 211

Cabinet Office, 39
Callinicos, Alex, 51
Cannadine, David, 19, 27
Capital
  cultural, 28, 89, 158
  diasporic, 70
  economic, 28
  financial, 58, 70, 144, 229
  foreign, 59, 74, 206, 229
  global, 144, 207
  holistic nature of, 204
  industrial, 59
  production, 203
  real, 139
  remittance-derived, 61, 139, 180
  social, 158
  symbolic, 28
Capitalism
  Golden Age of, 14, 15, 38
  nature of, 32, 33, 129
  neoliberal, 53, 74, 207, 211
  realism, 56
  relations in, 21

Capitalist economy, 104
  see also Economy
Capitalization of opportunities, 138
Case tudy(-ies), 11, 97, 99–110
CASMIN class scheme, 117, 120, 234 see also Social-class schemes
Caste system, 16
Cheliotis, Leonidas and Xenakis, Sappho, 54, 63, 232
Childrearing, 145, 146
Christodoulakis, Nikos and Kalyvitis, Sarantis, 61, 62, 67, 230
Churchill, Winston, 54
Civil sector, 3, 150, 191
Civil war, 53–7, 58, 60, 74, 78, 104, 191, 192–3, 218 see also Greek civil war
Class see social class
Classifications, 116, 120 see also under Social class
  consumption-based, 45
  conventional, 46, 49
  male-centred, 6
Clientelism, 177, 190–1, 194, 198, 209, 214
Clientelistic demands, 191
Clientelistic patterns of political relations, 191
Clientelistic relations/relationships, 69, 177, 191, 194, 196, 197–8
Closure, 32, 112, 222 see also Social closure
Coalition government in Greece, 55, 56
  see also Greek governments
Coalition government in the UK, 40
Cole, Mike, 45, 46
Collins, Randall, 200
Communism, 21, 27, 54
Communist Party of Greece, 56, 229
  see also KKE
Community, 28, 71, 99, 100, 103, 104, 119, 133, 134, 138, 154, 158, 166, 167, 172, 180, 185, 188, 192, 197, 209, 214, 215, 218, 219, 222, 227, 229
Commodity mode of production, 103
  see also Mode of production

INDEX

Competition, 35, 48, 51, 91, 93, 94, 142, 143, 144, 165, 183, 197, 214
Composition of socialism, 112
 see also under Socialism
Conditions of ideological transformation see Ideological transformation
Conflict
 social class, 47 see also under Socialc lass
 theories, 25
Conservative party in the UK, 40
 see also Political parties in the UK
Conservative party in Greece, 55–6, 104 see also Political parties in theU K
Credentials inflation, 200
Critical theorizing, 105
Crompton, Margaret, 17, 42, 43, 44
Cohen, Gerry, A., 47, 228
Council of Europe, 57, 218
Coup d'état (in Greece), 54, 55
Cultural
 relations, 33, 202
 values, 172

Dahrendorf, Ralf, 31, 125
De facto mobility rates see under Social mobility
Delphy, Christine, 42, 213
Democracy, 89
 liberal, 14, 15, 34, 37, 87, 195, 202, 218, 219
 parliamentary, 14, 55, 57, 76
 Westernp olitical, 14, 175
Democratization, 55, 56, 74, 76, 77, 78
Dependency, 117, 143, 161
Deprivation, 102, 155
Determinist thesis, 26
Dex, Shirley, 6, 42, 96, 105, 146
Dialectical relationship(s), 17, 51
Dictatorship, 55, 77, 78, 154, 193, 218
Differentiation, 16, 20, 23, 69, 71, 104, 121, 135, 138, 145, 147, 155, 156, 166, 174, 204, 205, 238
 social differentiation, 103, 119, 136, 234
Disability, 29, 106, 224

Disadvantages, 32, 77, 93, 127
 social disadvantages, 36, 112
Discrimination, 51, 106, 156, 165, 170, 173, 174, 180, 186, 188, 189, 193, 204, 205
Discriminatorys trategies, 189
Distribution of opportunities, 32, 45, 93, 101, 104, 106, 112, 113, 131, 196, 197, 198, 200
Division of labor, 37, 74 see also under Labor
Domestic work, 145, 146
Dominant and marginalized groups, 61, 105
Domination, 17, 45, 46, 120, 139, 167, 237

EAM/ELAS, 54 see also Andartes; resistance fighters
Economic base, 100
Economic boom, 76
Economic crisis, 4, 7, 13, 14, 61, 62, 86, 181, 211, 238
Economic development, 34, 35, 47, 58, 70, 77, 86, 91, 97, 100, 203, 228
Economic elite(s), 155, 211
Economic emigrants, 178
Economic growth, 10, 15, 35, 37, 38, 57, 58, 60, 61, 62, 66, 91, 92, 181, 183, 202, 203
Economic inequalities, 15, 31, 72, 103, 115
Economism, 26, 209
Economistic approach (to social mobility), 23, 33 see also under Social mobility
Economy
 capitalist, 104
 free-market, 95
 marketized (or market), 7
 political, 11, 15, 21, 47, 53, 56, 57, 58, 60, 61, 63, 75, 79, 80, 90, 99, 121, 134, 143, 178, 203, 205, 209, 211, 228, 229
Education
 as avenue par excellence of social mobility, 90, 153, 156
 compulsory, 77, 78, 81, 203

Education—*Continued*
  examinations, 78, 80, 84, 90
  and expansion, 94
  expenditures, 79
  higher, 73, 76, 81, 86, 118, 169, 203, 205, 209, 215
  over-education, 75, 85, 200
  qualifications, 3, 85, 86, 92, 163
  reform, 91, 156, 159, 168
  secondary, 76, 77, 78, 80, 81, 85, 101, 118, 153, 157 *see also* School, secondary
  selective function of, 161
  technical, 77 *see also* Technical education
  terminal, 76 *see also* Terminal education
  tertiary, 71, 76, 78, 82, 83, 84, 85, 149, 150, 165, 170, 199, 200 *see also* Higher education
  and testing, 90, 91
  vocational, 76, 77, 164
Educational accomplishments, 11
Educational achievement, 5, 88, 90, 92
Educational attainment, 2, 5, 41, 85, 86, 94, 100, 133, 153, 154, 165, 199, 201, 202, 221
Educational level, 72, 73, 74, 78, 112, 163, 166, 171, 173, 234
Educational mobility, 72, 73, 74, 106
  see also under Social mobility
Educational openness, 202
Educational participation, 75, 85, 104, 160, 165, 168, 234
Educational qualifications, 9, 28, 35, 38, 82, 88, 91, 92, 94, 95, 101, 150, 158, 163, 164, 172, 175, 195, 200, 202, 215, 233
Educational standards, 76, 156, 209
Educational underachievement, 16
Education-based meritocracy, 90, 92, 118, 162, 163, 183, 198
Educo-centric jobs, 201 *see also* Jobs
Effort, 80, 88, 91, 92, 94, 108, 119, 151, 156, 157, 208, 210
EGP class scheme, 120, 235
  see also Social-class schemes
Electrician *see* Occupations

Elite(s), 34, 81, 172, 204, 207
  economic, 211
Elster, John, 48
Embedded liberalism, 15, 202
  see also Liberalism
Embourgeoisement, 56, 70, 124, 160, 204, 206, 212, 237
Emigration, 5, 10, 61, 65, 70, 84, 100, 141, 177–82, 185, 187, 189, 190, 196, 198, 209, 212, 214, 215, 221, 223, 231
  pull factors, 182
  push factors, 182
  and repatriation, 62, 69, 145, 178, 182–9
Employment
  agricultural, 231
  in the civil sector, 150, 191
  industrial, 68, 142
  opportunities, 32, 141, 182, 193
  self-employment, 64, 103, 124, 128, 140, 145, 147, 162, 199, 212
  stories, 148
England, 20, 24, 25, 231
Endogenous transformations, 74, 100, 139
Episteme, 46
Equality, 34, 38, 76, 87, 89, 91, 92, 93, 95, 112, 227
  (of) opportunities, 34, 76, 87, 91, 92
Equalization of opportunities, 5, 101, 214
Equitable arrangements, 194
Erikson, Robert, 35, 39, 41
Esping-Andersen, Gøsta, 113
Ethnic
  differentiation, 138, 156, 204, 205
  (minority) groups, 42, 109, 120, 224, 227, 232
Ethnicity, 29, 43, 105, 107, 110, 194, 213, 224, 225, 227, 234
  see also 'Race'
Ethnicized differentiation, 204, 205
  see also Racialized differentiation
Ethnographer(s), 44, 108
  see also Methodology
Ethnographic research, 118, 234, 237
  see also Methodology

European and Monetary Union or Unification (EMU), 57, 207, 219
European Central Bank (ECB), 57, 208, 219
European periphery, 75, 179, 207
European Union (EU), 56, 57, 60, 61, 63, 64, 66, 79, 84, 86, 142, 143, 182, 206, 207, 211, 219, 230, 232, 233
Eurostat, 62, 63, 67, 86, 232
Examinations, 39, 78, 80, 84, 89, 90 see also under Education
Existing socialism, 27 see also Socialism
Exodus (from agriculture), 65, 70 see also Agricultural exodus
Exogamy, 187 see also under Marriage
Exploitation, 21, 23, 24, 33, 100, 116, 121, 122, 135, 137, 138, 143, 204

Factory
  owners, 117
  workers, 118, 121, 122, 140, 145, 163
Fairness, 41, 87, 96
Family
  background, 88, 90, 130, 157
  income, 41, 73, 139, 154, 158, 169
  system, 35, 71
Farmers see under Occupations
Featherman, David, 35
Feminist perspective, 42
Feminist researcher(s), 42
Filtering, 87
Fiscal and monetary policies, 14–15
Fisher, Mark, 56
Fluidity, 35, 37, 38, 114, 125, 126, 128 see also Social fluidity
Fordism, 208
Foregone income, 154, 155, 157, 166, 199 see also under Income
Foreign
  aid, 59
  workers, 145
Freedom of choice, 89
Free market(s), 14, 56, 76, 95, 120, 143, 177, 211 see also Market
Frontistiria, 79, 80 see also Private tuition

Functionalism
  Parsonian, 26
  structural, 25

Gastarbeiters, 178
Gekas, Rallis, 58, 65, 66, 67
Gender, 16, 42, 63, 85, 105, 107, 110, 135, 145, 148, 167, 213
  division of labor, 37, 74
  second shift, 148
  sexual, 146, 147
Generation, of 700 Euro, 151, 207
Germany, 163, 178–82, 231
Giddens, Anthony, 20
Glass, David, 26, 34, 35, 36, 37, 38, 40, 41, 42, 212, 227
Global
  capital, 144, 207 see also Capital
  economic crisis, 61
Globalization, 144, 206
Golden Age of capitalism, 14, 15, 38 see also Capitalism
Goldthorpe John H., 6, 32, 34, 35, 37, 38, 39, 40, 41, 42, 44, 45, 47, 49, 90, 91, 92, 94, 100, 105, 112, 114, 116, 117, 125, 162, 227, 233, 235, 237
Gramsci, Antonio, 46, 208
Great Depression, 14
Greece, 207–16, 221, 223, 224, 230, 231, 232, 233, 235, 237
Greek civil war, 54
Greek diaspora, 69, 70
Greek economy, 56, 57, 59, 60, 61, 62, 63, 64, 66, 68, 86, 133, 134, 143, 175, 183, 229
Greek education, 77, 79
Greek 'exceptionalism', 208
Greek governments, 57, 58
  coalition, 55, 56
Greek social structure, 69, 70, 71, 72, 74, 83, 204
Greek political parties see under Political parties, Greek
Greenspan, Alan, 211
Gregg, Paul, 41
Growth, 82
  in agriculture, 234

Growth—*Continued*
  demographic, 143
  economic, 10, 15, 35, 37, 38, 57, 58, 60, 61, 62, 66, 91, 92, 181, 183, 202, 203
  industrial, 58, 64, 73
  jobless, 62, 145
  population, 66, 70, 85, 102, 143, 191, 214
Gymnasium, 80, 81 *see also under* School

Hamilton, Malcolm and Hirzowicz, Maria, 16
Harvey, David, 202, 237
Hatcher, Richard, 45
Heath, Anthony, 34, 37, 42, 94, 236
Hegemonic discourse, 46
Hegemony, 17, 46, 172, 204
Hierarchal social formations, 20, 25, 227 *see also* Social formations
Higher education, 73, 76, 81, 86, 118, 169, 203, 205, 209, 215 *see also under* Education
Hill, Dave, 17, 27, 45, 46, 54, 205
Historical materialism, 44, 47, 49, 210, 228
  orthodox conception of, 47
Hobsbawm, Eric, 14
Holistic nature of capitalist production, 203–4 *see also* Production, capitalist mode of
Homogeneity, 103, 190
Honor, 25, 189
House construction, 103, 139, 179, 180, 183 *see also under* Occupations
Household, 102, 120, 135, 141, 142, 145, 147, 149, 150, 166, 168, 170, 181, 184, 232
  and division of labor, 146, 148, 169
  economy/consumption/income/budget, 63, 79, 80, 82, 154, 185, 232
  male head of, (in social classifications), 42, 73, 221
  strategies, 133
Housework, 146, 147, 169
Hout, Michael, 35, 41, 87, 114

Humanism, 76
Hungary, 84
Hypertrophy (in the civil sector), 3, 68, 150, 191 *see also* Civil sector
Hypostatization, 43

Identity (-ies), 27, 43, 103, 104, 105, 156, 221, 224
Ideological transformation, 159, 204
Idiaitera, 79, 80 *see also* Frontistiria; Private tuition
Immigrants, 42, 61, 62, 65, 76, 107, 143, 173, 182, 183, 189, 205, 221, 226, 229, 230, 231, 233
Income
  background(s), 94
  foregone, 154, 155, 157, 166, 199
  supplementary source of, 138, 142
Indigenous groups, 70, 182, 231
Individual liberty (-ies), 89, 167 *see also* Liberty
Individualism, 113, 210
Individuality, 27
Industrial
  growth, 58, 60, 64, 66, 73
  production, 66, 159
  proletariat, 70, 160, 206
  workforce, 67
Industrialization, 58
Industry, 15, 58, 62, 64, 66, 68, 70, 77, 82, 142, 143, 196
INE (Institute for Employment), 62
Inflation, 15, 172, 200, 207
Inheritance, 91, 92, 101, 188
Insider/outsider roles (in research), 109 *see also* Methodology
Intelligentsia, 155
Intermarriage, 104, 188, 189 *see also* Marriage
Intermediate class *see* Social class(-es)
Internal social stratification, 185 *see also* Social stratification
International Monetary Fund (IMF), 17, 57, 208, 219
Investment
  foreign, 60
  private, 79
  public, 59, 79

INDEX 267

IPPR (Institute for Public Policy Research), 112
IQ, 93, 157
  and effort, 88, 92, 93, 94
  and rewards

Jobless growth, 62, 145 *see also* Growth
Jobs *see also* Occupations
  education-based, 118, 201
    see also Educo-centric
  second rate, 138
  semiskilled, 138, 171
  unskilled, 138, 179, 194
Jonsson, J an.O., 94, 95
Jouganatos, George, 61, 178
Justification of the subordination (of the Roma and/or the working class), 156, 205

KANEP, 80, 82, 85, 232 (Centre for Development of Education Policy)
Kasimati, K oula, 71, 72, 73, 75, 117
Kazamias, Andreas, 76
Kerr, C lark, 35, 91
Keynes, J ohn, M., 202
Keynesian
  model, 202, 203
  phase, 82, 206
  turn, 82
Keynesianism, 15, 58
Kinship, 99, 103, 112
KKE, 56, 229 *see also* Communist Party of Greece
Knowledge, 28, 37, 44, 46, 72, 77, 78, 79, 92, 108, 109, 233, 234
Koliopoulos, John and Veremis, Thanos, 54, 59, 60

Labor
  and capital, 17, 21
  division of, 37, 74
  power, 118, 166, 235
  sexual division of, 146, 147
  unions, 15, 79
  wage, 21, 134, 179
Labor-market
  captivity, 207

  opportunities, 128
  passivity, 207
  rigidity (-ies), 145, 151
Lambiri-Dimaki, Jane, 71, 72, 83, 135, 234
Land
  arable, 102, 135
  for dwelling, 102, 135
  reform, 101, 102, 134, 138
Landed property, 21 *see also under* Property
Landlords, 20, 70, 125, 135
Landowners, 50, 69, 117, 118, 119, 120, 135, 136, 185, 236, 238
Landworkers, 103, 119, 135, 136
Late-developed countries, 134
Legitimization of social inequalities, 210
Levine, Andrew and Wright, Erik, O., 47, 228, 229
Liberal
  consensus, 38
  democracy *see under* Democracy
  democrats, 40
Liberalism, 15, 37, 202
Liberalization policies, 57
Liberal theory
  and industrialism, 35, 91
  of industrialization, 35
Liberty, 89, 167
Life chances, 9, 10, 22, 43, 56, 88, 90, 101, 124, 133, 138, 174, 182, 200, 201, 214
Lifestyle choices, 82, 166
Lipset, Seymour, M., 26, 34, 35
  hypothesis, the, 35
Livestock, 103, 117, 120, 134, 135, 146, 147, 167, 184, 185, 186, 238
Local oligarchies, 191
(The) LSE study, 35, 42, 227
  see also Social mobility studies
Loury, Glenn, 33, 42, 227

Machin, Stephen, 41, 94
Manual
  "communities", 99
  jobs, 141, 183

Manual—*Continued*
  occupations, 118, 124, 129, 137
  worker(s), 45, 83, 130, 141, 160,
    163, 237
Manufacturing, 15, 59, 64, 65, 67,
  114, 142
Marginalization, 103, 106, 144
Marginalized groups, 105, 190
Marital arrangements, 185, 187
Marital preferences, 189, 190
Marital strategies, non-mixing
  strategies, 189
Marital selection, 186, 187, 189, 190,
  234 *see also* Mechanisms of
  marital selection
Market
  capitalist, 77
  free, 14, 56, 76, 95, 120, 143, 177,
    211
  rigidities, 67
  situation, 22, 23, 32
Marketized economy, 7
  see also Economy
Marriage, 146, 148, 150, 169, 175, 177,
  184, 185, 186, 196, 198, 209,
  214, 215, 221, 238
  exogamy, 187
  intermarriage, 104, 188, 189
  mixed, 188, 189, 190
Marshall Plan, 54, 59, 218
Marx, Karl, 8, 19–22, 23–31, 44–52,
  115–16, 122–5, 209, 210, 228,
  229, 235
Marxism, 13, 24, 27, 47, 48, 49
  criticism of, 24
  neo-Marxism/neo-Marxists, 26
Marxist(-s)
  accounts, 13, 209
  conception of history, 45
  science of history, 45
  social science, 47
Mazower, Mark, 54, 55
Mechanisms
  of early selection and prevention, 190
  of justification, 156, 204
  of marital selection, 186, 187, 189,
    190, 234
  ranking, 87

sorting, 87
ofs ubordination, 156
Mediation, 3, 194, 195, 196, 197, 238
  see also Political mediation
Merit, 157, 159, 160, 162
Meritocracy, 75, 88, 89, 90–6, 157,
  162, 163, 195, 198, 202, 232
  ande ducation *see* Education-based
    meritocracy
Meritocratic
  failure, 95, 96
  ideal, 88, 174
  ideology, 95
  society, 114, 126, 128, 129
Mertens, Donna, 7, 106, 108
Meson, 3, 190, 194, 195, 196, 197
  as a corrosive social practice, 194
  the normalization of, 195
Methodology/methods, 44, 106
  atypicalc ases tudy, 99–101
  ethnographer(s), 44, 108
  ethnographic research, 118, 234, 237
  ethnography, 6, 108, 109, 234
  insider/ outsider roles
    (inr esearch), 109
  mixed-methods, 6, 105, 215
  observations, 105, 108, 109, 110,
    119, 148, 150, 215
  qualitative methods, 215
  quantitative methods, 107, 225
  semi-structured interviews, 6, 109
  survey, 42
  transformative–emancipatory
    approach, 6, 106, 119, 222
Milonas, Thedoros, 70, 75, 76, 78, 83, 85
Mode
  of life, 20
  of production, 18, 19, 20, 21, 47, 48,
    66, 71, 102, 103, 120, 134, 135,
    139, 143, 167, 180, 199, 202,
    208, 212, 214, 228, 231, 232
Modernization theory, 35
Monarchy, 54, 55, 218
Money, 59, 80, 103, 116, 117, 136, 137,
  139, 141, 151, 155, 156, 157, 158,
  161, 162, 168, 170, 179, 180,
  181, 185, 186, 187, 193, 194,
  195, 207, 213, 221, 229, 230

INDEX

Moral panic, 184
Moschonas, Andreas, 22, 72
Mouzelis, Nicos, 64, 66, 71, 191, 214, 229, 231
Musician(s), 138 *see also* Occupations

National Statistical Service of Greece (NSSG), 62, 66, 67, 68, 69, 81, 82, 230, 232
Nazism, 14
Nea Demokratia, 56, 57 *see also* Greek political parties
Negative discrimination, 170, 186
Neoliberalism, 15, 79, 80, 208
Neo-Marxists, 26 *see also* Marxist(-s)
New Labour, 128, 211
Non-mixings trategies, 189
see also Marital strategies
Northern Ireland, 35, 95

Observation *see* Methodology
Occupation(s) *see also* Jobs
  builder(s), 2, 118, 141, 161, 179, 181, 183, 237
  electrician(s), 118, 144, 145, 182, 196
  elite, 34, 81, 172, 204, 207
  farmers, 65, 70, 71, 83, 84, 110, 118, 119, 120, 121, 124, 125, 129, 130, 146, 148, 163, 178, 179, 234, 235
  house construction, 103, 139, 179, 180, 183
  middle-class, 73, 83, 93, 110, 155, 174, 199, 202, 212
  musicians, 138
  routine-manual, 129
  and social mobility movement, 43, 47, 127, 151, 201
  working-class, 70
Occupational careers, 141, 147, 150, 198
  experiences, 106, 133, 145, 177, 196, 236
  histories, 101
  insecurity, 144
  opportunities, 37, 96, 143, 151, 156, 164, 169, 177, 185, 194, 196, 199, 200, 201, 202, 209, 211, 212, 237

  prospects, 147
  situation, 62, 101, 148, 164, 181, 201
  status, 32, 72
Occupation-based approach to social mobility, 227 *see also under* Social mobility
Oddsr atios, 67, 66, 67, 70, 82, 83, 85, 108, 111, 119, 124, 125, 127, 128, 129, 130, <u>137</u>, *218*, **219**, 225
Oils hocks, 15
Openness
  educational *see* Educational openness
  and labor-market, 201, 209
  social, 34, 37, 93, 112, 114, 115, 125
Opportunity(-ies)
  deficit, 40
  educational, 28, 76, 172
  for movement, 39, 44
  occupational *see* Occupational careers, opportunities
Oppression, 24, 27, 47, 50, 105
Organisation for Economic Co-operation and Development [OECD], 57, 60, 61, 62, 63, 64, 65, 66, 67, 68, 69, 84, 85, 86, 207, 208, 219
Ossowski,S tanisław, 19
Ottoman Empire, 134, 191, 231

Pagoulatos, George, 58, 60
Pakulski, Jan and Waters, Malcolm, 17, 27
Panayotakis, Costas, 211
Papadimitriou, Dimitris, 62, 63, 64, 229
Parasitism (and civil sector), 68
  see also Civil sector
Pareto, Vilfredo, 34
Parliamentary democracy, 14, 55, 57, 76
  see also Democracy
Parsons, Talcott, 8, 25–6, 29, 31, 209
PASOK, 55–6, 57, 78, 79, 218, 219, 229 *see also* Greekp olitical parties
Patriarchal and capitalist relations, 42, 213
Patronage, 5, 10, 68, 175, 177, 190, 191, 194, 196, 197, 198, 209, 214, 215, 238

Patrons (political), 191, 194
Payne, Geoff, 32, 39, 112
Peasantry, 56, 69, 70, 83, 121, 129, 134, 135, 136, 137, 138, 140, 143, 146, 147, 163, 180, 185, 191, 206
Petmezidou-Tsoulouvi, Maria, 73, 117
Photopoulos, Takis, 64, 65, 68, 76
Polarization, 54, 55, 195, 196, 201, 210
Political affiliation, 192, 193, 196
Political economy, 4, 5, 8, 10, 11, 15, 21, 47, 53–75, 79, 80, 90, 99, 121, 134, 143, 178, 203, 205, 209, 211, 228, 229
Political mediation, 3, 194, 195, 197, 238
Political mediation and corruption, 196
Political parties, 22, 52, 90, 191
Political parties, British (or in the UK), 39
   Conservative party, 40
   New Labour, 128, 211
Political parties, Greek (or in Greece)
   Conservative party, 55–6, 104
   KKE, 56, 229
   Left, 15, 55, 56, 57, 104, 191, 192, 211, 218
   Nea Democratia, 56, 57
   PASOK, 55–6, 57, 78, 79, 218, 219, 229
   and polarization, 54, 55, 195, 196, 201, 210
   Right, 54, 55, 56, 57, 104, 191, 192, 211, 218
   and rousfeti, 196, 197, 238
   Synaspismos, 56
Population growth, 143 *see also* Growth
Post-modernism, 56
Poulantzas, Nicos, 18, 26, 44, 51
Power relations, 51, 105, 106, 214, 224
Precariat, 212 *see also* Socialc lass
Precariousness, 2, 4, 145, 237
Primary school *see* School
Private
   investment, 79
   sphere, 145, 146
   tuition, 80
Privatization, 60, 80

Privilege(s), 22, 39, 81, 89, 90, 91, 92, 108, 114, 125, 131, 141, 155, 156, 160, 185, 195, 200, 202, 228 *see also* Socialc lass
Production
   agricultural, 69, 102, 180
   capitalist mode of, 18, 19, 20, 21, 47, 48, 66, 134, 139, 199, 212, 228, 231
   corn, 102, 116, 147, 149
   meansof, 19, 20, 21, 22, 23, 33, 45, 49, 113, 116, 117, 121, 135, 136, 143
   mechanization of, 117, 180
   mode(s) of *see* Mode of production
   and organization, 7, 22, 208
   ownership of the means of, 21, 116, 120, 121
   relations of/in, 4, 19, 21, 68, 82, 105, 117, 118, 121, 122, 134, 137, 139, 143, 177, 178, 204, 228, 229
   tobacco, 66, 103, 117, 121, 147, 149, 157, 234
   wheat, 102, 116, 147
Proletarianization, 70, 122, 124, 159, 212
Proletarian/Proletariat(s), 19, 20, 24, 47, 50, 121, 122
   see also Working-class
   industrial, 70, 160, 206
   workers, 121
Property, 23, 49, 69, 71, 101, 116, 140, 146, 147, 186
   landed, 21
Proto-capitalist, 102, 120, 134, 135, 136
   mode of production, 199
Protopi
   division of labor, 103, 120, 121, 122, 134, 135, 136, 138, 139, 146, 147, 148, 154, 168, 170, 178, 183, 184, 232
   economy of, 102, 117, 134, 139, 141, 178
   educationi n, 104, 174, 199, 200, 234
   labor market of, 183

INDEX

Non- Roma (people/groups), 3, 4, 6, 103–10, 120, 133–44, 146–50, 151–66, 168–74, 178–90, 192–8, 199–205, 213, 225–6, 233, 235, 236, 237, 238
Roma (people/groups), 5, 103, 105, 120, 138, 181, 187, 197, 199, 201, 202, 204, 224, 225, 236, 238
 social groups in, 107, 110
 the socioeconomic development of, 100, 180, 198
Psilos, Diomedes, 59, 60, 229
Public sector, 46, 53, 67, 71, 89, 103, 149, 164, 180, 203
 employment, 203, 207
 growth, 68, 191, 193

Qualifications *see* Educational qualifications
Qualified workforce, 71, 172
Qualitatived ata, 6, 105, 109
 see also Methodology
Qualitativeme thods, 215
 see also Methodology
Quantitative data, 107, 225
 see also Methodology
Quantitative methodology, 106
 see also Methodology
Quantitative methods, 215
 see also Methodology

'Race', 27, 29, 194, 224 *see also* Ethnicity
Racialization, 104
Racialized differentiation, 204, 205
Recruitment, 28, 36, 48, 69, 83, 92, 112, 125, 126, 159
Relations
 antagonistic, 33, 45, 49
 exploitative, 20, 116, 122, 137
 of production, 228
 social, 5, 6, 18, 21, 50, 51, 82, 103, 122, 147, 148, 155, 160, 167, 178, 184, 193, 198, 203, 204, 214, 233
 working, 99

Remittance-derived capital, 61, 139, 180 *see also* Capital
Remittances
 contribution of (to the economy), 180
Reproduction of
 capitalism, 159
 class privileges, 89
 social inequalities, 89, 113
Republic of Ireland, 35, 95
Resistance fighters, 54
Rikowski, Glenn, 20, 21, 46, 47
Roberts, Ken, 26, 37, 112
Romania, 70, 84
Rousfeti, 196, 197, 238
Rural
 areas, 61, 68, 71, 75, 76, 77, 83, 85, 100, 104, 134, 153, 184, 191, 232
 population, 70, 77, 206
Russia, 70

Saunders, Peter, 92, 93
Savage, Mike, 29, 117
Scapegoats, 184
School
 lower (secondary), 81, 85, 154, 163, 164, 171
 upper (secondary), 78, 80, 81, 85, 154, 158, 162, 163, 228
 performance, 90
 primary, 3, 74, 77, 78, 104, 154, 155, 157, 161, 162, 165, 166, 167, 168, 169, 171, 185
 secondary, 1, 2, 74, 75, 77, 79, 80, 83, 84, 101, 144, 150, 154, 155, 156, 157, 158, 160, 161, 162, 163, 168, 169, 170, 171
 state, 80
Secondary sector, 62, 66, 117, 144, 230
 see also Industry
 employment in, 67, 142
Second shift, 148 *see also* Gender division of labor
Second World War, 5, 8, 11, 14, 34, 36, 53, 54, 58, 59, 71, 74, 77, 81, 87, 89, 91, 94, 114, 153, 159, 202, 203, 225, 231, 235, 238

Self-employment, 64, 103, 124, 128, 140, 145, 147, 162, 199, 212
Semi-structured interviews, 6, 109
  see also Methodology
Sexual division of labor, 146, 147
  see also under Gender
Sexuality, 27, 29
Situation
  class, 23, 130
  market, 22, 23, 32
Skin color, 16, 104, 238
Social action, 26 see also Action
Social antagonism see Antagonism
Social change, 4, 8, 10, 11, 14, 90, 199, 209, 234
Social class(-es)
  analysis, 17, 29
  antagonistic conception of, 45
  boundaries, 19, 25, 47, 103, 104, 107, 115, 167, 188, 190
  bourgeoisie, 19, 20, 46, 50, 59, 71, 118
  categories, 23, 24, 32, 42, 43, 44, 49, 116, 213, 214
  chances, 39, 127, 129
  classifications, 45, 46, 49, 116, 120
  conflict, 47
  consciousness, 10, 13, 21, 46, 47, 104, 160, 204, 212
  death of, 27
  destination, 93, 112, 125
  divisions, 36, 46, 56, 193
  dominant, 3, 5, 46, 103, 106, 155, 160, 161, 180, 184, 187, 197
  for-itself, 21, 46, 212
  formation, 4, 70, 71, 72, 97, 191
  inequalities, 39, 93
  inferior, 109, 141, 188, 227
  in-itself, 21, 212
  interests, 18, 22
  intermediate, 56, 70, 71, 73, 83, 118, 120, 121, 124, 125, 126, 129, 130, 131, 158, 159, 172, 191, 199, 206, 211, 212
  middle class, 50, 73, 83, 89, 93, 95, 110, 118, 122, 123, 125, 126, 155, 158, 159, 172, 174, 199, 202, 204, 206, 211, 212, 213, 236
  operationalizing (and operationalization of), 17, 25, 116, 119
  origins, 112, 123
  positions, 24, 36, 83, 112, 209, 211
  power, 159, 203
  practices, 33
  precariat, 212
  privileges, 89, 125, 131, 141, 202
  and productive activity, 20
  Proletarian/Proletariat(s), 19, 20, 24, 47, 50, 121, 122
  relations, 23
  ruling, 17, 33, 46, 48, 116, 117, 121, 122, 160, 206, 207, 208, 228, 235
  situation, 44
  strata, 43, 45, 50, 71, 89, 115
  structure, 186, 205
  struggle(s), 24, 26
  upper class, 44, 228
  working class, 15, 19, 23, 24, 25, 38, 45, 46, 70, 71, 73, 79, 83, 88, 89, 93, 99, 110, 118, 120, 121, 122, 125, 156, 159, 160, 174, 204, 205, 208, 212
Social and cultural processes, 133
Social-class schemes
  CASMIN, 117, 120, 234
  EGP, 120, 235
  traditional, 45, 105, 149, 201, 228, 237
Social closure, 32, 112, 222
Social cohesion, 36
Social differentiation, 103, 119, 136, 234
Social disadvantages, 36, 112
Social fluidity, 22, 34, 35, 36, 74, 115, 131
Social formation(s), 8, 18, 20, 70, 159, 172, 203, 207, 212, 228
Social hierarchy(-ies), 36, 49, 91
Social inequalities, 8, 11, 14, 19, 22, 24, 26, 27, 28, 29, 31, 35, 36, 38, 44, 45, 51, 89, 113, 115, 131, 201, 209, 210, 234

Social injustice(s), 210
Socialism, 27, 34, 47, 48
  composition of, 112
  existing, 27
Social justice, 106, 108
Social mobility
  as the 'anaesthetic' of class antagonisms, 210
  de facto mobility rates, 112
  downward, 41, 92, 95, 112, 113, 124, 126, 211, 235
  exchange, 9, 73, 111, 113, 114, 127, 128, 235
  experiences, 109, 111, 118, 151
  horizontal, 112, 113, 123, 124, 151
  immobility, 38, 124, 235
  life-course, 113, 133, 137, 142, 215
  long-range, 113, 124, 235
  measurement of, 32
  opportunities, 89
  pathways, 133, 175, 177, 190, 196, 198, 213, 214
  perfect, 43, 126, 235
  short-range, 36, 37, 113, 124, 126, 235
  structural, 95, 114, 127, 128, 131, 133, 235, 236
  upward, 16, 31, 48, 90, 93, 95, 112, 113, 123, 124, 158, 161, 164, 181, 200, 210, 235
  vertical, 112, 123, 124, 200, 235
  understanding of, 101
Social mobility studies, approaches to
  conventional (or dominant), 13, 17, 42, 43, 44, 45, 46, 49, 105
  economistic approach, 23, 33
  male-centred, 6
  Nuffield mobility study, 32, 37, 38, 42
  Oxford mobility Study, 4, 25, 37
  traditional, 42, 109, 209, 214, 222
Social openness *see* Openness
Social origins, 36, 91
Social polarization *see* Polarization
Social-status advancement, 187
Social stratification, 8, 11, 13–15, 16–25, 26, 29, 31, 32, 34, 43, 53–92, 99, 116, 156, 185, 214, 229
  approaches to (social stratification):
  liberal, 14

Marxist, 13, 24
  post-structuralist, 19, 27
  Weberian, 19, 24
  dual system of social stratification, 71
  integrating aspect of, 26
  pluralistic approach to, 22
  political and analytical dimensions of, 19
Social structure, 31, 36, 92, 93, 96, 111, 138, 202, 203, 206, 210, 232, 233
  analysis of/approaches to, 16–19
  in Bourdieu, 28–9
  in conventional mobility studies, 44
  economistic and structuralist approaches, 269
  in Glass, 36–7
  in Goldthorpe, 37–8
  in Greece *see* Greeks ocials tructure
  in M arx, 19–22
  in Marxism, 45–51
  in Parsons, 25–6
  in Protopi, 103, 120, 121, 122, 124, 125, 127, 128, 129, 131
  and social mobility, 112, 113, 114, 115, 117
  in Weber, 22, 24
Social system, 16, 19, 20, 22, 25, 33, 36, 39, 42, 53, 74, 87, 88, 93, 95, 112, 113, 115, 117, 125, 126, 131, 159
  distributional aspects of, 43
  rigidity of a s ocials ystem, 114
Solidarity, 103, 134, 138, 159, 204
Sorokin, Pitirim, 34
Sotiris, Panayiotis, 206, 207
Stability, 15, 39
Stagflation, 15
Stalin, Vladimir, 54
Standing, Guy, 212
State
  bureaucracy, 125, 140, 191, 192
  intervention(-ism), 14, 58, 91, 156, 191, 202
  school, 80
  sponsored mobility, 159, 206
  supported economy, 7
  welfare, 34, 76, 202, 208, 211

Stereotyping, 144, 170, 174, 188, 189, 224
Strata, 21, 43, 45, 50, 71, 89, 115
   see also Socialc lass,s trata
Strategies for social advancement, 159
Structuralism, 27
Structure
   of modern capitalist societies, 18
   monopolistic, 59
   oligopolistic, 59
Subjectivities, 27, 106
Subordination, 17, 18, 33, 89, 156, 205
Supplementary source of income, 138, 142 see also Income
Survey-method approach, 42
Sweden, 35, 41, 95, 178
Synaspismos, 56 see also Greekp olitical parties

Talent, 26, 126, 157
Taxation, 76, 134, 207, 230
Tayfur, Fatih, M, 59, 60
Technicale ducation, 77
Terminal education, 76
Testing, 90, 91, 208 see also Education
Themelis, Spyros, 90, 91, 93
Tourism, 69, 82, 178
Transformative–emancipatory approach, 6, 106, 119, 222
   see also Methodology
Transmission, 101, 161
   of disadvantage, 93, 95
   of privilege, 39
Treiman, Donald, 35, 91
Truman Doctrine, 54
Tsakloglou, Panos and Cholezas, Ioannis, 85
Tsoukalas, Costas, 69, 70, 71, 72, 134, 143, 191, 231
Turner, Ralph, 90, 91

Underdeveloped countries, 134
Unemployment, 1, 4, 15, 58, 62, 63, 64, 86, 145, 164, 172, 173, 178, 183, 194, 195, 200, 203, 207, 215, 230, 232

United Kingdom, 35, 40, 41, 52, 80, 88, 95, 220
United States, 59, 60, 84, 211, 231, 237
Universalism, 34
University
   degree, 83, 151, 158, 193, 194
   expansion, 86, 172
   graduates, 1, 3, 73, 83, 86, 87, 89, 164, 172, 203, 207
Unskilled jobs/ occupations, 137, 138, 179, 194 see also Jobs
Urban centres, 61, 62, 67, 69, 70, 71, 83, 143, 165, 206, 218
Urbanization, 53, 70

Values, 1, 2, 4, 7, 16, 27, 28, 33, 34, 106, 108, 150, 166, 172, 208, 222
Vergopoulos, Costas, 58, 63, 72, 134
Vocational
   qualifications, 3
   training, 144, 163
Voglis, Polymeris, 54
Voting rights, 197, 221

Wacquant, Loic, 208
Wage
   compression, 145
   labor, 21, 134, 179
Wealth, 9, 15, 33, 49, 59, 90, 91, 101, 116, 117, 134, 203
Weber, Max, 8, 19, 22–9, 31, 32, 89, 209, 210
Welfare, 14, 15, 34, 39, 76, 78, 157, 179, 202, 208, 211
West, Jackie, 42
Westergaard, John and Resler, Henrietta, 38, 49, 116, 117, 233
Western countries, 7, 8, 14, 53, 75, 77, 80, 88, 100, 202, 206, 212, 215
White-collar, 1, 45, 46, 70, 84, 127, 129, 135, 141, 183, 203, 233, 237
Willis, Paul, 108, 160, 205
Wolf, Alison, 82, 205
Workers

foreign, 145
industrial, 72, 73
proletariat, 19, 20, 24, 47, 50, 121, 122
Working-class *see also under* Social class
  communities, 99
  occupations, 70
  origins, 38, 174
Working relations, 99 *see also* Relations

Wright Erik Olin, 14, 16, 18, 23, 47, 50, 228, 229

Yiftoi, 135, 137, 138, 144, 161, 162, 170, 174, 184, 188, 190, 197, 232, 236
Young, Michael, 149

Zetterberg, Hans, L., 26, 35
Zouboulakis, Michel, 57, 59

GPSR Compliance

The European Union's (EU) General Product Safety Regulation (GPSR) is a set of rules that requires consumer products to be safe and our obligations to ensure this.

If you have any concerns about our products, you can contact us on

ProductSafety@springernature.com

In case Publisher is established outside the EU, the EU authorized representative is:

Springer Nature Customer Service Center GmbH
Europaplatz 3
69115 Heidelberg, Germany

www.ingramcontent.com/pod-product-compliance
Lightning Source LLC
LaVergne TN
LVHW011807060526
838200LV00053B/3688